MOUNTING FRUSTRATION

MOUNTING FRUSTRATION

THE ART MUSEUM IN THE AGE OF BLACK POWER

SUSAN E. CAHAN

DUKE UNIVERSITY PRESS

Durham and London

Text designed by Barbara Wiedemann
Typeset in Quadraat Pro by Westchester Publishing Services

Library of Congress Cataloging-in-Publication Data
Cahan, Susan, author.
Mounting frustration : the art museum in the age of Black Power /
Susan E. Cahan.
pages cm — (Art history publication initiative)
Includes bibliographical references and index.
ISBN 978-0-8223-5897-8 (hardcover : alk. paper)
ISBN 978-0-8223-7489-3 (e-book)
1. African American art—New York (State)—New York—Exhibitions—
History—20th century. 2. Racism in museum exhibits—New York
(State)—New York—History—20th century. 3. Museum exhibits—Social
aspects—New York (State)—New York—History—20th century. 4. Museum
exhibits—Political aspects—New York (State)—New York—History—
20th century. I. Title. II. Series: Art history publication initiative.
N6538.N5C34 2016
704.03'9607300747471—dc23
2015022351

ISBN 978-0-8223-7145-8 (paperback : alk. paper)

Cover photo: Black Emergency Cultural Coalition protest at the Whitney
Museum of American Art, New York, January 31, 1971. © Jan van Raay.

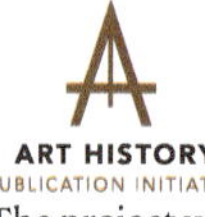 This book was made possible by a collaborative grant from
the Andrew W. Mellon Foundation.
The project was supported by the Creative Capital | Warhol Foundation
Arts Writers Grant Program.
This book was published with the assistance of The Frederick W. Hilles
Publication Fund of Yale University.
Publication of this book has been aided by a grant from the Wyeth Foundation for American Art Publication Fund of the College Art Association.
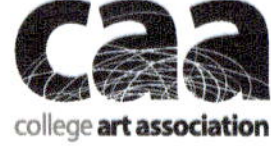 Illustrations in this book were funded by a grant from
the Meiss/Mellon Author's Book Award of the College Art
Association and by support from the Interdisciplinary Performance Studies initiative at Yale (IPSY), which is funded by
a grant from the Andrew W. Mellon Foundation.

CONTENTS

ILLUSTRATIONS

ACKNOWLEDGMENTS

The research for this book began in 1978 when I was hired as a high school intern at the Metropolitan Museum of Art. I was placed in the museum's Community Programs Department, created in 1970 to engage a wider public in the aftermath of the catastrophic exhibition *Harlem on My Mind*. The exhibition had been held in 1969 but, nine years later, was still fresh in the minds of the museum's staff members, and saying the words "Harlem on my mind" was like uttering an obscenity. I didn't know anything about the show or understand why it provoked such consternation, but even as a high school student, I could see that the Community Programs Department had an uneasy relationship to both the communities of New York City that it was meant to serve and the rest of the museum. Our offices were located in the museum's basement off a long, stark corridor. The exhibitions we mounted—of artworks created at social service organizations, such as senior citizens' centers—were mainly seen by the groups of schoolchildren who entered through the museum's side door. Two months after I began my internship Philippe de Montebello was appointed as the museum's director, succeeding Thomas P. F. Hoving, who had served since 1967. The Community Programs Department was disbanded. This ending reflected a broader shift in American social values and priorities: the reaction against the progressivism, civil rights advances, and power shifts of the 1960s.

For years I wondered about the significance of *Harlem on My Mind*. Why did the mere utterance of these words send shudders through so many people? How did this show relate to the museum's outreach programs? And how did these programs come to be seen as superfluous, or even opposed, to the museum's mission? As I progressed in my career—as an educator at the Museum of Modern Art (MoMA) during the controversial exhibition *"Primitivism" in 20th Century Art*, and later at the New Museum of Contemporary Art, where I worked on many shows, including *The Decade Show: Frameworks of Identity in the 1980s*—I became increasingly driven to understand the dynamics and contours of the art world, particularly in the period that directly preceded my own entry into the professional museum world in the 1980s. It was during planning meetings for *The Decade Show* that I learned there had been a movement in the 1960s and '70s among arts activists of color to bring the ethos of civil rights and the determination of the Black Power movement into the major museums. As Lowery Stokes Sims wrote in the catalogue for that exhibition, "Segments of the American people mounted an offensive to have their cultural values be recognized by the establishment, which up to that point had upheld Western culture as a sole criterion by which to judge such qualifiers as 'quality,' 'beauty,' and, yes, even 'truth.'"

I decided to research this history in order to understand the context for my own experience and was surprised to learn how central racial issues had been to major museums in the late 1960s and early '70s. Letters and internal memos in personal and museum archives indicate that for several years all of the major museums in New York City, including the Whitney Museum of American Art, the Met, and MoMA, engaged in daily confrontations with activists and heated internal debates about the character and the responsibilities of museums. This book is the result of that search.

Many of those who advocated for change in the major museums took great risks, forfeiting successful careers in the art world or losing their jobs. Some of the people I interviewed were eager and enthusiastic to have "their story" told, while others struggled with the sting of revisiting a painful, even frightening, time in their lives. Some insisted on keeping secrets, maintaining promises they had made four decades earlier, while others divulged astonishing revelations.

I would like to thank those who shared their stories and personal archives: Benny Andrews, Susan Badder, Flora Biddle, Betty Blayton, Marvin Brown, Mary Bundy, Mary Schmidt Campbell, Kinshasha Holman Conwill, Fred Eversley, Edmund

Barry Gaither, Linda Goode Bryant, Barkley Hendricks, Jon Hendricks, Janet Henry, John Hightower, Thomas P. F. Hoving, Manuel Hughes, Corinne Jennings, Werner Kramarsky, Gail Levin, Irvine R. MacManus Jr., Robert Malone, Sonia BasSheva Mañjon, Raphael Montañez Ortiz, Joe Overstreet, Harry S. Parker III, Thomas Patsenka, Howardena Pindell, Faith Ringgold, Arthur Rosenblatt, Allon Schoener, Lowery Stokes Sims, Robert Storr, Marcia Tucker, Marta Moreno Vega, Michele Wallace, William T. Williams, Philip Yenawine, and Elyn Zimmerman.

I would also like to thank the staff members in the institutions that assisted me with my archival research: MacKenzie Bennett, Michelle Elligott, Tom Grischkowsky, Michelle Harvey, and Elisabeth Thomas at the Museum of Modern Art; Carol Rusk, Anita Duquette, and Marianne Pegno at the Whitney Museum of American Art; Adrianna Del Collo and James Moske at the Metropolitan Museum of Art; Camille Billops and James V. Hatch of the Hatch-Billops Collection; Marisa Bourgoin at the Archives of American Art; Paul Karwacki at Penn State University; and most especially James Estrin and Jeff Roth at the *New York Times*.

Over the years of my work on this book, I have benefited from the support of many colleagues, particularly Norton Batkin in his former role as director of the Center for Curatorial Studies at Bard College; Mireille Bourgeois, who provided invaluable research assistance; my mentors and advisers at the Graduate Center of the City University of New York, Romy Golan, Patricia Mainardi, Stanley Aronowitz, Juan Flores, and Agustín Laó-Montes; Mark Anderson and Tom Radko; Ruth Bohan, John Hylton, Louis Lankford, and Jay Rounds at the University of Missouri–St. Louis; and my colleagues at Yale University, Mary Miller, Emily Bakemeier, James Bundy, Tamar Gendler, Joseph Gordon, Jonathan Holloway, Matthew Jacobson, Paul McKinley, Kobena Mercer, Sam Messer, Stephen Pitti, Joseph Roach, Mark Schenker, Robert Storr, Derek Webster, and Leslie Woodard.

Conversations with thinkers from a range of fields helped shape my approach to the material presented in this book, and for sharing their opinions and suggestions I am grateful to Bruce Altshuler, Julie Ault, David A. Bailey, David Bonetti, Claudine Brown, Lonnie Bunch, Melissa Rachleff Burtt, Darby English, Coco Fusco, Thelma Golden, Kellie Jones, Glenn Ligon, Carlos Manjarrez, Raymond J. McGuire, Toby Miller, Carrie Mae Weems, Laurie Woodard, and Deborah Willis-Braithwaite. Throughout the project Richard Meyer has been a trusted friend and mentor, and as the manuscript progressed, Kobena Mercer and Robert Storr offered invaluable critique and suggestions.

I would like to thank Ken Wissoker, editor in chief of Duke University Press, for his early support and patient, steady commitment to seeing this project through to fruition, and Elizabeth Ault, Heather Hensley, Bonnie Perkel, and Liz Smith for their extraordinary skill and collegiality. To the readers of the manuscript I say thank you for your firm guidance.

Finally, for all his openhearted support, unfailing confidence, and tender care, I thank Jürgen Bank.

Introduction

<blockquote>

Up until the sixties, the gallery system would have X number of artists, established artists—like, ten. Those artists very often decided who the one or two young artists would be to come in, like protégés, and then they would be nourished and they would become the next group. And for the average person—average artist—there was no way to enter unless they got, literally, what the slaves got: a note from the master to come in. You'd go to a gallery and if you didn't know some famous artist, they'd wonder: Why are you there? . . . The art criticism was just as impossible to deal with. You just sat there like you sat waiting for the morning paper to come. . . . And those criticisms were either devastating or they made you; the gallery dealers and curators just looked to what the critics were saying.

Benny Andrews, artist

</blockquote>

The institutions that make up the art establishment determine what constitutes high art through a process of selective acquisition and display. Until the late twentieth century, African Americans were virtually absent from this circuit as cultural producers and cultural consumers. Prior to 1967 one could count fewer than a dozen museum exhibitions that had featured the work of African American artists, with the exception of museums at historically black colleges and universities. On rare occasions when the work of African American artists was shown, it was typically in segregated contexts, as in *Contemporary Negro Art* at the Baltimore Museum of Art in 1939 and *The Negro Artist Comes of Age* at the Brooklyn Museum in 1945. In the late 1960s and early '70s, several large-scale exhibitions focusing on African American culture were mounted by major museums in the United States, including the Metropolitan Museum of Art, the Museum of Modern Art, and the Whitney Museum of American Art. The invisible yet very real boundary separating "African American art" from the universal notion of "art" had been pierced. Yet these shows did not bring about a seamless transition to integration. Each was a wildly contested event, a spark that ignited debate, dissention, and often protest, revealing divergent visions of progress.

This book excavates the moment when museums were forced to face artists' demands for justice and equality. What strategies did African American artists use to gain institutional access, and what tactics did museum professionals employ, as the establishment and the activists wrestled over power and control? What were the models for democratizing museums? Which actions brought success or failure? How did the adjustments of this period in American history both modify and preserve the racial system that was in place before the civil rights movement? And why, five decades later, do we find many of the same challenges in the major museums: a persistent belief that token inclusion is synonymous with institutional change; a scant number of people of color in curatorial and management positions; a preference for using guest curators of color over hiring permanent staff; and a dearth of consistent, sustained research that explores cross-cultural histories and relationships?

The art world has been particularly resistant to racial equality. By the time the civil rights movement reached the American art museum, the movement had passed its peak. The first public demonstrations to integrate museums occurred in late 1968 and early 1969, twenty years after desegregation of the military and fourteen years after the *Brown v. Board of Education* decision, five years after the great March on Washington, four years after the Civil Rights Act, and three years after the Voting Rights Act. Malcolm X, Martin Luther King Jr., and Robert Kennedy had all been assassinated. Stokely Carmichael had already espoused a philosophy of Black Power, and the Black Panther Party was already under investigation by the FBI. The museum establishment's failure to integrate during the prime of the civil rights movement meant that by the time artists began confronting arts institutions in the late 1960s, a liberal retreat from integration was already under way.[1]

Howardena Pindell, an artist and one of the few African Americans to have a curatorial career in a major museum in the 1960s and '70s, the Museum of Modern Art, has described the art world as a "nepotistic, interlocking network" in which artists and arts workers experience an "industry-wide 'restraint of trade'" that limits their ability to enter the system.[2] Since the founding of the first American museums in the mid-nineteenth century, social closure has been a barrier to change, and even though museums have become more populist in the last fifty years, the fact of racial discrimination persists.[3]

The art world explored in this book extends beyond the museum per se to encompass the system of galleries, museums, auction houses, private collections, schools, government funding agencies, art books, and magazines that together form the conduit through which art, and ideas about art, circulate through society. Museums exist within a self-perpetuating system of mutually reinforcing judgments that create informal consensus about the relative importance of a given artist or group of artists. Artists, curators, and art writers can enter in different ways, and in today's art world, once one is "in," it's possible to move from one role to another, or to occupy multiple roles simultaneously. But for artists of color there has not yet been such a thing as life membership.

Museum acquisition and exhibition records indicate that throughout the twentieth century there have been waves of abundant interest in African American art interposed with periods of dormancy. One of these waves occurred around 1940 and another around 1970. Often an artwork acquired during one of these phases was shown frequently at the time and then put into storage, perhaps to be brought out during the next wave. A case in point is Jacob Lawrence's *Migration of the Negro* painting series (1940–41), owned by the Museum of Modern Art (MoMA) in New York City and the Phillips Collection in Washington, DC.[4] The museums acquired the series in 1942 and sent it on a national tour for two years. Records indicate that the work was shown in its entirety at MoMA in 1944 and again in 1971.[5] Since then, this masterful, iconic series has been unified and shown in its New York City home only twice: in 1995 during the "multicultural" moment in which museums demonstrated a resurgence of interest in showing works by artists of color; and in 2015, a year when the United States was gripped by repeated incidents of police violence against African American men.[6] As curator Thelma Golden has observed, "The fact is that there have been waves. Everybody puts their big black shows on the books, they get their corporate funding, it goes all around the country, it's a big extravaganza, and then it's over."[7] Or, as Michele Wallace has expressed in more biting words, "Perhaps the dominant discourse is given to these lapses of amnesia because some ideas are so repugnant to Western culture that they are forced to emerge, again and again, as if new."[8] There is an undeniable correlation between racial politics in the United States and the visibility of artists of color in American museums.

Throughout much of the twentieth century, de facto segregation produced a separate world of African American art centers and museums. One of the most vital and influential was Augusta Savage's Studio of Arts and Crafts on West 143th Street, founded in 1933.[9] Savage's roster of students included Norman Lewis, Ernest Crichlow, Gwendolyn Knight, Elton Fax, and Kenneth B. Clark. Under the Federal Arts Project the studio evolved into the Harlem Community Art Center and continued to be a magnet for both recreational art study and professional training for many artists, including Jacob Lawrence. Later, in 1939, Savage opened the short-lived Salon of Contemporary Negro Art on 125th Street, which showed the work of her former students and others, including Richmond Barthé and Beauford Delaney.[10]

Another important venue, started in 1934, was "306," the studio of Charles Alston and Henry W. Bannarn, located at 306 West 141st Street. According to Romare Bearden, "At 306, Harlem artists, writers, dancers, poets, dramatists, actors, and intellectuals discussed ideas, aesthetic concepts, performances, and 'the news,' from a new play or book to a Supreme Court decision, focusing on the social and political implications for African-Americans. . . . More than anything, 306 evoked the feeling in African-American artists of belonging to a community, dedicated to the arts and to changing the image and status of black people."[11]

Prior to the 1960s, there were three types of patrons of African American art. Of prime importance were the historically black colleges and universities, which employed important African American artists and built outstanding collections of artwork. The earliest were the Hampton Institute Museum (now the Hampton University Museum), founded in 1868, and the Howard University art gallery, founded in 1928.[12]

In private philanthropy, the most prominent organizations were the Harmon Foundation and the Rosenwald Fund. Rosenwald gave grants directly to African American artists between 1928 and 1948; recipients included Gordon Parks Jr., Elizabeth Catlett, Augusta Savage, and Jacob Lawrence, who used the fifteen hundred dollars he received in 1940 to complete his *Great Migration* painting series. There were few strings attached to these grants.[13] The Harmon Foundation was started in 1927 by William E. Harmon, who died shortly after establishing the organization and whose work was continued by director Mary Beattie Brady with the guidance of philosopher and theorist Alain Locke. The foundation awarded annual prizes, sponsored projects, and between 1927 and 1935 organized a series of exhibitions of work by African American artists.[14] Many artists benefited monetarily from these awards, including Aaron Douglas, Hale Woodruff, Palmer Hayden, and Archibald J. Motley Jr., but the foundation's race-based approach was criticized by some as stunting artists' development. In 1934 Romare Bearden published an article in *Opportunity*, the journal of the National Urban League, denouncing the foundation's approach as "coddling and patronizing." The foundation, he wrote, "has encouraged the artist to exhibit long before he has mastered the technical equipment of his medium. By its choice of the type of work it favors, it has allowed the Negro artist to accept standards that are both artificial and corrupt."[15]

In the public realm, the federal arts programs of the 1930s provided unprecedented support for African American artists, who were hired in the various Works Progress Administration (WPA) art programs and offered opportunities through art education programs. Yet even the WPA was tainted by discriminatory practices;

African American artists were employed as muralists, easel painters, and teachers, but were barred from supervisory roles. In 1935 the Harlem Artists' Guild organized to oppose this policy, and eventually the group succeeded in overturning it.[16]

After the victories of the civil rights movement in the 1950s and '60s, artists of color began to stake their claim on the major museums. As the gatekeepers who determined what passed from the studio into the public realm, museums were viewed by many artists as critical conduits through which culture enters a continuum of history. As Raphael Montañez Ortiz, founder of El Museo del Barrio, contends, "The museum is important in affirming the particular culture process and the development of peoples. . . . The museum moves people's culture process out into the larger world."[17] Most of the great strides toward equality were spearheaded by artists themselves. They organized, protested, negotiated with large institutions, and held counterexhibitions that discursively engaged assumptions and omissions of the mainstream art world. Many themes of the 1930s would carry forward into the 1960s: the tension between an art based on racial identification and the desire to break out of race-based constraints; the relationship between white patronage and black self-determination; and equity and accountability in arts financing by the government.

As artists placed new demands on the art establishment, those who worked in museums responded energetically, from active resistance to fitful support. During the late 1960s and early '70s several large-scale exhibitions featuring African American art were mounted by major museums around the country. This unprecedented level of engagement with African American artists, who worked in a range of styles and from different philosophical viewpoints, raised more questions than it answered. Should these artists be shown in "black art" shows? Was there such a thing as a black aesthetic and, if so, what characteristics defined it? Who was qualified to organize exhibitions of work by African Americans? What knowledge and experience did a curator need? Could white curators understand African American art accurately, or did one have to be black to contextualize work by African American artists in ways it was meant to be seen?

In the 1960s—and this is still a view held today—most museum professionals believed the art system was a valid sifting mechanism that allowed quality to rise to the top as a result of critical consensus. If few artists of color made the grade, the shortcoming was considered the artists', not the system's. There were no formal laws against integration, but only a few artists of color had entrée into this circuit of relationships. Informal patterns of access and acceptance calibrated the relative degrees of institutional recognition and status.

De facto discrimination in the art system was not to be rectified by the passage of laws or demonstrations of unconstitutionality. Anxious to defuse conflict—and sometimes eager to defend the status quo—museum insiders were adept at devising seemingly race-neutral reasons for diminishing the roles of African Americans in positions of power and visibility. Artists of color, with occasional exceptions, were routinely dismissed as deficient, derivative, or simply out of sync with mainstream trends. The exceptions were cited as proof of the rule. Thus as soon as artists of color began to actively seek their place in major museums, progress became mired in what has been called "the quality debate," a debate about whether or not such discrimination existed at all. The practice of racism on the part of individual curators, directors, or trustees was legitimated as just that: a series of individual judgment calls, not institutional policy. When patterns of exclusion were pointed out, museums typically responded with platitudes and generalizations: it's not intentional and it's nobody's fault. African Americans, they said—often directly with no shame—simply lacked the education and opportunities to improve themselves and reach the level of accomplishment of their white counterparts. Their own ignorance was projected outward. Yet structural racism didn't obviate the need for personal responsibility. As legal and culture scholar Imani Perry has pointed out, "If we don't look at the actions of individuals . . . how do we believe in the capacity of citizens to affect change?" The role of the individual as an agent of racism does not deny the existence of racism; rather, it "allows us to recognize that we have a cultural practice that is diffuse."[18] Perry cites evidence that there are "cumulative patterns to be found in the choices that individuals make, patterns that are not readily identifiable if one looks at the actions or beliefs of an individual, but that emerge when one looks at how many individuals choose to act in the same way."[19]

This book presents case studies that examine the techniques used to both accommodate and manage the inclusion, for some the *intrusion*, of artists of color when the overt expression of racist attitudes and beliefs was becoming less socially acceptable. Taken together, these studies demonstrate a pattern of ambivalence toward integration on the part of individuals who constituted the museum establishment in the late 1960s and early '70s. Many of the financially and politically powerful trustees and administrators espoused support for the cause of civil rights in principle, but did not necessarily act in ways that supported cultural equity, particularly not in "their own" museums.

Chapter 1 focuses on the Studio Museum in Harlem, whose inception predates the movement to integrate the major museums and was an outgrowth of President Lyndon B. Johnson's antipoverty programs, drawing a direct line between the response to the civil rights movement at the federal level and the New York City museum world. The history of the Studio Museum is worthy of an in-depth study in and of itself; here its early history serves as an introduction to the racial politics of museums in the 1960s, the rise of "neighborhood," "community-based," "culturally based," and "culturally specific" museums, and the vital role they played in both opening exhibition opportunities for artists of color and serving as pressure valves for the release of racial tension.[20]

Chapter 2 looks closely at the events leading up to and surrounding the exhibition *Harlem on My Mind* at the Metropolitan Museum of Art beginning in 1967 and continuing through the show's run in 1969. *Harlem on My Mind* was celebrated by its organizers as "a community project," but despite its egalitarian objectives, the exhibition failed to galvanize support among cultural activists or African American artists, nor did it garner the confidence of the museum's conservative audiences and patrons.[21] For artists, the central problem was that this bastion of high culture chose to mount an exhibition of documentary materials—photojournalism and historical documents—without including works of art.[22] Up to that point the Met had never shown any photography, and in this case the photographs were not even shown in the original, but as reproductions mounted on large placards. The show didn't "make sense" within the logic of an art museum. Curator Allon Schoener intended the project to be a populist gesture, a challenge to the traditional hierarchy that privileged high art over mass culture. Yet by opting for photography rather than art, the exhibition perpetuated the corrosive prejudice that distinguished "art" and "African American art"—and excluded the latter. Rather than ameliorate de facto segregation, the show accentuated the problem.

This study adds texture to previous accounts of the exhibition and also demonstrates that the museum had both idealistic and pragmatic aims. The utilitarian goal of the show was to encourage support for the Met's plan to build several new wings and expand its footprint farther into Central Park. The unpopular plan was in jeopardy of failing without broad public support. *Harlem on My Mind* was part of a much larger public relations project. Out of this fiasco emerged two developments: the museum created a vast network of community outreach programs and a diverse community of African American artists and arts activists united around a common agenda. In the years following *Harlem on My Mind* other museums were forced to enter the dialogue.

Chapter 3 demonstrates how activists were thwarted by museums' "profound historicity," to borrow a term from Michel Foucault—that is, their investment in maintaining the status quo in order to preserve their sense of their own coherence.[23]

Through an analysis of *Contemporary Black Artists in America*, an exhibition held at the Whitney Museum of American Art in 1971, this chapter critiques one of the main curatorial strategies used to moderate and manage the incorporation of African American art in major museums: "black art shows," exhibitions composed exclusively of work by African American artists. The Whitney didn't invent this curatorial template. In fact, it was preceded by African American art shows such as *Art of the American Negro*, organized by Romare Bearden in 1966, and *Afro American Artists: New York and Boston*, organized by Edmund Barry Gaither in 1970.[24] But use of this exhibition format by the Whitney vividly demonstrated the limitations of this model when in the hands of a curator unfamiliar with his subject matter. The museum refused to engage an expert on African American art and instead delegated direction of the show to in-house curator Robert Doty, who had little knowledge of the subject. This led to a widespread sense among artists that their work would be misrepresented, and many withdrew from the exhibition. Bowing to prevailing trends, the curator privileged abstract work in his catalogue essay and in the show's layout. This pleased neither the artists working in an abstract vein, who objected to the show's race-based rubric, nor those making representational work, whose art was disparaged. Those with an overtly militant agenda saw the curator attempt to defang their work, to purge it of its potency and politics through the lens of high modernism. The show embodied a core contradiction: the artists were shown separately from their white peers, but their work was assimilated into a then dominant art historical narrative. This was segregation in the guise of integration, and it served as a cautionary example of inclusion as a double-edged sword. This example demonstrates how aesthetic ideas were used to advance political agendas that could not be expressed outright. In this case the Whitney Museum used aesthetic concepts to do the work of discrimination.

In each of these cases the leaders in the museums struggled to find ways to balance continuity and change in their respective institutions' missions, artistic scope, and constituencies. Chapter 4 looks at the Museum of Modern Art at a time when the museum was forced to wrestle with three intertwining questions: What was the museum's relationship to the work of living artists? What was the museum's responsibility to American artists of color? And how, if at all, did the museum's history of presenting non-Western art require reexamination and revision of its construction of modernism? Artists Faith Ringgold, Tom Lloyd, and Raphael Montañez Ortiz, as well as the museum's director from 1970 to 1972, John Hightower, worked to provoke introspection and change at MoMA. Hightower vowed to learn from the mistakes of other museums and undertook a program of experimental projects that addressed current hot-button political issues and supported increased engagement with African American and Puerto Rican artists and arts activists. These efforts, which included one-person exhibitions of work by Romare Bearden and Richard Hunt, ended abruptly in January 1972 when Hightower was fired after a trustee committee found artists' accusations of ethnocentrism "unfounded." These trustees presented an official recommendation that the museum maintain the status quo, citing its early exhibition program of artworks from Africa, Oceania, and Native cultures in the Americas that resonated with progressive—often non-naturalistic—twentieth-century art.[25] This thread in the history of the museum's exhibition program would be both glorified and distorted in its 1984 exhibition *"Primitivism" in 20th Century Art: Affinity of the Tribal and the Modern*, an anachronism in its own time that was as problematic as *Harlem on My Mind* had been in 1969. Like *Harlem on My Mind*, the show catalyzed a critical reaction: the development of an expanded history of art in the 1980s into what Kobena Mercer has called "Cosmopolitan Modernisms," the study of modernity and art of different cultures and nations throughout the world.[26]

The epilogue outlines the strategies ultimately devised by the major museums to manage and accommodate the call for racial justice: the creation of specific physical spaces within the museum in which to show works by artists of color; reframing the issues of cultural equity and accessibility as questions of "audience development"; and helping to create the wave of new culturally grounded museums, rather than revising their foundational art historical narratives. This last development, the emergence of culturally grounded art museums, marks the 1970s as the beginning of our own era, an era of new opportunities, but one that retains culturally coded pathways through the art world; systems that sift artists by "race" and ethnicity; and culturally separate institutions with managed crossovers.

Taken together, these stories demonstrate the complex relationships between the actions of individuals and the transformation of institutions. Each chapter aims to tease out the often elusive relationship between structural inequities and individual choices. I have chosen to focus on a single location, New York City, in order to delve deeply into the texture of a community and the multiple roles played by individuals within that community in different institutional contexts. New York City is dense with culturally, financially, and politically powerful individuals, and these individuals exercised disproportionate influence within the museum world. Nelson Rockefeller, for example, the governor of the State of New York, a presidential hopeful, and vice president of the United States under Gerald Ford, was a trustee of the Museum of Modern Art from 1932 to 1979 and a longtime board member at the Metropolitan Museum. C. Douglas Dillon, the secretary of the treasury in the Kennedy and Johnson administrations, was a Metropolitan trustee for more than fifty years, its president in the early 1970s, and a chairman of the Museum of Modern Art's International Council.[27] Privileged families and individuals moved seamlessly from one power center to another, keenly aware not only of the high stakes involved in the civil rights struggle, but also that the effort to integrate the art world was part of a much larger movement to address racial inequality and social injustice.[28] Armed with this knowledge, one key strategy for insulating their institutions from the conflicts that attended civil rights debates and actions was to deny that the art world was part of the larger sociopolitical system. This contention provided the rationale for simply rejecting calls for the redistribution of power as well as the justification for repudiating art that criticized the status quo.

Over the past three decades several scholars and critics have looked back to the late '60s and early '70s as a critical period not only in politics but also in the politics of art. The groundbreaking exhibition and catalogue *Tradition and Conflict: Images of a Turbulent Decade, 1963–1973*, organized by Mary Schmidt Campbell in 1985, documented an important history and provided a methodological key to researching this period.[29] The exhibition catalogue included excerpts from journals written by artist and activist Benny Andrews, underscoring the value of returning to primary sources in order to understand events that have been poorly documented in secondary texts. Artist and archivist Camille Billops and theater historian James Hatch have been visionary in their decades-long project to interview artists, curators, art historians, and arts writers and to organize panel discussions in order to record firsthand accounts of historic events. The pair not only collected materials but also produced and disseminated knowledge through their periodical *Artist and Influence*.[30] The writings of Kellie Jones on art of the 1970s, especially her essay "It's Not Enough to Say 'Black Is Beautiful' " and her exhibitions *Energy/Experimentation, Now Dig This!*, and *Witness: Art and Civil Rights in the Sixties*, are essential cornerstones for the study of this period and a foundation for much of this book. Jones has brought back to center stage work by artists who have been buffeted in and out of dominant art history and has reconnected African American art to conceptual and performative, as well as object-based, modes of art making. Michele Wallace and Faith Ringgold, participants in many of the events described in this book, have been stalwarts in telling it like it was and keeping alive narratives that help complete our understanding of this history.[31]

Over the past twenty years there have been several discussions of *Harlem on My Mind*, starting with Deborah Willis-Braithwaite's book on James VanDerZee and continuing with Steven Dubin's essay "Crossing 125th Street: *Harlem on My Mind* Revisited" and essays by Mary Ellen Lennon, Bridget Cooks, Margaret Olin, and myself.[32] The retelling of these events in this book situates the exhibition in relation to the specific conditions in the art world at the time, including the Met's physical expansion plans, in order to explore the confluence of factors that shape the way culture is imagined, discussed, and changed.

Romare Bearden and Harry Henderson's history of African American art, Mary Ann Calo's study of African American artists in the 1940s, Ann Gibson's revisionist history of Abstract Expressionism, and Patricia Hills's monograph on the life and work of Jacob Lawrence have built a foundation for critical understanding of African American artists in relation to arts institutions and art criticism. In the same vein, the exhibition and publication *Theater of Refusal: Black Art and Mainstream Criticism*, organized by Charles Gaines and Catherine Lord in 1993, explored the construction of African American artists' careers in the 1980s and '90s through exhibition thematics and art criticism.[33]

Some of the culturally grounded organizations considered in this study have been discussed in books addressing the alternative arts movement of the 1960s through the 1980s.[34] While valuable for documentary purposes, the clustering of artists of color, women, and other groups under the banner "alternative" is problematic because it perpetuates a racialized and gendered concept of margin and center.[35] Particularly strong, in-depth work on Puerto Rican, Nuyorican, and, more broadly, Latino cultural institutions has been done by Arlene Dávila, Agustín Laó-Montes, and Yasmín Ramírez.[36]

In recent decades many artists of color been given exhibition opportunities in major museums, and some have had their work collected. Many more commercial galleries feature artists of color, and some represent several of the artists discussed in this book. But the most significant change since the 1970s has not been full integration or equality, but the development of a two-tiered system of cultural institutions, one "mainstream," the other "culturally specific." In this new equilibrium, many culturally grounded institutions have become feeders to the major museums, but patterns of differential treatment persist. With some notable exceptions, presentations of work by artists of color in the major museums have been subject to a series of curatorial trends: from ethnicity- and identity-based shows to "other" art histories; from "artists' choice" curatorial interventions to public service projects.[37] Currently, the preferred exhibition model for showcasing artists of color is the one-person exhibition, a model that holds good potential for focusing in depth on an individual's work but subscribes to what theorist James Banks has called the "additive" approach to multicultural reform, which safely avoids radical revision.[38] And by privileging artists who have reached a certain level of recognition in the public eye and within the marketplace, this model limits the range of art shown.

The story of racial equality in major museums is not simply one of struggle to overcome past exclusions. The dichotomy between inclusion and exclusion does not adequately account for developments in museum practice during the post–civil rights movement era. Instead, this book explores a history of power struggles. By digging deep into this history of advances and regressions during this troubling and electrifying era, this book aims to frame our understanding of the present.

Electronic Refractions II
at the Studio Museum in Harlem

On September 25, 1968, the *New York Times* reported the grand opening of a new art museum: "White-gloved waiters plowed through the milling crowds with trays of drink and hors d'oeuvres. Friends greeted friends with little cries and social pecks on the cheek. The air conditioning broke down, and a drunk lurched against a programed sculpture, smashing part of its protective glass. 'This is as normal a museum opening as I've seen,' Thomas P.F. Hoving, director of the Metropolitan Museum of Art, sighed as he mopped his sweaty brow with a handkerchief."[1] And why wouldn't this opening be "normal"? This was the opening of the Studio Museum in Harlem, the first museum in the United States founded to show the work of African Americans alongside artists of all other backgrounds, and in 1968, this wasn't the norm.

The Studio Museum had been conceived three years earlier, in 1965, by an interracial group of artists and educators together with several philanthropists, art collectors, a social worker, and two aspiring politicians (fig. 1.1). The institution grew out of alliances that cut across racial lines at a time when the hope of eradicating racial inequality through integration had powerful currency. At the grand opening of the Studio Museum on that September evening, its director, Charles Inniss, said he hoped the museum would be a place for good black artists to exhibit, a place where black people would be able to see each other's work, "But more than that we want to be a ground where the black and white art worlds can really meet."[2] And meet they did, but not in the way Inniss had hoped. The members of the founding board were condemned by local arts activists as introducing an "alien culture" into Harlem, and a leadership change in 1969 brought a new vision based on black nationalism that continued until the mid-'70s.[3]

When the Studio Museum was conceived in 1965, interracial partnerships appeared to hold the promise of disrupting patterns of de facto segregation in the New York art world. But by the time the Studio Museum opened in 1968, Black Power had become the dominant unifying theme for movement to the next stage in the struggle for racial equality, an understanding among African Americans that "they, independent of whites, can achieve liberation by the creation and maintenance of black institutions that serve the best interests of black people."[4]

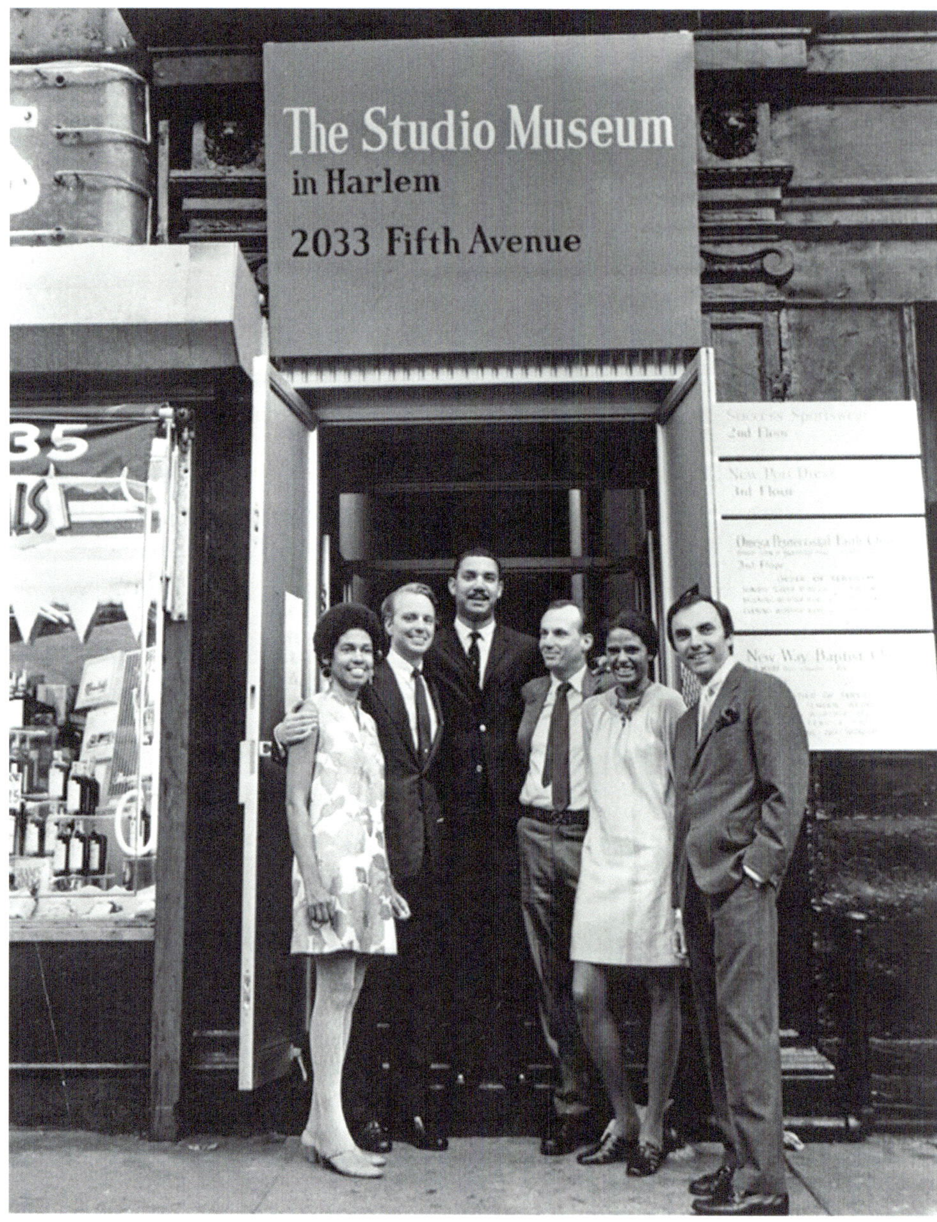

Fig. 1.1 The Studio Museum on opening night, September 24, 1968. From left: Eleanor Holmes Norton, vice president; Carter Burden, president; Charles Inniss, director; Campbell Wylly, trustee; Betty Blayton, secretary; Frank Donnelly, vice president. Courtesy of the Studio Museum in Harlem.

The creation of culturally specific museums was a significant institutional expression of a new racial order that reflected a belief in culture as a means of affirming the existence of those groups that had historically controlled "no means of production, no land mass," and in the 1960s little "meaningful participation in formal public politics."[5] If the historical mission of the American museum was to preserve the past, the culturally grounded museum was designed to broaden the American notion of its past. The early years of the Studio Museum embody the range and complexity of concepts of racial discourse of the mid- to late 1960s, from desegregation and equality to freedom and liberation. The museum was a cipher for the hopes and aspirations of integrationists that was quickly converted by separatists into the country's first, and eventually foremost, museum of African American art.

Betty Blayton, a painter, educator, and key figure in the creation of the Studio Museum, moved to New York City in the summer of 1960. Born in Newport News and raised in Williamsburg, Virginia, she had attended Syracuse University with her tuition fully paid by the State of Virginia, as the state was still segregated and there was no African American college in Virginia that had an accredited arts program. In 1959, she graduated with a degree in art, spent a short time in Washington, DC, then went to St. Thomas, where she taught high school art for a year. After her arrival in New York, she started looking for an artists' community, and soon she started taking classes at the Art Students League with Charles Alston.

Blayton also studied education and psychology at City College of New York, where Kenneth B. Clark was teaching.[6] Clark, the social psychologist whose research conducted with his wife Mamie Phipps Clark was instrumental in the 1954 *Brown v. Board of Education* school desegregation decision, was in the process of developing an empowerment program for teenagers living in Harlem. In 1962 Clark was commissioned by the President's Committee on Juvenile Delinquency and Youth Crime and the City of New York to study the conditions of the lives of teenagers. From 1962 to 1964 he headed a team of researchers who studied manifestations of juvenile delinquency—from dereliction to criminal behavior—as a symptom of the larger problems of poverty and racial discrimination.[7] Clark believed that juvenile delinquency would persist until the larger problems of financial insecurity and social and political disaffection were addressed.[8] Blayton heard about the project and immediately identified with its goals. She signed on to help write the proposal for the arts and culture program directed by the musician Julian Euell (fig. 1.2).

In 1964 Euell invited Blayton to a gathering of the Spiral group to meet two other artists who were going to teach in his program, Norman Lewis and James

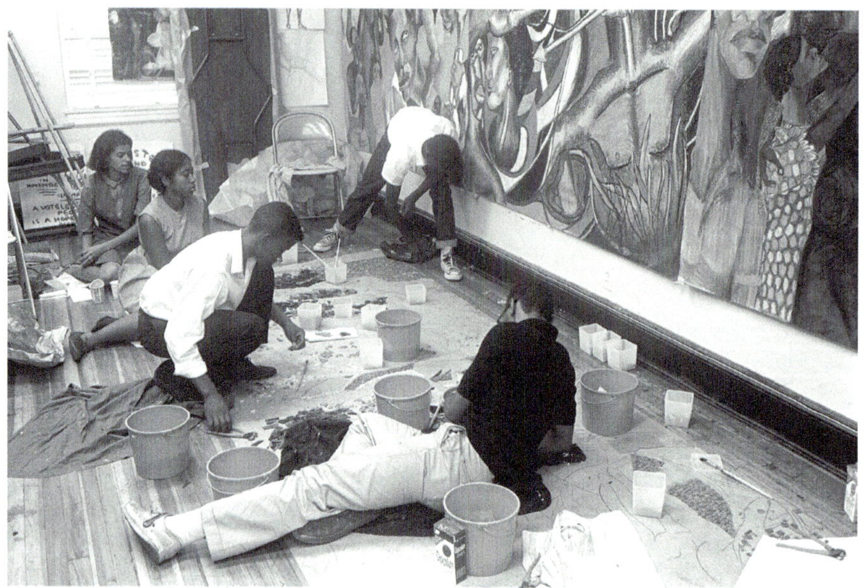

Fig. 1.2 Artist and HARYOU-ACT instructor Betty Blayton looks on as students work on a wall mosaic in a class being conducted at the YMCA. August 26, 1964. Photo: Robert Walker / The New York Times / Redux.

Yeargens. The Spiral group had formed in 1963 to discuss ways that artists could participate in the civil rights struggle and cultivate a culture of mutual support.[9] Talking with the members of the Spiral group heightened Blayton's consciousness of discrimination in the art world, not only because of the artists' political engagement but because of the personal sting of their stories: "When I first met the Spiral group they were talking about the problems with their galleries, of the lack of galleries. I have always been a proactive kind of person; when I saw this gorgeous work I was just amazed they were having problems. Romy [Bearden] and Norman [Lewis] weren't that much older than my father. How could they be doing this work all this time and I never heard of them? I was enraged."[10]

In April 1964 Kenneth Clark delivered to the President's Committee on Juvenile Delinquency his report, "Youth in the Ghetto: A Study of the Consequences of Powerlessness and a Blueprint for Change."[11] The report proposed a program called Harlem Youth Opportunities Unlimited, known as HARYOU, that would bring seven thousand young people in Harlem into a network of job training, educational, social, and arts activities. Unlike the social programs in which participants received services from professionals who were not from the community, Clark's action-oriented vision was to organize a large group of Harlem residents, young and old, who were "disciplined and politically sensitive" to gain the power to reverse the conditions of poverty themselves.[12] "Otherwise," he wrote, "these vast and wide-ranging programs of reform would only amount to benevolence from outside the community, vulnerable to control and abuse, and tending to encourage further dependency."[13] Clark wrote that HARYOU seeks to engender "an increasing sense of pride, confidence, and initiative in the youth themselves."[14] The program received $1 million in federal funds, and the City of New York allocated $3.5 million from its federal antipoverty program funds. An additional $500,000 was paid by the Department of Labor to train and place the program's workers. All participants—teachers and students—would receive stipends.

Between HARYOU's planning and implementation stages, Congressman Adam Clayton Powell introduced his own initiative, Associated Community Team (ACT), which received equivalent funding without conducting a planning study. According to sociologist Noel Cazenave, ACT's funding was part of a quid pro quo deal between Powell and the Kennedy administration intended to secure the congressman's support for another program of the Department of Health, Education, and Welfare.[15] Under political pressure, in 1964 the two organizations merged to form HARYOU-ACT. Clark withdrew from the organization and immediately began developing a framework for assessing the effectiveness of community action programs, a model increasingly favored by private foundations and policy makers.[16]

Despite this political jockeying and, in subsequent years, the program's financial problems, HARYOU-ACT gave thousands of teenagers life-changing opportunities. The Arts and Culture section enabled students to write plays, perform drama and dance, make music, and produce films. Program participant Janet Henry (fig. 1.3) recalls, "There was a place to practice. There was a place to meet other people who thought of themselves as artists, and to work with adults who worked as artists."[17] The Arts and Culture program consisted of six divisions: Graphics and Plastics; Commercial Art; Fashion; Journalism; Film and Sound; and Photography.

It was open by application to teenagers who lived in Harlem; candidates had to demonstrate both an aptitude and an interest in art. Some, like Henry, who would later become a professional artist and administrator at the New York State Council on the Arts, attended the city's specialty arts high schools.[18] During the summer, the students worked with HARYOU-ACT five days a week, learning art techniques in all media, making individual studio-based work, and collaborating on group projects, such as mosaics and vest pocket sculpture parks. These small parks were urban

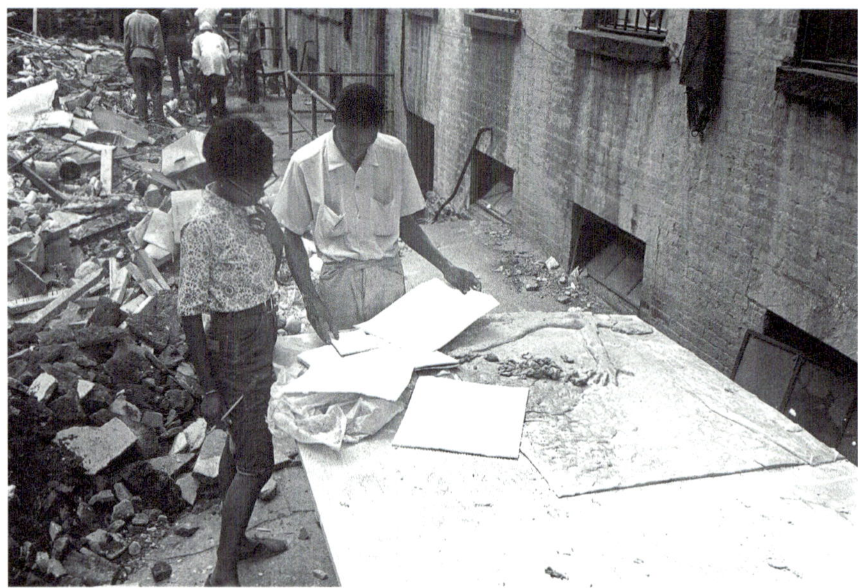

Fig. 1.3 Artist and HARYOU-ACT sculpture instructor Arnold Prince looks over the sketchbook of Janet Henry, August 26, 1964. Henry's clay mold is at right. Photo: Robert Walker / The New York Times / Redux.

oases created in unused building lots through a city program promoted by New York City mayor John V. Lindsay and parks commissioner Thomas P. F. Hoving. During the academic year, the students came to HARYOU-ACT after school. They not only created art; they also had opportunities to interact with working artists. Henry recalls that on one very special occasion Romare Bearden gave a lecture for students in the Arts and Culture program, about a hundred in all.[19]

Blayton taught in HARYOU-ACT for two years, from 1964 through 1966. As an extension of the program, she began sending her students downtown to view works of art at the Museum of Modern Art at 11 West Fifty-Third Street. She soon discovered that when the teenagers arrived at the museum, they were turned away, refused entrance by the museum's security guards. Blayton contacted her friend Frank O'Hara, the poet, who was the museum's associate curator of painting and sculpture, and he, along with public relations director Elizabeth Shaw, saw to it that the students were admitted. According to Blayton, before the students set out for the museum, she would call and alert Shaw, who would then see that the guards didn't "give them a hard time."[20] Eventually Shaw and O'Hara arranged for admission passes.

After a while the students began to see MoMA as a place of their own. Henry recalls, "I'd take my sisters and cousins too, because they gave us free passes. Going to the Museum of Modern Art was one of the things we'd do, as a bunch of teenage girls." She remembers Picasso's *She-Goat* as one of their favorite pieces: "We liked the pregnant goat, the *She-Goat*. . . . In fact, when our church had a boat outing and docked over on the West Side in midtown, my mother drove us across town and I made her go down Fifty-Fourth Street so we could see the goat in the museum's courtyard. . . . It became a kind of family event."[21] During these years, Henry doesn't recall seeing other people of color visiting the museum.

Frank Donnelly, a member of the Museum of Modern Art's Junior Council and a social worker with the Citizens Committee for Children (CCC) in Harlem, saw potential for a closer relationship with HARYOU-ACT. The CCC was a children's advocacy and service organization that had a constituency of supporters in the arts, including some art world luminaries, such as Alfred Barr, founding director of the Museum of Modern Art, and Thomas Hess, the editor of *Art News*. According to Blayton: "MoMA was interested in finding out what they could do for the cause that everyone was so anxiously pursuing. And they came up to Harlem, to HARYOU, to see if there was some way that MoMA, through the Junior Council, could be of service to the art department. . . . I met with them and told them I thought it would be very interesting to have the teenagers who were involved come down to the museum on Saturdays and have rap sessions about the museum's collection."[22]

MoMA's Junior Council had been formed in 1949 for younger members of the museum's inner circle of supporters as an in-house training ground for trustees, a "peaceable cutting garden out of which ornamental blossoms might be plucked to replenish the bouquet."[23] The members of the Junior Council undertook projects that extended the reach of the museum, such as producing Christmas cards and an annual calendar illustrated with works from the collection.[24] Their most ambitious initiative was the Art Lending Service, through which commercial galleries would loan works to the museum, which in turn could be borrowed by museum members.

For over a year, between 1965 and 1966, the curator of the museum's Art Lending Service, Campbell Wylly, met with the group of fifteen or so students every month. Sometimes he invited artists, such as Claes Oldenburg, Robert Indiana, and Jim Dine (fig. 1.4). Often the conversations were attended by members of the Museum's Junior Council who, according to Blayton, wanted to hear what these young people had to say: "Teenagers in Harlem are very sophisticated, on the surface. For a lot of the Junior Council members, who came out of very sheltered environments, these teenagers were extremely interesting."[25]

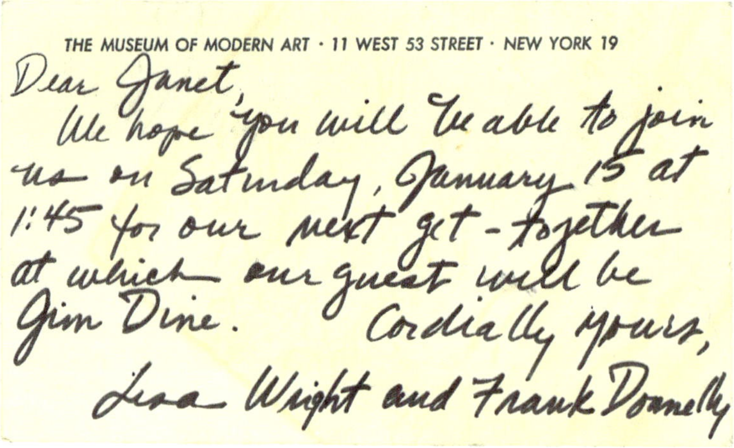

Fig. 1.4 Postcard invitation from Lisa Wright and Frank Donnelly to Janet Henry, January 1966. Courtesy of Janet Henry.

With their students now "regulars" at MoMA, Blayton and Donnelly began talking about the fact that there was no museum in the students' own neighborhood. As President Lyndon B. Johnson's War on Poverty became a social ethos as well as a public policy goal, large, established arts institutions became targets of criticism as hoarders of financial resources. Neighborhood museums, or what would be called "community-based," "culturally specific," or "culturally grounded" museums, were conceived to redistribute the financial wealth and validate a broader spectrum of cultural experiences.[26] The HARYOU-ACT teens were enlisted to talk with social groups and church groups to gauge support in the community for such a venture. Henry, one of the students who canvassed the neighborhood, has recalled that she was "held up as an example of the kind of person the place would be good for."[27]

Donnelly brought in other members of MoMA's Junior Council, including Charles Cowles, the publisher of *Artforum*; Carter Burden, a candidate for the New York City Council whose father had been president of MoMA in the 1950s; J. Frederic Byers III, a collector and sponsor of the Bykert Gallery whose father-in-law, William S. Paley, would become the museum's president in 1968; and the collector Barbara Jakobson. Jakobson has recalled, "In terms of our involvement with the black community, this was something that we sought out more than they. I did not feel pressure upon the Museum, during those years, from the black community. It was much more something we felt we wanted to do."[28] These individuals worked on the project outside their formal roles as members of MoMA's Junior Council.

Still, before proceeding with the formation of a Studio Museum development board, they sought and received the approval of Bill Paley. Also enlisted to work on the project were Eleanor Holmes Norton, a lawyer with the American Civil Liberties Union who would go on to serve on the New York Human Rights Commission and the Equal Employment Opportunities Commission and would become a member of Congress in 1990; Theodore Gunn, an artist; and Robert Macbeth, director of the New Lafayette Theater. On March 13, 1967, artist Mahler Ryder became the executive secretary of the Committee to Form the Harlem Museum, Inc. Donnelly served as chairman.

Blayton asked Romare Bearden to join the board, but he refused, stating that the whites who were involved were there for their own gain. There is evidence to support this view. Carter Burden, for example, was campaigning for the post of New York City councilman in the Second District, which ran from Twenty-Second Street to 109th Street on the East Side of Manhattan, where he lost, and then in the newly rezoned District 4, which incorporated both the Upper East Side and Harlem from Fifty-Ninth Street to 131st Street and the East River to Fifth Avenue. There he eventually won. During Burden's 1969 campaign to win the District 4 primary election, he and his family were profiled in the *New York Times*: "For the last three years, [Burden] has tried to rid himself of an image as a socialite fop and to renounce his unofficial title of crown prince of fashion society. . . . Mrs. Burden has stopped going to fashion shows, although she is still seen lunching at fashionable French restaurants. . . . Mr. Burden has been listening, and learning, and taking private lessons in urban Puerto Rican Spanish."[29] No doubt Burden's involvement in the Studio Museum starting in 1967 and his eventual ascent to the role of board chair in 1969 was part of this project to cultivate a more populist public image.

An advisory board of professionals included Thomas P. F. Hoving, newly appointed director of the Metropolitan Museum of Art, and Bates Lowry, who was then the director of the Museum of Modern Art. Also involved was Kynaston McShine, who at the time was temporary director of the Jewish Museum in New York. McShine had previously served at MoMA in the Circulating Exhibitions department and would soon return there as an associate curator. In the mid-'60s, he was the only person of color in a curatorial position at a major museum.[30] The Studio Museum's first director was Charles Inniss, who had previously been a manager with the business information research firm Dun & Bradstreet. Inniss was not familiar with art, but he had organizational skills and had been born in Harlem.

The initial programmatic vision consisted of four areas: exhibitions of newly commissioned art; guest-curated exhibitions; a film workshop; and an artists-in-residence program. The driving vision behind the artists-in-residence program was that of painter William T. Williams, who joined the museum's staff after graduating from the Yale School of Art in spring 1968. Williams proposed that artists be given studio space and support for making art that would then be exhibited at the museum. In addition to helping the artists, the residencies were designed to demystify the art-making process by involving local young people as apprentices.

The Studio Museum differed from Harlem's existing cultural organizations because its structure mirrored that of the major museums downtown, and many of its leaders came from outside Harlem. The active arts groups in Harlem at the time were, for the most part, artists' collectives. In 1963 a group of African American photographers had formed the Kamoinge group. Their aims were "to view and critique each others [sic] work in an honest and understanding atmosphere, to nurture and challenge each other in order to attain the highest creative level."[31] The name "Kamoinge," which came from the Gikuyu language of Kenya, means "a group of people acting together." The group was committed "to seek out the truth inherent in our cultural roots, to create and communicate these truths with insight and integrity."[32] Roy DeCarava was a major catalyst in giving the group direction and served as Kamoinge's first director.[33]

A coalition of over fifty artists, the Twentieth Century Creators, had come together after an art exhibition at the 125th Street Harlem Branch of the NAACP in 1964. Headed by James Sneed (Jemisi Obanjoko) and Malikah Rahman, the group staged two major exhibitions: an outdoor show along Seventh Avenue between 127th and 135th Streets in the summer of 1964 and *Creative Profile*, an exhibition with accompanying lectures and workshops held between October 1964 and February 1965 at the Community Center of the Abraham Lincoln Houses, a large public housing project spanning East 132nd Street to East 135th Street between Fifth and Park Avenues. Ideological differences led the group to split, with Sneed and artist Babatunde Folayemi (Tony Northern) eventually forming the Harlem Art Gallery located at 2133 Seventh Avenue between 126th and 127th Streets. The remaining members joined together as the Weusi group—"Weusi" derives from the Swahili word for "blackness"—and began organizing Afrocentric cultural events, including an annual outdoor celebration combining dance, fashion, and art that continued through 1977.[34] In 1967 five members of Weusi formed Nyumba Ya Sanaa Gallery ("House of Art" in Swahili) at 158 West 132nd Street on the corner of Seventh Avenue.[35] One of its leaders, Ademola Olugebefola (Bedwick Thomas), also created the House of Umoja, which offered clothing and consciousness raising aimed at promoting a black aesthetic.[36]

Babatunde (Michael) Olatunji, a celebrated drummer from Nigeria, had come to the United States in the 1950s to study at Spelman College and then at New York

University. In 1965 he founded the Olatunji Center for African Culture in Harlem with money he had made organizing music performances at the 1964 World's Fair. The center offered classes in African dance, music, language, folklore, and history for two dollars a session; and teacher training. On Sundays there was the Roots of Africa concert series, featuring performances by such legendary musicians as Yusef Lateef, John Coltrane, and Pete Seeger.

The most prominent local arts organization was the Harlem Cultural Council, founded in 1964 as part of a revitalization and economic growth plan for the Harlem area.[37] Its vibrant and popular Jazzmobile and Dancemobile programs, funded by the New York State Council on the Arts, provided public performances on an outdoor, mobile stage. Romare Bearden was its first director, and artist Charles Alston served on the board, along with Robert W. Dowling, the city's cultural executive.[38] The exhibition *Art of the American Negro*, organized by Bearden and sponsored by the council, took place in 1966 at 144 West 125th Street, in the basement of the Kenwood furniture store.[39] This address would become the home of the Studio Museum in 1979.

In his work on behalf of the Studio Museum, Mahler Ryder encountered artists across a broad spectrum of social aesthetics, from those who wanted access to the mainstream gallery and museum world to others who were more concerned with culture as a collectivist, mobilizing social force: "The organizations most concerned with an aesthetic based on Africanism had political underpinnings that did not embrace art created in the spirit of individualism."[40] Many eyed the Studio Museum with caution.

From the early planning stages of the Studio Museum there were tensions between the "uptown" and "downtown" players. While Ryder spread the word and garnered support in Harlem among "pimps, prostitutes, [local] politicians, solid citizens and their children," closed decision-making meetings simultaneously took place in "mid-Manhattan, Wall Street and the Hamptons."[41] Ryder described one of the clashes in vivid detail:

> One memorable afternoon, after much preparation, the chairman of the committee [Frank Donnelly] and I made a presentation to a ministers' convention. While ad-libbing the text, the chairman stated that one of his primary concerns was to make "the streets of Harlem safe for Europeans." The day, as I recall, was very warm and many [members of the audience] had large fans decorated with various religious motifs. I watched with a mixture of horror and fascination while, as if on cue, the movement of the fans stopped, then, one by one, they began to move very rapidly. Not a word was

spoken, although one very large woman shifted her body noticeably. As our chairman took his seat in the rear of the large church, I was summoned to a small annex, where I received a severe tongue-lashing from two ministers who made it very clear that they were more interested in making the streets of Harlem safe for black people. The episode was the first of several snafus.[42]

According to poet Ed Spriggs, who would soon become the Studio Museum's second director, "Harlemites considered Harlem to be under attack by white institutions." The museum was only one of several interracial ventures in Harlem in the 1960s. On July 17, 1968, just two months before the Studio Museum opened, the securities brokerage firm Shearson Hammill announced its intention to open a branch in Harlem at 144 West 125th Street, the very location of the *Art of the American Negro* exhibition and the future location of the Studio Museum. The idea had been proposed by Russell L. Goings Jr., a registered representative for Shearson Hammill who served as branch manager. Ten days after the announcement, the chairman of the Harlem branch of the Congress of Racial Equality (CORE) denounced the move, calling the plan "a conspiracy by state, municipal, and Wall Street high-finance interests to take over Harlem."[43] CORE members picketed the branch. Shearson Hammill agreed to pay 7.5 percent of its gross revenues to the Atticus Foundation to support projects within the Harlem community.[44]

Attacks on Harlem's culture core seemed to be coming from all sides. In the fall of 1968 the New York Public Library threatened to close the Arthur A. Schomburg branch, which had been an intellectual and artistic center in Harlem since the 1920s. Columbia University had, a year earlier, tried to expand through Morningside Park into Harlem. The Metropolitan Museum of Art was in the midst of extracting local support and expertise for its forthcoming exhibition *Harlem on My Mind*, a gesture viewed by many as misguided, if not outright exploitative. All these events led Spriggs to declare, "It seems to me, that the vision of any alien group attempting to establish an institution in any given neighborhood should and must emanate from the combined experiences and creative inventory of the people it seeks to serve."[45]

Blayton remembers a widespread feeling within the Harlem arts community that the leaders of the Studio Museum lacked an organic relationship to the neighborhood. The planning committee sought endorsement from the Harlem Cultural Council without success. Its director, Ed Taylor, accused those involved with the Studio Museum of going over to "the enemy."[46] Janet Henry doesn't recall hearing any overt opposition, but did get the sense that people felt skeptical: "We don't have any money. What do we need a museum for? We could spend the money on something else."[47] In retrospect, Blayton believes she was "politically ignorant" at the time; few of the board members "were sincerely interested in the arts as it related to black people."[48] William T. Williams remembers that "there was never any talk about aesthetics. It was always social talk. It was political talk."[49] Although he participated in the museum from 1968 to 1969, Williams feared that "the Studio Museum could become a means of pacifying black artists and preventing them from pressuring other institutions—like the Museum of Modern Art or the Whitney—that needed to be pressured."[50] Some disparaged the Studio Museum as a revival of the kind of "white slumming" that took place in the 1920s.[51]

As executive secretary of the museum Mahler Ryder faced hurdles that reflected the mistrust between local residents and museum board members. In Harlem, he was turned away from local banks "with a mixture of disbelief and rhetoric" because of a perception that the museum was "white controlled."[52] At the same time, the museum's board prohibited Ryder from using any African American printer because the Harlem-based printer he first chose was housed in a decrepit building that made calibration of the printing "a nightmare."[53] Eventually, because he was engaged to a white woman, Ryder felt that "his impending interracial marriage would further tax the situation."[54] After making all the necessary arrangements for the first exhibition, scheduled to open in fall 1968, he quit so as to try and shield the work he and others had done from local criticism.

According to artist Benny Andrews, the white sculptor John Chamberlain was one of the first people the museum wanted to show, but the trustees thought it wiser to inaugurate the museum with an African American artist. They chose Tom Lloyd, an African American sculptor who worked in the medium of light (fig. 1.5). Born in 1929 in New York City, Lloyd was trained at the Pratt Institute and the Brooklyn Museum School of Art. Since 1965 he had had a string of shows at prestigious museums and galleries, including a solo exhibition at the Wadsworth Atheneum in Hartford, Connecticut, in 1966.[55] During the Studio Museum show he had work in the exhibition *30 Contemporary Black Artists*, which was circulating nationwide, and in April 1968 his work had been included in a benefit exhibition at the Museum of Modern Art honoring Martin Luther King Jr.[56] Lloyd called his show at the Studio Museum *Electronic Refractions II*. Looking back, Blayton thinks Lloyd may have been used as something of an instrument by the downtown contingent. She has recalled, "People on the board wanted the museum to be a Happening and Tom Lloyd was the closest thing they could come to."[57]

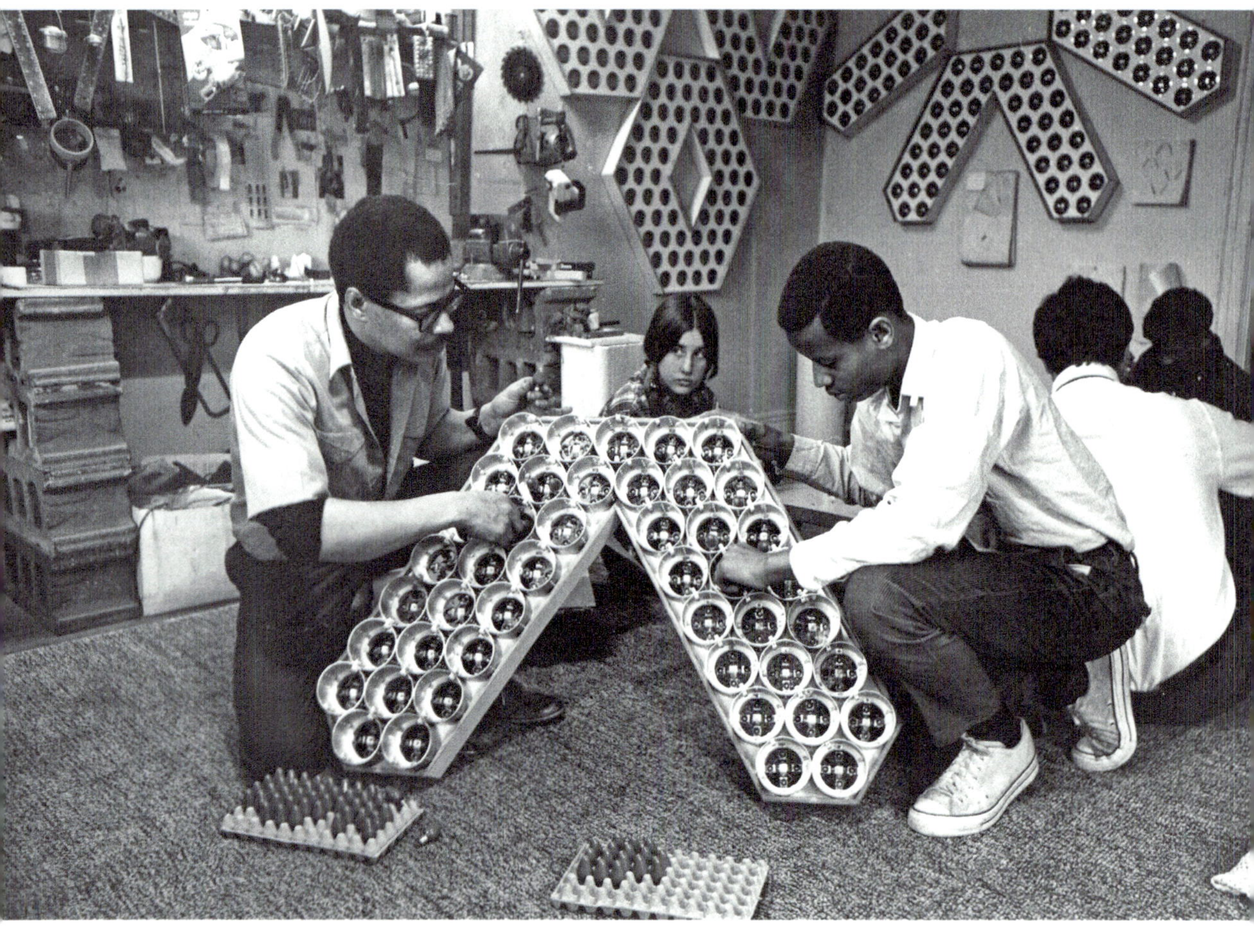

Fig. 1.5 Tom Lloyd (left) working with apprentices in his studio in Jamaica, Queens, 1968. Courtesy of the Studio Museum in Harlem.

Electronic Refractions II opened on September 24, 1968 (figs. 1.6 and 1.7). Ed Spriggs came to the opening straight from a meeting to discuss the possible closing of the Schomburg Library, which had served as the country's main repository of research on global African and African diasporan cultures since the Harlem Renaissance. As he approached the museum, he saw TV cameras, bright lights, and a "half dozen sleek limousines with waiting chauffeurs [lining] the block from corner to corner."[58] Inside he witnessed an unforgettable event: "As I reached for my second helping of something on an imported cracker, we heard a brother screaming out, 'God damn it! This shit ain't no *black* art. This ain't no black *museum*. You said this was gonna be a *black* museum. Get this shit out of here!' Then his fist came crashing down on one of the light tables. The smashing sound was like an immediate aftershock following the standstill silence that his screams had just created" (emphasis original).[59]

Opinions differ over the exact nature of the incident. Grace Glueck wrote in the *New York Times* that "a drunk lurched against a programed sculpture, smashing part of its protective glass," and *Artnews* reported that "one of the works was mysteriously broken."[60] Benny Andrews witnessed the destruction of two or three pieces.[61] The reaction to the museum surprised and disappointed William T. Williams:

> You had Olatunji and his group, who were coming from one direction, and another group, Weusi Artists were coming from another. . . . You had all these people outside. And here I am in the middle, showing up from my loft on Broadway, with my new little suit that I had bought because I had never owned a suit, right? I'm showing up at this place, and God, I feel on top of the world, right? We finally got a place, we're gonna do it now. . . . And I see people, kicking Tom Lloyd's sculpture in. . . . Literally breaking them.[62]

According to Blayton, "The Tom Lloyd show got a very big reaction from the community. The community reviewed it without having to write a word."[63] She noted, "The general feeling was that whitey was bringing what it thought was good art and they had no real feeling for it, and that if this was the kind of thing that was going to be shown that they didn't feel it was going to be speaking to the people."[64] The day after the opening Ted Gunn told the *New York Times*, "It's a new program and it will have to prove itself to the community."[65]

On November 22, 1968, Charles Inniss resigned as the Studio Museum's director. Gunn has recalled that "there was so much discontent that they were ready to close the museum."[66] But Gunn agreed to stay on and run the organization for a year, along with Williams and the board. The inaugural show of Lloyd's work was

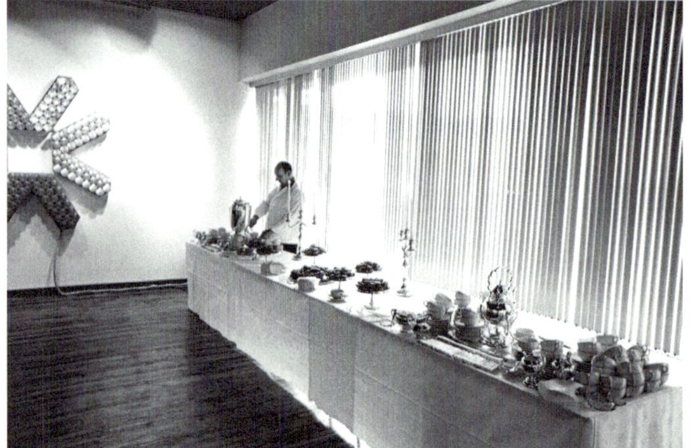

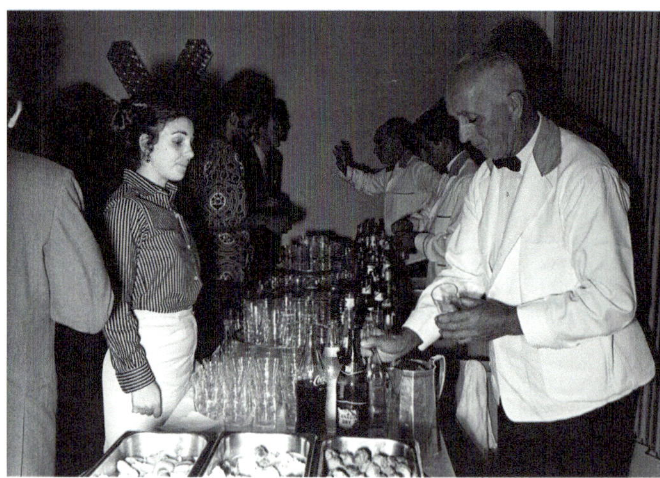

followed by *Invisible Americans*, a rebuttal exhibition to a show at the Whitney Museum of American Art, *The 1930's: Painting and Sculpture in America*; the Whitney show had failed to include a single African American artist. The next exhibition featured Afro-Haitian art and was followed by an exhibition of photographs of the Black Panthers by Ruth-Marion Baruch and Pirkle Jones. In June Williams had the opportunity to organize his first show, *X to the Fourth Power*, which included his own work, as well as that of Sam Gilliam, Melvin Edwards, and Steve Kelsey. The show was met with controversy revolving around two points: the inclusion of a white artist (Kelsey) and the focus on abstract work. The *New York Times* gave the show a positive review, but Williams was accused of being "anti-progressive," particularly by some members of the board.[67] He left the museum shortly thereafter.

Harlem Artists 69, organized by Ted Gunn and Betty Blayton, opened on July 22, 1969, featuring fifty-four artists from throughout New York City.[68] The curators had originally anticipated including only artists who lived in Harlem, but as word of the show spread, artists from elsewhere expressed interest. The curators explained in the exhibition brochure: "Harlem has for many years been the center of Black America, the spiritual and cultural home for tens of thousands of black people across the country."[69] Ed Spriggs took the helm as soon as the show opened, timing the start of his tenure to coincide with the project so as to express his alignment with its new nationalist focus.

Spriggs had moved to New York in 1965 after graduating from San Francisco State College, where he was a founding member of the journal *Black Dialogue*. He'd been on the New York scene as a printmaking instructor at LeRoi Jones's Black Arts Repertory Theater School and was conversant in Harlem's cultural politics. The school operated under the auspices of HARYOU-ACT until federal officials and the popular media began to criticize the program for being "racist" and "antiwhite."[70] Like many government-funded arts programs of the mid- to late '60s, the Black Arts Repertory Theater occupied a paradoxical position as a state-funded black nationalist organization whose leader advocated militancy. In 1966, when the program's leaders defiantly refused to allow white government officials to enter its building, funding was terminated.[71]

Spriggs brought a new philosophy to the museum. The Studio Museum would reject its former leaders' stance on integration. The board was reorganized to include cultural leaders living in Harlem, including Babatunde Olatunji. Spriggs has described the museum as a failed experiment in race relations, but a success in becoming a place with an undeniably special mission as a "black art museum."[72] At a colloquium on neighborhood museums in November 1969 Spriggs repudiated the Studio Museum's founders, pressing the question, "What right has any external cultural or colonial body, organization, or council to impose its establishment values and mores upon a different people?"[73] According to Mary Schmidt Campbell, Spriggs, whom she describes as a cultural activist, "really did lay the sort of cultural content groundwork for the museum."[74]

While developing the Studio Museum, Mahler Ryder met with many artists inside and outside Harlem and "found that a lot of fence-mending was needed to bring them together."[75] There were resentments based on ideological differences as well as socioeconomic positions. There were artists who sought mainstream attention and those who considered such attention irrelevant, or even exploitative. There were those who worked communally and those who pursued individual artistic practices. In 1985 Ryder reflected on those years and what would soon follow: "The healing process would not take place . . . until the ill-fated 'Harlem On My Mind' exhibition at the Metropolitan Museum . . . but that is another story."[76]

2. *Harlem on My Mind*
at the Metropolitan Museum of Art

You can't hide when you're as wealthy as the men who governed the Met. They lived an insular life. They had chauffeurs and they could keep the window closed, so to speak. But they couldn't avoid seeing in the newspaper, on the television, what was really happening. And they couldn't stand it.

Robert Malone, artist and exhibition designer of *Harlem on My Mind*

On the night of January 16, 1969, three dozen artists staged a protest outside the Metropolitan Museum of Art on New York City's Upper East Side. The occasion for the protest was the black tie opening of the Metropolitan Museum's exhibition *Harlem on My Mind*. As partygoers made their way inside sporting tuxedos and evening gowns, members of an activist group called the Black Emergency Cultural Coalition and their supporters marched back and forth along Fifth Avenue bundled in overcoats and gloves handing out leaflets that read "Soul's Been Sold Again!!!" and carrying signs that called the museum's director, Thomas P. F. Hoving, "Massa Hoving" (fig. 2.1). They implored the museum's guests to join their ranks. The protestors opposed what they saw as the misrepresentation of African Americans in this large exhibition about the social history of the Harlem neighborhood in New York City. The show's contents included documentary photographs and newspaper texts presented in the form of slide projections, photo blowups, audiotapes, text panels, and videos. The aim of the curator, Allon Schoener, was to demonstrate the Met's willingness to embrace a broad spectrum of community and cultural interests and to recast the role of the museum from connoisseur of precious objects to participant in contemporary cultural debate. Yet the exclusive use of journalistic media implied that African American artists had no place at the Met. The protestors' leaflet read: "Black people puzzled and anxious to learn of their heritage and of some meaning in their lives, can find very little enlightenment in this fantasia." They mocked the show's white organizers as the "latest experts on the Black experience." The protest marked a turning point. According to Lowery Stokes Sims, a longtime curator at the Metropolitan Museum, "The reaction against *Harlem on My Mind* is comparable to Woodstock, the March on Washington,

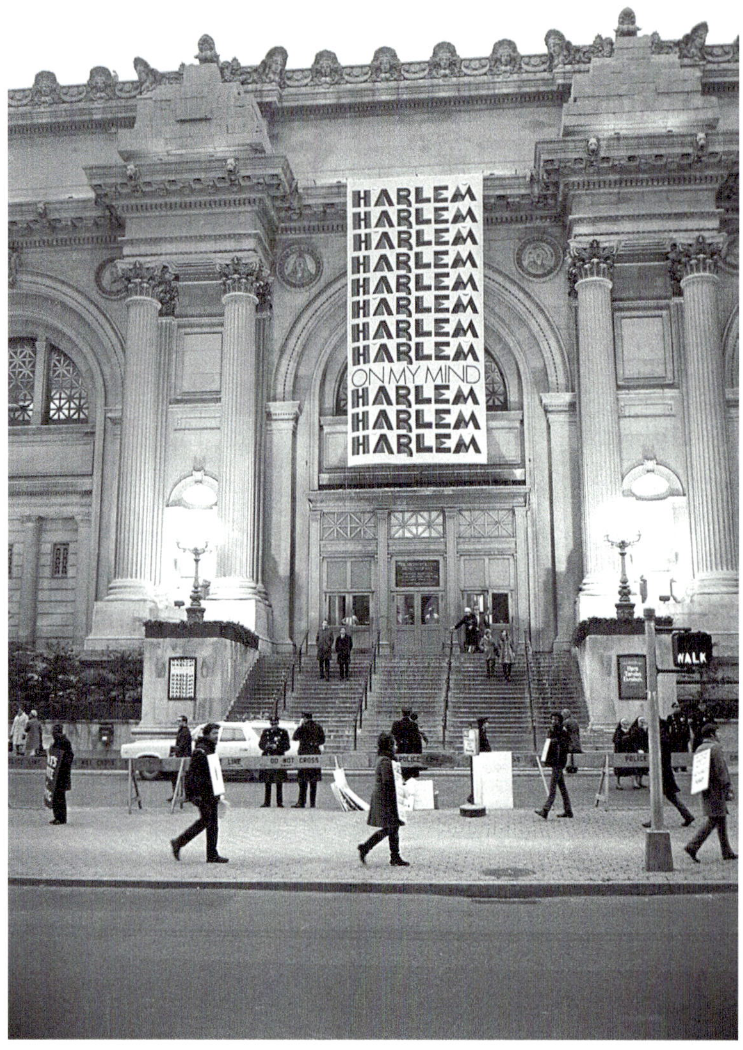

Fig. 2.1 Protest at the Metropolitan Museum of Art, January 16, 1969.
Photo: Jack Manning / The New York Times / Redux.

all these large manifestations that really gave people an inkling of their entitlement and their ability to make change within institutions."[1] The artists jolted the Metropolitan Museum out of the past and brought the civil rights movement to the museum's front door.

Photography had been shown in exhibitions and collected by museums since the beginning of the twentieth century.[2] Yet, as the artists pointed out, the Met had never done any exhibitions of photography, not even exhibitions of photographs by white artists. The museum's acceptance of photography as an art medium would not be formalized until 1992 with the establishment of its Photography Department. Some of the artists who picketed the museum wore signs that read, "Visit the Metropolitan Museum of Art Photography."[3]

The curator had several reasons for focusing on photography and for using only reproductions in his show. First and foremost, Schoener excluded traditional art media as a challenge to prevailing cultural hierarchies. He considered photographic reproduction an inherently democratic mode of cultural production that dissolved the aura of exclusivity that surrounded the unique art object.[4] Beyond this, the use of photography reflected Schoener's desire to convey truth. He believed in the veracity and objectivity of photographs as documents. His selection of photos and newspaper texts was intended to convey a feeling of reportage, the sense that the viewer was experiencing Harlem's history "as it happened."[5]

As a socio-documentary exhibition of photo-reproductions and media, *Harlem on My Mind* didn't "make sense" within the logic of an art museum. Looking back, even staff members who were directly involved with the project were vexed. As Harry S. Parker III, who was working in the director's office at the time, recalls: "Here it was [an exhibition] at the Metropolitan Museum of Art, but it ignored African American art. Which was amazing. . . . I remember thinking how stupid we were to ignore art when, here, that's the medium that we're theoretically the most interested in. When the show started to come together why weren't any of us out there saying, 'Well, aren't you going to include some art, Allon? This is an art museum.' "[6]

From its founding in 1870 up until the 1960s, the Metropolitan Museum had been a bastion of elite culture that had studiously avoided substantive involvement with contemporary art and issues of the day.[7] Conceived and founded as an encyclopedic museum, the collection had begun with the purchase of 174 European paintings from the sixteenth to nineteenth centuries, mostly seventeenth-century Dutch and Flemish works. The collections would soon grow to include Egyptian artifacts excavated on museum-sponsored archeological expeditions, Greek and

Etruscan vases, Chinese jades, and Italian Renaissance paintings purchased, donated, or bequeathed by the "men of fortune" who sat on the museum board.[8]
These treasures were displayed in lavish galleries often designed to evoke the ex-
travagant interiors of collectors' homes. For example, Heber R. Bishop, who bequeathed his collection of over a thousand Chinese jades in 1902, stipulated that
they be installed at the museum exactly as he had had them in his home. Upon
the death of the financier George Blumenthal in 1941, the museum inherited a reconstruction of a two-story courtyard from a Spanish castle built around 1515; Blumenthal had bought the structure and rebuilt it as a room in his townhouse on the
corner of Fifth Avenue and Seventieth Street. The Wrightsman period rooms of
French decorative arts from the ancien régime allowed visitors to ogle the lifestyle
of the ruling class on the eve of the French Revolution.[9] Prior to donating their
collection to the Met throughout the 1960s and '70s, Jayne and Charles Wrightsman had lived with these furnishings, which included a red lacquered and gilt
bronze desk commissioned for Louis XV for Versailles and a console that had belonged to Marie Antoinette. As Carol Duncan has observed, the galleries at the Met
"collect and idealize ancestral identities from other times and places—past royalty,
aristocracy or . . . well-bred, AngloSaxon stock—and ritually transfer them to the
conglomerated elites of the present."[10]

The Met's board was stocked with some of the most powerful men in New York,
prominent patricians who often had connections to government and finance, such
as J. P. Morgan and Nelson Rockefeller.[11] Moreover, they were a long-serving crew.
It was not unusual to find among the museum's roster of trustees individuals who
had served on the board for twenty or thirty years, or even longer. In 1969, at the
time of the *Harlem on My Mind* show, twelve of the museum's thirty-seven trustees
had been on the board for at least twenty years; one had served since 1934.[12]

Until the late 1960s, the Metropolitan Museum of Art was an extension of a
small, elite social world. Public openings were not yet common practice. Harry
Parker, who joined the museum's staff in January 1964, has described the social
milieu:

> When I came to the Met, a typical social event would be the acquisitions din-
> ner at which the acquisitions committee and the curators would all dress in
> black tie for the evening meeting. Everybody would have a couple of drinks
> and sit at a formal table with all the waiters and the glasses of wine and all
> the rest of it. One curator would present the object that he thought ought to
> be bought. And another curator would get up and do the same. But it was all

presented as a social occasion for the eight or ten members of the acquisition committee who would sit and debate the presentation. . . . The events were meant to support and sustain [the trustees'] sense of importance and their collegiality. They all knew each other. They all went to each other's parties and they all were part of a social world.[13]

In the late 1960s the cast of leaders at the Metropolitan began to change. Arthur A. Houghton Jr., who had been on the board since 1952, became president in 1964 and chairman in 1970. His brother was the American ambassador to France under John F. Kennedy. Douglas Dillon, a powerful member of the board who would succeed Houghton as president in 1970, had been undersecretary of state for the Kennedy and Johnson administrations. These men were tied into the Kennedy spirit and the concerns of a younger generation. Thomas P. F. Hoving, who was appointed director of the Met in 1966, would launch a new, progressive agenda.

The museum's previous director, from 1955 to 1966, had been James Rorimer, a medieval scholar who had joined the museum's staff in 1927 at the age of twenty-two directly from his studies at Harvard. With the exception of army service during World War II, Rorimer had never worked anywhere but the Met. Like Alfred H. Barr Jr., the founding director of the Museum of Modern Art, he had studied art history at Harvard with mentor Paul Sachs, who taught a graduate course specifically designed to train future museum curators. Rorimer's triumph, an accomplishment that contributed to his ascendance to the directorship nearly a quarter of a century later, was his supervision of the establishment of The Cloisters, a satellite of the Metropolitan Museum located in Upper Manhattan's Fort Tryon Park, which was completed in 1938.[14]

Like Rorimer, Hoving was a medievalist and widely viewed as a brilliant art historian. The two men met when Hoving delivered a student paper at a symposium sponsored by the Frick museum in 1959. Rorimer picked Hoving out of the lineup and made him his protégé. He hired him at the Met, took him on trips to Europe, eventually promoted him to the position of curator of The Cloisters, and groomed him to be his successor as the museum's director. In 1965, when Hoving took a sabbatical from the museum to work for the mayoral campaign of John V. Lindsay, Rorimer was puzzled and hurt. He saw politics as a debased arena and did not share the values that drove Hoving to leave the very position that Rorimer himself had relished. When Lindsay was elected mayor and appointed Hoving as parks commissioner, Rorimer disparaged the post as a lowly form of bureaucratic civil service.[15]

In the spring of 1966 Rorimer died suddenly of a heart attack. During the year-long interregnum, a committee of curators ran the museum under the direction of board president Arthur Houghton. Hoving was the top contender for the director's job despite his hiatus from the museum and Rorimer's disdain for his political activities; many members of the board were ready for a breath of fresh air. Hoving was given the position in late 1966 and in March 1967 officially took charge as director. In a single year a generational shift had occurred. Hoving was thirty-six years old, twenty-five years younger than his predecessor, and although he possessed classical art history training, establishment credentials rivaling any curator in the country, and a first-class mind, there was also throughout Hoving's life a rebellion against the standards of the traditional world into which he'd been born. He had been kicked out of prep school. His wife Nancy was working for Phoenix House, a drug rehabilitation program. As Harry Parker put it, "There weren't many museum curators whose wives were working for drug addicts. . . . Hoving came in full of piss and vinegar supported by trustees who wanted to see change."[16]

Parker recalls that very few people of color were associated with the museum at that time. The only African Americans he recalls seeing at the Met, until *Harlem on My Mind*, were on the maintenance and custodial staff: "There were no black curators, no black administrators, no black secretaries, and there were certainly no black trustees. It was a totally upstairs, downstairs situation."[17] Arthur Rosenblatt, Hoving's deputy parks commissioner and the Metropolitan Museum's vice director for architecture, recalls that if an African American person approached the museum's door there was a second glance and a reaction of suspicion.[18] Hoving puts it even more strongly: "When I arrived [at the museum] I found that the Irish guards at the main entrance actually turned away African Americans and Hispanics saying that the MMA was a private club. (I guess it was, but it didn't stay that way very long after I arrived.)"[19] *Harlem on My Mind* was designed to transform the museum. "I looked upon 'Harlem on My Mind' as a turning point. It was going to justify my view of the museum as a moral, social, and educational force."[20]

The *Harlem on My Mind* exhibition was the brainchild of Allon Schoener, an art historian and curator who was working as director of the Visual Arts Program at the New York State Council on the Arts when he proposed the project to Hoving in January 1967. Schoener's career had always been focused on populist endeavors. He had studied art history first at Yale University, then at London's Courtauld Institute with the Marxist art historian Anthony Blunt. His first museum job, in the early 1950s, was at the San Francisco Museum of Modern Art producing a Sunday morning television show called *Art in Your Life*.[21] The show presented interviews with artists, painting demonstrations, and gallery talks. The gallery talks were conducted in mock exhibitions created in the studio especially for the program. Foreshadowing Schoener's exhibition technique in *Harlem on My Mind*, in place of actual artworks, the production crew used reproductions, framed photographs of paintings printed to actual scale. Although it was broadcast in black and white and was only a faint echo of the actual museum experience, Schoener took pride in the fact that the show reached eighty thousand people every Sunday afternoon, half the number of people who came to the museum in an entire year. Working on this television program shaped Schoener's belief in the power of communications technology.[22] His enthusiasm for television was part of a widespread belief in the 1950s that television would be the great leveler, bringing high culture to mass audiences. Schoener's TV program in San Francisco was one of the many that delivered dance, theater, music, and the visual arts directly into viewers' living rooms.

Schoener left San Francisco to become curator, and later director, of the Contemporary Art Center in Cincinnati. He arrived in New York City in 1964, and after brief stints as an art dealer at Marlborough Gallery and a staff member at the Brooklyn Museum, he landed the position of assistant director at the Jewish Museum. Then known as an innovator in the fields of contemporary art and exhibition practice, Jewish Museum director Sam Hunter asked Schoener if he would be interested in organizing a show about the Lower East Side, an idea that had been under discussion at the museum for several years. Schoener agreed and decided to structure the show as a collage of sounds and both moving and static images that told the story of Eastern European Jews who had emigrated to the Lower East Side between 1870 and 1925, struggled to adapt to American life, and were eventually assimilated into New York City's mixture of cultures.[23] Schoener was excited by the opportunity to apply multimedia communications technology to an exhibition. *Portal to America* was by all measures a great success. Crowds lined up around the block and the critical response was good.

As a social history exhibition about one of New York City's most distinctive ethnic neighborhoods, *Portal to America* was the model for *Harlem on My Mind*. Like the Jewish Museum show, *Harlem on My Mind* would tell its story exclusively through documentary materials—photographs, videotapes, and primary texts—presented in the form of slide projections, photo blowups, audiotapes, text panels, and video projections. The idea came to Schoener while he was taking two Harlem ministers through the Lower East Side exhibition. The two shows differed, however, in one key respect: *Portal to America* explored Schoener's own cultural history and the neighborhood where his father had lived as a boy; Harlem was a neighborhood

Schoener did not know and to which he had no personal connection. Moreover, while the Jewish Museum had an ongoing relationship with the constituency portrayed in *Portal to America*, the Metropolitan Museum of Art had no such relationship with the communities of Harlem.

The title of the show, *Harlem on My Mind*, also grew out of the Lower East Side exhibition. The phrase comes from a song that composer and lyricist Irving Berlin wrote for his 1933 Broadway musical *As Thousands Cheer*. In the production, Ethel Waters performs the song "Harlem on My Mind" in the guise of a character based on the expatriate singer and dancer Josephine Baker. The Baker character sits alone in a Paris café pining for her former Harlem haunts singing the lyrics "I've a longing to be low down and my *parlez-vous* will not ring true, with Harlem on my mind." Perhaps Schoener considered Fifth Avenue and Eighty-Second Street to be as distant from Harlem as Paris. *As Thousands Cheer* was based on the structure of a daily newspaper; each scene of the show brought a different section of the newspaper to life. (One of its best-known numbers is "Heatwave," which was based on the weather report.) Schoener no doubt saw an affinity between his exhibition methodology, which drew heavily on newspaper source material, and Berlin's musical.[24] Irving Berlin was one of the Lower East Side's most dramatic success stories.

Born Israel (Izzy) Baline, Berlin was a Russian Jewish immigrant who rose to become one the most lauded songwriters in American history. Irving Berlin epitomized the triumph of poor Jews and their full integration into American society. Schoener saw *Portal to America* as a symbolic culmination of the Jewish immigrant's success story in the United States, paralleling the trajectory of Berlin's life, since the show took place at a museum that was the former mansion of a wealthy and distinguished Jewish family, the Warburgs. Schoener viewed the staging of an exhibition on the history of blacks at the Metropolitan, the country's most exalted museum, as a matching achievement. "If telling the story of poor immigrant Jews in the former Warburg mansion at 92nd and Fifth Avenue was of interest," he thought, "telling the story of blacks in Harlem should also be of interest, and should happen at the Met."[25] Berlin's song "Harlem on My Mind" bridged *Portal to America*, the story of struggling Jews, with the story of African Americans.

Berlin bore another relation to the Metropolitan Museum that Schoener may or may not have been aware of. In 1926 Berlin married Ellin Mackay, the daughter of Clarence H. Mackay, one of the richest and most prominent men in New York society and a devout Catholic. Clarence Mackay had inherited a fortune from his father's Nevada mining business and enlarged this wealth by becoming a controlling investor in utilities and telegraph companies.[26] When Ellin Mackay became engaged to Irving Berlin, her father forbade the marriage because Berlin was

Jewish. Mackay and Berlin ended up eloping, against the wishes of her father, who disinherited her. Clarence Mackay was a collector of arms and armor, as well as Italian painting and sculpture. He was also a major supporter of the Metropolitan Museum of Art throughout the mid-1920s and a member of the board of trustees from 1929 through 1932. *Harlem on My Mind* would not only bring images of African Americans into the museum's hallowed halls but would also admit Irving Berlin, a Jew who had been shunned by a member of the Metropolitan Museum of Art's power elite.

The exhibition's subtitle, "Cultural Capital of Black America," alluded to the idea that Harlem was the cultural homeland of all African Americans. The phrase was adapted from James Weldon Johnson's famous essay "Harlem: The Cultural Capital," written in 1925 and published in *Survey Graphic* magazine. This essay lays out Johnson's vision of Harlem as a center of intellectual, cultural, and economic power, exerting influence throughout the world.[27]

Schoener joined the staff of the New York State Council on the Arts (NYSCA) in 1967 as the Visual Arts Program director. In this role he was responsible for a broad program that included financial aid to museums, traveling exhibitions, artists' studio visits for college and university students, and an initiative designed to foster new techniques in exhibition production. When Schoener arrived at NYSCA, he was still riding the wave of public success he had achieved with *Portal to America*. At the council Schoener had the opportunity to further develop his ideas about the use of reproducible media in exhibition practice with the support of its director, John Hightower, also a populist, who was developing a reputation as a maverick in the burgeoning field of public arts funding. Schoener's first major project at the council was a show commemorating the 150th anniversary of the Erie Canal. The project's main innovation was its location: the exhibition took place on a barge that traveled along the canal from town to town, making stops where an advance team of NYSCA staff members had organized festivals and "happenings." Like *Portal to America, Erie Canal: 1817–1967* relied heavily on archival photographs reproduced on large placards. Schoener saw traveling exhibitions as a form of mass culture. Indeed, *Harlem on My Mind* was originally conceived as traveling to multiple venues.[28]

As a liberal thinker with leftist leanings, Schoener saw *Harlem on My Mind* as a chance not only to explore new exhibition techniques but also to be a civil rights activist. He had not participated in the Freedom Rides and civil rights marches in the South like many of his contemporaries with similarly liberal political views. Psychologically and spiritually, however, he felt that he was there. He asked himself, "What can I do that will contribute to what is happening in the country today? I knew how to make exhibitions, so I thought, why not make an exhibition that's revolutionary?"[29] Schoener's ambitions were grand, but not entirely unfounded. The New York State Council on the Arts had been a model for the creation of the National Endowment for the Arts in 1965 and for arts councils in every state of the country and most of the U.S. territories.[30] With the creation of these state and federal funding agencies Schoener had witnessed the expansion of arts patronage beyond the scope of private interests into the public realm.

Tom Hoving shared Schoener's sense of civic duty and public mission. As New York City's parks commissioner under Mayor John Lindsay from 1965 until his appointment as the Met's director in December 1966, Hoving had been deeply involved in the racial politics of New York City. His office took a proactive role in quelling racial tensions by sponsoring events in public parks that allowed supervised chaos. "Most of my summer games and circuses, concerts and 'Happenings,'" said Hoving, "were intended to keep the city cool." In his view, "it worked. New York City didn't get torched as did so many around the U.S.A."[31] Hoving also had a history of taking liberal stands on controversial issues. During his tenure as parks commissioner he was asked by Mayor Lindsay to assess a plan that would have allowed Columbia University to build a controversial gym in Harlem's Morningside Park. The plan was controversial not only because it gave a private university use of public lands and thus infringed on a public entitlement of Harlem residents, but also because its plans to allow gym access by the neighborhood's African American residents relegated them to an entrance on the lower floors of the building in what amounted to de facto segregation. One journalist termed the situation "apartheid."[32] Hoving argued against Columbia's encroachment on Morningside Park and advised Lindsay that using public lands for private interests would set "a very, very bad precedent."[33] The controversy over the building of the gym would, in 1968, spark the student uprising that shut down Columbia University.[34]

On the surface, *Harlem on My Mind* seemed to fly in the face of the Metropolitan's traditional interests and such staples of traditional curatorial concern as connoisseurship and provenance. Many of the photographs included in the exhibition were by unknown photographers and had been obtained from United Press International (UPI) and the local history collection of the New York Public Library. In many cases, even if their makers were known, the photos were not attributed. Most importantly, these photographs were presented in reproduction, not in the original. Nonetheless, the exhibition's focus on pedagogy had a history at the Metropolitan Museum. As Hoving reminded readers in the preface to the *Harlem on My Mind* catalogue, the museum's mission was "to relate art to practical life and practical living to art."[35] Since its founding, the Metropolitan had gone through phases in which public service was its primary emphasis. From 1940 to 1954 the museum had launched several projects with explicitly pedagogical and populist aims under the direction of Henry Francis Taylor, a pioneer in the field of museology who advocated that museums be places for public education.[36] While the tenure of Hoving's immediate predecessor, James Rorimer, was marked by retrenchment, the Hoving era swung the pendulum back in the direction of public service. Harry Parker recalls that the late 1960s was a time when people of conscience felt both a sense of social responsibility and a feeling of empowerment that they could make a positive impact on society even from within an elite institution like the Metropolitan Museum of Art. As Parker recollects, "You've got to put it in context. In the mid-'60s what we were all saying is that there are some issues that were so important that every institution had to get involved in them. You can't afford to be saying . . . that's somebody else's problem. So what everyone was crying for was: No. You're rich. You're powerful. You're a big institution. You have to take an interest in problems of the day."[37] All of this set the background for *Harlem on My Mind.*

Beyond these social ideals, there was another reason Hoving embraced the show when Schoener proposed it to the museum. In April 1967, the first month of Hoving's tenure as director, President Lyndon B. Johnson announced that the Metropolitan Museum of Art had been awarded custodianship of the Temple of Dendur.[38] The Temple had been removed from an area on the Nile River in Egypt to save it from engulfment in water when the Aswan Dam was constructed in 1963. The structure was given to the United States as a gift from the Egyptian government in exchange for financial aid to restore another archeological landmark, the ancient temple of Abu Simbel. Selected by a presidential commission from among proposals submitted by museums around the country, the Met planned to encase the temple, measuring fifty by thirty feet and twenty feet high, in a large glass wing that would have an open-air feel without subjecting its ancient stones to the harsh effects of the northeastern climate. In September 1967, the museum revealed that the new wing for the Temple of Dendur was the first phase of a major expansion plan.

Over the next two years Hoving would develop a full scheme to transform every inch of the Metropolitan Museum. In addition to the Temple of Dendur, which would extend the museum to the north, the museum planned to build a second wing, equally large, on the south side, to house the collection of the Museum of Primitive Art, which Nelson Rockefeller donated to the museum in May 1969. This would become the Michael C. Rockefeller Wing, named after Nelson's son who had disappeared while leading an expedition in New Guinea in 1961. But this was not all. Robert Lehman, who headed the prestigious and lucrative Lehman Brothers investment bank, promised to donate his entire collection of European paintings, drawings, sculptures, medieval illuminated manuscripts, and modern art, valued at $100 million, if, and only if, the museum agreed to build an entire wing exclusively devoted to this work. Lehman died in 1969, and the bequest came to the museum under those terms. And as if this weren't enough, Hoving envisioned substantial renovations to the American galleries, a redesign of the museum's façade, major renovations to the Great Hall, and upgrades for all of the museum's two hundred galleries. In total, the plan increased the space of the museum from seven to seventeen acres. The price tag in 1970 was $50 million. Hoving called this the Master Plan.

The museum's planned expansion was carefully calculated to ensure that every inch was within the legal boundaries of land within Central Park that had been allocated by the city when the museum was chartered in 1870.[39] Nonetheless, park preservationists recoiled at the museum's desire to encroach further into the beloved urban sanctuary. Robert Makla, a lawyer and conservationist, expressed the sentiment of many in a letter to the editor of the *New York Times*, claiming, "Central Park is threatened on all sides. Its irreplaceable green fields, recreational areas, woods and lakes must be spared if we are to know the rewards of nature which have succumbed to urban sprawl everywhere."[40]

Conservationists weren't the only opponents. On December 15, 1967, the New York City Planning Commission conducted its usual hearing on proposals for city construction projects. The museum had put in a request to the commission for $1.68 million. In the public hearing, the museum's funding request for the Temple of Dendur was pitted against requests for improvements to city psychiatric facilities; heating at a center for mentally handicapped people; and educational facilities at community colleges. The commission would have a hard time justifying an appropriation to the Met in the face of these pressing needs. Speaking out against appropriations for the museum, Assemblyman Bill Green from the Sixty-Sixth District said, "The Temple of Dendur may be one of the gems of Egyptian civilization, but Central Park is one of the gems of our civilization." He suggested that the building be put "in some economically depressed area of the city like Harlem."[41]

Robert Makla's letter to the *New York Times* editor also proposed finding an alternative location: "Cultural decentralization is the only policy to pursue today. Entire communities are still untouched by the cultural explosion which has enriched central Manhattan, while the museum's stupendous ten acres buildings [*sic*], stretching from 80th to 84th Street, saturate Fifth Avenue with art."[42] Hoving resented the opposition to the Met's expansion and defended his plans, saying, "Decentralization is mostly a coverup for the rabid park person who doesn't want us to build on our own property."[43]

Yet the call to decentralize the Met reflected the tenor of the times. Nationally, decentralization was at the core of Lyndon Johnson's antipoverty programs. To Sargent Shriver, widely viewed as the architect of these programs, decentralization was a civil rights issue: "We are asking those who hold power in the community to 'move over' and share that power with those who are to be helped. We insist that this can't be just token involvement. It must be a real one."[44]

In New York City decentralization was a major theme in education reform. In 1966 over half of New York City's 1.1 million school children were identified as "Negro and Puerto Rican," yet segregation was increasing because African Americans and Latinos tended to cluster in particular neighborhoods and whites were fleeing from the city to the suburbs.[45] The New York state legislature agreed to give New York City public schools increased financial aid on the condition that the city "afford members of the community an opportunity to take a more active and meaningful role in the development of educational policy related to the diverse needs and aspirations of the community."[46] In April 1967 Mayor John Lindsay created an advisory panel headed by McGeorge Bundy, president of the Ford Foundation, to devise a plan for decentralized school governance.[47] The panel came to the conclusion that the city's schools were caught in a "spiral of decline" due primarily to the size and complexity of the citywide education bureaucracy. Decentralizing governance and replacing New York City's school bureaucracy with a system of local community boards was designed to "liberate new constructive energies and rebuild confidence in all parts of our educational system" by allowing parents in communities of color to have greater say over the education of their children.[48]

Decentralization was also a hot topic in city government. Right after his election Mayor Lindsay had called for the creation of "Little City Halls," neighborhood offices throughout the city to give residents a line into City Hall when they wanted answers or action on problems like better streetlights, vandalism, or landlord-tenant disputes. Some critics disparaged the idea as "nothing more than municipal service stations for minor repairs," but by the end of 1967, Lindsay had managed to start six Little City Halls in Washington Heights in Upper Manhattan; Flushing-Corona and Flushing-Hillcrest in Queens; Brownsville and Fordham–East Tremont in the Bronx; and East New York in Brooklyn.[49]

Finally, in the museum field, decentralization was the impetus behind the creation of satellite museums. The first, the Anacostia Neighborhood Museum, opened to the public on September 16, 1967, as a branch museum of the Smithsonian Institution.[50] Located in Southeast Washington in a building that had once been a dance hall, the museum was overseen by thirty-year-old director John Kinard. The inaugural exhibitions included a Mercury space capsule that visitors could enter and operate; a small theater with closed-circuit television over which children could watch themselves rehearse and perform; and a walk-through reproduction of an Anacostia store of the 1890s furnished with goods that visitors could touch.[51] Another early satellite museum initiative was the National Museum of Afro-American Art, a joint venture of the Elma Lewis School and the Boston Museum of Fine Arts, which was conceived in 1967, was incorporated in 1968, and opened in 1969 under the direction of Edmund Barry Gaither. Gaither's exhibitions focused on art.

The concept of decentralization did not have an exact definition. In fact, its meaning was a point of debate at the NYSCA seminar on "neighborhood museums" held in November 1969. Ed Spriggs, shortly after his appointment as director of the Studio Museum in Harlem, delivered a fiery presentation advocating repatriation of African art and criticizing the Met's plans. He said: "This is the age of the master plan. I am sure that we have all become aware of master plans in the last few years—plans of the masters. [Laughter] It's the age of hidden agendas, which characterise and camouflage white imperialism and racism; white nationalism; white regionalism; white provincialism, as well as institutional racism. . . . I'd like to see the major institutions begin to redistribute the wealth of continents like Africa that has been ripped off over the years, raped, plundered, etcetera, for the benefit of private collections and museums in this country."[52]

Various parts of the Met's Master Plan required approvals from different New York City offices. Parks Commissioner August Heckscher reviewed all the museum's plans and had the authority to refer or not refer them on to the New York City Arts Commission. The Arts Commission, which Heckscher also headed, then had to approve all parts of the plan, since the museum, built on city land and supported in part by city funds, was city property. These approvals were all that was needed for the Lehman Pavilion, since this section was underwritten by the Lehman bequest; however, this part of the plan was as controversial as the rest and was opposed by the Art Workers' Coalition, which staged a protest at Lehman Brothers headquarters at One William Street parodying the museum's expansion by deploying a large inflatable sculpture by artist Gilles Larrain that blocked traffic in the narrow streets (figs. 2.2–2.4). Other parts of the plan were to be implemented with city funding, such as the Temple of Dendur, which required approval by the City Planning Commission, the budget director, the Finance Committee of the City Council, and the Board of Estimate. In addition, the Landmarks Preservation Commission had to ratify any exterior changes whether public or private funds were used, since the museum was a city landmark. In short, the museum needed to mount a massive

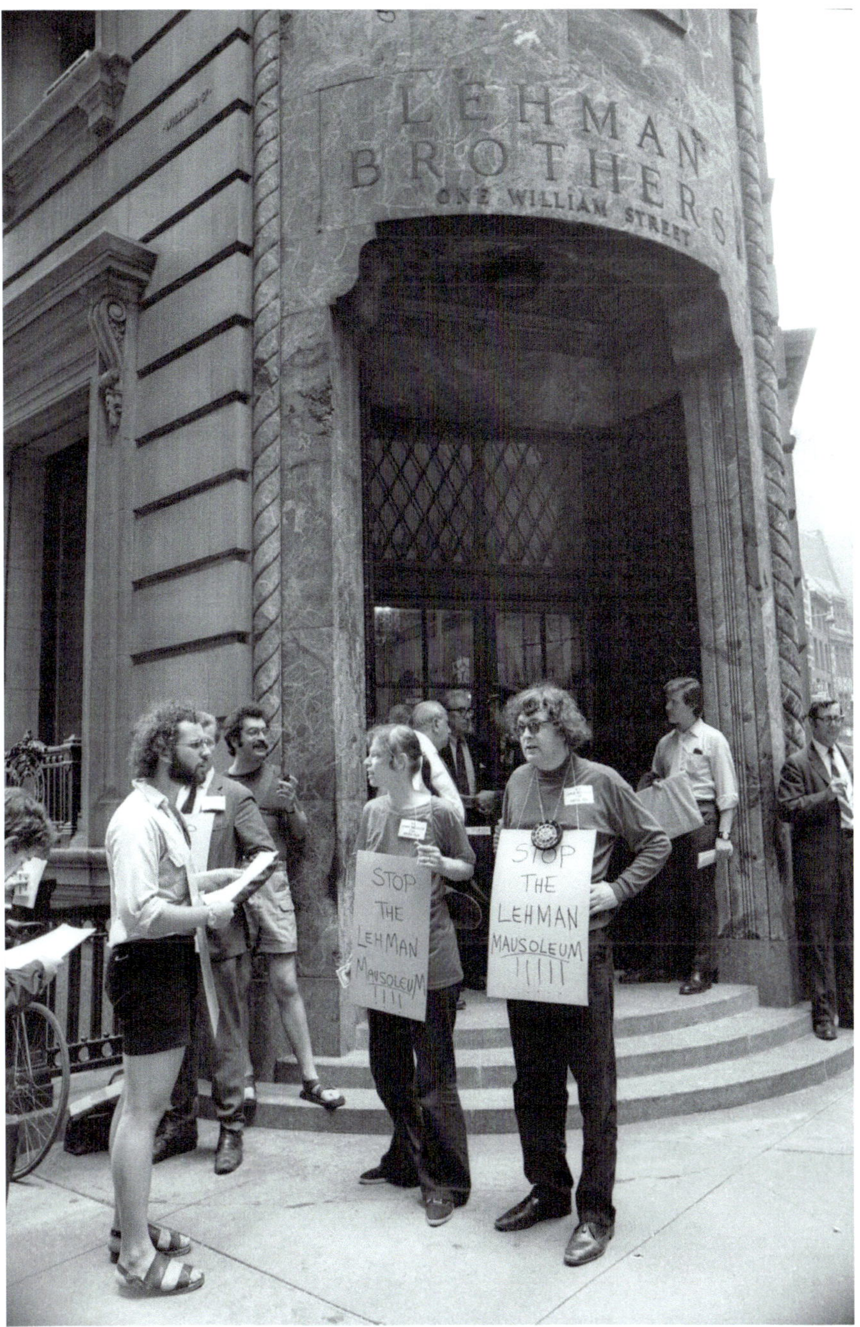

Fig. 2.2 Art Workers' Coalition protest at Lehman Brothers, One William Street, New York City, against planned expansion by the Metropolitan Museum of Art for the Lehman Wing, June 12, 1970. © Jan van Raay.

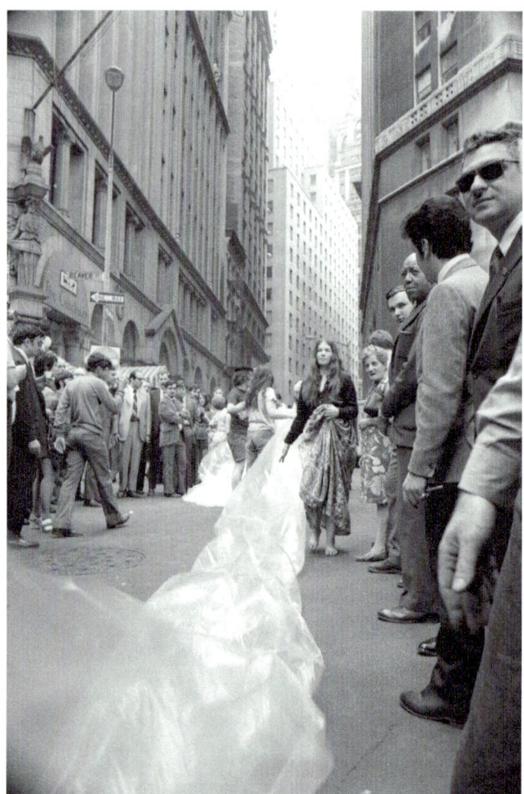

Fig. 2.3 Art Workers' Coalition protest at Lehman Brothers, One William Street, New York City, against planned expansion by the Metropolitan Museum of Art for the Lehman Wing, June 12, 1970, with inflatable by Gilles Larrain. © Jan van Raay.

Fig. 2.4 Art Workers' Coalition protest at Lehman Brothers, One William Street, New York City, against planned expansion by the Metropolitan Museum of Art for the Lehman Wing, June 12, 1970, with inflatable by Gilles Larrain. © Jan van Raay.

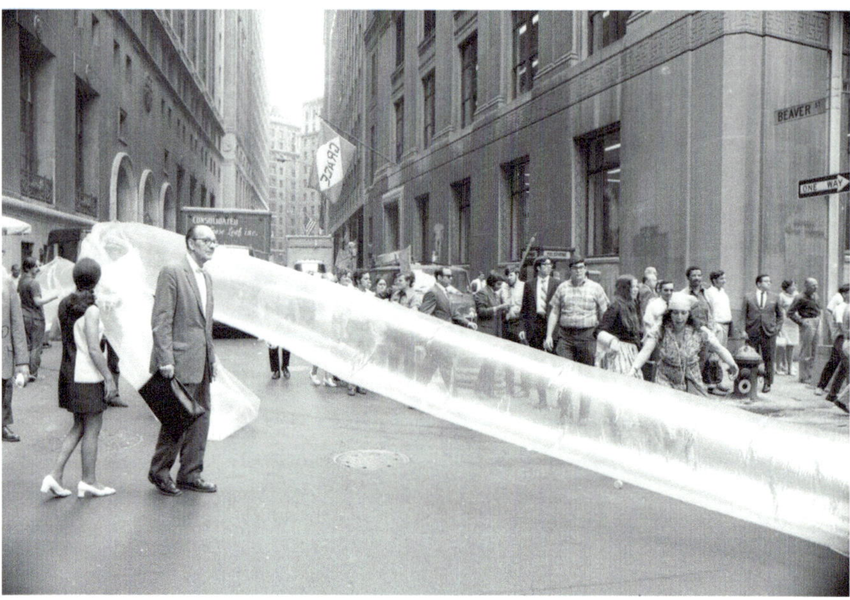

public relations campaign that would generate support from politicians throughout the five boroughs of New York City. Harlem was not a borough, but like the Bronx, Brooklyn, and Queens, it had its own arts association, the Harlem Cultural Council.

Sheer pragmatism drove the Met to embark on a systematic program of community outreach—decentralization—to extend its services deep into each of the boroughs in order to garner the support it needed to obtain both the formal approvals from the various New York City agencies and boards and the acquiescence of the city's elected politicians. The community outreach program, which began with a small staff and a focus on cultivating community relationships, would eventually encompass the creation of four museums, eight major exhibitions, workshops and training programs for museum professionals entering the field, summer internships for college students, and programs of exhibitions highlighting the cultural activities of over a hundred community organizations.[53] The museum's campaign to expand farther into Central Park would succeed, but only after the museum's mammoth investment of time, money, and political know-how.

Architect Arthur Rosenblatt, first hired to oversee the expansion project, soon saw his portfolio expand to include community relations (fig. 2.5). Rosenblatt was familiar with the city's various neighborhoods because he had previously designed playgrounds in New York City and was active in city politics—he and Hoving had met in the late '50s when Hoving was a curator at The Cloisters; both men had campaigned for John Lindsay in the 1965 mayoral election; and when Hoving was appointed parks commissioner, he chose Rosenblatt as his deputy. Hoving asked Rosenblatt to employ the lessons they had learned in city government, and Rosenblatt understood his charge: "It became clear that the Met was going to have to play politics" in order to appease its critics.[54]

Throughout 1968 and 1969, Rosenblatt undertook a campaign to present the museum's designs and concepts to community boards throughout the city. Rosenblatt recalls: "We . . . had to present all of these designs and all of these concepts to community boards *everywhere*, and so one of my jobs was to make presentations to community board number 2, community board number 5, community board number 8, etc."[55] Rosenblatt hired Susan Coppello, whose instructions were to "inform herself about New York's many communities and to suggest ways in which the Museum could relate to them more effectively."[56] To this end, she visited each city councilman to learn about his district and hear his assessment of what the Metropolitan Museum meant to his constituents.

To support the *Harlem on My Mind* show, the museum solicited endorsements from political figures, including Harlem congressman Adam Clayton Powell and

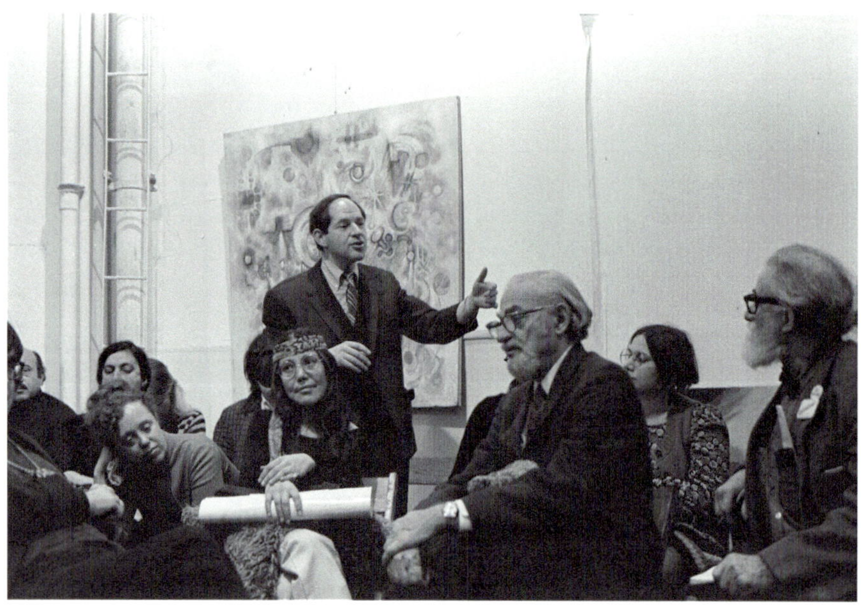

Fig. 2.5 Arthur Rosenblatt, in charge of architecture and planning at the Metropolitan Museum of Art, speaking at an Art Workers' Coalition meeting, March 23, 1970. © Jan van Raay.

William H. Booth, chairman of the city's Human Rights Commission, whom they hoped would deliver their constituents as fans of the museum. But the courting of these politicians would become a sore point among artists who opposed the exhibition. Why curry favor with politicians while ignoring artists? These artists would later see, after a series of public hearings on the museum's expansion plans, that *Harlem on My Mind* was part of the larger public relations campaign. Little did Hoving know that the exhibition would alienate a large portion of the very constituency it was designed to court.

To fund the exhibition, Hoving asked the Henry Luce Foundation for full support. He and Schoener found Executive Director Martha Wallace and Luce family member Beth Moore, Henry Robinson Luce's sister, extremely sympathetic to their vision. Socially driven projects were part of the foundation's mission, and *Harlem on My Mind* might have held a special appeal for the Luce family because of its affinity with the populist and photojournalistic bent of *Time* and *Life*, two of the magazines from which Henry Robinson Luce, founder of the foundation, had made his fortune. Moreover, the Luce Foundation had just acquired an enormous bequest when

Luce died suddenly in February 1967. This bequest quadrupled the foundation's assets to over $80 million.[57] The Luce Foundation joined the *Harlem on My Mind* project as its sole funder by providing $225,000.[58] The New York State Council on the Arts made an in-kind contribution in the form of Schoener's salary, which came to about $25,000. Thus support for the show was a public and private partnership.

Once funding had been secured, Schoener began to build his team. He hired three African American staff members: Reginald McGhee as director of photographic research, Donald Harper as audio curator, and A'Lelia Nelson as administrator. McGhee (fig. 2.6) was a freelance photojournalist whom Schoener had met through Vinnette Carroll, director of the New York State Council on the Arts' Ghetto Arts Program, which "provide[d] artists in ghetto communities with the opportunity to develop their talents and present their work, and act[ed] generally to encourage activities that relate art to the everyday life in the ghetto."[59] McGhee had worked as a photographer for NYSCA and the Studio Museum in Harlem, as well as *Jet*, *Ebony*, and the Magnum Agency. Reginald McGhee brought in A'Lelia Nelson, a Harlem resident and a close friend of the family of the famous turn-of-the-century beautician and entrepreneur Madame C. J. Walker; she was named after Walker's daughter. Donald Harper (fig. 2.7) had been trained as an electrical engineer and had worked as an audio producer in television and theater.[60]

From the outset, Schoener knew he needed to enlist the support of opinion leaders in the community to help legitimize the project and its claim that the show was being developed with the participation of "the people of Harlem." He set about creating an exhibition research committee. Schoener did his homework and stocked this committee with individuals who had both credentials and credibility among Harlem's intellectual community. First and foremost was John Henrik Clarke, a scholar of African American history and an editor of *Freedomways*, an influential leftist African American journal that published political and cultural commentary as well as poetry, fiction, and drama. Schoener invited Clarke to work with him on the show in the summer of 1967. Clarke had been active in the Young Communist League in the 1930s, and during his tenure as editor, *Freedomways* provided a venue for politically engaged literature, art, and social commentary, giving both older and emerging artists a vehicle for linking their work to the liberation struggle in the United States and the independence movements in Africa, Asia, and Latin America. Clarke's leftist orientation may have appealed to Schoener, a self-proclaimed Marxist.[61]

Clarke was also the director of the Heritage Program of the Harlem-based youth program HARYOU-ACT. Initially, Clarke and Schoener envisioned that some of

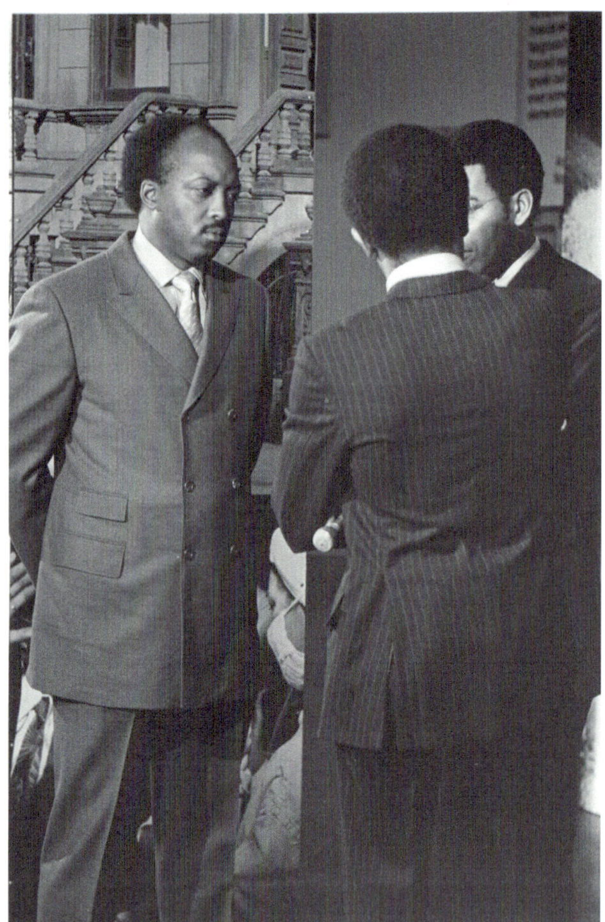

Fig. 2.6 Reginald McGhee (left) and Donald Harper (right) at *Harlem on My Mind* exhibition with unknown person. Photo: Thomas Patsenka. Courtesy of Robert Malone.

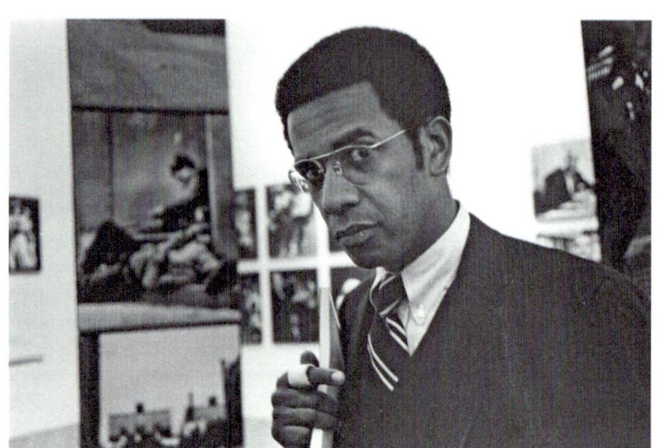

Fig. 2.7 Donald Harper at *Harlem on My Mind* exhibition. Photo: Thomas Patsenka. Courtesy of Robert Malone.

the teenagers involved in HARYOU-ACT would play a role in the *Harlem on My Mind* exhibition as assistants and exhibition installers, but the collaboration between HARYOU-ACT and the Met never came to fruition. Nonetheless, Schoener turned to Clarke for historical insight and viewed him as a possible essayist for the exhibition's publication. Clarke would provide the scholarly backbone of the exhibition, drawing on the frameworks for Harlem's history that he had previously developed in his two edited anthologies, *Harlem U.S.A.* and *Harlem: A Community in Transition*, both first published in 1964.

A second core member of the exhibition research committee was Jean Blackwell Hutson, a curator at the Arthur A. Schomburg branch of the New York Public Library, located in Harlem at 135th Street and Lenox Avenue. The third key member of the research committee was Regina Andrews. Andrews had moved to Harlem in the early 1920s and had been a librarian at the Schomburg Library during the Harlem Renaissance. She was, in fact, the first black librarian in New York City. This position brought her into contact with many important literary and artistic figures, and her home was a social and intellectual meeting place.[62]

With this team in place, Schoener had strategically surrounded himself with people who would perform key roles. Staff members Reginald McGhee and Donald Harper would coordinate the concrete aspects of the show; advisers Jean Blackwell Hutson, John Henrik Clarke, and Regina Andrews would give the project scholarly legitimacy; and A'Lelia Nelson, a well-connected Harlem socialite, would add a bit of luster.

As Schoener has recounted, things got off to a rocky start. On his first visit to Harlem Hutson arranged for Schoener to have lunch with John Henrik Clarke. Over lunch Clarke told Schoener about his experience of being a *shabbas goy* working with the Jews on the Lower East Side, performing tasks forbidden to Jews on the Sabbath. "Then," Schoener has recalled, "he turned to me and looked at me straight in the face and said, 'If you're another downtown Jew come up here to rip us off, go away.'"[63] Schoener had no clue as to the seriousness of this statement. He just took it for granted that black/Jewish relations were tense.

Did Clarke's comment reflect simply healthy skepticism or an unusually high degree of hostility toward whites in general and Jews in particular? Clarke was a leading scholar of Harlem history, and he would go on to become one of the preeminent figures in the Afrocentric movement. Driven and confident, Schoener did not let Clarke's challenge deter him: "I never felt guilty about being a Jew and wanting to do this stuff."[64]

One of the biggest issues that arose early in the planning process was the use of expertise from the Harlem community. Staff members Donald Harper and

Reginald McGhee fulfilled Schoener's race-conscious vision of the project team, but neither had lived in Harlem, therefore local cultural leaders questioned whether they would accurately reflect a Harlem-based perspective. McGhee and Harper dismissed these concerns. In an article published in the *New York Times* when the show opened in January 1969 McGhee said, "You know, we get a few people complaining about Don and me because neither of us is *from* Harlem. I'm from Milwaukee and he's from Chicago. But how many New Yorkers are from any part of New York? What people don't realize is that there's an awful lot of pride in Harlem. A black man may live better somewhere else—in better circumstances, you know—but when he gets to Harlem, he knows he's home. You don't have to be born there to *know* Harlem. You've just got to be black" (emphasis original).[65]

Schoener and his staff vastly underestimated the importance of hiring members of the Harlem community and the concept of community control. Schoener was shooting from the hip, and nowhere was this more apparent than in his invitation to Edward K. Taylor to join the exhibition staff, an invitation he would later retract. Taylor was a community organizer, singer, and voice teacher who would be appointed executive director of the Harlem Cultural Council in early 1968. In November 1967, Schoener invited Taylor to serve as "staff production consultant." As Schoener stated in a letter to Taylor, "You will be paid at a monthly rate yet to be established. . . . The exact nature of your duties to be performed during the varying phases of the preparation of the exhibition will have to be defined."[66] This lack of clarity about Taylor's role would prove to be a critical mistake for Schoener, as Taylor, feeling that he had been duped when his position failed to materialize and believing that his community had been treated unjustly, would become one of the most outspoken opponents of the show.

By the fall of 1967 the museum was ready to publicly announce the exhibition. Mel Patrick, who was the community board coordinator for Manhattan borough president Percy Sutton and was also serving as an informal adviser to Schoener, recommended announcing the exhibition in Oak Bluffs, Martha's Vineyard, an exclusive vacation community of wealthy blacks where A'Lelia Nelson had a home. Schoener, Harper, and McGhee went to the Nelson house for the kickoff party. Later, on November 15, 1967, a press conference was held at the Schomburg Library. The press release read: "At no time in this country's history has there been a more urgent need for a creative confrontation between white and black communities than today. In the belief that the Metropolitan Museum of Art has a deep responsibility to help provide the opportunity for such an exchange, an exhibition of Harlem's rich and varied sixty-year history as the cultural capital of Black America will be shown in the Museum's major exhibition galleries in October of 1968."[67] At the Schomburg event, Hoving introduced the exhibition flanked by Mayor John Lindsay on one side and Percy Sutton on the other. He announced, "This isn't going to be a hand-out to Harlem. . . . The museum's role is simply that of a broker for the channeling of ideas."[68] Both politicians heartily endorsed the show.

The following day the *New York Times* ran a long article portraying the exhibition as a celebration of Harlem's achievements. In line with the museum's promotional materials, *Harlem on My Mind* was described as a project that would be developed with the direct participation of members of the Harlem community. The show was also announced in the January 1968 *Metropolitan Museum of Art Bulletin* as an exhibition that would travel throughout the country as part of an "unprecedented movement toward a world community of museums and institutions."[69] Despite this utopian rhetoric, the article revealed the foreignness of African American culture to the conventional concerns of the Metropolitan Museum: Hoving called *Harlem on My Mind* the museum's "most exotic" exhibition of the coming year—more exotic in his mind than the other shows covered in the same issue, which included displays of artifacts from fourth- to seventh-century Byzantium, pottery from the fifteenth- and sixteenth-century Ottoman Empire, and bronzes from third-millennium BCE Anatolia.

The exhibition team had a downtown office at NYSCA, which was then located on West Fifty-Seventh Street, and an uptown office at the Schomburg Library. As he rode the subway to the Harlem office, Schoener imagined that he was crossing a color line: "I used to have this experience where I'd go uptown to work at the Schomburg and then I'd take [the subway] downtown to where we lived at Lexington Avenue and Ninetieth Street and I used to feel like I was changing color myself. For a short period of time I thought I was able to really identify with black society or understand it."[70] Schoener had the idealistic, some might even say arrogant, belief that he could transcend the social markers of his identity even as he instrumentalized the identities of others. Indeed, his desire to fit in is illustrated in a publicity photo taken in front of a mural-size reproduction of a photograph by James VanDerZee of a Sunday school class from the Abyssinian Baptist Church led by Reverend Adam Clayton Powell Sr. The VanDerZee photo was enlarged and cropped to fit on the wall of a long gallery so that the figures were represented in life size. Schoener visually inserted himself into the scene by standing in front of the photo on a ladder that elevated him close to Powell's height and, implicitly, his stature. Metaphorically, he incorporated himself into the community (fig. 2.8).[71] But although Schoener could perhaps forget that he was white, others did not.

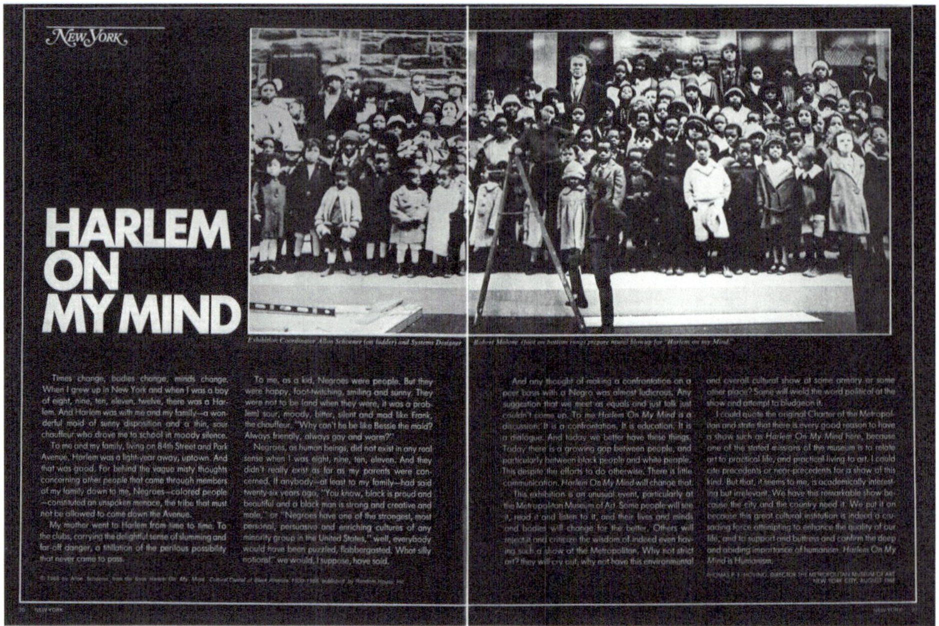

Fig. 2.8 *New York* magazine article on *Harlem on My Mind* exhibition, January 20, 1969, 20–21. Courtesy *New York* magazine.

According to Schoener, Donald Harper had a standing joke: "He'd say, 'It's just like the Cotton Club, black talent and Jewish bosses.'"[72]

Though he was never credited for playing this role, John Henrik Clarke and his two published anthologies, *Harlem U.S.A.* and *Harlem: A Community in Transition*, provided the thematic framework for the show. This framework was a chronological survey of Harlem history that began with the settlement by African Americans at the end of the nineteenth century; the creation of black organizations and institutions such as the National Association for the Advancement of Colored People (NAACP) in the early twentieth century; the New Negro movement and Marcus Garvey's Back-to-Africa movement; the Harlem Renaissance; the economic oppression of blacks during the Great Depression; the rise of the civil rights movement; and militancy and the Black Power movement. To illustrate this timeline, Reginald McGhee pounded the pavement looking for photographs and memorabilia and found photographer James VanDerZee. Over fifty of the seven hundred photographs in the show were chosen from his work. These photographs included the full range of VanDerZee's work from the 1920s and '30s, including street scenes;

studio portraits of both famous figures and ordinary families; church groups, schools, and social clubs; and pictures of Marcus Garvey, for whom he was the official photographer.[73] Donald Harper made recordings and researched music that was piped into the exhibition through ceiling-mounted speakers; this music served as its "sound track" and as the basis for a record album sold in a museum shop at the end of the show.

Work on the catalogue had begun before the exhibition team was assembled. Schoener originally planned to publish the book with Holt, Rinehart and Winston, the press that produced the catalogue for *Portal to America*, and had begun negotiations with Holt's editor in chief, Arthur A. Cohen, as early as March 1967. But a series of disagreements plagued Schoener and Cohen's plans for the book, causing Cohen to oscillate from what he described as "continued enthusiasm for the project to extreme bleakness."[74] Cohen wanted an established writer for the introduction and a postscript. Without consulting Schoener, he had met with Ralph Ellison, best known for his 1952 novel, *Invisible Man*, and also a prolific critic and social commentator. Ellison agreed to do the essays, but Schoener was dead set against engaging an established writer.[75] In a letter to his literary agent, he complained: "Ralph Ellison would not have been my choice to write an introduction to the book because he is a literary figure, not a person who has been identified with the social situation in Harlem."[76] Schoener's preference was to have the catalogue provide a platform for an unknown talent. In June 1967, Schoener conceded that if an established figure were to be used, he would accept Kenneth Clark. But by January 1968, Schoener had become adamant once again that he did not want someone who had been accepted by the mainstream. Now he demanded that if a known figure were used, it must be H. Rap Brown, a black activist and the national director of SNCC (the Student Nonviolent Coordinating Committee), who was denouncing the pacifist tactics of the civil rights movement and espousing the militant rhetoric of black nationalism.[77] To imagine that one of the country's most visible proponents of Black Power would be interested in writing a catalogue essay for the Metropolitan Museum of Art was probably wishful thinking and revealed Schoener's presumption that the museum held a universal value that others would argue it clearly did not.

As the conflict with Cohen grew deeper, Schoener sought other options. In January 1968 Reginald McGhee suggested that he read a research paper on Harlem written by a young woman who was working as an intern in the NYSCA office. The paper, written by Candice Van Ellison, a student at Theodore Roosevelt High School in the Bronx, quoted heavily from the anthologies edited by John Henrik

Clarke, *Harlem U.S.A.* and *Harlem: A Community in Transition.* Schoener read the paper, then sent it to Clarke with a note saying that he'd like to use it as the introduction, and he'd appreciate Clarke's opinion. The paper was essentially based on Clarke's books, and it received the scholar's approval.

In the weeks that followed, differences between Schoener and Cohen came to a head, and on January 22, 1968, Holt, Rinehart and Winston dropped the project. In a letter explaining the decision, Cohen contrasted *Harlem on My Mind* with *Portal to America*, pointing out: "The real problem, as an ideological problem (not unrelated to the question of sales) is that by and large the immigrant story is a success story and the experience of the black community in America is still an unrelieved tragedy." In a prescient statement Cohen also said, "Moreover, it is my feeling, in checking with some of my Negro friends [about] their own reactions to the book as a concept, that there is going to be one helluva lot of political hostility generated by the show and the book. This can work miracles for a $5.95 book, but I think may work precisely opposite for a $14.95 book."[78] The book would ultimately be picked up and published by Random House.

Cohen's incisive comment about the different experiences of American Jews and African Americans would become the central issue in the show's failure to analyze and appropriately position the idea of African American identity in the United States. From the 1940s through the late 1960s, the dominant paradigm for understanding race in America was based on ethnicity theory, that is, the view that African Americans in the United States are equivalent to ethnic groups and that their processes of assimilation are like those of European immigrant groups. When ethnicity theory was developed in the 1920s and '30s, it represented a progressive step toward greater equality because it displaced biological theories of race that justified slavery on the basis of inherent racial inferiority. The ethnicity paradigm posited race as a social category. Yet this paradigm was solidly based on the framework of European (white) ethnicity and could not account for racialized inequality, in which many legal barriers to equality had been removed yet discrimination in the United States continued. The immigrant analogy was not applicable to the experience of African Americans, and among the whites involved in the *Harlem on My Mind* project, only Arthur Cohen seems to have understood that Schoener's success with *Portal to America* was not an accurate indicator of his ability to succeed with *Harlem on My Mind*.[79] Schoener himself never grasped this critical difference.

Throughout the exhibition planning process, Schoener, his staff, and his advisers were forced to grapple with issues of representation: Who is qualified to define the history of Harlem? Who is qualified to speak for whom? Minutes from the advisory committee meetings reveal a tug-of-war in which the process of "community participation" suffered from an ill-defined leadership structure. Were the community experts to provide the leadership, with Schoener acting as a facilitator, or was Schoener directing the show himself? At a meeting held on May 1, 1968, Schoener told the exhibition research committee that while he knew they did not represent the entire community, he was relying on their help to ensure as complete a view of the community as possible. Regina Andrews pointed out that in order for the consultants to be effective, they must know more about the structure of the exhibition. Schoener responded by stating that it was impossible to know at that point what different directions the show would take and that those directions would depend on their input. And so the discussions went round and round, with Schoener insisting that he wanted "community participation" but leaving the nature of that participation ambiguous.[80] He later openly admitted that he did not want any interference with his vision, even though the idea of creating the advisory board was his own.[81] When it became clear to the research committee members that they were being used as window dressing, the sting of betrayal was intense. The hypocrisy would provoke profound criticisms of Schoener, the Metropolitan Museum of Art, and the whole *Harlem on My Mind* endeavor.

By far the most important point of contention that would become a focus of protests against the show was whether the exhibition would include works of art. African American artists in New York not only were beginning to organize and protest their chronic exclusion from exhibitions in mainstream museums; they had also begun to create their own exhibition opportunities. In 1967 Betty Blayton had organized an exhibition entitled *Counterpoints* at Lever House through her connection with Richard V. Clarke, an art enthusiast and founder of the nation's first recruitment firm specializing in diversity hiring, whom she had met while job hunting.[82] The show included artists Tom Lloyd, Mahler Ryder, Arnold Prince, Faith Ringgold, Benny Andrews, Reggie Gammon, Al Hollingsworth, Earl Miller, Jack White, and Blayton herself. In total Blayton invited fifteen African American artists, but the artists "did not want to have an all-Black show," so she asked each to invite another artist of his or her choice of some other ethnic or racial background. This process led to the title. As Blayton put it, the show offered "counterpoints to the mainstream art world."[83]

With the help of Campbell Wylly, curator for the Museum of Modern Art's Art Lending Service, Ruder & Finn remounted the show, but chose to feature only the African American artists. *New Voices: 15 New York Artists* opened at the American Greetings Gallery in the Pan American Building next to Grand Central Station in

1968.[84] The Studio Museum in Harlem was listed as a cosponsor. After this New York showing, the exhibition traveled to five major museums—including the Minneapolis Institute of the Arts, the High Museum, and the San Francisco Museum of Art—as *Thirty Contemporary Black Artists*, with the addition of Emma Amos, Romare Bearden, Floyd Coleman, Sam Gilliam, Felrath Hines, Richard Hunt, Daniel LaRue Johnson, Jacob Lawrence, Richard Mayhew, Betye Saar, Raymond Saunders, and others. According to Mahler Ryder, through these early shows many young African American artists had their first taste of public recognition.[85]

When these and other artists learned of the *Harlem on My Mind* project, many thought this was finally their chance to show in a major New York City museum. It was unfathomable to them that an art museum would mount a show about the culture of Harlem without including African American artists. But from his earliest conception, Schoener had seen the *Harlem on My Mind* show as a social history display, not an art event.

The use of large-scale photo blowups harked back not only to Schoener's own *Portal to America* exhibition but also to *The Family of Man*, an exhibition organized by Edward Steichen at the Museum of Modern Art in 1955.[86] *The Family of Man* was a panoramic installation of photo-reproductions based on pictures taken by some of the best-known photojournalists of the day. The installation was designed by Paul Rudolph to function like a giant picture magazine in installation form (fig. 2.9). Eric Sandeen has cogently argued that *The Family of Man* was designed to diffuse public anxiety about global tension produced by the Cold War and portray a world of stability and peace.[87] Though Schoener denies any influence, *Harlem on My Mind* resonated with *The Family of Man* exhibition in both its aim of addressing social anxieties and its form.

The *Harlem on My Mind* exhibition itself, according to Schoener, "was conceived as a communications environment, one that parallels our daily lives in which we are deluged with information stimuli. Images and sounds—documentary in character—have been organized into a pattern of experiences recreating the history of Harlem as it happened."[88] The show was intended to mirror the disjunctive quality of contemporary experience by overloading the viewer with a collage of stimuli rather than providing a linear, explanatory experience, and it thus put the process of sifting and making meaning into the viewer's hands.

Schoener maintains that *Harlem on My Mind*'s "communications environment" was primarily inspired by the exhibition design theories of Charles and Ray Eames, whom Schoener had met in the late 1950s while he was on staff at the San Francisco Museum of Modern Art and was the producer of the museum's weekly educational

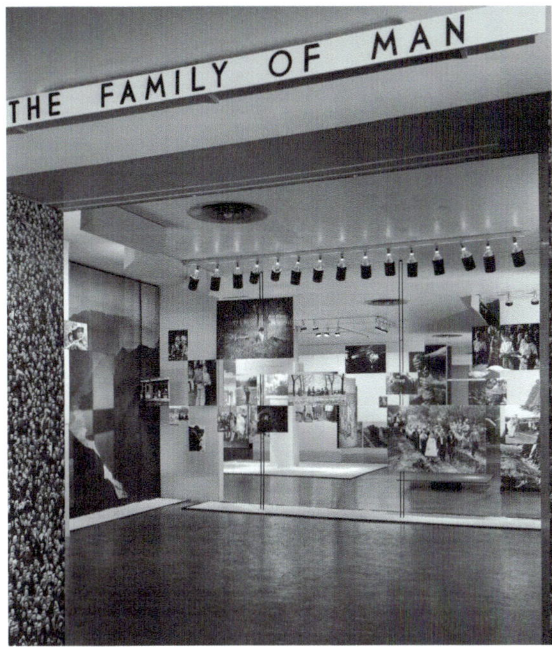

Fig. 2.9 Exhibition entrance, *The Family of Man*, Museum of Modern Art, January 24–May 8, 1955. © Ezra Stoller/Esto.

television program.[89] Although the Eameses were best known for their furniture designs, their work of the late 1950s focused primarily on exhibitions, books, and films—what they referred to as information and communication systems. These media projects were produced as government, industrial, or educational commissions that drew on the imagery of daily rituals, vernacular culture, and ordinary objects to reflect and interpret American culture at home and overseas.[90]

Following the Eameses' visit to the San Francisco Museum of Modern Art, Schoener and Charles Eames developed a professional friendship, and on one occasion the designer invited Schoener to join him for a showing of his "Circus" slide show at the architecture school of the University of California at Berkeley.[91] "Circus" was a 180-image three-screen slide show accompanied by a sound track featuring circus music and other recorded sounds.[92] The presentation's central message was that the circus, which appears to be made up of freewheeling spontaneous expressions, is instead a tightly knit and masterfully disciplined accumulation of people, energies, and details.[93] For the Eameses, the circus offered "a multitude of experiences for the visitor—something for everybody, and more than could be taken in in one viewing or visit."[94] This philosophy appealed enormously to Schoener, who used a similar strategy in *Harlem on My Mind*. He has described his participation in the "Circus" presentation as a catalytic experience.[95]

Through his association with the Eameses, Schoener began to see the potential for creating exhibitions as what he called "spatial films."[96] In a 1968 article on his exhibition philosophy Schoener described a "new iconography of creativity" based on processes, not objects. To Schoener, the Eameses and their close colleague, the designer George Nelson, epitomized this new aesthetic. In an article on his exhibition aesthetic published in the fall of 1968, Schoener wrote: "Eames and Nelson used slides, films, sounds, music, narration, and odors to develop high-speed techniques of exposing relationships between seemingly unrelated phenomena. They have continued to approach the mixed media environment as a communication experience in which their designs are based upon a systems approach applying industrial methods. These new media-mix environments can be communication experience, entertainment experience, or simply events in themselves which are to be appreciated as multi-sensory experiences."[97]

The project that influenced Schoener the most was one that the Eameses were producing when he met them: *Glimpses of the U.S.A.*, a multiscreen film for the American National Exhibition in Moscow for the 1959 USSR-USA Exchange in Sokolniki Park.[98] *Glimpses of the U.S.A.* was a montage of 2,200 images selected to create a collective portrait of American life. The images were presented on seven 35mm film reels projected simultaneously on 20-by-30-foot screens installed in a 250-foot geodesic dome designed by Buckminster Fuller (fig. 2.10). The presentation ran for ten minutes, beginning with images of the land and people's various relationships to it, then moving on to scenes of waking, eating, commuting to jobs: a collective day in the life of America. The final scenes showed symbols of love and friendship, including, at the very end, a picture of a bunch of forget-me-nots. The romantic humanism of this pastiche was designed to encourage Soviet citizens to identify with their counterparts in the United States while also illustrating the material abundance of the American middle class.[99] In *Harlem on My Mind*, Schoener drew not only on the Eameses' formal and technical innovations but also on their social philosophy. Just as *Glimpses of the U.S.A.* was a multimedia display that would reach across political and cultural differences dividing the people of the United States from those in the Soviet Union during the Cold War, so too might *Harlem on My Mind* bridge the gap between blacks and whites in America.

Despite percolating opposition from artists, Schoener adhered to his position that visual arts such as painting, sculpture, or printmaking had no role in his project: "I thought they [African American artists] deserved to have their art dignified

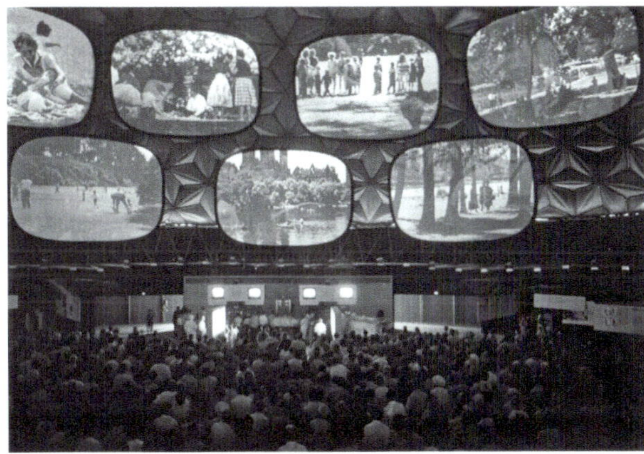

Fig. 2.10 Charles and Ray Eames, *Glimpses of the U.S.A.*, Moscow Fair Auditorium with geodesic dome by Buckminster Fuller, 1959. Courtesy Eames Office.

by being presented in the Metropolitan Museum—I never questioned that. . . . But I didn't see that as my responsibility."[100] Schoener's rationale for excluding artists led to striking omissions. Perhaps the most egregious exclusion was Aaron Douglas's suite of paintings titled *Aspects of Negro Life*, a series of four monumental works from the 1930s depicting vignettes in the imagined collective history of African Americans from freedom in Africa through slavery and reconstruction in the United States. These paintings hung in the Schomburg Library, the very building that housed *Harlem on My Mind*'s uptown office. Art historian Richard Powell has written that the specific intent of these works was "to celebrate past and present African American achievements and to help viewers link art with struggle."[101] Their inclusion would have hit the sweet spot of Schoener's social goals.

During the 1960s Harlem was experiencing what Henry Louis Gates Jr. and others have called a second Harlem Renaissance.[102] Artists Faith Ringgold, Romare Bearden, and Jacob Lawrence all lived there and made work that intimately and powerfully conveyed their visions, ideas, and experiences. Their work would have also addressed Schoener's social goals. Indeed, many artists all over the country were dealing with themes related to black cultural identity and the struggle for power. The artists who took issue with Schoener's decision to omit the fine arts did not see it as a question of curatorial methodology. Rather, they saw the curatorial strategy as a rationale for their continued systemic neglect.

There was a brief period during the exhibition planning process when Schoener agreed to include photo-reproductions of artworks, a move that would have enabled him to appease the artists—or so he thought—while adhering to his curatorial vision of a show composed solely of documentary materials. But whereas presenting photo-reproductions of artworks may have been sufficient in his San Francisco television show, it was grossly out of place at the Metropolitan Museum of Art's galleries. The idea was dropped.

As early as January 1968 exhibition adviser Regina Andrews raised concern that the omission of visual artists from the exhibition and the curatorial process weakened the project. She contacted Romare Bearden to enlist his participation in the show. Bearden was an inspired choice not only because he was a respected member of the New York City art community and the organizer of two previous important art exhibitions—a show of contemporary art held in 1966, *Art of the American Negro*, and the 1967 exhibition *The Evolution of Afro-American Arts: 1800–1950*—but also because he was a painter who had employed photographic techniques in his work.[103] Bearden's *Projections* of 1964 had translated collages into large-scale Photostats. Indeed, the photography historian Van Deren Coke admired the *Projections* in ways that make clear how Bearden's aesthetic might have amplified Schoener's curatorial aesthetic: "[Bearden's *Projections*] retain the immediacy of newsphotos and, through his use of optical shifts and arrangements similar to jigsaw puzzles, cover much more ground factually and metaphorically than a group of photographs presented in a conventional fashion."[104]

In March, Bearden was invited to join the exhibition planning team as "fine arts consultant." Having followed the saga, he politely declined, citing previous commitments.

At the March 6 exhibition committee meeting, Reginald McGhee made the well-taken point that individual artistic visions were all to take second place to the larger portrait of Harlem created by the total exhibition.[105] Nonetheless, in April exhibition research committee member Jean Blackwell Hutson informed Schoener, his staff, and the other committee members that the Harlem Cultural Council was beginning to question why established artists were not to be included in the show. At the May 1 exhibition research committee meeting Hutson suggested Bruce Nugent as another possible fine arts consultant. There was no follow-up to this recommendation. On May 16 Ed Taylor sent a letter to Schoener expressing consternation about the show. He began by lamenting the ill-defined nature of his role: "In the original letter concerning my formal connection with the exhibit, you called my position one of 'Staff Consultant' and said that the *production phase* would start immediately and continue throughout the exhibit. . . . At this point, it is not very clear just exactly what I'm supposed to be doing. It's obvious that I have not been functioning according to the original premise since so much has happened that affects the production aspects of the show that I have neither been consulted about nor informed of" (emphasis original).[106]

Taylor went on to criticize the exhibition's title. "After taking the pulse of community reaction, I feel that the title of the show is an unwise one. There is much adverse feeling towards it because of its lack of *dignity* and *respect* and because of its white Irving Berlin origin" (emphasis original). But his strongest words were reserved for the issue of artists' exclusion: "I find it distressing that a Beardon [*sic*], Critchlow [*sic*], or DeCarava has not been added. . . . As one very young photographer put it: 'How can we have a show of such major proportions without some of the truly great Afro-American artists being involved.'" These conflicts would not be reported in newspapers or made public until six months later, in November 1968. But the damage to the museum's community relationships was already becoming irreparable. As Taylor states later in his letter, "Much of the controversy that exists within the community with regard to the show would not be there if there was a black group or person from the community assisting in the total coordination [of the exhibition]."[107]

Unbeknownst to Schoener, Taylor and exhibition adviser John Henrik Clarke were sharing their doubts about the show. Clarke wrote to Schoener three weeks after Taylor, suggesting that the show be either substantially changed or cancelled: "As I have told you there are several things that the community is just not going to accept, and rather than completely antagonize people, it might actually be best to phase the show out, or else start immediately to work in the interests of the kind of a show that the community as a whole would want. For one, as I have told you, something must be done as to the title, 'Harlem on My Mind.'" Alluding to the short-lived idea that works of art might be included in the form of reproductions, Clarke went on to say: "I know the artists are not going to tolerate color transparencies of their work in an Art Museum. As I see it, the sort of show you are putting together should be in the Museum of the City of New York, the New York Historical Society, or some similar place."[108]

Clarke's letter must have carried some weight, because five days later, on June 11, 1968, the museum sent artist Romare Bearden a note thanking him for joining the *Harlem on My Mind* exhibition staff as curator of an art exhibition. But the letter was not signed by Schoener. Rather, it came from Eleanor Falcon, the museum's public relations manager. Demonstrating a level of naïveté that was typical of the times, Falcon's invitation to Bearden included advice on what to include.[109] Schoener himself has no recollection of Bearden's appointment to the exhibition staff, and his short-lived involvement with the museum had no discernible impact.[110]

Discussions about how to deal with the fine art issue proceeded into the summer. On June 25, the Metropolitan Museum's Community Relations staff member, Susan Coppello, met with a group of Harlem-based artists led by Sol Battle at the Weusi-Nyumba Ya-Sanaa Gallery, located in a brownstone on West 132nd Street near Seventh Avenue. The artists associated with this group had an Afrocentric aesthetic quite distinct from those artists who had been lobbying the Metropolitan, who were relatively established within the mainstream gallery system and aspired to show their work in museums. In a memo to Tom Hoving following the meeting, Coppello reported that the artists "are tired of exhibits about their past and feel they are the present and the future of Harlem and must be included."[111] Coppello went on to say, "I made the mistake of telling them the amount of the grant from the Luce Foundation [$225,000]. They demanded that this money, and in fact the entire exhibit, be put in their hands."[112]

On September 24, 1968, the research committee met to further discuss the issue. As documented in a follow-up letter by Bearden—written because, as he tartly points out, no minutes were taken at the meeting—several conclusions were reached. Among them, Bearden confirmed that a separate art exhibition was to take place concurrently with *Harlem on My Mind*, and he reminded Tom Hoving that the research committee had recommended that two individuals serve as members of a selection panel. The first was James Porter, an artist and art historian, who had written the landmark survey *Modern Negro Art* (1943) and was head of the Art Department and director of the art gallery at Howard University. The second was Carroll Greene Jr., art historian and cocurator, with Bearden, of the exhibition *The Evolution of Afro-American Artists: 1800 to 1950*, held at City College in 1967. The letter also mentioned an agreement reached that Hoving would meet with Roy DeCarava to reopen the discussion about including his photos in the exhibition.[113] It is unclear whether this meeting ever took place.

Instead of heeding Bearden's advice to bring in James Porter or Carroll Greene, the museum turned the exhibition over to James Sneed, Taiwo Yusef Shabazz [DuVall], and Ademola Olugebefola. Sneed was a local artist who had previously worked with some of the artists in the Weusi group and had organized, with Malikah Rahman, the Twentieth Century Creators. Olugebefola was a founder of the Weusi-Nyumba Ya Sanaa group.[114] Once Sneed and Olugebefola were engaged for the exhibition, Schoener referred all inquiries from artists to them.[115] He wanted no part in the art exhibition. On January 12, 1969, the *New York Times* ran an article about *Harlem on My Mind* parenthetically mentioning that a contemporary painting and sculpture show was scheduled to open at the museum in February. An article appeared in the February 8 edition of the *Amsterdam News* that even mentioned the title, *Inner World of the Black Movement*, and listed the artists: Al Hollingsworth, Tony Northern [Babatunde Folayemi], Jim Janulo, Ahmado Wachuco, George Wilson, Charles Hudson, John Johnson, and Sneed himself.[116] Yet not until March 10, two months after *Harlem on My Mind* opened, was a letter sent by Sneed to "Fellow Artists" inviting submissions for a juried show for which the museum would exert as little curatorial effort as possible. Sneed's letter said: "All works are to come to the receiving entrance of the Metropolitan Museum of Art, 84th Street and 5th Avenue, March 17th, 18th & 19th between the hours of 11:00 a.m. and 4:00 p.m. Each artist can bring in two paintings. No paintings are to be larger than 40 × 60 inches. Pick out your most powerful pieces and enter them."[117]

Few, if any, serious artists submitted their work. In the end this project turned out to be too little, too late. According to Benny Andrews, "It was not something that we gave any importance to 'cause it was not being approached in a way that was really going to *mean* anything. . . . I'd been exhibiting on Madison Avenue, like one or two of the other people, so we knew what good exhibitions were. We were not that hungry to have something thrown at us."[118] The painting and sculpture show never occurred.[119] However, the museum did mount a show in its children's wing, the Junior Museum, of art by youngsters who lived in Harlem. This show foreshadowed the way in which the Metropolitan Museum's egalitarian impulses would be later channeled primarily into the area of education, a trend also seen in other museums.[120]

As the exhibition research committee members dissociated themselves from the museum, they built alliances with the artists who opposed the show. In the growing conflict, the museum tried to replenish its troops by strengthening the ranks of its community participants. In September 1968 the museum created an even larger committee of about fifty African American leaders and Harlem residents called the Community Advisory Committee, which included politicians; religious leaders; local heads of community groups such as CORE, the Urban League, and the NAACP; prominent lawyers, doctors, and businesspeople; and a handful of cultural figures. In the Artists and Writers category were artists Bearden and Sneed and writer Larry Neal. This committee, which was described as working in an "advisory and liaison capacity," allowed Schoener to disengage from the disgruntled circle of initial advisers and start with a fresh group whose charge was simple and clear: to promote the show.[121] A memo sent to the Community Advisory Committee in September read: "The Research Phase of the exhibition is completed. We are now entering a new phase—Community Relations; therefore, we need a new group of consultants with a different orientation."[122] The formation of the committee was part of a large and ambitious publicity campaign. Promoting the museum's populist image was, from the beginning, one of the aims of the project, and despite the candid words of caution from the exhibition advisers, Schoener and Hoving stayed their course.

The first meeting of the Community Relations committee took place on October 1, 1968. Schoener structured the meeting so that Hoving addressed the group on behalf of the museum.[123] He stressed the philosophy behind the *Harlem on My Mind* project and how it created a new role for the museum. Exhibition staff members Donald Harper and Reginald McGhee described their sound and photo research and the contents of the exhibition, and Schoener gave an overview of the exhibition structure. Hoving then wrapped up by reiterating the role of the committee: to help the museum directly reach the "black community." The names of the committee members would be announced in a press release, and the museum would try to place stories about its formation in African American newspapers such as the *Amsterdam News*, the *Pittsburgh Courier*, and the *Chicago Defender*, as well as on the local black radio station, WLIB. Subsequently, a second press release would be issued giving information about the exhibition and containing quotes from committee members and their reactions to the museum's plans. Again, the museum would seek editorial coverage, this time in a wider range of publications, including mainstream outlets such as the *New York Times*, *Daily News*, and *New York Post*.

As the exhibition grew nearer, tensions continued to mount. Schoener began to sense the seriousness of the pressures and the need for damage control. He conveyed his apprehensions in a memo to public relations manager Eleanor Falcon: "It is the firm recommendation of the exhibition staff that every attempt possible should be made to obtain interpretation of the exhibition and its content which is compatible with the point of view of the exhibition and which reflects an attitude that will generally meet with the approval of the Harlem community. We believe that such an approach to publicity is, without question, in the best interest of the Metropolitan Museum."[124]

Schoener's quest to win the approval of the "Harlem community" was futile because the "community" itself encompassed many points of view, from the politicians who endorsed the show, such as Percy Sutton, to community leaders such as Jean Blackwell Hutson, who wanted to see the project succeed but felt frustrated and withdrew her support, to more militant constituencies who would probably never have been satisfied by the undertaking, particularly given that the project was led by a white curator. As curator Edmund Barry Gaither has put it, "There are some things that outsiders can't say because it creates rage."[125] Aside from the question of whether or not one could claim such a thing as a single Harlem "community," unresolved conflicts over the direction of the exhibition had already compromised the approval of Schoener's advisers. It was difficult to see how the show could have averted major criticisms. Schoener grasped at straws by urging Falcon to find African American voices to legitimize the project: "Although two articles are under way with *Vogue* and *McCall's*, we regret that it was not possible to insist that black writers, who can meet the specifications which are stated above, were not commissioned by these publications to prepare their articles. Considering the lethargy with which white publications engage black writers to interpret black material, we believe that it is important to insist that with all future magazine publicity opportunities that black writers be engaged to prepare these articles."[126]

The letter included a list of nine suggested writers. There was a certain irony in Schoener's insistence on the involvement of African American writers in the publicity for the show considering that he himself had neglected similar advice by African American scholars, artists, and activists.

By mid-November 1968 relations between Schoener and the original members of the research committee had reached a crisis point. This tension was exacerbated by the opening of an exhibition at the Whitney Museum of American Art on October 15. The show was *The 1930's: Painting and Sculpture in America*, and the curator, William Agee, had completely excluded African American artists despite their well-documented presence, especially in the WPA Arts Programs (fig. 2.11). In response, Faith Ringgold, Benny Andrews, and others, including Henri Ghent, director of the Community Gallery at the Brooklyn Museum, picketed the Whitney on November 17 and mounted a counterexhibition at the Studio Museum in Harlem, *Invisible Americans: Black Artists of the 1930s*, which opened on November 19 and ran through January 5, 1969.

Convinced that they had been duped by Schoener's claims of community involvement, on November 22 the Harlem Cultural Council held a press conference at the YWCA on 125th Street to announce the withdrawal of its endorsement of *Harlem on My Mind*. The event featured appearances by Benny Andrews, Romare Bearden, and Roy DeCarava.[127] Grace Glueck reported the event in the *New York Times*, stating, "Harlem's leading cultural organization has withdrawn its endorsement of the Metropolitan Museum of Art's multi-media exhibition, 'Harlem on My Mind,' scheduled to open January 18. The Harlem Cultural Council cited a 'breakdown in communications' between itself and the Metropolitan as reason for the action."[128] Glueck went on to say that John Henrik Clarke and Jean Blackwell Hutson claimed their ideas had been ignored in favor of those of two "out of towners," Reginald McGhee and Donald Harper. "Both are also Negro," noted Glueck.

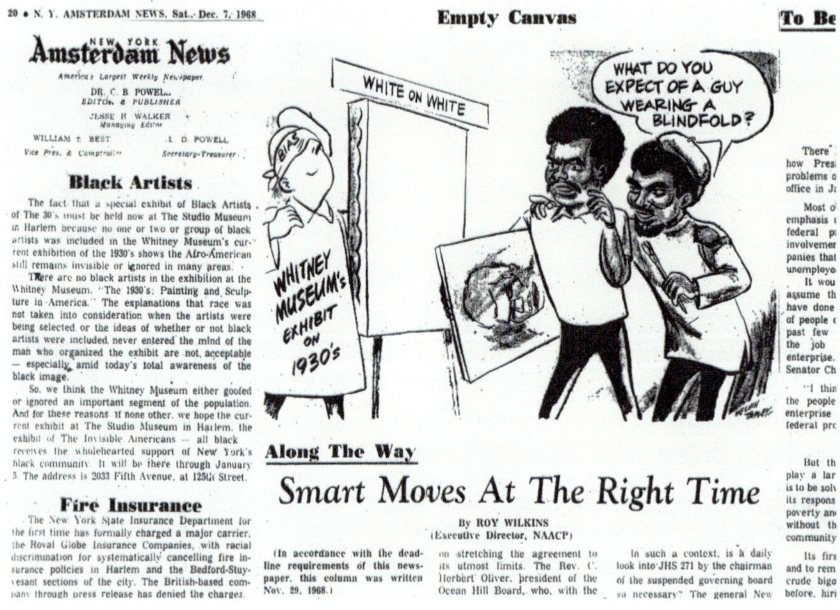

Fig. 2.11 *Amsterdam News*, December 7, 1968. Artist: Melvin Tapley.

A week later, Jack Whitten hosted a meeting with a group of other artists that included Benny Andrews, Tom Lloyd, Daniel LaRue Johnson, Jack White, and others. Joining forces with the defecting advisers were others who were similarly dismayed by the museum's neglect of art, including Henri Ghent, Romare Bearden, Merton Simpson, and Roy DeCarava. The attitude of the group was concisely summed up in a letter from John Henrik Clarke to Romare Bearden written at the end of August: "The basis of the trouble with this project is that it never belonged to us and while a lot of people listened to our suggestions about the project. Very few of these suggestions were ever put into effect."[129]

On November 26 Schoener sent a long memo to Hoving refuting the criticisms cited in Glueck's article. Schoener wrote, "Although we have an air-tight case against Ed Taylor personally with our correspondence, I would not bring this up directly. . . . To engage in direct controversy with him is to help build his position."[130] Schoener discounted John Henrik Clarke's contributions, writing, "Although we know that John Hendrik [*sic*] Clarke did a bad job for us, this should also not be mentioned. I have found enough critical statements by black writers—Harold Kruse [*sic*] in particular—to put John in his place." Astonishingly, Schoener refuted the claim that the show should have included works of art by invoking Hilton Kramer's position on the burgeoning "quality debate." He said: "Ed Taylor, Henri Ghent, Romare Bearden, and their supporters want to bargain with the white establishment on the basis of their 'Blackness,' not artistic merit. Hilton Kramer made this very evident of his review of the Studio Museum show [*Invisible Americans: Black Artists of the 1930s*]. Kramer's review is evidence of the falseness of their position and its ultimate futility. If the work is no good, no reputable art organization anywhere in the world will endorse it."[131]

Schoener concluded by chalking up the problems of the exhibition to the historic isolation of blacks and whites: "How can we expect either blacks or whites to perform miracles and do something super by getting along with each other as effective cultural equals—that neither one has ever done?"[132] Quick to portray blacks and whites as equally guilty of discrimination, he ignored the power imbalance inherent in racial inequality. Thus the museum hobbled toward opening day desperately trying to salvage some semblance of credibility in the face of deteriorating community support.

Tension continued through the start of the new year. On January 7, with the press opening just one week away, Tom Hoving called Henri Ghent to urgently request a meeting the next day. On January 8, Romare Bearden, Henri Ghent, Edward Taylor, and Cathy Aldridge, a writer for the *Amsterdam News*, met with Hoving and with the Metropolitan Museum's European Paintings curator, Theodore Rousseau, and the executive director of the New York State Council on the Arts, John Hightower. The specifics of the meeting were not documented, but clearly the discussion didn't satisfy the artists. On January 9, Bearden, Ghent, Taylor, Norman Lewis, Mahler and Karen Ryder, Cliff Joseph and his family, Bill Durante, Joan Sandler, Bob Carter, Russ Thompson, and a few others met at Benny Andrews's studio to organize the first of many demonstrations against the exhibition and form an organization called the Black Emergency Cultural Coalition (BECC).[133]

At this meeting, the group decided to picket the museum and stage media events to publicize their position. Their primary demands were twofold. First, they protested the absence of African Americans in curatorial positions at the Metropolitan Museum, and second, they rejected the idea that an art museum would have an exhibition of African American culture that contained no painting or sculpture. They called for the immediate cancellation of the show; the appointment of African Americans to policy-making and curatorial positions; and a more "viable relationship" between the museum and the "total Black community."[134] The group's most articulate statement of purpose, written a few months later, is worth quoting at length. The statement said:

The Black Emergency Cultural Coalition came into being in response to what its founders deemed a travesty of the cultural ethic. An institution invested with the guardianship of our society's cultural integrity, on January 18th, 1969, presented an exhibition entitled "Harlem on My Mind." That institution, The Metropolitan Museum of Art, hired Allon Schoerner [*sic*] as the exhibition coordinator. He sought to, "prove that the black community in Harlem is a major cultural environment with enormous strength and potential and that this community has made major contributions to the mainstream of American culture in music, theater and literature." The museum's director, Thomas P. Hoving [*sic*], stated that the purpose of the exhibition was, "a sincere effort to increase the knowledge and understanding of the cultural history of Harlem." Both the exhibition coordinator and the museum director failed to meet their stated objectives.

They failed because they omitted painters and sculptors who also contributed to the cultural development of Harlem, misused and otherwise ignored the body of black advisors to the exhibition, so that their own ignorance assisted by their arrogance, became their only guidelines, imported people from outside the Harlem community to work on the exhibition and ended up producing an audio-visual exposition with neither logical sequence nor adequate explanatory information.[135]

The first public demonstration against *Harlem on My Mind* was held on Sunday, January 12, at 1:00 p.m. (figs. 2.12 and 2.13). Marching directly in front of the museum, protestors handed out leaflets informing passersby of the issues and imploring them to boycott the show. The second demonstration took place on Tuesday, January 14, during the exhibition's press conference.[136] These two actions were then followed by a campaign to encourage African American leaders not to attend the opening night festivities, to return their invitations, and to join the protest. Henri Ghent sent telegrams to Mayor Lindsay, Percy Sutton, and Kenneth Clark, but failed to enlist their support. The protests did attract historian Eugene Genovese, who would publish a powerful critique in *Artforum* magazine.

The picketers turned to the media in order to bring more attention to their cause. Andrews has said, "That's all we had. We had no money. We had no influence. We had no entrée into the white museum structure."[137] According to the artist, race relations were so hyped up that any racial conflict could be made newsworthy with the right staging. The media loved the spectacle of protesting African Americans, and the Met was one of the country's premier art institutions where

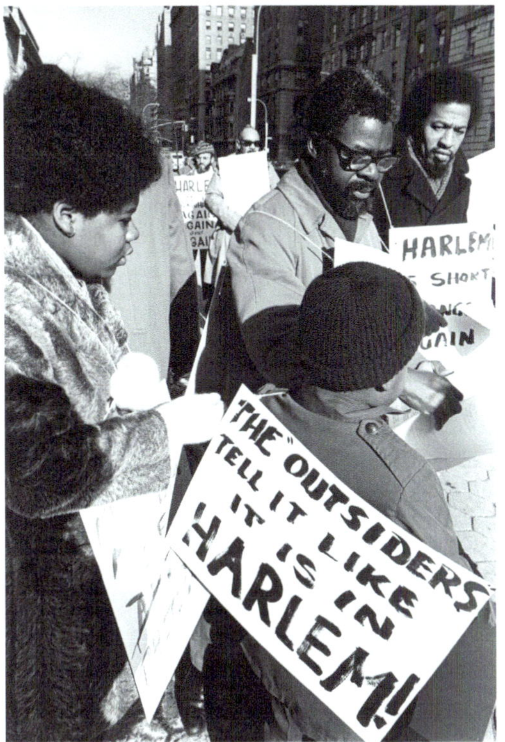

Fig. 2.12 Protest at the Metropolitan Museum of Art, Cliff Joseph (center), January 12, 1969. Photo: Thomas Patsenka. Courtesy of Robert Malone.

Fig. 2.13 Protest at the Metropolitan Museum of Art, January 12, 1969. Photo: Thomas Patsenka. Courtesy of Robert Malone.

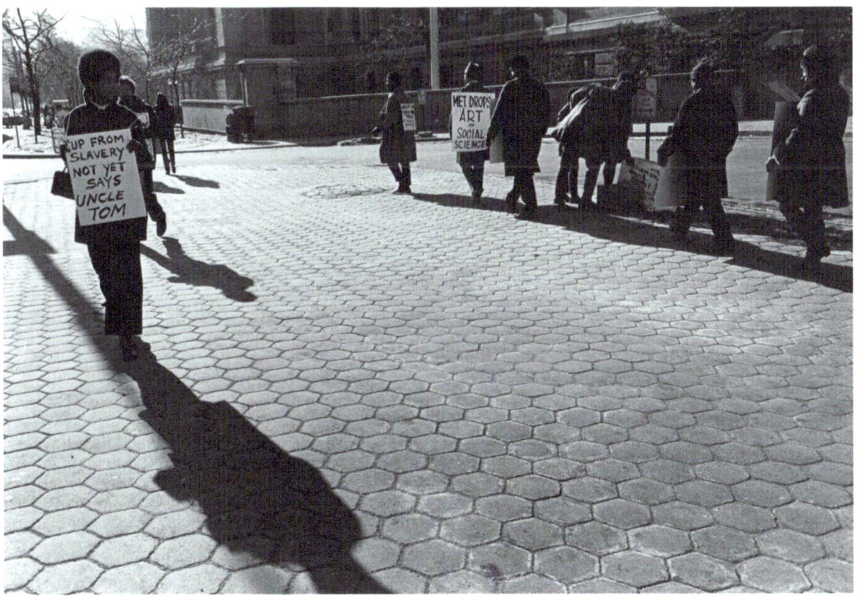

anything that happened was news. The members of the Black Emergency Cultural Coalition did their best to offer good television. Says Andrews, "I'll never forget how little we looked there. . . . Fortunate[ly] for us we got window dressing because the police came, set up barricades. . . . It was almost like giving us some clothing to wear." The light-skinned Andrews also recalls, "Henri [Ghent] was our front piece 'cause in my case, with my complexion it was very hard at that time for me to be out there on television. . . . They basically wanted a black person who was very specifically militant in their minds . . . and Henri was also articulate, which was an added plus."[138] After the first two protests, a small article appeared in the *New York Times* on January 15: "Bearing signs that read, 'Tricky Tom at it Again?' and 'That's White of Hoving!' about 15 black and white demonstrators picketed the Metropolitan Museum last evening. . . . Urging the entire black community to boycott the show, the leaflets demanded that the museum appoint blacks to policy-making and curatorial positions, and that the Metropolitan Museum 'seek a more viable relationship with the total black community.' "[139]

These pickets were not something the artists took lightly. Though they were critical of the museum, even they respected the Met as an old dowager. According to Andrews, "It was like picketing your grandmother. . . . I mean, the Met was almost like the Vatican."[140] Yet, on the night of the opening dinner, Thursday, January 16, the demonstration was ramped up (figs. 2.1, 2.14, and 2.15). The long roster of participants included Romare Bearden, Norman Lewis, Roy DeCarava, Tom Lloyd, Reginald Gammon, Earl Miller, Richard Mayhew, Calvin Douglass, Felrath Hines, Russ Thompson, Frank Sharpe, Vivian Browne, Mahler and Karen Ryder, Charles Creary, Raymond Saunders, Barbara Carter, Joan Sandler, Bill Durante, John Dobbs, Henri Ghent, Ed Taylor, Benny Andrews, Cliff Joseph, Tecla (Selnick), Zeb and Francesca Burgess, Alice Neel, Mel Ramos, and others.[141] Protestors wore placards that characterized the show as latter-day slavery: "On the auction block again—Sold out by Massa Hoving." They hooted and yelled at the people entering the museum. Some visitors—both African American and white—came over to talk with the group and others actually joined the picket line, while inside, partygoers toured the exhibition.

But this protest was overshadowed in the next day's news by another event. On January 16, during a private daytime preview of the show, ten paintings hanging in the museum's galleries were scratched with the letter *H*. Based on statements by museum officials, newspaper accounts connected the vandalism with the African American protestors and speculated that the *H* stood for "Harlem" or "Hoving." The *New York Times* reported the incident on the front page. A *Daily News* headline

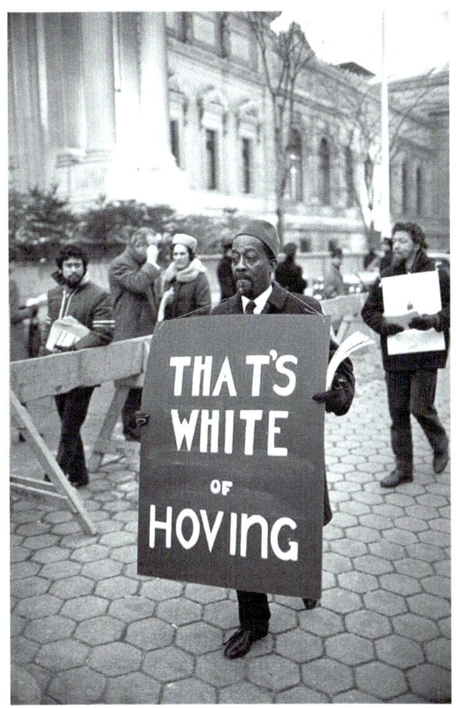

Fig. 2.14 Protest at the Metropolitan Museum of Art, Norman Lewis (foreground) and Benny Andrews (background), January 16, 1969. Photo: Jack Manning / The New York Times / Redux.

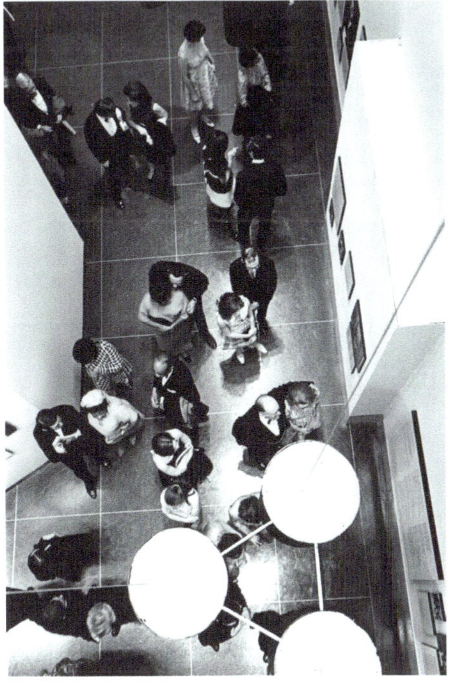

Fig. 2.15 Opening reception of *Harlem on My Mind* exhibition at the Metropolitan Museum of Art, January 16, 1969. Photo: Thomas Patsenka. Courtesy of Robert Malone.

screamed, "11 [*sic*] Met Paintings Slashed in 'Racist' Furor," while in smaller type in the second paragraph the article conceded that the "damage was slight."[142] *Muhammad Speaks*, the paper of the Nation of Islam, embraced the idea that African Americans were responsible for the acts and defended the incident: "The insult of the 'Harlem on My Mind' exhibit at New York City's Metropolitan Museum of Art was that it mainly portrayed white minds' attitudes towards Black Harlem. Because of this colonial and condescending attitude, Afro-Americans retaliated by defacing some so-called classical western art in the museum."[143]

The meaning of the letter H and the identity of the perpetrator have remained a mystery to this day. One possible association is the book *Uncle Tom's Cabin*, which features a character who is branded with the letter H. George is a runaway slave who escapes from the Kentucky house of his master, Mr. Harris, to meet his wife Eliza and his son in Canada, and eventually flee to Africa. Traveling to Canada incognito, George wears gloves to conceal the letter H branded on his hand and passes for a dark-skinned Spaniard rather than a light-skinned African American.[144] Whether the H was a reference to this narrative of bondage and escape, subterfuge and subversion, is impossible to say. One way or another, the protestors made amply clear that they would not behave as "Uncle Toms" in Tom Hoving's museum.

The protests on January 16 brought another surprise. As the artists were picketing on the museum's plaza, they were startled to find they had been joined by other protestors. Several Jewish groups, led by the Anti-Defamation League and including the Jewish Defense League and the American Jewish Congress, accused the museum of propagating anti-Semitism, citing offensive statements in the exhibition catalogue. What sparked their opposition was a passage in the introduction to the *Harlem on My Mind* book written by high school student and NYSCA intern Candice Van Ellison. In choosing a high school student over a recognized author, Schoener had imagined that the essay would bring an air of authenticity to the *Harlem on My Mind* project, but in a section on "intergroup relations" Van Ellison included several comments that incensed organized Jewish groups. The most objectionable sentences read: "One other important factor worth noting is that, psychologically, Blacks find that anti-Jewish sentiments place them, for once, within a majority. Thus, our contempt for the Jew makes us feel more completely American in sharing a national prejudice." Jews were up in arms.

This incident merely ignited an already incendiary situation. Tensions between blacks and Jews had come to a head during a teachers' strike in the fall of 1968, and when *Harlem on My Mind* opened in January 1969, the aftershocks of the school controversy were still being felt.[145] In 1968 the Ford Foundation, whose director,

McGeorge Bundy, had headed the Mayor's Advisory Panel on Decentralization of the New York City Schools, agreed to underwrite the cost of establishing three experimental decentralized school districts with local governance in Harlem, Lower Manhattan, and the Ocean Hill–Brownsville section of Brooklyn. In Ocean Hill–Brownsville, one of the poorest neighborhoods in the United States (with a population that was about 70 percent African American and 25 percent Puerto Rican), the experiment would result in a head-on collision with the powerful teachers' union, the United Federation of Teachers. The confrontation began in May 1968 when the district's new governing board dismissed thirteen teachers and six administrators. The union feared that community control would threaten their constituency and destroy their power. They demanded that the teachers be reinstated. When the governing board refused, the teachers union went on strike on Monday, September 9, the first day of the school year. Throughout the fall of 1968 three strikes would be held, crippling public education in New York for over 1 million students.

The conflict polarized African Americans and Jews because the largely Jewish teachers' union, headed by Albert Shanker, was seen as standing in the way of the African American and Puerto Rican parents' desire to educate their children the way that they saw fit. On the flip side, Jews felt angry at what they saw as a betrayal by liberals, including Mayor Lindsay, who sanctioned the experimental districts. The American Jewish Committee saw decentralization as subsidized anti-Semitism.[146] Having been accused of favoring African Americans in the schools controversy, Lindsay came out swinging against the Metropolitan Museum and issued a statement condemning the exhibition catalogue:

> [The catalogue's] statements on intergroup relations contains [*sic*] remarks which can only be described as racist. It suggests that black Americans have joined a national majority not by their efforts for justice and dignity, but through anti-Semitic feelings.
>
> This is a slander on both the black and the white community, as well as an insult to the Jewish community.[147]

Lindsay called for the withdrawal of the offending catalogue introduction. According to Hoving, "Lindsay was in deep trouble with the middle class and at that moment with the Jewish middle class. He was beginning his run for the second term and I guess he thought 'book burning' in the form of the Harlem catalogue was hunky-dory."[148]

Harry Parker recalls, "When it started to deteriorate, it deteriorated very fast."[149] There was an endless meeting going on in Hoving's office all day as he repeatedly called his old friend and former boss, Lindsay, to ask his advice. Arthur Rosenblatt has recounted that Random House was being pressured to withdraw the catalogue by the Metropolitan Museum's own trustees, those more conservative members of the board.[150] The publisher urged Hoving to eliminate the introduction. Hoving was furious with Random House for agreeing to print the catalogue then back-pedaling when the controversy intensified.

The Anti-Defamation League took an even sharper tone than the mayor. National chairman Dore Schary called the introductory essay "an insult and attack on Jews." He went on to excoriate the Met: "Random statements of anti-Semitism always plague the Jewish community and in normal circumstances we would be inclined to dismiss a statement by a 16-year-old girl ridden with frustration and anger. But we cannot ignore a great institution as respectable as the Metropolitan Museum of Art giving such a statement credence or significance."[151]

The American Jewish Congress took out a full-page ad in the *New York Times*. The headline read, "The Enemy is Silence," and their statement began, "It is important that every American understand the anger and dismay that swept the Jewish community when the Metropolitan Museum of Art published the racist catalogue for its exhibit, 'Harlem on My Mind.' We have had a long experience with the big lie—in this case, the lie that the Negro plight is the result of some kind of conspiracy by the Jews. . . . What troubled us profoundly was the silence of those (black and white) who, by failing to speak out, gave their consent to group libel and the scape-goating of a people."[152]

Lindsay was up for reelection that year, and politically he could not afford to alienate Jewish constituencies. After several days of public conflict, he not only denounced the catalogue but also threatened to rescind the museum's city funds, which amounted to a whopping $3.5 million.[153]

The American Jewish Committee issued a press release on January 16 hailing Mayor Lindsay's condemnation of the catalogue essay: "We heartily support the forthright position taken by Mayor Lindsay in condemning what he rightfully called the 'racist' views expressed in the introduction to this book."[154]

At first, Hoving defended the catalogue. But as the pressure mounted, on the evening of January 17, the day before the show was scheduled to open, he authorized the insertion into the catalogue of a disclaimer by Van Ellison. Worked out with her by one of Hoving's assistants, the statement read: "In regards to the controversy concerning the section in my introduction dealing with inter-group relations, I would like to state that the facts were organized according to the socio-economic realities in Harlem at that time, and that any racist overtones which were inferred from the passages quoted out of context are regrettable."[155]

The staff worked all night to duplicate the disclaimer and insert it into the book. When this failed to quell the storm, the museum inserted a second statement five days later, an apology signed by Hoving in which he personally accepted responsibility for his "error in judgment." The sheet, printed on museum letterhead, explained that the introduction had been written by a high school student, a fact omitted from the book itself. It went on to denounce the essay, stating that when he approved the inclusion of the piece, Hoving "wholly failed to sense the racial undertones that might be read into portions of it. . . . I now fully recognize that her essay was not appropriate as an introduction to the catalogue and offer my deepest apologies to all persons who have been offended."[156]

Ultimately, on January 24—less than a week after the show opened—Hoving agreed to withdraw the catalogue from sale. In retrospect Hoving has said, "I never forgave him [Lindsay] and his advisors for forcing us to stop selling those catalogues. Yet, I caved, so maybe I should direct my anger at myself."[157] The museum had purchased forty thousand softcover copies from Random House. Fourteen thousand had been sold. The remaining twenty-six thousand were taken out of circulation and stashed in the museum's basement. (Later they were given to schools and community organizations.) By the end of February, Random House, which had also inserted a disclaimer, had sold five thousand hardcover copies. The Book-of-the-Month Club bought five thousand copies but never offered them to its members. The essay was suppressed.

Meanwhile, Schoener insisted that his scholarly freedom was being infringed upon.[158] He worried that the withdrawal of the catalogue would be professionally damaging because it implied a failure on his part as editor.[159] Schoener maintains that he had no idea Lindsay was pressuring the New York City Council to withdraw the museum's funds or that Hoving's job was on the line with his board of trustees.[160] He desperately tried to keep the book available for sale, and when he failed, he obtained legal counsel in order to get the softcover copies distributed through some other means. Later, he tried to obtain the mechanicals or film that would have enabled him to have the book reprinted on his own, but was unsuccessful. The book, however, was reissued in 1978 by Dell Publishing with Van Ellison's essay replaced by an introduction written by Nathan Irvin Huggins, a widely published African American writer and editor. To make the book appear timely, Schoener added a chapter on the 1970s.[161] In 1995 and 2007 the New Press reprinted the original catalogue for new generations of readers complete with Van Ellison's text.

Werner Kramarsky, who was Mayor Lindsay's special assistant, the chair of the board of estimate, and the head of Governor Hugh Carey's New York State Human Rights Commission, says that looking back, the withdrawal of the catalogue was probably an infringement on free speech, but there was no one to publicly refute the mayor, and the only member of Lindsay's administration to voice opposition was Kramarsky himself. Kramarsky, a First Amendment rights expert, explained the legal and ethical implications to Lindsay, but the mayor held to his position and instead decided to capitalize on the opportunity to curry favor with the powerful constituency that opposed the show.[162] Did Lindsay have the authority to rescind the city funds? According to Kramarsky, probably not.[163] That would have taken a vote of the New York City Council. Indeed, such a move on Lindsay's part may have even been illegal. But his political purposes were served by threatening such a gesture.

During all of this, Schoener concealed an important piece of information. The offending catalogue statement had actually been paraphrased from a well-known book by Nathan Glazer and Daniel Patrick Moynihan called *Beyond the Melting Pot*. In Van Ellison's original term paper, the text had appeared as a quotation: "One other important factor worth noting is that psychologically Negroes may find that 'a bit of anti-Jewish feeling helps make them feel more completely American, a part of the majority group.' "[164] In the catalogue, however, not only were the quotation marks removed, but the third-person pronoun "them" was changed to "us" and anti-Jewish feelings were characterized as a national prejudice: "One other important factor worth noting is that, psychologically, Blacks find that anti-Jewish sentiments place them, for once, within a majority. Thus, our contempt for the Jew makes us feel more completely American in sharing a national prejudice."[165]

The uproar might have been avoided had the catalogue specified the source of the statements in Glazer and Moynihan's book, or the fact that the essay was based on a high school term paper. But the author was identified merely as "Candice Van Ellison / Harlem, 1967."

Schoener's objective in editing Van Ellison's paper was to give the impression of authenticity. He wanted to avoid the appearance that this young black woman was discussing her own identity in terms that were borrowed from white men. As Adolph L. Reed has pointed out, at a time when black nationalism was on the rise, "Truth became a feature of the speaker's 'blackness,' i.e. validity claims were to be resolved not through discourse but by the claimant's manipulation of certain banal symbols of legitimacy."[166] Schoener understood this; if he hadn't, he certainly would not have omitted the citations from Van Ellison's essay. He legitimized his own prerogative to speak about African American culture by speaking through Van Ellison's voice. According to Schoener, "Everyone was into black nationalism and black identity and it was very important for black statements to be listened to by white people. So for me to say in the introduction that this was a young black women who was borrowing from white intellectuals would have been very inappropriate."[167] Ironically, because he attributed Glazer's words to Van Ellison, Schoener's quest for authenticity brought just the opposite. It was staging of identity that put words in the writer's mouth. Schoener's elimination of the student's citations also transformed her essay from being a product of intellectual research into a "natural" expression of personal angst. Schoener failed to see that his editing of Van Ellison's catalogue essay constituted a far more virulent form of manipulation and co-optation than her own decision to include quotations from white authors.

The ultimate source of the offending text was revealed in a small neighborhood newspaper from the Upper East Side, *Park East News*. Writer Morton Lawrence obtained a copy of Van Ellison's original term paper and revealed not only the source of the objectionable idea but also the sources of a number of other borrowed ideas in the text.[168] In her original paper Van Ellison had actually cited nine sources in twenty-four footnotes. In the published *Harlem on My Mind* version, all twenty-four quotations were either deleted or paraphrased, and all the citations were omitted, including references from John Henrik Clarke's *Harlem: A Community in Transition* and *Harlem U.S.A.* Furthermore, Schoener omitted Van Ellison's introductory statement that the essay was "a combination of fact, observation, and opinion."[169] And finally, Schoener "radicalized" Van Ellison's text by substituting the words "black" or "Afro-American" everywhere she had used the word "Negro." Schoener lifted the quotation marks from Van Ellison's essay because he thought that a direct statement from a "ghetto resident" would provide a more compelling first-person account of Harlem life. The truth—that this student had written a well-researched academic paper drawing on sources written by whites as well as African Americans—was much less provocative than the stereotypical image of a young black woman giving an unmediated, eyewitness account of her personal experiences.

When Hoving learned that the controversial statement had been borrowed from *Beyond the Melting Pot* and that Schoener had omitted the source, he was furious. But Hoving himself was not immune to charges of falsifying the truth. In his own preface to the catalogue he had fabricated a fictitious childhood complete with a Negro maid named Bessie who was always "friendly, always gay and warm," and Frank, a dour chauffeur who was "sour, moody, bitter, silent and mad."[170] He claimed that his mother used to go "slumming" in the clubs of Harlem for exotic titillation, and that to him as a kid, "Negroes were people, but they were happy, foot-twitching, smiling and sunny. . . . Negroes, as human beings, did not exist." Perhaps he created these caricatures to illustrate for an elite white audience how far he himself had evolved. He has since said, "When I read my embarrassing text in galleys, I asked Schoener if I could rewrite it, but he discouraged me, saying he liked the confessional tone and especially the part about the maid and the chauffeur. So I let the foreword go unchanged."[171] All of the participants in the *Harlem on My Mind* controversy strove to speak from positions of authority. For Hoving, this meant portraying himself as the child of white privilege who had recognized the injustice of racial discrimination and was now able to make amends.

Ironically, the Jewish groups' criticisms of the show enabled the African American activists to gain more media attention than they would have otherwise. Not until the catalogue controversy appeared on the front page of the *New York Times* did the Harlem community's criticisms receive wide newspaper coverage. Had Jewish groups remained quiet, the African American artists' concerns might have slipped under the radar, buried on page 41 of the newspaper, as was the first article in the *New York Times* reporting their protest.[172]

The museum's staff anticipated a large turnout for *Harlem on My Mind* based on the record-breaking attendance of Schoener's previous exhibition, *Portal to America*, held at the Jewish Museum a few years earlier, and the publicity engendered by the controversy no doubt drew even more people to the spectacle. Elaborate traffic flow plans were developed to control the crowd. Schoener envisioned a long line that would wind down the stairs, through the Roman and Greek gallery, to the Great Hall, and flow out of the museum onto the sidewalk. The throng of waiting visitors would then form a queue southward down Fifth Avenue.

The exhibition itself was divided into six chronologically and thematically structured sections: "1900–1919, From White to Black Harlem"; "1920–1929, An Urban Black Culture"; "1930–1939, Depression and Hard Times"; "1940–1949, War, Hope, and Opportunity"; "1950–1959, Frustration and Ambivalence"; and "1960–1968, Militancy and Identity." Each section presented a combination of photo blow-ups, voice sound track, music, and texts based on newspaper article excerpts and primary documents. Some rooms presented film and slide projections, and each decade included a timeline of significant events. In keeping with Schoener's intent for the exhibition, overlapping sounds and images created a chaotic atmosphere, even though the show itself comprised a highly structured sequence of fifteen consecutive galleries with one point of entry, one path through, and one way out.

Schoener wanted viewers to experience the exhibition as if they were watching a film. He did not want people to dwell on written texts, so he did not include captions with any of the images. Instead, each room contained a single diagram identifying its contents. Moreover, none of the photographs in the galleries were identified by maker. The point was to draw the viewer into the subject matter of the images, not to showcase individual artistic vision or interpretation. (By contrast, *The Family of Man* exhibition had included the country of origin and maker of each image on a small label attached to the bottom of each photograph.)

It was not uncommon to see objects displayed with no attribution at the Metropolitan Museum of Art. Many of the collections—Egyptian, ancient Near East, Islamic, early Christian, medieval—contain items where the maker is unknown or the object was made through a collective process, rather than by an individual. What made the absence of photographers' names such an anomaly in *Harlem on My Mind* was that the images were recent and, in most cases, their makers were known. Schoener also neglected to identify the subjects in many of the images, thus undermining the pedagogical character of the show. In retrospect Schoener felt that the omission of captions was a mistake, but at the time his aim was not to disrupt the viewers' flow. Schoener wanted people to "read experientially."[173]

Synthesizing, organizing, and formulating methods for presenting the vast catalogue of raw material collected for the show fell to exhibition designer Robert Malone, who designed and fabricated the display systems (fig. 2.16). Malone devised structures and solutions for the cohesive presentation of a massive collection of disparate research materials. The show began with the *Harlem on My Mind* logo in the form of a slide projection (fig. 2.17). As visitors passed through the hallway, they were greeted by a sound track featuring street sounds recorded in Harlem. The first gallery focused on African Americans in New York during the eighteenth and nineteenth centuries. An array of historical documents reproduced on wall panels charted a skeletal history of African American life from slavery through emancipation. A broadside from 1731 stated regulations restricting the activities of "Negroes and slaves" in the City of New York after sunset. A 1788 runaway poster advertised a fifteen-dollar reward for a slave from an owner on Long Island. There was the front page of an 1837 issue of *Freedom's Journal*, the first African American newspaper in the country, a copy of the Emancipation Proclamation, and the frontispiece of Sojourner Truth's *Narrative of a Northern Slave*. A notice from 1867 from the African Mutual Instruction Society in downtown Manhattan offered a school for "colored Adults of both Sexes." These documents were presented with a sound track of Paul Robeson singing spirituals.

The next two rooms addressed Harlem's transformation around the turn of the twentieth century from a white neighborhood to one that was mostly African American. A picture from 1902 showed a group of affluent white women in bustles and large wide-brimmed hats being rowed on the Harlem River by men in sleeveless

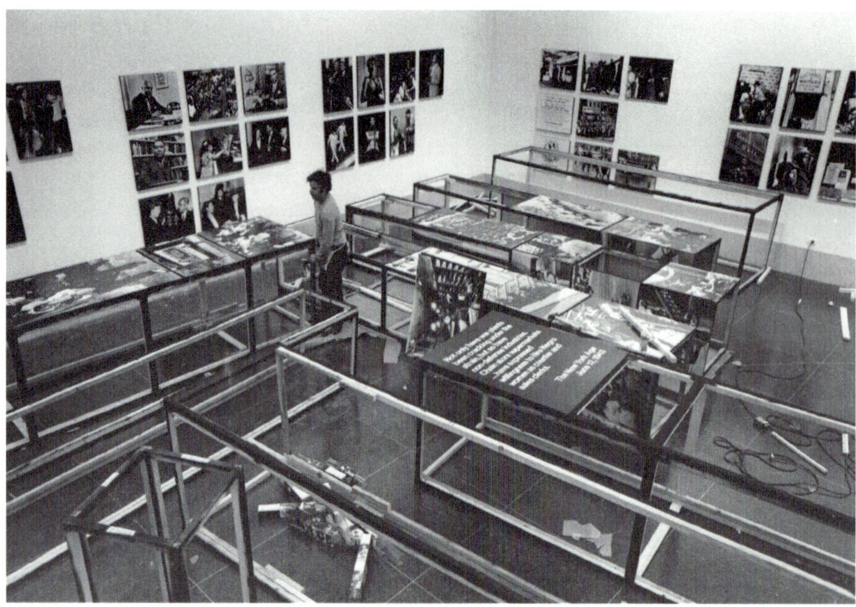

Fig. 2.16 Installation of the *Harlem on My Mind* exhibition at the Metropolitan Museum of Art. Photo: Thomas Patsenka. Courtesy of Robert Malone.

tops. There were photos of smartly dressed customers sitting in a beer garden in 1912, and three photographs showing modes of transportation: bicycling on Fifth Avenue in 1897, a horse-drawn carriage circa 1900, and an early automobile from 1908. There was a grand Victorian house on the corner of Fifth Avenue and 130th Street and a picture of Harlem Hospital. A photo blowup of an advertisement offered "Apartments to Let" at 44 and 46 West Ninety-Ninth Street, 236 West 134th Street, and East 103rd Street on the corner of Park Avenue. These photos were followed by images of neighborhoods that were predominantly African American at the turn of the century, Chelsea and San Juan Hill, on the West Side of Manhattan.

The first rooms depicting Harlem populated by African Americans covered the 1910s. Featured in a film presentation was one of the neighborhood's oldest residents, Alice Peyton Brown, known as "Mother Brown" (figs. 2.18 and 2.19). A brief text panel explained that "Mother Brown" had been born a slave in Lexington, Virginia, on November 17, 1853, and moved to New York City in 1891. In 1907 she arrived in Harlem. A film projection showed "Mother Brown" celebrating her

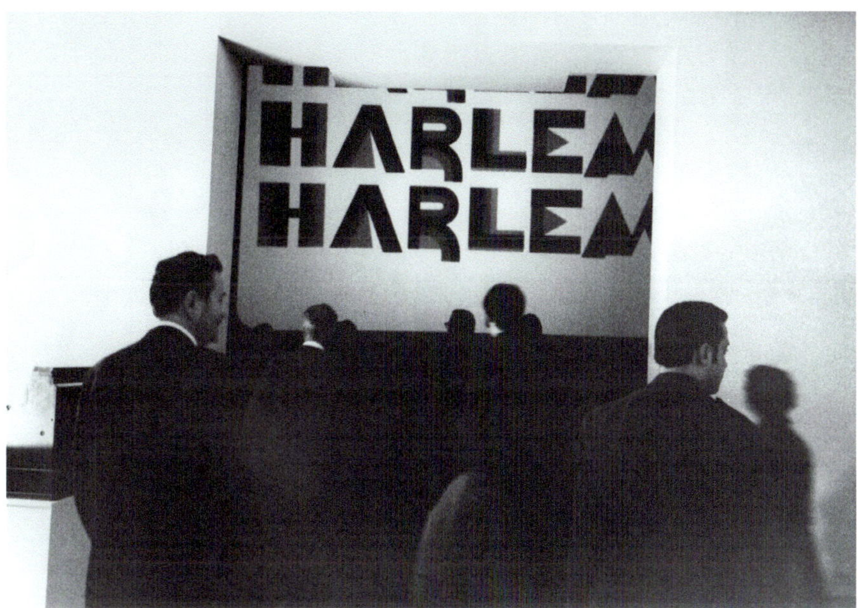

Fig. 2.17 Entrance, *Harlem on My Mind: Cultural Capital of Black America, 1900–1968*, the Metropolitan Museum of Art, January 18–April 6, 1969. Photo: Thomas Patsenka. Courtesy of Robert Malone.

115th birthday, just two months before the exhibition opened, surrounded by "friendly faces," as Schoener called them in his exhibition notes, singing "Happy Birthday." The film also included interview footage shot in various locations, including Brown's apartment, the Friendship Baptist Church to which she belonged, and a Harlem street. The script for the voice-over piped into the gallery added little in the way of information, but presented "Mother Brown" as a witness to history:

> NARRATOR: On November 17, 1853, Alice Payton Brown, the daughter of Louise and Joe Payton, was born a slave on Sam Hollman's plantation about twelve miles from Lexington, Virginia. . . . Slavemaster Holloman did not believe in schooling for slaves; therefore Mother Brown never learned to read or write. Mother Brown remembers that she was about twelve when the Civil War began and that many slaves ran away to join "Mr. Lincoln's Army." This is how she remembers being a slave.

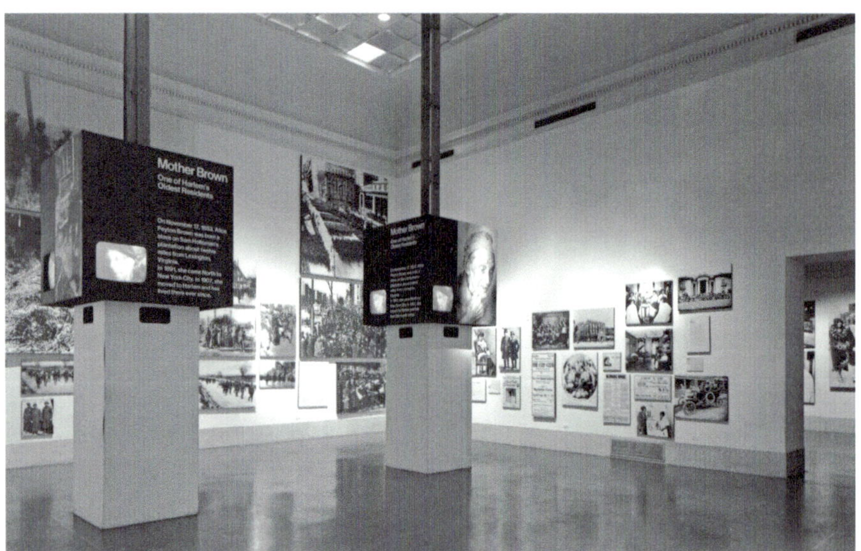

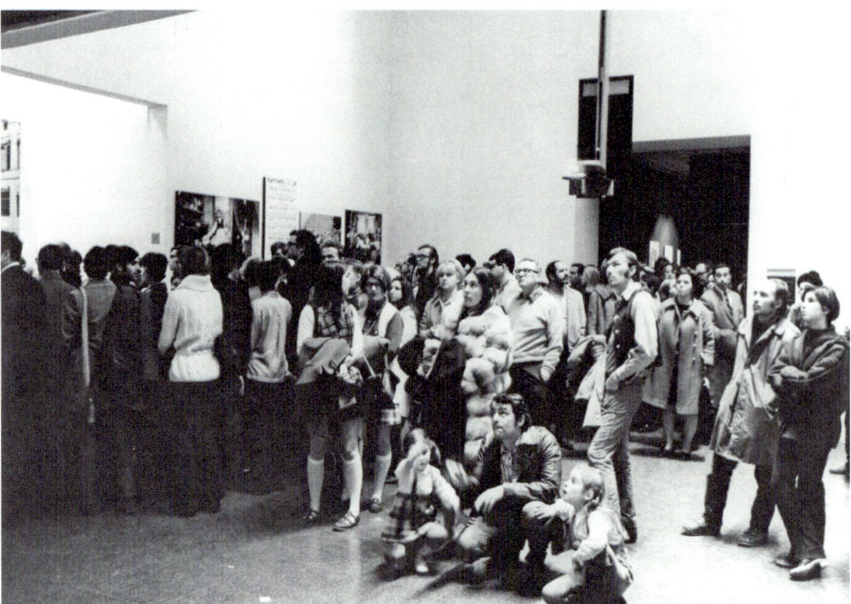

Fig. 2.18 Installation view of "1900–1919, From White to Black Harlem," *Harlem on My Mind: Cultural Capital of Black America, 1900-1968*, the Metropolitan Museum of Art, January 18–April 6, 1969. Image © The Metropolitan Museum of Art.

Fig. 2.19 Installation view of "1900–1919, From White to Black Harlem," *Harlem on My Mind: Cultural Capital of Black America, 1900-1968*, the Metropolitan Museum of Art, January 18–April 6, 1969. Photo: Thomas Patsenka. Courtesy of Robert Malone.

"Mother Brown" was presented as an artifact, a symbol of the transition from slavery to freedom, past to present; the mere sound of her voice, a testament to the spirit of survival; her face, an image of triumph over adversity.

The section on the 1910s also contained photographs of African American soldiers from World War I, members of the 369th Infantry, who were called the "Harlem Hell-Fighters." One of these images showed the soldiers marching down Fifth Avenue directly in front of the Metropolitan Museum of Art, but because there were no wall labels, this detail was not pointed out. In the next gallery visitors were confronted with a floor-to-ceiling photo-mural of a Harlem side street circa 1915 with several men staring out at the viewer (figs. 2.20 and 2.21). The enormous scale of the image, the one-point perspective of the cobblestone street, and the intense gazes of the men created the effect of bridging the space between the viewer and the scene and accentuated the curatorial intention of making viewers feel that they were witnesses to history.

The next two rooms focused on the years 1920–29 and the rise of an "urban black culture" represented by scenes of daily life and the rapidly growing number of black social institutions in Harlem, such as schools, churches, libraries, and social clubs. One entire wall measuring eighteen by fifty feet contained a photo mural of a Sunday school class from the Abyssinian Baptist Church led by Reverend Adam Clayton Powell Sr. (fig. 2.22). The picture had been taken by James VanDerZee and was enlarged so that the figures appeared life size. Another room presented great men and women of the Harlem Renaissance, including Langston Hughes, Duke Ellington, Florence Mills, Zora Neale Hurston, W. E. B. Du Bois, and others. This section was the only part of the exhibition to include source material by a visual artist, photo-reproductions of woodcut prints by Aaron Douglas illustrating plays by Alain Locke and Montgomery Gregory, and *God's Trombones* by James Weldon Johnson. There were also cover pages from the magazines *The Crisis* and *Opportunity* and a sound track of poetry by writers of the Harlem Renaissance.

An array of photographs of Marcus Garvey, leader of the Universal Negro Improvement Association (UNIA) and the Back-to-Africa movement, depicted the massive leader riding through the crowded streets of Harlem, a ship from Garvey's business venture the Black Star Line, and Garvey being led off to prison in 1925 when he was charged with mail fraud (fig. 2.23). An audiotape of Garvey delivering

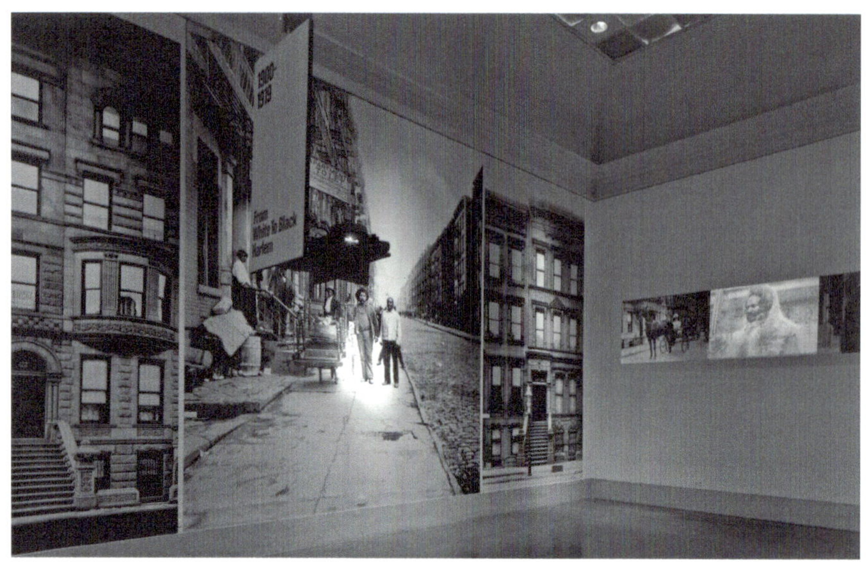

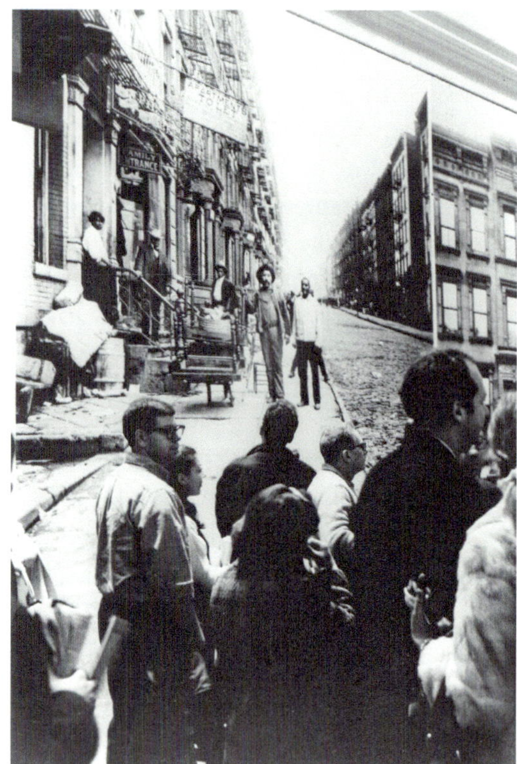

Fig. 2.20 Installation view of "1900–1919, From White to Black Harlem," *Harlem on My Mind: Cultural Capital of Black America, 1900–1968*, the Metropolitan Museum of Art, January 18–April 6, 1969. Image © The Metropolitan Museum of Art.

Fig. 2.21 Installation view of "1900–1919, From White to Black Harlem," *Harlem on My Mind: Cultural Capital of Black America, 1900–1968*, the Metropolitan Museum of Art, January 18–April 6, 1969. Photo: Thomas Patsenka. Courtesy of Robert Malone.

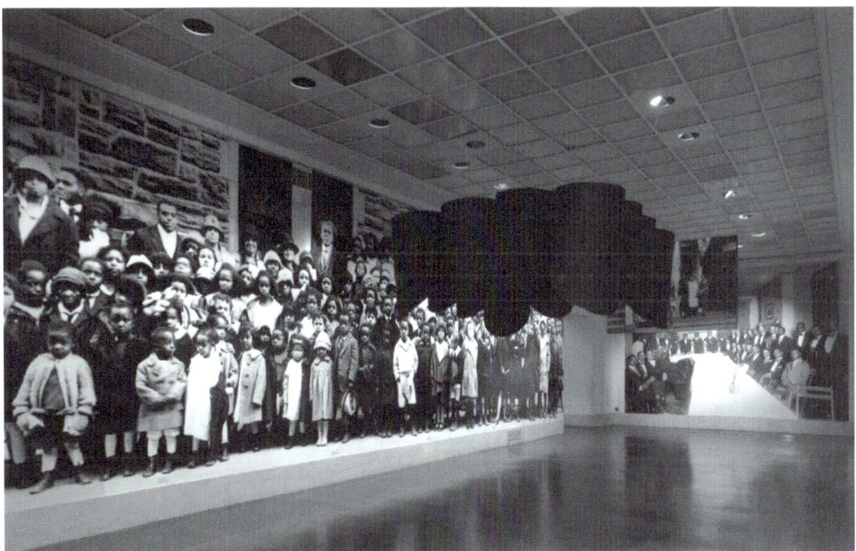

a speech played in the gallery. The second of the 1920s galleries was outfitted with tables and chairs, with jazz band music piped in to suggest the atmosphere of a nightclub. Schoener hoped the music would prompt people to dance.[175]

The next two rooms, "Depression and Hard Times," focused on the 1930s. A wall-size photo-mural of a repeated image of a bread line ran the full length of one gallery (fig. 2.24). The room was devoid of a sound track, a choice intended to induce a somber mood. A second gallery devoted to the '30s featured photos of Harlem leaders, including Father Divine and his followers. Billie Holiday's blues filled the space (figs. 2.25 and 2.26).

In the room labeled "1940–1949, War, Hope, and Opportunity," images hung from pylons in the center of the room (fig. 2.27). Once again, there were portraits of major figures, including performers Paul Robeson, Pearl Bailey, Ella Fitzgerald, Charlie Parker, and Count Basie, author Richard Wright, and sports heroes Joe Louis, Sugar Ray Robinson, and Jackie Robinson. A sound track of bands of the '40s included Dizzy Gillespie. Street scenes showed children playing war in an abandoned lot with wooden rifles, the 1943 Harlem riot, and Helen Levitt's enchanting photograph of a building façade with the words "Button to Secret Passage Press" written in chalk, one of the show's few moments of poetry (fig. 2.28).

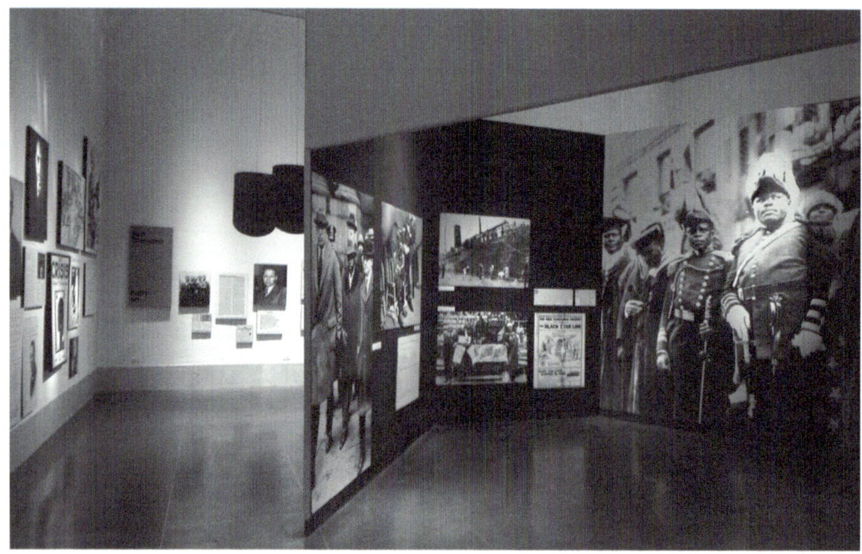

Fig. 2.23 Installation view of "1920–1929, An Urban Black Culture,"
Harlem on My Mind: Cultural Capital of Black America, 1900–1968, the
Metropolitan Museum of Art, January 18–April 6, 1969.
Image © The Metropolitan Museum of Art.

The next room, "1950–1959, Frustration and Ambivalence," contained over a dozen photographs of Malcolm X during the early phase of his participation in Elijah Muhammad's Nation of Islam. Other public figures in this section included Ralph Ellison, Willie Mays, and Martin Luther King Jr. The sound track featured cool jazz by Miles Davis (fig. 2.29).

Finally, the section "1960–1968, Militancy and Identity" had three rooms. One was totally dark and had banks of slide projectors simultaneously casting nine sets of images onto Mylar screens across the room (fig. 2.30). Each set of images was devoted to one year leading up to the opening date of the show in January 1969. The electronic timeline contained pictures of significant African American figures and major events. Loud rock music was piped into the space. A second room, dedicated to "Harlem Today," contained the only color images in the show, street scenes taken by Leroy Lucas, a photographer commissioned by Schoener to create the work especially for the exhibition.[176]

The last room summarized the show in a "Hall of Heroes," a grid of photo blowups of black faces, many of which were seen earlier in the galleries and cropped to serve the format (fig. 2.31). The images included W. E. B. Du Bois, Claude McKay,

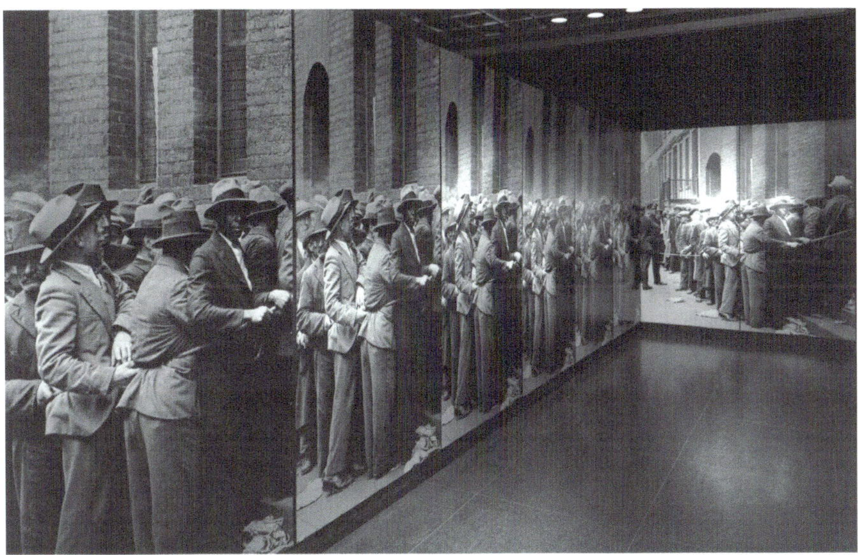

Charles Mingus, Malcolm X, and Mohammad Ali, as well as anonymous men, women, and children. The gallery resembled the "Faces" section of the *Family of Man* show (fig. 2.32), which was designed to encourage identification with the subjects portrayed.[177] The "Hall of Heroes," however, fostered both identification and confrontation. This ambiguity was reflected in the poem "Love Your Enemy":

> *Brought here in slave ships and pitched over board.*
> *Love your enemy.*
> *Language taken away, culture taken away.*
> *Love your enemy . . .*
> *Lynch your father.*
> *Love your enemy.*
> *Bomb your churches.*
> *Love your enemy.*
> *Kill your children.*
> *Love your enemy . . .*
> *Love for everybody else.*
> *But when will we love ourselves?*[178]

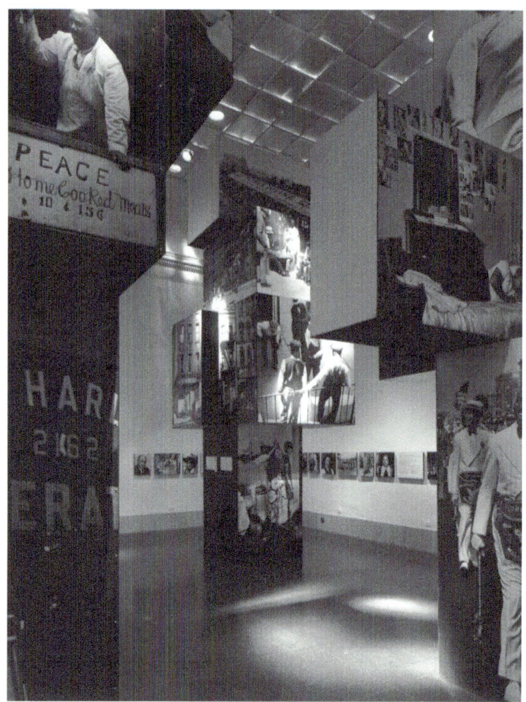

Fig. 2.25 Installation view of "1930–1939, Depression and Hard Times," *Harlem on My Mind: Cultural Capital of Black America, 1900–1968*, the Metropolitan Museum of Art, New York, January 18–April 6, 1969. Image © The Metropolitan Museum of Art.

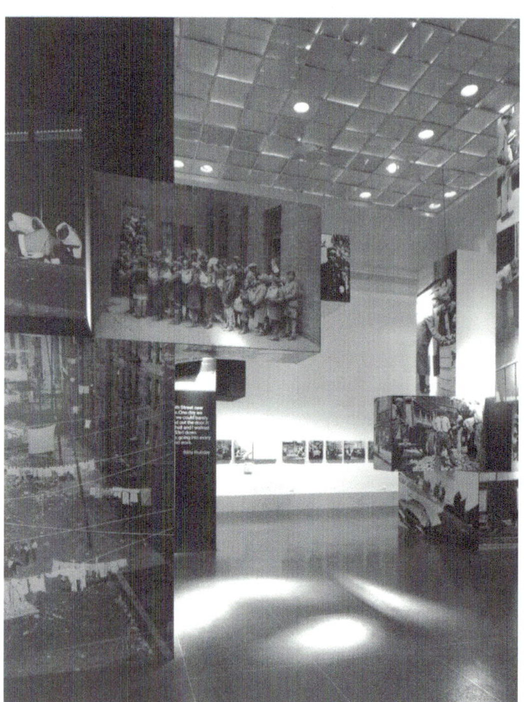

Fig. 2.26 Installation view of "1930–1939, Depression and Hard Times," *Harlem on My Mind: Cultural Capital of Black America, 1900–1968*, the Metropolitan Museum of Art, New York, January 18–April 6, 1969. Image © The Metropolitan Museum of Art.

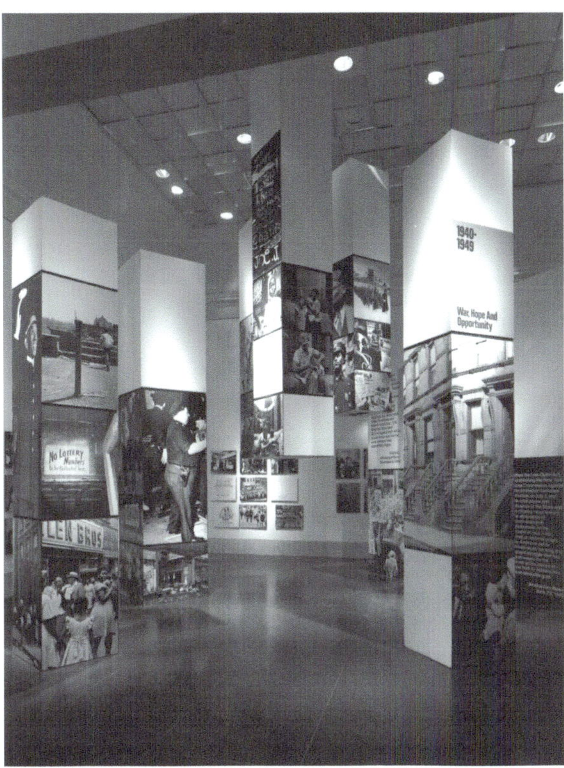

Fig. 2.27 Installation view of "1940–1949, War, Hope, and Opportunity," *Harlem on My Mind: Cultural Capital of Black America, 1900–1968*, the Metropolitan Museum of Art, January 18–April 6, 1969. Image © The Metropolitan Museum of Art.

Fig. 2.28 Helen Levitt, *New York [Button to Secret Passage]*, 1938, gelatin silver print, 5⅜×7⅝ ins. © Estate of Helen Levitt.

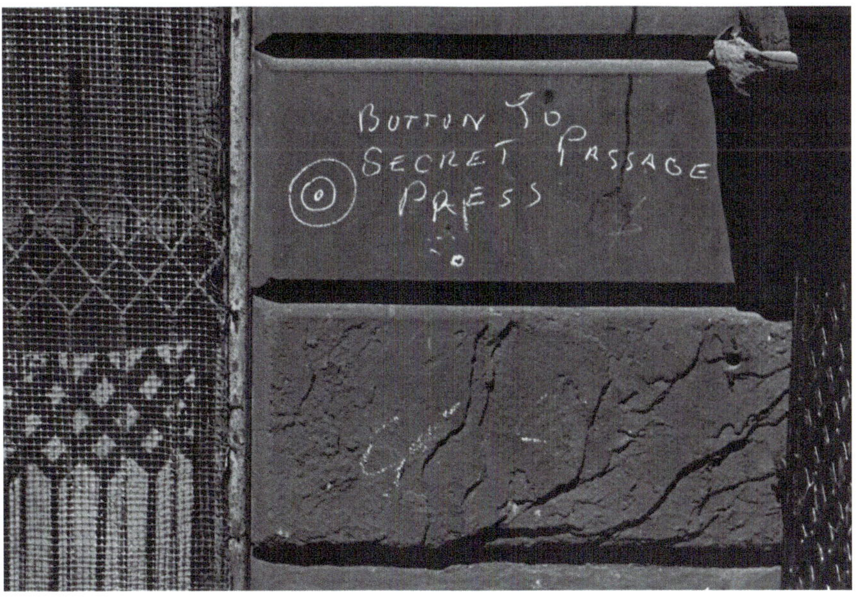

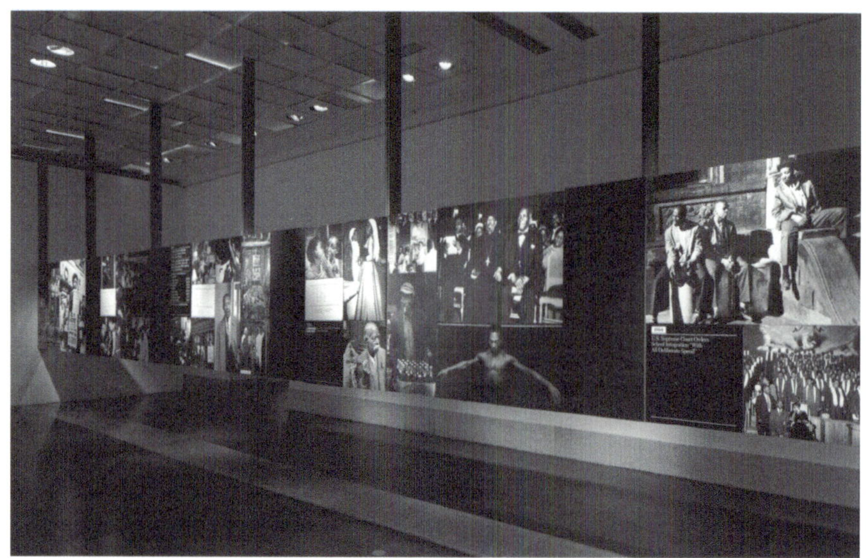

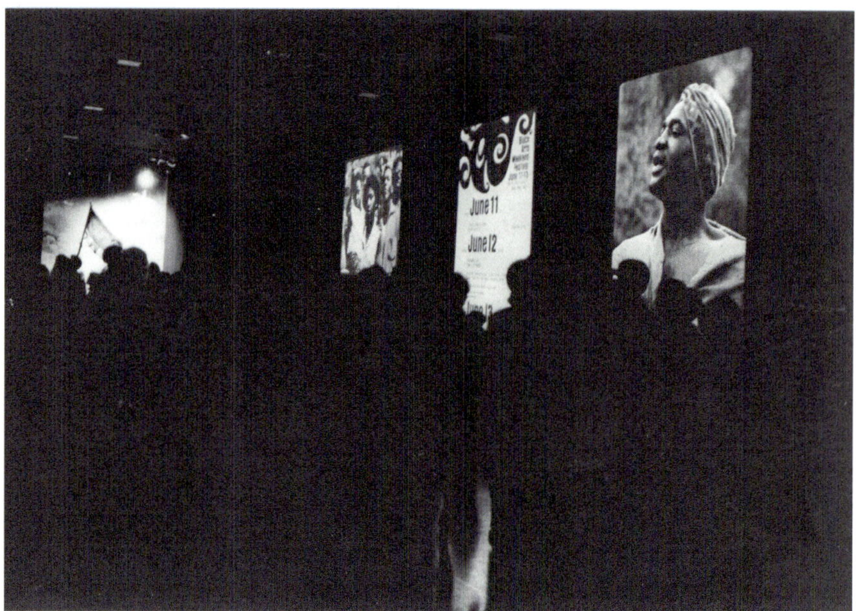

Fig. 2.29 Installation view of "1950–1959, Frustration and Ambivalence," *Harlem on My Mind: Cultural Capital of Black America, 1900–1968*, the Metropolitan Museum of Art, January 18–April 6, 1969. Image © The Metropolitan Museum of Art.

Fig. 2.30 Installation view of "1960–1969, Militancy and Identity," *Harlem on My Mind: Cultural Capital of Black America, 1900–1968*, the Metropolitan Museum of Art, January 18–April 6, 1969. Photo: Thomas Patsenka. Courtesy of Robert Malone.

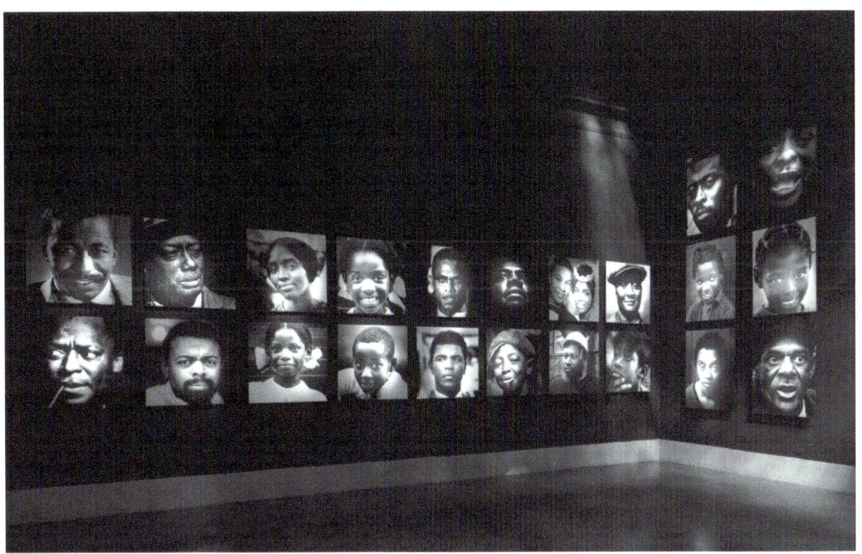

Fig. 2.31 Installation view of "Hall of Heroes," *Harlem on My Mind: Cultural Capital of Black America, 1900–1968*, the Metropolitan Museum of Art, January 18–April 6, 1969. Image © The Metropolitan Museum of Art.

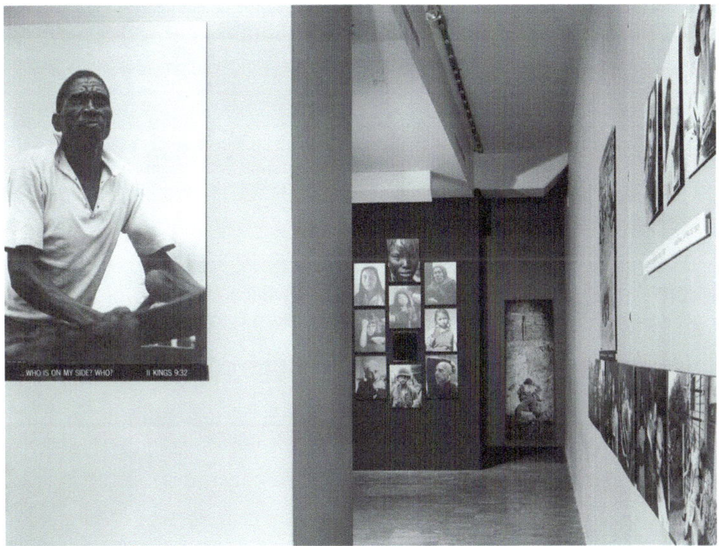

Fig. 2.32 Faces exhibit, *The Family of Man*, the Museum of Modern Art, New York, January 24–May 8, 1955. © Ezra Stoller / Esto.

The poem, written by Yusef Iman, chronicled a history of violence against blacks in the United States. Printed on a placard and played over the sound system, the recitation linked past to present in a rhythm as relentless as the cruelties themselves. One of the few parts of the show attributed to its creator, the poem embodied a situated voice, that of one African American addressing others, at once refreshing and jarringly out of sync with the exhibition as a whole. Again, we see the curator manipulate a sign of authenticity without exposing his own identity.

As visitors exited the exhibition, they passed through a room with a sales desk featuring the *Harlem on My Mind* phonograph record and the catalogue (priced to be affordable at $1.95)—until the museum pulled the book from its shelves. The record, produced by the exhibition's sound consultant, Donald Harper, contained a medley of twentieth-century African American musical genres performed by Hank Johnson and the Jazz Heritage Ensemble, including ragtime, New Orleans blues, swing, big band, bebop, cool jazz, and bossa nova, ending with an upbeat pop number reminiscent of the contemporary musical group the Fifth Dimension.[179] There were also anonymous voices recounting personal memories of Harlem.

Overall, the exhibition was designed to create "encounters." Pictures were given corporeal presence by being hung on pylons and blown up to life-size. Voices were piped into the galleries to create the sense that the rooms were filled with actual beings. At the same time, the exhibition drained the photographs of their own integrity; pictures were enlarged, reduced, cropped, repeated. They were used as the building blocks of Schoener's narrative.

This treatment of the photography medium accounts for Roy DeCarava's absence from the show, even though his photographs of Harlem were the most famous—and powerful—of the time. Schoener and McGhee knew DeCarava's work. He was an accomplished artist who had been born in Harlem in 1919 and lived there his entire life. In 1952 DeCarava had received a Guggenheim Fellowship to produce a series of photographs documenting Harlem. In 1955 Simon and Schuster published the photos accompanied by a text by Langston Hughes in a book called *The Sweet Flypaper of Life*.[180] The book was a huge success; the initial publication of 3,000 clothbound and 22,000 paperback copies was soon supplemented by a second printing of 10,000 copies. Schoener and McGhee invited DeCarava to be in the show, but the artist informed them that his pictures were meant to be seen as a group. Schoener's concept for the show did not allow for any such groupings; he claimed that the emergence of an individual artist's aesthetic would disrupt the show's narrative and refused to comply with DeCarava's request. The artist chose not to participate.[181]

DeCarava's approach to photography differed radically from Schoener's. In 1951 the artist had written, "I want to photograph Harlem through the Negro people. Morning, noon, night, at work, going to work, coming home from work, at play, in the streets, talking, kidding, laughing, in the home, in the playgrounds, in the schools, bars, store, libraries, beauty parlors, churches, etc." DeCarava wanted "to heighten the awareness of my people and bring to our consciousness greater knowledge of our heritage," an aim also expressed by Schoener—but that's where any commonality in the two men's goals ends. DeCarava wanted "to show the strength, the wisdom the dignity of the Negro people. Not the famous and the well known, but the unknown and the unnamed, thus revealing the roots from which spring the greatness of all human beings. . . . I do not want a documentary or sociological statement, I want a creative expression, the kind of penetrating insight and understanding of Negroes which I believe only a Negro photographer can interpret."[182] Among DeCarava's best-known pictures is a girl in a communion dress standing alone in an empty lot illuminated by sunshine. In another, a couple talks intimately on a subway platform locked in each other's loving gaze. A man tenderly holds a baby engulfed in womblike darkness (fig. 2.33).

DeCarava's photographs of Harlem have an atmospheric beauty, an intimacy, a weightiness that not only describes things but also carries feeling. The formal qualities of DeCarava's works are paramount to their impact. As Sherry Turner DeCarava has pointed out, because the artist explored the "landscape of emotions . . . grain becomes a tool that he can selectively employ. Focus, blur, and motion are other techniques used to produce visible texture that diffuse the descriptive aspects of the field."[183] None of these formal qualities would have been conveyed to viewers given Schoener's curatorial strategy. Indeed, presenting the works in reproduction would have negated their intrinsic aesthetic. DeCarava's poetic images had no place in Schoener's vision, and in the final analysis, the absence of his works epitomized the museum's failure to acknowledge the existence of art by African Americans.

In the seven hundred or so photographs that Schoener brought together for the project, few stand out for their aesthetic power, save those of James VanDerZee.[184] In her monograph on VanDerZee, Deborah Willis-Braithwaite cogently argues that VanDerZee's images often projected an identification and intimacy with his subjects that gave his pictures a distinctive feel.[185] Schoener, on the other hand, opted for images that gave an emotionally detached view of their subjects. For instance, the image Schoener selected of opening night of *Voodoo Macbeth* at the Lafayette Theatre in 1936 is shot from across the street (fig. 2.34). The photograph

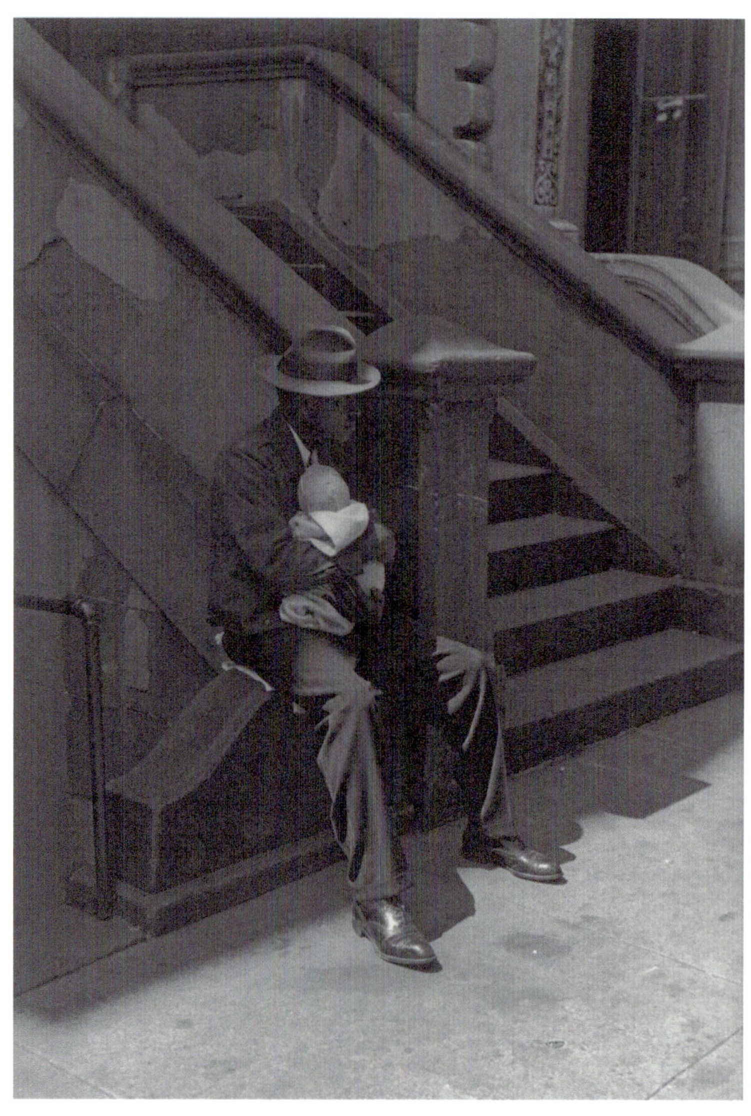

Fig. 2.33 Roy DeCarava, *Man on stoop with baby*, 1952, gelatin silver print.
© The Roy DeCarava Estate and Sherry DeCarava 2014.

documents the façade of the theater, its architecture and signage. The photographer has no interaction with the crowd. The faces and expressions of the figures are impossible to discern. A large car parked in front of the theater contains several white passengers, who regard the scene from inside their car, also from a distance. By contrast, another photo taken by the same photographer on the same night has a far more engaged feel (fig. 2.35). The image tightly frames a view of the crowd. The people look directly into the camera, laughing, smiling, and waving. The photograph does not reinforce a sense of separation. This photo may not have appealed to Schoener because it does not show the marquee containing the theater's name. Yet a third photo is even more compelling in that it conveys the flavor of the event: the crush of excitement among the theatergoing crowd, the contrast between the spectacle created by the spotlight and the nonchalant postures of the silhouetted figures matter-of-factly operating the equipment. The viewer feels vicariously the sensation of being on the street among the clubs and bars (fig. 2.36). The scene is overwhelmed with light—from the bulbs on the marquee to the neon shop signs to the immense spotlight itself—all competing with each other to grab attention and combining to create the palpable sensation of collective excitement. This photograph conveys the kind of experience Schoener aspired to create in *Harlem on My Mind*.

Schoener selected most of the images for the show from the picture press, with a few exceptions—notably, images by VanDerZee, Gordon Parks, Aaron Siskind, and Helen Levitt. This choice caused the exhibition to reproduce the status quo representations of blacks encountered in daily newspapers and magazines. A critique of such representations and a search for a more authentic photographic "voice" was the mission of the Kamoinge group, a collective formed in New York in 1963 to address the underrepresentation of black photographers in the art world.[186] DeCarava was one of its leaders. In 1966 the international photography journal *Camera* had published a portfolio of the Kamoinge group's photographs—their work was known—but none of these photographers were included in the show.[187]

Several elements of the exhibition were envisioned, but never realized. In the last gallery Schoener wanted to have a media room that would play all the local radio and TV stations simultaneously so that visitors would see the exhibition juxtaposed with up-to-the-minute news. This proved logistically impossible. Schoener had also wanted to create a two-way video phone linking the galleries of the Metropolitan Museum of Art with Harlem. The uptown unit was to be housed in a mobile studio parked at the corner of 125th Street and Seventh Avenue that

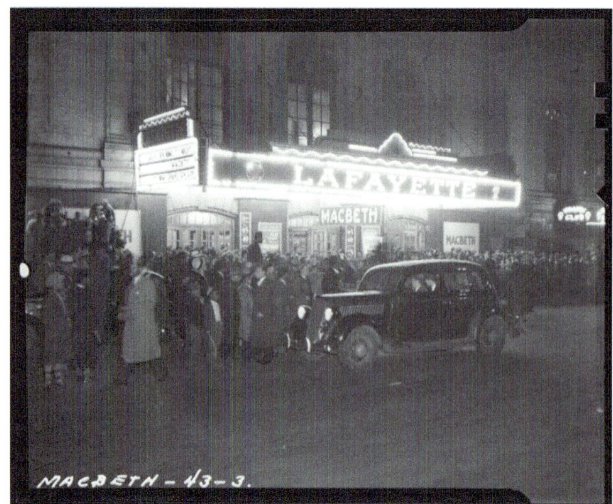

Fig. 2.34 Opening night of *Macbeth*, New Lafayette Theater, 1936. Library of Congress, Music Division, Federal Theatre Project Collection.

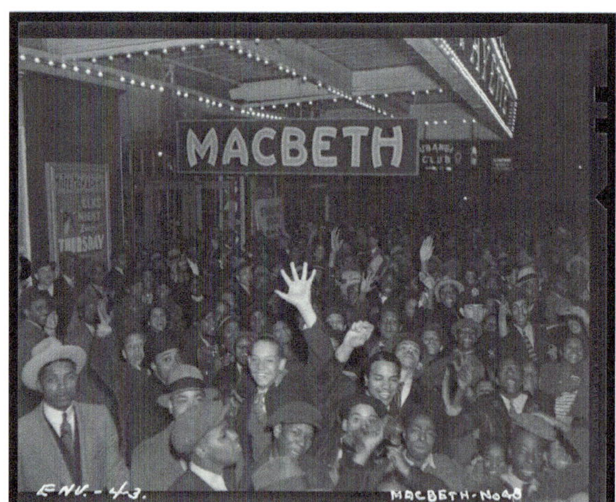

Fig. 2.35 Opening night of *Macbeth*, New Lafayette Theater, 1936. Library of Congress, Music Division, Federal Theatre Project Collection.

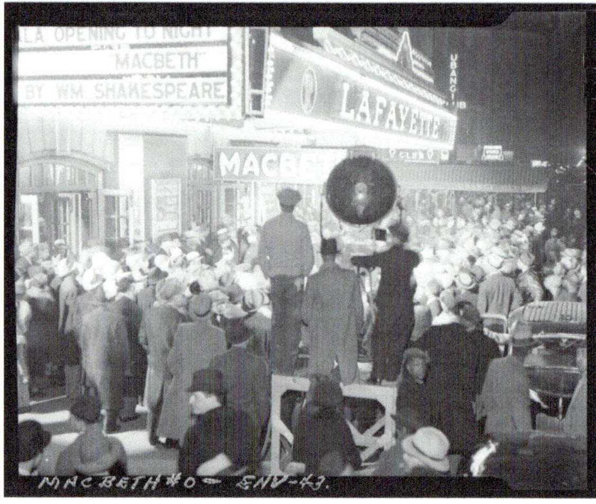

Fig. 2.36 Opening night of *Macbeth*, New Lafayette Theater, 1936. Library of Congress, Music Division, Federal Theatre Project Collection.

would periodically travel the streets making visits to homes, churches, and other sites. The museum unit, equipped with a camera, several phones, and a large viewing screen, was to be placed in one of the exhibition galleries. The project was intended to foster dialogue between the people in the museum and those uptown, bridging a geographic distance of only twenty blocks, but a social distance thought to be much wider.

Another project that was discussed but never realized was a room that would have paid homage to Martin Luther King Jr., who had been assassinated on April 4, 1968. When the Exhibition Research Committee met on May 1, exhibition staff member Reginald McGhee proposed devoting one gallery at the end of the exhibition exclusively to King, with a single photograph of the civil rights leader accompanied by recordings of some of his speeches. There was little support for his proposal. Exhibition adviser John Henrik Clarke pointed out that there would be many memorials to King in the ensuing months. Clarke and another of the advisers, Jean Blackwell Hutson, suggested that if there were to be a dedication, it should be to someone more directly a part of the Harlem community, such as Langston Hughes, who had died in 1967. A'Lelia Nelson countered that the exhibition was intended not to celebrate the accomplishments of one individual, but rather to commemorate the achievements of the Harlem community as a whole. McGhee pressed his point, but in the end Schoener capped the discussion by emphasizing that any dedications would undermine the basic structure of the exhibition, which was the story of Harlem. In the end, the show featured very few references to Martin Luther King Jr.; instead, Malcolm X emerged as the dominant African American leader. Malcolm X was more identified with Harlem than King, and his politics may have seemed more in tune with the ideology of Black Power gaining momentum in the late 1960s.[188]

The show drew the largest audience of any exhibition at the Metropolitan Museum of Art up to that time, 450,000 people over a period of sixteen weeks. (A typical show drew 50,000 to 60,000.) Mahler Ryder of the BECC lamented that "sadly, many black people who hungered for their images crossed the picket line, including lots of teachers who took black children across the picket line."[189] A colleague from NYSCA hired to evaluate the techniques used to manage the volume of traffic reported a rowdy crowd that swarmed the main staircase and ignored the instructions of a lone security guard.[190]

Schoener had calculated the optimum number of visitors and prescribed a pathway through the show. Sound elements were timed to loop every four or five minutes, "pulsing" visitors through to the next gallery, but few followed the path laid out for them.[191] Visitors passed quickly through the rooms with photomurals, causing bottlenecks in the more densely hung galleries.

Many reviews of the show noted a chaotic atmosphere. Perhaps the most vivid description was published in the neighborhood paper *Manhattan East*. Critic David Noble wrote:

> Stepping into the first gallery, one finds himself in the vice-like grasp of the multi-mixed-media wizards who set up the display. And it is not until leaving that one breathlessly regains his sense of intellectual and visual freedom. By that time, the viewer-victim's feeling is one of having been thoroughly worked over, if not pummeled, battered and bruised. . . . [The exhibition] is a mind-fatiguing, futuristic nightmare. Names, dates, images blink on and off against a background of distracting sounds. While one tries to read one poem, another is coming over the loudspeaker and those of us with but a single mind begin to wish we had none as we are swept along in the crowd.[192]

In his weekly photography column in the *Village Voice*, photography critic A. D. Coleman dismissed the exhibition as a meaningless jumble and a disservice to the medium of photography:

> There is evidence aplenty that Allon Schoener, coordinator of the exhibit, and his fellow workers have read Marshall McLuhan and really tried to do something original and avant-garde. There are photos all over—on towering columns, on walls, on ceilings, on TV screens, everywhere photographs, more than you can shake a stick at. But one can look at just so many photographs on any subject unaccompanied by informative text before they all begin to look the same. Here they are lumped together, in no order save chronology, hung in clumps on the walls, grouped in fives and sixes for no apparent reason, certainly without any visual harmonies or correlations. What a waste of so many fine photographers.[193]

Critics of every stripe, from the most liberal to the most conservative, denounced the show's political message. Liberals who might have been sympathetic to Schoener's politics saw his use of photo-reproductions as a means of replicating mass media stereotypes.[194] Conservative critics, such as Hilton Kramer, lamented the jettisoning of traditional artistic values in favor of photojournalism. In his review for the *New York Times* Kramer condemned the show as an "amateur exercise in social evangelism" and criticized Hoving for "abandoning art for a cheap form of photo-audio journalism."[195] Kramer cautioned that *Harlem on My Mind* was a threat to one of the world's great institutions of high art:

> There are undoubtedly many intelligent and socially concerned people in our midst who, in measuring the pressures of current social grievances against the often very private and specialized emotions of contemporary art, have decided to wash their hands of art altogether and devote their energies to a more immediately constructive task. What is odd, not to say alarming, is to discover this point of view harbored in the mind of the director of one of the greatest art museums in the world—a mind that shows itself increasingly impatient with the kind of slow, and in the short run anyway, often unmeasurable benefactions that a deep attachment to the art experience bestows on our spirit and on our emotions.[196]

Taking this exhibition as a sign of Hoving's aims for the entire museum, Kramer indicted him as an enemy of art.

John Canaday, the chief art critic for the *New York Times*, wrote an article arguing that, as an art critic, he was unqualified to review the show since he saw it as an exhibit of sociological documentation. He flatly stated that the show did not belong at the Metropolitan Museum of Art and would be better suited to the Museum of the City of New York.[197] Ironically, conservative art critics, such as Canaday and Kramer, were united with the protesting artists in their mutual disdain for the exhibition's emphasis on sociological content. A flyer handed out by the BECC expressed precisely the same opinion as Canaday's review: "Those persons coming to the exhibit, in the world's major museum, expecting to see the aesthetic dimensions of the Black American experience will be disappointed—THE MET HAS GIVEN UP ART FOR SOCIAL SCIENCE."[198]

Perhaps the most incisive review appeared in *Artforum* and was written by the scholar of African American social history Eugene Genovese, who was teaching at Yale at the time. It is significant that *Artforum*, known for its formalist orientation during the late '60s, chose to commission a historian to review the show, rather than an art historian or art critic. On the one hand, this reflected the exhibition's antipathy toward engaging African American culture in aesthetic terms. On the other hand, since *Harlem on My Mind* was a show about social history, Genovese's credentials as a historian—particularly as a white historian and a leading authority on slavery in the United States—made him uniquely qualified for the task. Genovese's article deconstructed Schoener's representation of Harlem and criticized the curator's cavalier attitude toward the responsibilities of a historian. According to

Genovese, Schoener was out of his depth. He based his argument on a critique of the types of subjects Schoener selected and the weight he gave to each. Using the example of Malcolm X, whose image was not only prominently featured in the show but whose picture also appeared on the cover of the catalogue, Genovese wrote: "A large amount of space is given to Malcolm X, whose prestige in Harlem remains strong and probably grows stronger. There are pictures of Malcolm the Muslim minister and street-corner speaker and of Malcolm the corpse, together with indifferent excerpts from his magnificent autobiography. The exhibit immediately involved political decisions: Should you emphasize the early or the late Malcolm? Malcolm the uncompromising nationalist or Malcolm the man who ended his life edging toward a new position? . . . Who is making the decision to interpret Malcolm?"[199]

Genovese questions why W. E. B. Du Bois, the most significant leader in the founding of the National Association for the Advancement of Colored People (NAACP) and a figure cited by many African American historians as the most influential African American intellectual of the twentieth century, is given little space in the show, while Marcus Garvey, the father of the Black Nationalist movement, is featured prominently. In the end, Genovese reached a conclusion similar to Kramer's and Canaday's: "Mr. Hoving has a responsibility toward the art world in general, toward those black artists who have been shamelessly neglected for so long, and toward the white and black communities of New York City, but that responsibility consists of strengthening the Museum as a vehicle for the presentation and development of the arts, including Afro-American arts. It does not consist of his intrusion into matters beyond his competence and beyond the Museum's proper institutional function."[200]

Echoing this message, the prevailing reaction of the museum's staff was self-righteous indignation. According to Harry Parker, the museum's curators saw the negative press as vindication of their misgivings about the show. Parker recalls that most of the staff had balked from the outset and asked, "What do we think we are? . . . This institution is about preserving the art of the ages, and we don't have a role in contemporary social concerns. That's not our business."[201]

One of Schoener's pet projects as visual art director at NYSCA was a program of traveling exhibitions composed of reproductions. These exhibitions could be produced in multiple copies and sent to many sites simultaneously, creating what Schoener called "a total information system for the State."[202] Schoener had always hoped that *Harlem on My Mind* would travel to other venues after its debut at the Met. In fact, in the January 1968 *Metropolitan Museum of Art Bulletin*, Hoving stated that the show was being designed to travel throughout the country.[203] Schoener's impulses were admirably populist, but because of the controversy and the fact that his methodologies were ill-suited to the traditions of the art museum, after the show closed, the pictures in the exhibition were discarded. Jean Blackwell Hutson, one of the early advisers to the exhibition and a librarian at the Schomburg, salvaged them, and that is where they remained for nearly forty years, hanging anonymously on office and reading room walls before being donated to South Carolina State University in 2006.[204]

Harlem on My Mind proved to be a public relations disaster in the museum's effort to establish itself as a "people's museum," but the institution had a mission to complete: to obtain city approval for its expansion plans. In November 1969, the Met's board president, Douglas Dillon, appointed a trustee committee on decentralization and community needs. Reporting for the *New York Times*, Grace Glueck wrote, "Formation of the committee comes at a time when the Metropolitan and other art museums in the city have been under pressure not only to extend their community services, but to make their central facilities more 'relevant' and available to minority people."[205] The purpose of the committee was "to study the cultural needs of New York communities not directly served by the Metropolitan or by other major art museums."[206] Funds were allocated to create a series of pilot projects, including "technical help, cooperation in the development of new cultural programs, and loan of art objects from the Museum's collections."[207] The following month Harry Parker was promoted to vice director for education, a position equal in rank to the museum's other vice directors in curatorial affairs, administration, and finance. According to Parker, Hoving recognized that education was an area in which the museum could deliver on some of its more "idealistic ventures."[208]

The Metropolitan's staff and board conducted its community outreach experiments even as opposition to the museum's Master Plan intensified. In spring 1970, Paul O'Dwyer, vying for the Democratic nomination for U.S. senator from New York, said, "The plans of the Metropolitan Museum for massive expansion at its present site seem to be totally inappropriate. . . . The Board of Trustees seems to be oblivious to the many problems which beset us in an overcrowded city. It must be made to understand that to be worthwhile its tremendous interest and dedication must be expanded in such a way as to make museum facilities equally available to the most culturally deprived of our people."[209] Ted Sorenson, also running for the Democratic nomination, denounced the project as "a blunder of major proportions."[210] One opponent suggested that the newly acquired Lehman collection be sent to "Brooklyn, or Queens." Others proposed that the museum build a branch in the South Bronx, the Fulton Fish Market, or the U.S. Customs House at Bowling Green (on the lower tip of Manhattan), or take a floor or two of the World Trade Center, which was currently under construction.[211]

In an effort to bring order, closure, and the appearance of transparency to his process of adjudicating the museum's expansion proposal, the New York City Parks commissioner, August Heckscher, called for public hearings, one held in June 1970 at the Museum of Natural History and a second in August 1970 at the Landmarks Preservation Commission. Benny Andrews attended the second hearing on behalf of the BECC to advocate for the placement of Rockefeller's "primitive" art collection, which had recently been donated to the museum, in an African American neighborhood, but there were dozens of speakers, and the hearing dragged on for hours. A battle-fatigued Andrews, who at the time was ensnared in negotiations with the Whitney Museum of American Art over the *Contemporary Black Artists in America* show, left without saying his piece.[212]

A transcript of one of the hearings lists forty-three speakers almost evenly divided between supporters and detractors, including architects Marcel Breuer, who had recently designed a new building for the Whitney Museum of American Art, and Philip Johnson, who had designed wings for the Museum of Modern Art. The architects supported the museum. Hoving argued that the Met could both build new wings and decentralize. "Decentralization means different things to different people," Hoving said. "I don't want to lop off sections of the Metropolitan and put them down in the Bronx or Queens. I'd rather extend all the help we can give—loans, curators, advice—to cultural centers run by the people themselves, not by us."[213]

The Art Workers' Coalition also opposed the expansion, prompting Arthur Rosenblatt to address the group at one of its weekly meetings in March 1970. On October 20 the activists staged a spectacular indictment of the Met's trustees in the museum's own galleries (figs. 2.37 and 2.38), but unbeknownst to them, the board had already made plans to placate their political opponents by pouring hundreds of thousands of dollars into community outreach programs. On September 24, 1970, the board approved the following resolution: "The Board of Trustees approves the exploratory program prepared by the Museum's staff to extend the Museum's resources and services to local communities and, furthermore, intends to make available works of art to local museums, community cultural centers and other qualified local facilities on the basis of short-term loans, long-term loans or outright gifts, within the limits of any conditions in the case of objects given to the Museum, established by the donor at the time the gift was made."[214]

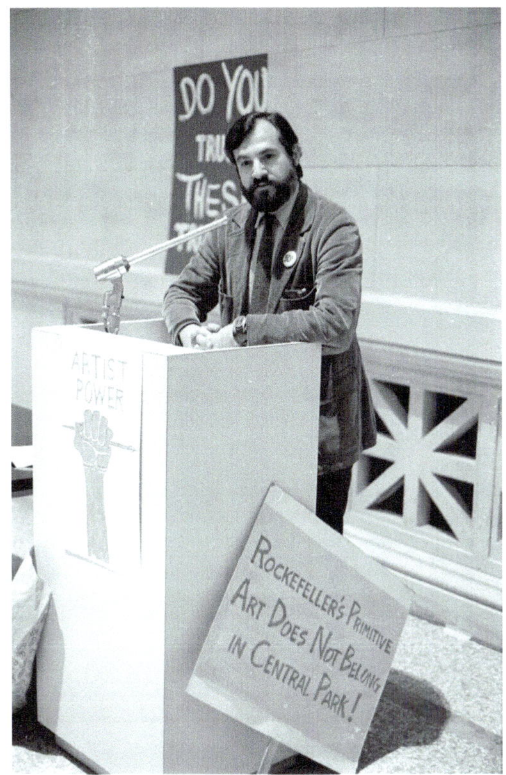

Fig. 2.37 Art Workers' Coalition protest at the Metropolitan Museum of Art, October 20, 1970. Hans Haacke at the podium. © Jan van Raay.

Fig. 2.38 Art Workers' Coalition protest at the Metropolitan Museum of Art, October 20, 1970. Alex Gross at the podium. © Jan van Raay.

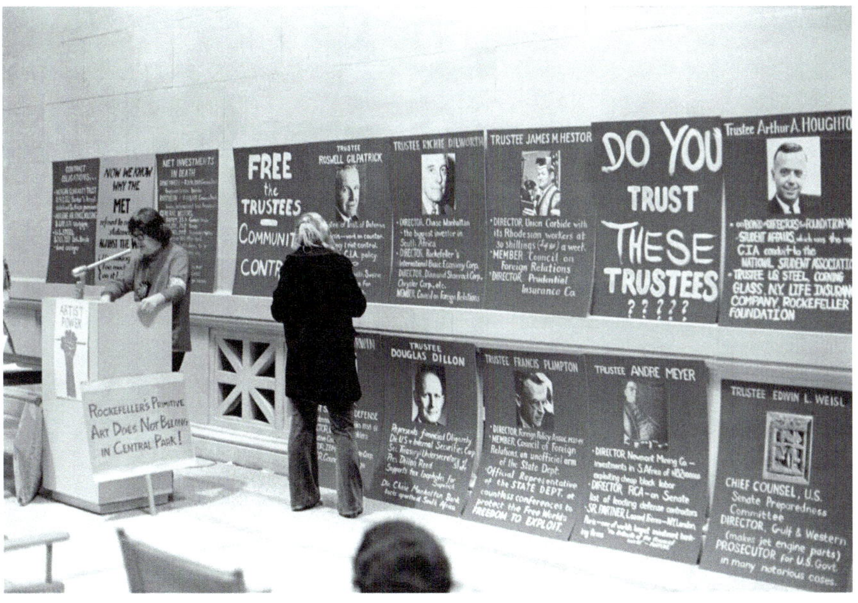

Four months later, on January 20, 1971, August Heckscher called a news conference to announce his approval of the Met's expansion plans: "I am today announcing the approval of the Parks, Recreation and Cultural Affairs Administration of the comprehensive architectural plans of The Metropolitan Museum of Art." Heckscher's statement addressed all the points of controversy, including which elements would be built with private funds and which with public, and the fact that this was to be the "completion" of the museum, that is, the very last of the museum's expansions in Central Park. He ended by addressing the issue of decentralization that had been in debate for almost four years: "We have been concerned lest the tremendous effort involved in completing this plan should lead to a neglect by the Museum of responsibilities to the neighborhoods and the boroughs of the City. As an answer to this the Trustees appointed a special committee on decentralization, and in September, 1970, voted approval of a program of decentralization. . . . This goes further than the Museum has ever done in asserting its City-wide role."[215]

Between 1971 and 1978 the museum embarked on a systematic program of community outreach to extend its services deep into each of New York City's five boroughs.[216] The program began with a small staff but eventually came to encompass the creation of four museums throughout New York City's boroughs, major exhibitions held at eight off-site locations, workshops and training programs for young museum professionals, summer internships for college students, and education programs for over a hundred community organizations. The campaign to obtain city approval for the expansion in Central Park succeeded after a mammoth investment of time, money, and political know-how.

Heckscher's statement in January 1971 ended with a flourish: "Greatness at the center is not at odds with decentralization. On the contrary, it is only a strong institution, self-confident and capable of attracting wealth, which can extend to institutions in other borough the services, the technical advice, the exhibitions, and the long-term loans which will help give New York a diversified and decentralized cultural life."[217] This argument was a variation on trickle-down economics, which had the same underlying theory: advantages provided to the privileged magically benefit society as a whole. The powerful deny the existence of divergent interests and absorb conflict into the ostensibly benign maintenance of their own privilege.

The *Harlem on My Mind* controversy was part of a larger chapter in the history of New York City and the history of race relations in the art world. Some believe that if Allon Schoener had been African American, there would not have been dissent among African American artists and community leaders. Yet this sentiment reflects a continuing blindness to the fact that racism entails differential access to power, for I would venture to say that if Allon Schoener had been African American, he would not have been given the opportunity to mount a show at the Metropolitan Museum of Art in 1969. In the words of Patricia Mainardi, "When the powers that be first take notice, they always want one of their own."[218] This is exactly what occurred over the next two years at the Whitney Museum of American Art.

3 Contemporary Black Artists in America
at the Whitney Museum of American Art

A statistic is a statistic, and an issue is an issue, and you can put them up on the wall and label them, and they're nice and safe and comfortable, but when they finally arrive on your doorstep in the presence of somebody, rather than an issue, it becomes much, much different.

Ralph Burgard, director of Arts Councils of America
and author of *Arts in the City* (1968)

Galvanized by *Harlem on My Mind* and determined to achieve change, the BECC turned its attention to the museum that defined the boundaries of "American" art: the Whitney Museum of American Art.[1] In spring 1969 the artists initiated a two-year negotiation that challenged the museum to embrace a fuller spectrum of the American experience. Primed by a confrontation in fall 1968 when the artists protested the exhibition *The 1930's: Painting and Sculpture in America* and mounted a counterexhibition at the Studio Museum in Harlem, the Whitney's administrators quickly agreed to organize a large survey exhibition of work by African American artists. Already stung once by the artists, and having witnessed the chaos at the Met, they needed surprisingly little convincing to set this exhibition in motion. The show would be called *Contemporary Black Artists in America*.

But this exhibition was only one of the artists' demands; they sought not only a platform for African American artists' work but also systemic, institutional change: they wanted the museum to hire a cocurator who had knowledge of African American art. When the museum refused this request and the depth of its resistance became clear, twenty-four of the seventy-eight artists invited to participate boycotted the show.[2] There were many contested issues: Was it acceptable for a white curator to organize the show, or would a black curator or cocurator have brought a more informed perspective? Was the exhibition "socially driven" or conceived for "aesthetic" reasons? What types of compromises were and were not acceptable to the artists approached for inclusion? What were the trade-offs for agreeing or refusing to participate in a racially defined exhibition? Like other museum managers at the time, the Whitney's administrators refused to cede authority. Instead, they tried to demonstrate that they were no longer impediments to African Americans' access, but rather facilitators of that access. *Contemporary Black Artists in America* is a particularly useful case study because the tensions around the exhibition manifest themselves in a concrete, large-scale, highly visible manner. The show exemplified both the desire to change and the resistance of many museums throughout the country.

The "black art" survey show was the exhibition model most favored by museums as a means of integration at this time. Previous neglect had created a vast pool of African American artists and other artists of color who suddenly had new relevance to the mainstream as museums responded to pressure to integrate. Between 1969 and 1973 literally hundreds of African American artists were featured in contemporary art exhibitions in an attempt to hustle these artists into the major museums.[3] While these efforts offered a new level of visibility for African Americans, such large group exhibitions often brought artists together in motley assortments whose only commonality was their perceived racial identity. Through this strategy institutions quickly added long lists of African American artists to their exhibition rosters while avoiding the more daunting task of questioning past practices, analyzing past oversights, and revising the canonical histories of art that almost universally omitted these artists. The large, identity-based survey show also provided a "safe" way to show groups of artists without formulating an exhibition thesis or identifying an artistic trend or tendency, as did the most important and influential shows of the period, such as *Information* (1970), organized by Kynaston McShine at the Museum of Modern Art, which presented Conceptual Art to a wide audience, and *Anti-Illusion: Procedures and Materials* (1969), curated by Marcia Tucker and James Monte at the Whitney, which showcased Process Art. In short, the identity-based survey exhibition became the dominant paradigm for integrating museums by satisfying demands for inclusion without attendant historical revisions. And *Contemporary Black Artists in America* was no exception: it enabled the Whitney to contain the "disruption" to the historical narrative of American art as it had been written by the museum up to that point through its exhibitions, publications, and collecting practices. Adding insult to injury and further marginalizing the artists, the museum paternalistically described the show as an act of "support and encouragement," not a scholarly or artistic endeavor.[4] Thus the exhibition served as a vehicle for both promoting and containing the artists' work.

The black art show seemed simple on the surface, but artists, critics, and museum professionals disagreed about the definition of "black art." Was "black art" based on the identity of its maker, or on a particular aesthetic? Some wondered whether it existed at all. Several documents of the time demonstrate the diversity of opinions. In the Metropolitan Museum of Art's symposium titled "The Black Artist in America," published in the January 1969 issue of the *Metropolitan Museum of Art Bulletin* to coincide with the opening of the *Harlem on My Mind* exhibition, Romare Bearden, Hale Woodruff, Jacob Lawrence, Sam Gilliam, Richard Hunt, Tom Lloyd, and William T. Williams vigorously debated the meaning of the terms "black art" and "black artist."[5] On one end of the spectrum, Tom Lloyd said that his marginalization on the basis of race was a defining factor in his identity as an artist. He claimed, "The white community hasn't accepted Black artists for years and years, and they're not even ready now, really. And so, I'm not just an artist. Therefore I'm a Black artist."[6] Lawrence retorted: "I think you are an artist who happens to be Black, but you're not a Black artist."[7] Williams weighed in: "It seems to me we're belaboring the label Black art for nothing. What you're [Tom] saying is that you should have a commitment to the Black community, to educate them to the visual world. We're not talking about Black art per se."[8] Hale Woodruff favored a cultural definition over a political one: "If there's to be a *Black art*—not just something made by a Black artist—there must be certain outer manifestations so it can be identified, as you can identify Oriental art or pre-Columbian art or Eskimo art" (emphasis original).[9] Richard Hunt denied the existence of race-based art world discrimination and rejected the concept of "black art" completely:

> Well, "the aesthetics of Black art" is a problem I really don't address myself to, in either my work or my thinking. The problem of the Negro in terms of the contemporary situation in art—showing in museums and galleries and all those things—seems to be more or less tied up with the prevailing currents in art itself. For instance an artist working in kinetic, light, or minimal things might have a better chance of breaking into the scene than somebody who's painting figuratively. All these things don't really seem that much different from the problems that white artists or any other kinds of artist have.[10]

This symposium documented the Gordian knot confronted by curators who mounted "black art" shows. The conversation exposed intergenerational differences, ideological disagreements, and a range of individual attitudes set against a backdrop of particular institutional histories, customs, values, and political pressures.

Specific notions of black art did, however, exist. The artists of the Black Arts movement developed a philosophy about the roles of art, and culture more broadly, in processes of political change. Larry Neal, one of the movement's primary spokespersons, described the Black Arts movement as a critical force for change based on art's ability to affect consciousness: "The Black Arts movement preaches that liberation is inextricably bound up with politics and culture. The culture gives us a revolutionary moral vision and a system of values and a methodology around which to shape the political movement. When we say 'culture,' we do not merely mean artistic forms. We mean, instead, the values, the life styles, and the feelings of people as expressed in everyday life."[11]

The artists of the Black Arts movement often drew on African (or what were considered to be African) subjects, stylistic elements, and artistic modalities. Poet Ron Milner has pointed out, "The whole concept of the Black Arts Movement, the whole definition of the art really was an African concept that art should be functional. You don't carve to carve. You carve a chair, you carve a spoon. You carve something useable and you make that beautiful."[12] The idea of functionality extended into the political realm. According to playwright August Wilson, poets and artists needed to ask themselves, "How does this contribute to the liberation of black people? How does this contribute to Black Power? How does this contribute to us moving forward collectively as a people? If it didn't contribute in any way then it wasn't Black Art. It was something else."[13] The Chicago-based art collective AfriCOBRA developed an aesthetic theory and practice combining inspiration, education, and exuberant color and form. These and other art collectives favored public spaces and the creation of work that "African people can relate to directly and without formal art training and/or experience."[14] In New York, the Weusi group combined art, education, spirituality, and fashion to advance an agenda of cultural and political empowerment.

The Black Arts movement had a parallel in the Chicano Arts movement. Chicano art of the 1960s and '70s melded political activism and cultural production and, in the words of art historian Tomás Ybarra-Frausto, sought "to link lived reality to the imagination."[15] Impelled by the efforts to unionize the California farmworkers beginning in 1965, the rural-land-grant uprisings in New Mexico, the labor struggles of undocumented workers, and the broader civil rights and antiwar activities, Chicano artists brought aesthetic practice to bear on social realities and were integrated into the various political fronts of the Chicano movement. Their work challenged the hierarchical distinction between "fine art" and "folk art" and displayed what Ybarra-Frausto has called a "visual biculturalism" through the reclaiming, remixing, and recontextualizing of vernacular traditions, handicrafts, mass culture, and fine art.[16] This strategy can be seen in the political posters of Carlos Cortes, Rupert Garcia, and Ester Hernandez; the collective murals painted throughout Chicano neighborhoods; and the performances of the Asco group.

Similarly, by the 1970s, a feminist aesthetic was beginning to emerge that also sought social transformation. Faith Ringgold began to make paintings on cloth that would later lead her to produce painted storytelling quilts. Ringgold's quilts infused this traditionally "women's" medium with urgent contemporary content. In 1972 the Feminist Art Program at the California Institute of Arts (CalArts), headed by Judy Chicago and Miriam Shapiro, produced *Womanhouse*, a series of installations in which the artists transformed the rooms of a vacant house into artworks addressing—and critiquing—domesticity, nurturance, maternity, and other things associated with women to challenge prevailing concepts of femininity.[17] Some feminist artists, most notably Judy Chicago, gravitated toward vaginal or gynocentric imagery. Others appropriated masterpieces by men and injected them with feminist content, such as Mary Beth Edelson's *Death of the Patriarchy / A.I.R. Anatomy Lesson* (1976), in which the faces of the medical students in Rembrandt's famous painting *Anatomy Lessons of Dr. Nicolaes Tulp* (1632) are replaced by women artists and the corpse—"The Patriarchy"—appears very dead.

This advancement of art as a site of political empowerment through the assertion and embodiment of community values migrated into museums and mutated into the identity-based exhibition. Both during the 1970s and since, the identity-based exhibition paradigm has had remarkable appeal for the major museums, starting with *Contemporary Black Artists*, held at the Minneapolis Institute of Arts in 1969 with a subsequent nationwide tour; *Afro-American Artists: New York and Boston*, held at the Museum of Fine Arts in Boston in 1970; and *Two Centuries of Black American Art*, organized at the Los Angeles County Museum of Art in 1976.[18] Exhibitions since the 1970s include the controversial *Hispanic Art in the United States: 30 Contemporary Painters and Sculptors*, organized by the Museum of Fine Arts in Houston in 1987, which toured nationally, and, as recently as 2007, *New Perspectives in Latin American Art, 1930–2006: Selections from a Decade of Acquisitions at the Museum of Modern Art*.[19]

The value of identity-based exhibitions in ameliorating systemic discrimination is debatable.[20] Definitions of group identity are empowering when self-generated, but limiting when imposed by others. Black identity had been used as an organizing principle for art exhibitions since the Harmon Foundation shows of the 1930s and had been a controversial model almost from the start.[21] This model redressed the exclusion of African Americans from the dominant institutions while simultaneously perpetuating segregation. In the 1960s and '70s the term "black art" was employed by some African American artists to describe their own work in a spirit of self-definition, but carried different connotations, or simply lacked the specificity to be artistically meaningful, when applied extrinsically by individuals or institutions. Most obviously, the identity-based art show maintained a literal, physical separation between artworks by African Americans and other artists of color, and those produced by whites. This reflected and maintained the perceived cultural difference and the real social separation between groups. And most importantly, identity-based shows implied a circumscribed role for the artist: the work of a defined group of artists was presented as if primarily, indeed exclusively, engaged in an identity-based discourse. Shows like *Contemporary Black Artists in America* manifested segregation in the guise of integration, operating as ostensible acts of inclusion that maintained separation.

Some artists embraced the term "black art," but others found it constraining. Many were ambivalent and caught in a double bind; they wanted exhibition opportunities but did not want to be marked as "other" or pigeonholed by assumptions about their aesthetic interests. A common misperception in the 1960s was the idea that "true" African American art always addressed racial struggle or contained obvious visual references to African forms (or what were construed to be African forms). Another was the equation of African American art with a particular style, ranging from "primitivism" to social realism. Well into the 1990s, the notion persisted that African Americans were more inclined to create figural rather than abstract art.[22] These generalizations and stereotypes are problematic not only because they presume to know identities a priori and thereby become prescriptive and proscriptive, but also because they obfuscate differences among members of the defined group and similarities between members of the target group and others. The free play of identifications and affiliations that is critical to the formation of self-defined communities of shared interests is suppressed as a marginalized identity construct becomes itself a centering mechanism.[23]

Contemporary Black Artists in America was grounded in a race-based selection process, though curator Robert Doty simultaneously, and in curious contradiction, attempted to disaggregate identity and aesthetics. He posited that some African American artists were able to "transcend" their identities through the use of abstraction, which embodied ostensibly universal values. In his catalogue essay, he contrasted these artists with others who were trapped exploring their "blackness" through representational strategies that ultimately communicated only specific interests and narrow agendas.

Doty's application of this idea in 1971 looks back to the post–World War II and Cold War era. As Ann Gibson has suggested in her study of the rise of Abstract Expressionism, in the 1940s and '50s abstraction could be a "vehicle of integration" because it held "the potential to diffuse the burden of difference that white culture imposed on African Americans."[24] It also anticipates the "postracial" discourse of the 1990s, the uncoupling of the concept of an artist's identity from the interpretation of that artist's work. The notion of abstraction as a liberatory aesthetic mode has been celebrated by art historian Darby English, who devised the term "strategic formalism" to describe the importance of extricating works of art from presumed a priori ideological contexts. Attending to the specific physical, visual attributes of works of art, "the peculiarity of works" can be a pathway to free African American artists from the continual burden of "representativeness." English has praised Robert Doty for his formalist approach to the work in *Contemporary Black Artists in America*.[25]

While recognizing the merits of English's theoretical proposition, I question its applicability to *Contemporary Black Artists in America*. I contend that Doty's celebration of abstraction as the highest calling for artists was not free of ideology, but rather distorted—and limited—interpretation of the artists' work. When we read his catalogue essay and look at the show in the context of the Whitney's own institutional history and ambitions, we see that the curator harnessed the artists in *Contemporary Black Artists in America* to advance an institutional agenda, and instrumentalized them even as he celebrated them.

Because of the museum's peculiar history—founded as a private club driven by an individual, and in the 1960s aspiring to be seen as a peer to New York City's other major museums—the Whitney strove to build its reputation as a public institution through image management played out in its exhibition program, as well as its public relations activities. Other museums in New York City—and most museums around the country—had been founded with institutional status from the start; they had boards of trustees and mission statements and civic agendas. Not so at the Whitney. The Whitney had to earn its stature.

One indicator of the museum's challenge is suggested in an essay by Henry Geldzahler, the curator of contemporary art at the Metropolitan Museum. Small in size, but a giant in the New York art world—a man who championed the avant-garde, kept company with Andy Warhol, and later become the commissioner of cultural affairs for the City of New York—Geldzahler organized the popular and influential 1969 exhibition *New York Painting and Sculpture: 1940–1970*. In his catalogue introduction, the curator charted the roles of New York's museums in writing the history of "advanced" art. The Museum of Modern Art is cited as the institution whose collecting practices most "helped make New York a major international center for painting and sculpture after 1940."[26] MoMA and the Guggenheim are lauded as meeting places and discussion centers for "the serious artist and the student who had to come to grips with Cubism and its aftermath."[27] The Jewish Museum is mentioned for its "valuable" midcareer surveys of the postwar artists Frankenthaler, Rauschenberg, Johns, and Noland, as well as the "important" sculpture exhibition *Primary Structures* (1966). Geldzahler offers the Whitney little more than a pardon for its absence from this history:

> It has been the Whitney Museum's function, especially during the fifties and sixties when so much varied work was on view every year in New York's many galleries, to recapitulate the season, impartially, in the mammoth Annuals devoted in alternate years to sculpture and painting. . . . For many of us growing up in New York, the Whitney Annual was always a much-anticipated event, for it allowed us to see in one large exhibition much of the best that was being produced along with the most stagnant, least provocative art imaginable. Thus the viewer was thrown into the healthful turmoil of doing what some consider the museum's job—of deciding, comparing, rejecting, and accepting until he felt, often after several visits to the same Annual, that he was able to find his own way to what constituted quality in contemporary American art.[28]

According to this characterization, the Whitney was barely a museum at all.

I offer the hypothesis that Geldzahler's image of the museum declared in print what many in the art world thought: the Whitney simply wasn't a relevant player in writing the history of modernism. The celebration of abstraction in *Contemporary Black Artists in America* was, among other things, a rejoinder to this perception.

Given the longstanding neglect and at times outright resistance to showing the work of African American artists, what drove museums, including the Whitney, to accept African American art in the late 1960s? A convergence of interests brought the goals of the dominant museum culture into alignment with those of excluded groups. The National Endowment for the Arts (NEA) was founded in 1965 as the first federal program to provide direct support for the arts since the end of the Federal Art Program of the WPA in 1943; likewise, the creation of state arts councils was a phenomenon of the 1960s.[29] The availability of state and federal funds provided an incentive for museums to broaden their constituencies. In order to justify their receipt of government funding, museums had to demonstrate willingness to serve a broad public. It is too simplistic to say that the one who pays the piper calls the tune. Nonetheless, government funding created new opportunities and a new accountability among museums that received these funds.[30]

Prior to the 1960s, with the exception of the Harmon Foundation, patronage of African American art and artists had been most consistently provided by the historically black colleges and universities, which had been collecting African American art for decades. Only during isolated periods, such as the WPA art projects of the 1930s, had African Americans been given nearly the same opportunities as whites through government programs that employed artists.[31] These programs had provided critical support for Aaron Douglas, Charles White, Charles Alston, Hale Woodruff, Archibald J. Motley Jr., Norman Lewis, Eldzier Cortor, and others, as well as funding the Harlem Community Art Center, run by Augusta Savage, where Jacob Lawrence and many other artists studied.

As the U.S. government turned its resources toward the war effort in the early 1940s, the WPA arts programs were phased out. After the war, as the Cold War heightened, the WPA was accused of serving as a breeding ground for communists, an accusation that tainted the very idea of government funding for art during the McCarthy era and that has persisted in related forms since then. Instead of focusing on funding for artists at home, arts advocates of the 1950s championed the touring of exhibitions of American art abroad through the United States Information Agency (USIA) and through Nelson Rockefeller's Office of Inter-American Affairs. In the context of the Cold War, art became exported as a symbol of American freedom and a vehicle for cultural diplomacy, particularly to emerging countries in Latin America, as the United States tried to tamp down leftist politics and activism.

In the 1960s government arts funding returned to the domestic scene. The United States had ascended to the position of leading world power, and culture was seen as an essential feature of a nation with economic and military strength; the 1960s saw an explosion of new government state and federal funding agencies. Yet among conservatives, the memory of the McCarthy era was still fresh. The creation of the NEA in 1965 reawakened fears that artists were communist infiltrators who should not be subsidized by the American government.[32] Indeed, in the early years of the NEA the clash of cultural values in the United States led some to resurrect McCarthy era arguments that artists were categorically "subversive" or "un-American." When the first reauthorization of the NEA was debated in Congress in 1968, Representative Paul Albert Fino of New York argued against grants to individual artists, warning it would mean that "taxpayer dollars can be spent to subsidize anti-Vietnam movies made by European Communists or antiwhite plays written by black nationalists like Leroi Jones."[33] The conflation of the antiwar movement, communism, and black nationalism reflected a conservative Cold War formulation: the United States had a global responsibility to defend democracy around the world by preventing communism and any perceived subversive infiltration at home and abroad.

Ironically, coexistent with the fear that government support for art would foster anti-American activities was the concept that public funding would place the controlling hand of the American government too heavily on artists. In 1967 Roger Stevens, the NEA's chairman, wrote, "One has only to see the works of 'socialist realism' in Communist cultures to get an acute case of indigestion at the mere mention of 'official art.' "[34] Whether it manifested itself in fear of excessive government control or anti-American subversion, clearly the specter of Cold War politics hung over the debate.

In order to dissociate the NEA from the work programs of the WPA and the taint of a domestic form of socialism, arguments in favor of the agency downplayed direct support for artists. Instead, the creators of the NEA took pains to emphasize the agency's role in arts education. The rhetoric surrounding the creation of the NEA stressed how it would enable Americans to enjoy the arts during their ample leisure time.[35] Senator Claiborne Pell, the main sponsor of the bill that created the NEA, sketched out a vision in which art would elevate American society by liberating the concept of prosperity from consumerism. In a 1965 address to the National Society of Arts and Letters Pell said:

> Throughout our history, America has been known as the land of the free. Traditionally, these words have described our national heritage of independence. Today, however, we are a free people in yet another way; we have more free or leisure time than any people have ever had at any time or any place on earth. . . . One recently published estimate forecasts that, before another 25 years have passed, 2 percent of our population will be able to produce all the goods and food which the remaining 98 percent can possibly consume. If this should happen, our leisure time would grow to truly astronomical proportions. . . . Let us make sure that we use our new leisure time, our new free time well—and that the working artist, who can so immeasurably invigorate this newly gained time for us all, is given the maximum climate for developing his or her creative and imaginative spirit.[36]

Support for the arts would ice the cake of affluent America.

Clearly, when Pell spoke these words he did not have in mind the 32 million people who were living in poverty in the United States in 1965. The NEA was sold to Congress as one of the benefits of affluence, not a handout to the poor, though both the arts and humanities federal endowments and the antipoverty programs of the 1960s were part of President Johnson's Great Society, and many NEA grants went to programs addressing "underserved" constituencies that were far from affluent. In 1969, the NEA supported the Harlem School for the Arts youth training programs in dance, art, music, and theater; the New Thing Art and Architecture

Center, a grassroots workshop program for "inner-city residents" in Washington, DC; and other such programs.[37]

In addition to the creation of the NEA, all fifty states and the U.S. territories created state arts councils in the 1960s. The first was NYSCA, the New York State Council on the Arts, a pilot project begun in 1960 by Governor Nelson Rockefeller to explore the role that a state agency could play in supporting the visual and performing arts. Members of the Rockefeller family had long been major arts philanthropists, and Rockefeller used his powers as governor to extend this philanthropic activity into the public realm. NYSCA became a model for other state arts councils, and by 1970 these agencies existed in every state and most of the U.S. territories.[38]

The New York State Council on the Arts was formally established in 1965 after a five-year exploratory phase.[39] The law establishing NYSCA reads: "Many of our citizens lack the opportunity to view, enjoy or participate in living theatrical performances, musical concerts, operas, dance and ballet recitals, art exhibits, examples of fine architecture, and the performing and fine arts generally. It is hereby found that, with increasing leisure time, the practice and enjoyment of the arts are of increasing importance."[40] The founding language of NYSCA echoed the NEA's emphasis on audiences, not makers. By 1967 the council's programs expanded to address heightened concern about social and economic inequality and the increasing incidence of urban violence that it was causing. A new concern emerged: how to use the arts to heal social rifts and ameliorate social ills. That year, the New York state legislature appropriated $1.3 million, an increase of almost 40 percent over its 1966 budget of $772,000, to have the council "investigate how the arts could help illuminate some of the frustrations of the ghetto." In NYSCA's 1967–68 annual report, Executive Director John Hightower wrote: "Too often museums and orchestras as well as opera and dance companies have been limited to the cautious stewardship of our cultural past. Until now public funds have not been available to permit them a concern for what is immediately critical, even explosive, in our society. In the next decade, however, the attitude of arts institutions will change. One of the reasons will be the amount of public funds available for productions, exhibitions, and performances that relate directly to current problems of our society."[41]

The summer of 1967 had been "explosive" indeed: according to the Report of the National Advisory Commission on Civil Disorders (popularly known as the Kerner Report), which was published in 1968, riots or uprisings had taken place in 150 cities throughout the United States during the summer of 1967. The commission studied twenty-three of these cities—including Detroit and Newark, where the most damage took place. In most of the cities where mass violence had occurred, the commission found discriminatory police practices, unemployment, and inadequate housing, as well as poor public recreational facilities and programs.[42] So traumatic had been the summer of 1967 and so urgent was the commission's desire to makes its findings public that the report was released on March 3, 1968, four months before the deadline set by President Johnson, so as not to "forfeit whatever opportunity exists for this report to affect this year the dangerous climate of tension and apprehension that pervades our cities."[43] The commission feared that summer would again become "riot season."

In 1969 NYSCA created a "Ghetto Arts Program," which provided arts management training to "ghetto students" and free performances of "relevant" theatrical material to "ghetto residents."[44] The council also offered grants to organizations that blended art with community development initiatives. Among the 1968–69 grantees were the newly formed Dance Theater of Harlem; the Puerto Rican Community Development Project, which presented theatrical performances designed to raise awareness of Puerto Rican cultural heritage; and the Brooklyn Museum, for the creation of a community gallery.[45] Undoubtedly, some of these programs were also intended to help quell violence in the city's streets.[46]

The Whitney Museum of American Art was one of the first museums to receive public funding from NYSCA, in 1962, an early sign of the museum's evolution from a private club into a public institution.[47] The museum had begun as the Whitney Studio Club, a salon founded in 1914 by Gertrude Vanderbilt Whitney and Julianne Force that provided a sympathetic exhibition space and social environment for the work of American artists who sought independence from the academic system of patronage and exhibition. Whitney had inherited a fortune from her father and used this money to support young artists. The club, located at 8 West Eighth Street, held annual nonjuried members' exhibitions from which Whitney consistently purchased artwork.[48] From its earliest days as the Whitney Studio Club, and later as a museum, the organization was a booster for American art, focusing less on collecting masterpieces than on nurturing young American talent and providing support for artists in need. The club's aesthetic orientation reflected the interests of the museum's founder, herself a realist sculptor, and its director, Julianna Force. Whitney and Force were allied with the cause of American realism and threw their considerable weight behind those artists who reacted against the National Academy of Design, the most powerful of the various exhibition societies of the time and the most conservative.[49]

The Whitney Studio Club was started just one year after the Armory Show of 1913, which had introduced Americans to the avant-garde work of European artists

Georges Seurat, Paul Gauguin, Henri Matisse, Wassily Kandinsky, Ernst Ludwig Kirchner, Odilon Redon, Constantin Brancusi, and Francis Picabia, among others, and of course Marcel Duchamp and his notorious *Nude Descending a Staircase* (1912). The Armory Show was to have an indelible effect on the development of American museums, as the Museum of Modern Art's founding director, Alfred Barr Jr., wrote in 1949: "In a sense, the epoch-making Armory Show was the real beginning of the Museum [of Modern Art]."[50] But Gertrude Vanderbilt Whitney herself wasn't interested in the European avant-garde and did not even see the show.[51] Nor was Whitney interested in the work of Alfred Stieglitz, whose 291 Gallery had held the first exhibition of Cézanne's work in the United States in 1911 and had by the 1920s shown work by the European artists Matisse, Pablo Picasso, and Henri de Toulouse-Lautrec, as well as American moderns John Marin, Max Weber, and Alfred Maurer. According to the art historian Avis Berman, Gertrude Whitney and Julianna Force were "not only not persuaded by modernism, but determined to ignore it."[52]

If there is one exhibition that can be said to have catalyzed the Whitney Studio Club, it was the exhibition of the Eight in 1908. When Robert Henri, who had just been elected to the National Academy of Design, was unsuccessful in advocating for the inclusion of his cohort in the academy's spring 1907 exhibition (with the exception of John Sloan), he announced a group show that included Arthur Davies, William Glackens, Ernest Lawson, George Luks, Maurice Prendergast, Everett Shinn, Sloan, and himself.[53] The Eight, also known as the Ashcan School for the group's gritty depictions of urban life, made work that was bold, fresh, and concerned with social conditions in the United States. Whitney and Julianna Force appreciated the artists' lively humanism and strong subject matter. They bought four paintings from the show for a total of $2,225.[54]

By 1930 Whitney had amassed a large collection of about six hundred works of contemporary American painting and sculpture by artists including Sloan, Luks, Edward Hopper, and Thomas Hart Benton and early modernists such as Stuart Davis, Charles Demuth, and Charles Sheeler. The case for American art had advanced considerably in the fifteen years since the Studio Club had opened. In the wake of the founding of the Museum of Modern Art in 1929 and after weighing a number of options—in 1929 Whitney offered her collection to the Metropolitan Museum of Art but was rebuffed, and from 1929 to 1931 the Whitney functioned as a commercial gallery—Gertrude Vanderbilt Whitney announced the establishment of the Whitney Museum.

For the first decade of the museum's life, Gertrude Vanderbilt Whitney continued to dominate the museum's activities. Indeed, the day after the opening, on November 17, 1931, the *New York Times* reported: "Throughout, the Museum reflects the personal taste of Mrs. Whitney. In each case final choice of a work of art depended on her, since there is no board of trustees."[55] But upon Whitney's death in 1942, the future of the museum was uncertain. Having outgrown its space on Eighth Street, the museum was now left to devise a new solution if it was to survive. Negotiations with the Met about acquiring the Whitney's collection were reopened and continued over a six-year period, protracted by World War II and the uncertainty of building costs after the war. Ultimately, the Met refused the acquisition once again, but in 1949, Gertrude Vanderbilt Whitney's nephew John Hay "Jock" Whitney, who was then the chairman of the Museum of Modern Art, arranged to offer the Whitney a piece of land adjoining MoMA's at 22 West Fifty-Fourth Street between Fifth and Sixth Avenues. Gertrude's daughter, Flora Whitney Miller, who had assumed the reins after her mother's death, gladly accepted.

Relocated to Fifty-Fourth Street, the Whitney reopened to the public and provided a counterpoint to MoMA. Like MoMA, the Whitney showcased recent art, but with exclusive emphasis on artists born in the United States rather than the European avant-garde or even European-influenced American art. Whitney's early support of artists associated with the Ashcan School and realists such as Edward Hopper, whom the Whitney Studio Club had given his first one-person exhibition in 1920, led to a collection initially composed of artists working primarily in a figural vein.[56]

Though the Whitney Museum was founded during the Depression, Gertrude Vanderbilt Whitney's wealth was sufficient to assume the full cost of the museum's operations and acquisitions until the 1950s, when increasing costs combined with dwindling family resources put the museum on shaky financial ground. The descending net worth of the generations that were to follow required an infusion of funds from other sources. In 1956 the museum established the Friends of the Whitney, a group of collectors and art patrons that supported the museum through membership dues and donations. In exchange, members were not only invited to parties but also received the privilege of borrowing works of art from the collection to hang in their homes when those works weren't needed by the museum.

According to John I. H. Baur, a curator at the museum starting in 1952 and its director from 1968 to 1974, rather than a general membership that would have been priced at about $10 a year, the museum decided to offer memberships on a more selective basis to people who could afford to pay more. The museum considered a membership fee as high as $500, the equivalent of $4,500 in 2015 dollars, and eventually settled on $250. One of the reasons for creating a more exclusive membership program was to maximize net income, since lower-level membership programs can eat up half their revenue in expenses. But another, as Baur has described, was not to dilute the intimacy of contact between the museum's patrons and artists.[57] The Friends of the Whitney didn't fundamentally change the character of the museum; it merely expanded the size of the club.

Five years later, the Whitney underwent another significant change, this time in its governance. The Whitney's board of trustees had always comprised members of the Whitney family, but as Gertrude Vanderbilt Whitney's fortune slowly disappeared, the family made a dramatic change of policy.[58] In 1961 the museum's constitution and by-laws were rewritten, and the board was enlarged to include ten new members, with provisions made for future expansion. Among the first group of new trustees were Jacqueline Kennedy; the financier Roy R. Neuberger, who would later establish the Neuberger Museum at SUNY Purchase; and David M. Solinger, a lawyer and art collector who had been one of first members of the Friends of the Whitney and would serve as the museum's board president during the turbulent years 1967 to 1974. (By 1974 the Whitney family represented only about one-quarter of the board.) Further expanding its base of support, in 1966 the Whitney received a ruling from the Internal Revenue Service that the museum had been declared an educational institution, enabling donors to take as tax deductions gifts of art, cash, or securities in amounts totaling up to 30 percent of their net adjusted income. This was significant because the Tax Reform Act of 1969 would differentiate and give higher tax benefits for gifts to "educational and charitable organizations" than those given to museums. No longer was the museum supported by just one family.[59]

The move to Fifty-Fourth Street was a temporary solution, and in 1963, when MoMA decided to reclaim the space, the Whitney acquired its own land and announced another move. The museum would build a new building at the corner of Madison Avenue and Seventy-Fifth Street designed by architect Marcel Breuer (fig. 3.1). The intent was not only to increase the amount of space available for exhibitions and storage, but to make a bold architectural statement rivaling that of Frank Lloyd Wright's Solomon R. Guggenheim Museum, completed in 1959 fourteen blocks uptown. The new building was designed to consolidate the Whitney's reputation as the leading museum of American art, as August Heckscher expressed at the cornerstone ceremony on October 20, 1964. Heckscher, New York City Parks commissioner and administrator of cultural affairs, who had been President Kennedy's adviser on arts policy, proclaimed, "From now on [the Whitney] can hardly fail to be considered a national institution. It will surely play a national role."[60] Heckscher's imprimatur helped the museum fulfill this prophesy.

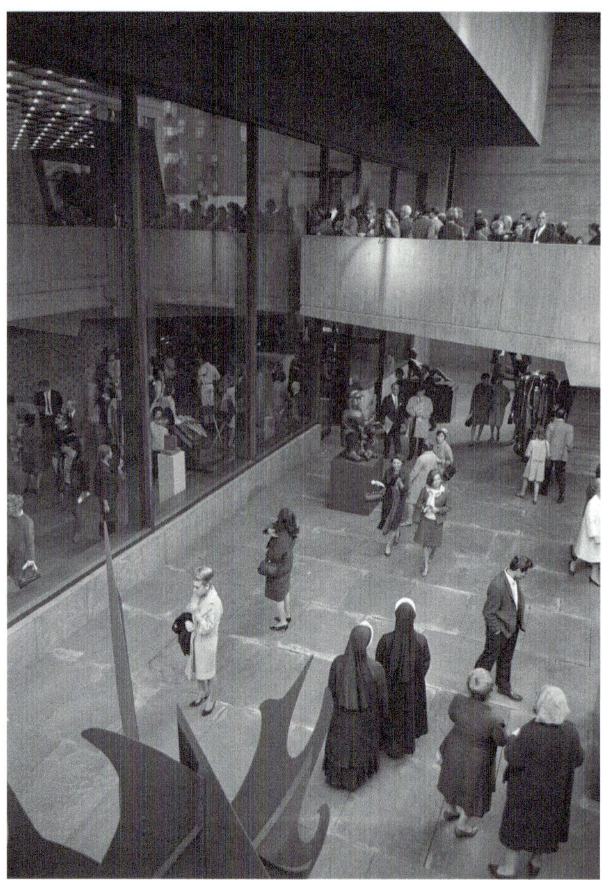

After the opening of the Seventy-Fifth Street building, other major changes transformed the museum from a private club run by a single family into a public institution. In 1967 David M. Solinger became the first president of the board who was not a member of the Whitney family. On January 1, 1968, John I. H. Baur became the director, succeeding Lloyd Goodrich, who had been on staff since the museum opened and had served as director since 1958. Baur had also been involved with the museum since its early days, but was twelve years younger and more attuned to recent developments in art.[61] Reflecting the maturation of the museum, Gertrude Vanderbilt Whitney's granddaughter, Flora Miller Biddle, noted how important it was that the museum's director support "*all* American art, rather than just the realistic work that not only they, but also my grandmother and Juliana Force, much preferred."[62]

The professional staff grew at a fast pace. In 1966 Stephen Weil was appointed to the newly created position of administrator. The same year a young curator named Robert M. Doty was appointed as associate curator. Doty was interested in photography and had come to the museum from the George Eastman House in Rochester, New York. His résumé included positions at the Victoria and Albert Museum in London, the Albright-Knox Art Gallery, and the Yale University Art Gallery. In January 1969, when Marcia Tucker and James Monte joined the staff as associate curators, Doty, known to his colleagues as Mac, was promoted to full curator.

To qualify for its new tax-exempt designation as an educational institution and reflect its new public identity, the museum created its first formal education program in 1966.[63] Called the Arts Resource Center, the program was headed by Douglas O. Pederson, the museum's first education director. According to Baur, Pederson "had devised a number of progressive education programs at the Princeton Day Schools. . . . He was full of ideas for revolutionizing the teaching of art particularly at the public school level and among poor children and ghetto children."[64] In January 1967 the museum received $250,000 from the Carnegie Corporation, and in 1968 NEA funds, to start a program designed to "provide an opportunity of positive expression for alienated youth of junior high and high school age."[65] The Carnegie Corporation had a history of funding educational programs for African Americans, including community art education programs in Harlem in the 1930s.[66] Alain Locke had been one of their advisers.

Pederson's vision had three parts. The first was to set up a studio program for junior high, high school, and college students. The second involved a lecture program featuring critics and artists. The third element was a program to "reeducate" public school teachers in order to make them "more conscious of the seriousness of art," rather than "treat it as a kind of artsy craftsy kind of thing."[67] The social goals were clearly stated in the museum's 1966–67 *Review*: the Arts Resource Center was to be "an active agent which seeks to break down those invisible barriers now isolating cultural minorities from cultural majorities." It was also designed to "help reduce ethnic controversy by fostering cooperation among diverse forces in the community."[68] Its constituents were described by Baur as "kids who are having trouble, but have shown some aptitude, and if possible, marked aptitude for art but who are in trouble otherwise with their academic studies."[69] The transformative—somewhat unbelievably so—power of art education was illustrated by the example of one such student who was profiled in the 1967–68 *Whitney Review*: "Classed as uneducable with grades in the sixties, he had been openly defiant to school authorities. His grades are currently in the nineties; and though his candid opinion of the school authorities has not changed, he no longer feels the necessity to challenge them overtly."[70]

Pederson engaged Julian Euell, who had formerly directed the creative arts programs of HARYOU-ACT. The two recommended that the museum target a constituency in an area of the Bronx that encompassed predominantly African American and Puerto Rican residents. Teachers in this geographic area were invited to participate in a summer training course for which they would receive a stipend. Upon returning to teach in the fall, they would be expected to make use of the Arts Resource Center that the museum intended to establish.

The first teacher training program took place on an estate near Baltimore that belonged to the Smithsonian Institution. The estate had old barns and stables that were converted into studio spaces for the teachers, and in exchange for use of the property, the Whitney agreed to give $25,000 of its Carnegie grant to the newly formed community-based Anacostia Neighborhood Museum. As Baur later recounted without providing details, the Whitney staff and the teachers found little common ground. The situation was rife with tension, so much so that the living quarters were divided into two camps—staff on one side and teachers on the other. Baur's interpretation of the problem was that the teachers "didn't want to be exposed to serious criticism of their own art, they didn't want to be serious artists themselves."[71] Despite this racially neutral assessment of the program's tensions, one wonders what values each side brought to the table, what interpersonal dynamics took place, and what aesthetic criteria were used to evaluate and critique the teachers' work.

After the unexpected outcome of the summer program, Pedersen resigned and was succeeded by Eugene Lewis and, eventually, David Hupert as head of the Education Department. Plans for the resource center in the Bronx were scrapped, and another site was located for the program: an old warehouse at 185 Cherry Street in Manhattan's Lower East Side. The location was chosen, according to Hupert, because it was at the "borderline of a Chinatown-Puerto Rican community, a Negro community, a strong Italian community; it's quite a mixture. . . . For the Whitney Museum, that was an ideal choice because Whitney becomes, in a sense, a community museum for the larger community of New York."[72] The education staff renovated the site and built studios and a gallery space to house both the youth program and a newly founded Independent Study Program for college students.[73]

While these education programs were being developed off-site, on September 28, 1966, the Whitney opened its new building with the inaugural exhibition *Art of the United States: 1670–1966*, a grand gesture signaling the museum's emerging position as the institutional authority on American art. The show presented 366 works of painting and sculpture by 277 artists. What vision of the United States did this show present? For one, it dramatically minimized the presence of African Americans. Only two African American artists were included: Jacob Lawrence, represented by *Tombstones* (1942), and Horace Pippin, represented by *Cabin in the Cotton* (1944). Neither artist's work was illustrated or discussed in the catalogue. The book covered art from colonial times through the present yet mentioned neither slavery nor its abolition. Despite the exhibition's virtual purging of African Americans from American history, the show didn't provoke visible opposition or the kind of counterexhibitions that would confront subsequent Whitney shows.

By 1966, several works by African American artists had been acquired for the Whitney's collection but were passed over for inclusion in the *Art of the United States* exhibition. The list of works by African Americans acquired up to that date is relatively short and can be related here in its entirety. The museum's first acquisition by an African American artist was *Ethiopian* (1912) by Arthur Lee, purchased in 1931. *Rhythm* (before 1930), also by Lee, was purchased in 1933. *The Blackberry Woman* (1932), by Richmond Barthé, was purchased the year it was made. Horace Pippin's *The Buffalo Hunt* (1933) was bought in 1941. Jacob Lawrence's *Tombstones* (1942) was purchased in 1943 after the Museum of Modern Art and Phillips Collection acquired the *Migration of the Negro* series (1940–41). In 1966 David Solinger gave the museum two watercolors by Lawrence: *Tombstones*, a work related to the 1942 painting of the same name, and *Depression* (1950). Roy Neuberger and his wife donated Lawrence's fourteen-painting set *War Series* (1946–47) in 1951. Charles White's magnificent *Preacher* of 1952 was purchased the year it was made, as was Charles Alston's *Family* (1955). Richard Hunt's *Horizontal Extending Form* (1958) was purchased and given to the collection by the Friends of the Whitney Museum of American Art. Richard Mayhew's *Morning Bush* (1960) and Raymond Saunders's *Winterscape* (1962) were purchased through the Ford Foundation Purchase Program in 1962 and 1964, respectively. And Thomas Sills's *Green Wind* (1963) was purchased in 1964.[74]

The Whitney's tendency toward what appeared to be tokenism began to emerge in the 1960s. The museum's group shows of this period each typically included one or two African American or Latino artists. The pattern is striking. In 1965 the museum mounted *Art USA: The Johnson Collection of Contemporary American Painting*, a group show that featured *The Library* (1961) by Jacob Lawrence. The museum's next show, *A Decade of American Drawings 1955–1965*, included *Nuance* (1964) by Richard Mayhew. *Young Americans 1965: Thirty American Artists under Thirty-Five* included three works by Raphael Montañez Ortiz from the *Archeological Find* series. *Contemporary American Sculpture—Selection 2*, held in 1969, included the Puerto Rican–born artist Raphael Ferrer. Robert Doty's 1969 exhibition *Human Concern / Personal Torment: The Grotesque* in *American Art* included one work by Daniel LaRue Johnson, *Yesterday* (1963), and one piece by Raphael Ortiz. Also held in 1969, *111 Masterpieces from the Collection of Edgar William and Bernice Chrysler Gurisch*, circulated by the American Federation of Arts, included one work by Joshua Johnston. The 1969 exhibition *Anti-Illusion: Process and Materials*, organized by Marcia Tucker and James Monte, reprised an appearance by Raphael Ferrer. Tucker's *The Structure of Color*, held in 1971 at the same time as *Contemporary Black Artists in America*, included a piece by William T. Williams, *Doctor Buzzard Meets Saddlehead* (1970). This pattern seems to indicate an unwritten policy—conscious or not—that cut across the museum's exhibition program and was perhaps intended to inoculate the museum against charges of racial exclusion.

There were some group shows that didn't include any artists of color and two in particular where African American artists were conspicuously omitted. The first was the exhibition *Light: Object and Image*, held from July 23 to September 28, 1968, and organized by Robert Doty, who would later organize the *Contemporary Black Artists in America* exhibition. Given the museum's previous record of including one or two artists of color, it is notable that *Light: Object and Image* did not feature the work of Tom Lloyd. Lloyd had been in several exhibitions, and his work was concurrently on view in the inaugural exhibition at the Studio Museum in Harlem.[75] Did Doty have a specific reason for leaving Lloyd out (later he would be included in *Contemporary Black Artists in America*), or was Doty simply unaware of his work?

Another noticeable absence was the omission of Barkley Hendricks from the exhibition *22 Realists* organized by James Monte in 1970, just a few months before the opening of *Contemporary Black Artists in America*, in which Hendricks was featured. Was the Whitney "saving" Hendricks for the latter? Was Monte unaware of Hendricks's work?

Hendricks himself was certainly aware of Monte's show. On July 16, 1970, he wrote the following letter to Robert Doty:

> Dear Mr. Doty,
>
> A fellow artist informed me your museum is planning a Black Artist Exhibition in the Spring of 1971. If your invitation or jury list has not previously been selected I would like to be considered as a possible exhibition candidate.
>
> I have shown at the major museums and galleries in Phila., the National Academy of Design N.Y., Butler Ins. of Art. Ohio and others.
>
> My work can be seen at the Kenmore Galleries in Phila., where I'm represented. Color slides are at your disposal upon your request.

I would also like to be considered for any other future exhibitions. I'm especially interested in future exhibitions. I'm especially interested in future Realist exhibition[s].[76]

This letter suggests Hendricks's willingness to participate under any rubric, but his more pointed eagerness to be featured in an exhibition with an aesthetic premise.

There was one exhibition in which the full exclusion of African American artists incited action. In the fall of 1968, on October 15, the Whitney opened an exhibition entitled *The 1930's: Painting and Sculpture in America* organized by associate curator William Agee.[77] The show included over one hundred works by eighty artists but failed to include a single work by an African American, even though the exhibition covered a period when a relatively large number of African American artists were known to be working in the mainstream through the WPA art projects. Omitted from the show were such senior and established figures as Romare Bearden and Jacob Lawrence (see fig. 2.11). "In presenting a period where black artists were active and were part of the exhibiting scene, to eliminate them was really to distort history, because they were there," observed art historian Mary Schmidt Campbell.[78] As Romare Bearden pointed out in an article in the *Amsterdam News*, "It was in the 1930s that black artists emerged in appreciable numbers. The Federal Arts Projects were important in this since they supported the artists while providing unaffordable technical training and materials, a chance for blacks to meet other artists, and practical experience in painting, sculpture, and the graphic arts."[79] Henri Ghent, director of the Brooklyn Museum's Community Gallery, called a meeting at the Studio Museum in Harlem, and at this meeting a group of artists, including Faith Ringgold and her daughters Michele and Barbara, Benny Andrews, and others decided to stage a protest on November 17. Ringgold belonged to the Spectrum Gallery, located a few blocks away from the Whitney, on Seventy-Ninth Street, and arranged to have the artists use the gallery "as a meeting place for everybody to come there, get your signs, make up your signs." As a group they proceeded four blocks to the Whitney to demonstrate.[80]

The newly founded Studio Museum in Harlem, which had just closed its inaugural show of work by Tom Lloyd, quickly mounted and added to its schedule the exhibition *Invisible Americans: Black Artists of the 1930s*, organized by Ghent and several artists. Opening on November 19, 1968, *Invisible Americans* presented about fifty works by over twenty African American artists who were active in the 1930s. The show included Charles Alston, Richmond Barthé, Romare Bearden, Joseph Delaney,

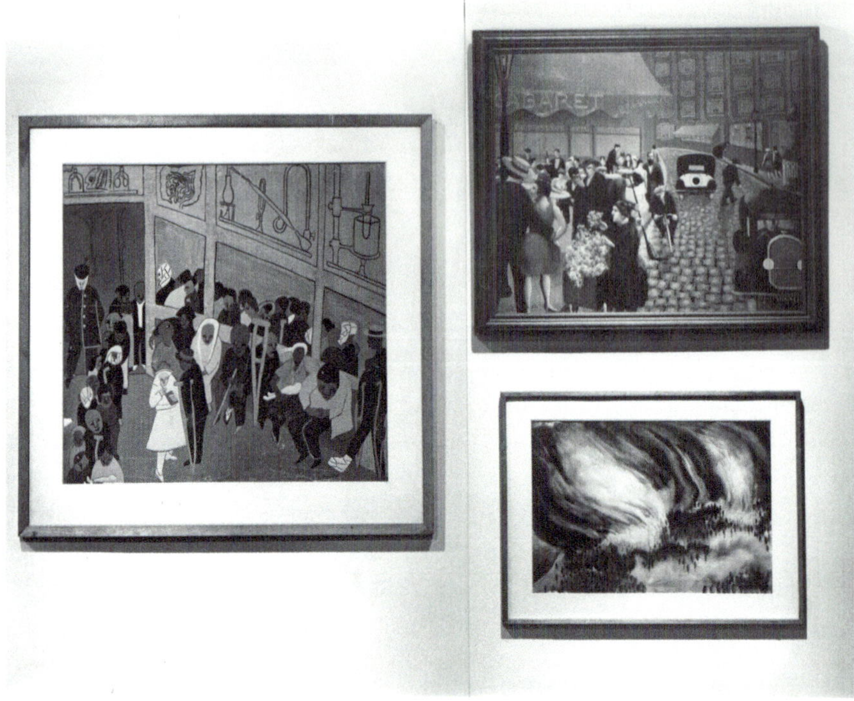

Fig. 3.2 Installation view of *Invisible Americans: Black Artists of the 1930s* exhibition at the Studio Museum in Harlem, New York, November 19, 1968–January 5, 1969. Left: Jacob Lawrence, *Free Clinic* (1937), © The Jacob and Gwendolyn Knight Lawrence Foundation, Seattle / Artists Rights Society (ARS), New York; upper right: Archibald J. Motley Jr., *Dans La Rue* (n.d.), © Valerie Gerrard Brown and Mara Motley, MD; lower right: Hale Woodruff, *Forest Fire* (1939), © Estate of Hale Woodruff / Licensed by VAGA, New York, NY. Photo courtesy Jeff Craig Associates.

Aaron Douglas, Palmer Hayden, Malvin Gray Johnson, William H. Johnson, Jacob Lawrence, Norman Lewis, Archibald J. Motley Jr., Douglas Pippin, Augusta Savage, and Hale Woodruff (fig. 3.2).[81] *Invisible Americans* displayed a wealth of talent that had been written out of Agee's show.

In an exhibition review defending Agee and the Whitney Museum, Robert Pincus-Witten wrote in *Artforum*: "Their [the artists'] charge, it seems to me, if it is to be given credence at all, should have been predicated on the possibility that sources normal to a practicing curator, written history particularly, would have, from the very outset, excluded black material and that, if this is so, then even the most assiduous museum researcher would not have been aware of black achievement in the 1930s (or of any decade for that matter)."[82]

Pincus-Witten might not have been aware, as William Agee surely would have been, that the Whitney's own holdings included work from the 1930s by Richmond Barthé, who had exhibited at the museum in 1933 and from whom the Whitney had purchased three sculptures.[83] Barthé may have been omitted because his figural art conflicted with Agee's curatorial interest in abstract art. Yet other artists working outside abstraction, such as Ben Shahn and Thomas Hart Benton, were included in the show as representatives of what Agee considered the minor contemporaneous current of social realism. Was there no place for Charles White or Dox Thrash in this group, or for Aaron Douglas or William H. Johnson among the artists working in a more abstract vein?

The previous year, in 1967, Romare Bearden and Carroll Greene Jr. had organized a major exhibition, *The Evolution of Afro-American Artists: 1800 to 1950*.[84] Spearheaded by the Harlem Cultural Council and the New York Urban League, the show was held in the Great Hall at City College in order to reach a broad audience and presented over 150 works by fifty-five artists, beginning with Joshua Johnston and including Barthé, Henry Ossawa Tanner, Edmonia Lewis, Palmer Hayden, Aaron Douglas, William H. Johnson, Augusta Savage, Jacob Lawrence, Beauford Delaney, Charles Alston, Charles White, Eldzier Cortor, Hughie Lee-Smith, Hale Woodruff, Humbert L. Howard, Haywood Rivers, Richard Mayhew, Merton Simpson, John Farrar, and Bearden himself. The show was accompanied by a catalogue that contained a complete checklist, illustrations of forty-four of the works in the exhibition, and short biographies of each artist.[85] If Agee had missed this show, he certainly had not consulted all of the sources "normal to a practicing curator."

Agee's aim was to revise the history of the 1930s and amplify the importance of abstract work. His revisionist view of the decade would not have been nearly as provocative if he had called the exhibition "Abstract Art of the 1930s." (In fact, the Whitney had done a show of abstract American work in 1935 that included a nearly identical roster of artists.)[86] By generalizing and presenting abstraction as if it were the only artistic mode of lasting importance, Agee used aesthetics to purge politics from art history. The implications for the 1960s were clear to most critics. Lawrence Alloway put it most succinctly: "Agee . . . is looking at the thirties in an anti-period way. He searched for, and found, the works closest to the currently reputable image of modernism."[87] In attempting to put the Whitney on track with the then dominant mainstream paradigm, he erased African American artists— both abstract and figural—from the history of art.

The Studio Museum's *Invisible Americans* featured a stylistically heterogeneous range of work, including Hale Woodruff's stunning watercolor *Forest Fire* (1939) (fig. 3.3), which even the conservative critic Kramer had to admit "would not have

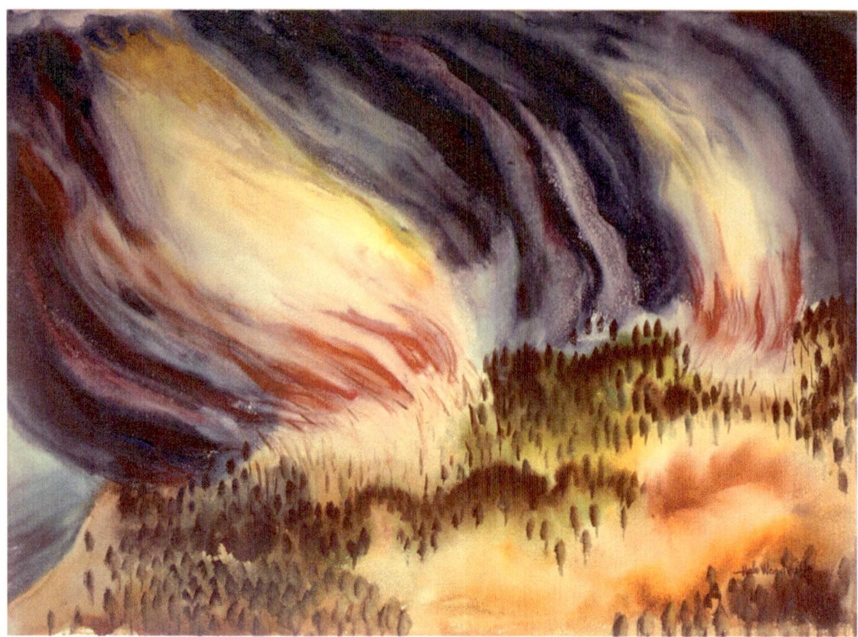

Fig. 3.3 Hale Woodruff, *Forest Fire*, 1939, watercolor, 14×18 ins. Photo: Harry Henderson. Penn State University Archives, Pennsylvania State University. Art © Estate of Hale Woodruff / Licensed by VAGA, New York, NY.

been out of place in the Whitney show," though he goes on to opine that Woodruff "is apparently a very uneven artist; his other contributions to the [*Invisible Americans*] exhibition—another watercolor and a group of woodcuts—are not in the same class."[88] Kramer is a crisp writer, and his use of the word "apparently" seems to imply that he was not familiar with Woodruff's work.

Provoked by the challenge posed by *Invisible Americans*, Baur defended the 1930's show, claiming, "It is not true that Agee didn't take Negro artists into consideration. He selected the art that he felt was best for the exhibit and the question of whether there were Negro artists included *never entered his mind*" (my emphasis).[89] There is no reason to doubt Baur's statement that including "Negro" artists never entered Agee's mind, but this in and of itself may define the problem at hand. A position of racial privilege allows one not to have to think about race.[90] Moreover, Baur's statement prompts the question: Is there such a thing as race-neutral decision making? And, if so, how are we to know when a decision reflects conscious discrimination, when it reflects unconscious discrimination, and when it is a truly nondiscriminatory case of race-neutral thinking? Many factors suggest that despite white critics' and curators' claims that their decisions were driven by purely objective standards of quality, there is evidence to suggest a racialized double standard.[91] Consider Hilton Kramer's discussion of *Invisible Americans*. While Kramer has no trouble describing the show as a protest against the omission of "black artists" from the 1930s exhibition, he chokes on the phrase "white artists." Kramer writes: "Mr. Ghent [the curator of *Invisible Americans*] is inviting us to judge black artists by standards greatly inferior to those we bring to the appreciation of—the term is absurd but unavoidable—white artists."[92] For Kramer the term "white artist" was absurd because for him whiteness was normative.

The *New York Times* was clearly stirred by both *The 1930's* and *Invisible Americans*; the paper published two reviews and an article on the question of quality by Kramer, one news article about the artists' protest, and two letters to the editor.[93] In his first review Kramer compared the two exhibitions, noting the incompatibility of art as "an instrument of political action" with "the esthetics of modernism." Kramer clearly favored modernist aesthetics, even to the point of disparaging the Whitney's own collecting history: "Not the least interesting thing about [the 1930's exhibition] is that the Whitney is sponsoring it. For the Whitney was an active patron of American art in the thirties, and this exhibition strongly suggests that its patronage was very often woefully misplaced."[94] Kramer conceded that there were some artists of quality in *Invisible Americans*, but didn't consider their omission from the 1930's show to be representative of the larger problem of discrimination, offhandedly remarking, "There are too many artists in this exhibition as it is."[95] So the result of this skirmish was two mutually exclusive exhibitions on art of the 1930s, one white, the other black. In the words of cultural critic Michele Wallace, "It boggles the mind."[96]

A two-year-long power struggle ensued on April 24, 1969, when Benny Andrews and Henri Ghent met with Baur to discuss the role of African American artists at the Whitney Museum. Andrews began the discussion by saying that even though there had been a lot of general talk in the art world about the relationship between museums and black artists, nothing tangible had been done to provide greater opportunity. Andrews wanted to open up a dialogue between the museum and the Black Emergency Cultural Coalition in the hope of devising ways they could do something "solid and meaningful" together. At this meeting, Baur suggested that the gallery on the first floor, off the lobby, be used for exhibitions of work by African American artists who had not had previous museum exposure. Several other points were discussed, including greater participation by African American artists in the Whitney annuals, more purchases of artworks, and the appointment of a guest curator to organize an exhibition of work by African American artists. Andrews left encouraged. He wrote in his journal that Baur was "very gracious and seemed to be very receptive to our opening remarks."[97]

After their initial meeting with Baur, the BECC met in Andrews's studio to talk about next steps.[98] The group came up with a list of five demands: (1) an exhibition of contemporary black artists' work; (2) at least five or more "one-man" shows during the year; (3) an increase in the number of black artists in the Whitney Annual and the inclusion of a black curator on the selection committee; (4) more purchases of works by black artists for the permanent collection; and (5) black curatorial staff to coordinate these endeavors.[99]

On May 1, 1969, Benny Andrews, Henri Ghent, Vivian Browne, and Mahler Ryder met with Baur again. Baur informed them that he had talked with his staff and several trustees and that the museum agreed to all points demanded by the group with one exception: but they would not agree to hire an African American curator. The following week, Andrews, Ghent, Ryder, and Cliff Joseph went back to the museum to continue negotiations. Again, Baur reported that the museum would not agree to the group's proposal to hire an African American curator. Negotiations were put on hold for the summer.[100]

The artists and museum staff returned to the table in September 1969. After two more meetings on September 11 and 18, involving Andrews, Joseph, Ryder, Ghent, Reginald Gammon, and Frank Sharpe on behalf of the BECC and Baur, Stephen Weil, and Robert Doty on behalf of the museum, the artists thought they had reached agreement. What they had agreed, however, was not that the museum would hire an African American curator, but merely the language that would be used in the press release announcing the survey exhibition, *Contemporary Black Artists in America*. Andrews wrote in his journal:

> We finally agreed to the Whitney's press release and decided to wait awhile before meeting with them again, so as to be able to judge by their action . . . whether or not they are putting into practice the agreed upon proposals. . . . This meeting was for all practical purposes the end of this particular phase with the Whitney Museum. We gained a respectability (something that was non-existent when we first approached them) and we also gained a major exhibition for black artists, promises to look at more unexposed black artists' work. They will seek more participation by black artists, and we did get them to publicly say they would deal with and consider black people for curatorial positions. It was a good step, not fantastic, but good.[101]

The report on the outcome of the negotiations that Baur submitted to the museum's president, David Solinger, had a different slant. Baur's letter to Solinger, dated September 18, 1969, indicated that the museum had no intention of hiring a black curator, but merely offered noncommittal language in order to placate the artists. The museum made only those concessions needed to avoid an escalating confrontation and no more. In his letter soliciting Solinger's approval for the *Contemporary Black Artists in America* press release, Baur wrote:

> We met today with our Black friends and after long discussions and two relatively minor changes in the wording of our statement—which I do not think vitiate its contents—we have parted amicably. . . . We have made it clear that we could not appoint a Black guest curator for the Black show, the Annuals or any of our other activities. We have said only that we would consider qualified Black candidates when a regular curatorial opening occurred, but that our final choice would be based on the ability and experience of all candidates. . . . The only new sentence added to the release says that we will consult Black art experts in the "survey" phase of our large Black exhibition, "wherever feasible." . . . Since the sentence simply states what we would normally do anyway, I think there is no harm in including it.[102]

Enclosed with the letter was a copy of the press release announcing the exhibition and other African American art initiatives:

> The Whitney Museum of American Art announced today that it was taking several steps for the support and encouragement of Black artists throughout the United States. These include a major exhibition of work by Black artists from all parts of the country and the establishment of a special fund for the acquisition of work by young and lesser-known Black artists, supported by a promised grant for this purpose from an anonymous donor.
>
> The Museum's new projects have evolved from a growing awareness of the special problems facing Black artists in America. In formulating them, the Museum has the benefit of close consultation with a group of artists representing the Black Emergency Cultural Coalition, as well as a number of other Black painters, sculptors and educators.
>
> The Museum's exhibition, scheduled for the 1970–71 season, is designed to assess the contribution which the best Black artists are making to the creative life of America today. The grant will enable the Museum to acquire some of the paintings and sculpture discovered in its survey, as well as works from other sources.

Before the final sentence there was a handwritten insertion: "In making its nation-wide survey of the work from which it will choose the exhibition, the Museum will utilize the advice of leading Black art experts wherever feasible."

The BECC issued a statement, unsubstantiated by the real outcomes of the negotiation, that Baur had agreed that the black art exhibition would be selected by a "two-man committee" consisting of one of the museum's curators and a "qualified Black art expert acceptable to both parties."[103] The group communicated this technically inaccurate information to Grace Glueck, who reported the development in an article in the *New York Times*.[104] When the Whitney failed to fulfill this expectation, the artists pointed to Glueck's article as "proof" that it had reneged on its promise. Yet the press release issued by the museum merely announced its intention to consult with black art experts. The commitment was minimal, and either the artists' hopes were a case of wishful thinking or the group knowingly misled the writer.

Despite Baur's continual denials that pressure from artists was impacting curatorial choices, the Whitney Annuals at this time (precursors to the Whitney Biennials) included more artists of color than previously. Prior to 1969 scarcely any artists of color were featured. By contrast, the 1969 Painting Annual included Malcolm Bailey, Romare Bearden, Frank Bowling, Marvin Brown, Sam Gilliam, Jacob Lawrence, Richard Mayhew, Jack Whitten, and William T. Williams. The 1970 Sculpture Annual featured Barbara Chase-Riboud, Melvin Edwards, Frederick Eversley, Richard Hunt, and Betye Saar. All of these artists would be invited to participate in *Contemporary Black Artists in America*, though many would refuse.

The Whitney also immediately began to organize small one-person shows of African American artists. From 1969 to 1971 every other exhibition held in the Lobby Gallery featured the work of an African American artist, including Al Loving, Melvin Edwards, Frederick Eversley, Malcolm Bailey, and Frank Bowling. These artists alternated with Stephan von Huene, Morris Louis, Ray Johnson, Raphael Ferrer, Lucas Samaras, Manfred Schwartz, and Mark Tobey. In 1972 and 1973 the frequency of shows by African American artists slowed, but those whose work appeared did include Alma W. Thomas, Joseph E. Yoakum, Robert Reed, and Mahler Ryder. Following this initial burst of activity, in 1974 and '75 the museum showed Jack Whitten, Betye Saar, and Minnie Evans.[105] After 1975, until the directorship of David Ross in the early 1990s, the museum showed few African Americans or other artists of color.[106]

The Whitney's solo exhibitions were in some ways the least "problematic" ideologically. With solo exhibitions individuals may be added to the canon of art history without a revision of the premises on which that canon is based and without any questioning of the reasons for more pervasive exclusion. It is true that solo exhibitions are generally considered strong endorsements by museums that lift one artist out of the pack and offer visibility and recognition. However, the Lobby Gallery shows, like the "Projects" exhibitions that were started at MoMA in 1971 and similar initiatives at other museums, enabled the Whitney to exhibit individual artists' work without the imprimatur of a main space exhibition. The lobby shows provided a compromise solution: they enabled curators to grant moderate exposure to some artists while withholding the unequivocal stamp of approval that comes with a major one-person show.

In an article published in *Arts* magazine in the summer of 1970, Andrews spelled out the qualities that the BECC thought a curator must have to successfully address work by African American artists. He wrote that a qualified curator must have "1. A lifelong identification with the entire spectrum of the 'black experience' and 2. a well-rounded formalized study of all available historical data on the history of black artists in America."[107] Though the BECC did not promote the idea that such a curator must be African American, this was implied. But the group sought expertise, not tokenism, and saw these qualities best embodied in Edmund Barry Gaither, director of the National Center of Afro-American Art in Boston, who held a joint curatorial appointment at the Museum of Fine Arts, Boston.

Contemporary Black Artists in America was put under the direction of in-house curator Robert Doty. Doty's previous shows had included an exhibition on the Photo-Secession movement, a survey of the work of Adolph Gottlieb, and a group show entitled *Human Concern / Personal Torment: The Grotesque in American Art*.[108] In planning *Contemporary Black Artists in America*, he proceeded as he would have with any other show. He asked colleagues to suggest artists, combed through catalogues and documentation of other shows, traveled around the country making studio visits, and fielded a range of unsolicited material submitted by artists who had heard about the forthcoming exhibition.

Contrary to the BECC's claims that Doty did not consult African American experts, he did in fact have ongoing contact with David Driskell, head of the art department at Fisk University in Nashville, Tennessee, who wrote to Baur in April 1970:

Several black artists in this area read with interest an article which appeared in October 1969 in the NEW YORK TIMES concerning an exhibition of works of "major black artists" that is being planned for presentation at the Whitney Museum during the 1970–71 season. Since the article stated that the exhibition would be "designed to assess the contribution that the best black artists are making to the creative life of America today," it would seem that more information or inquiries would have been made of artists from various parts of the nation. Perhaps it is assumed that all available information concerning the contributions that black artists are making to American culture has already been collected.

. . . There are several black artists in this vicinity whose work should be screened by your committee. They have not been informed of your proposed show and I hope that you will allow them the chance to be involved.[109]

This began an ongoing correspondence between Doty and Driskell.

On a trip to Los Angeles, Doty sought out Samella Lewis, who had recently been hired as the education coordinator at the Los Angeles County Museum of Art and was a professor at Scripps College. Lewis had coedited, with artist Ruth Waddy, an anthology of work by contemporary African American artists and was in the process of preparing a second. She found her encounter with Doty cursory and unsatisfying and came away unimpressed. " 'We didn't discuss the show at all,' " Lewis said to the *New York Times* writer Grace Glueck. " 'He talked in generalities about his philosophy. It didn't seem to me he was looking for new artists—he had his list, and everything else seemed to be an accommodation.' "[110]

Recalling her studio visit with Doty, artist Vivian Browne has described how "he walked in, went from the front to the back of the studio, and back around again, and was on his way to the elevator. That fast he went. I realized that the art community that he represented was not mine."[111] A perusal of Doty's correspondence files for *Contemporary Black Artists in America* reveals a higher comfort level and greater degree of candor about his lack of expertise when the curator communicated with his white colleagues. In January 1970 while preparing for his research trip to Los Angeles he wrote to Betty Asher, assistant to Maurice Tuchman, the modern and contemporary art curator at the Los Angeles County Museum of Art, and a collector in her own right:

Dear Betty:

Jim [Monte] has referred to me a letter from Dita Deanin Abbey [*sic*] concerning her work. I am directing the exhibition we will do for the black artists so he felt her material should come to me. Is she a black artist, or does the title of that exhibition refer to black as the medium?

Sometime in the near future, I expect to be in Los Angeles to work on the show. If you could write and give me your candid appraisal of the work by black artists in the area, I would be most grateful.[112]

Asher replied:

Dear Mac:

That is a good question. I asked three black people at this Museum to tell me if Rita Deanin Abbey is black, a determination I expected them to make from the photograph of her and her work. All three thought she was white but I have no idea how this decision was reached. The only thing left to do would be to write and ask her which isn't easy.[113]

Correspondence from later that year shows Doty still hunting. On September 2, 1970, he wrote to Lehigh University's art gallery:

Dear Sirs:

I noticed in the recent journal of the College Art Association that you showed the work of Henry Eatkin, Dewitt Hardy, Avel Deknight [sic], and Richard Mayhew.

I am organizing an exhibition of work by Black artists so the last two names are familiar. I would like to know if Eatkin and Hardy are Black, and if so, would you please send me their addresses. I would be very grateful to have a brochure or catalogue if one was published for the exhibition.[114]

Contemporary Black Artists in America became a sieve that separated African American artists from white. Other Whitney curators began to channel all the correspondence they received from African American artists to Doty. Whenever an unsolicited letter arrived from an artist discerned to be African American, it was passed on to Doty, who would reply that yes, he would look at the work for consideration in "our black art show."[115] Within this catch-22, being considered for exhibition at the Whitney went hand in hand with being marginalized.

Doty's steep learning curve was apparent to many of the artists considered for *Contemporary Black Artists in America*. Artists reported to the BECC that studio visits with Doty were exercises in frustration in which the curator would look only at work he had already seen elsewhere or work that he had been advised to select for the show by a third party. It was obvious to these artists that Doty's knowledge of African American art was insufficient and his openness to new material limited.[116]

Nonetheless, Doty traveled all over the country to visit the artists recommended to him by various curators and carried on a lively correspondence with Driskell. Driskell strongly influenced the course of Doty's research and his ultimate selection of artists not only for *Contemporary Black Artists in America* but for several of the small one-person shows that he also organized at the Whitney. Of the exhibitions of work by African American artists featured in the museum's Lobby Gallery, several had been affiliated with Fisk, where Driskell headed the art department. Richard Hunt (who dropped out of the *Contemporary Black Artists in America* show) had been a visiting professor at Fisk in 1968. Vincent Smith had had a solo show there in 1970. Doty organized Alma Thomas's 1972 show at Driskell's urging, accompanying the exhibition with the same interview that had been published in the exhibition catalogue for a show Driskell had organized at Fisk the previous year.[117]

Despite the increase in exhibitions of work by African American artists in the Annuals and Lobby exhibitions, members of the BECC were disappointed and angered by the absence of African American leadership in the development of *Contemporary Black Artists in America*. From the end of 1969 through the opening of the show in April 1971, BECC members worked both individually and as a group to persuade Baur to hire an African American cocurator. On March 31, 1970, Henri Ghent wrote to the director:

> I am extremely disenchanted that the suggestions to use a qualified black man or woman in the selection of works to be shown have been ignored. Quite frankly, I would think that everyone at the Whitney who's even vaguely involved with this project would be only too pleased to have such assistance, especially since it's such a delicate situation. I do hope you realize that you're only letting yourself in for possibly another fiasco like "Harlem On My Mind." What is being done at the Whitney is precisely what Hoving did! I needn't remind you that his utter imprudence, particularly in this instance, proved to be his undoing.

Ghent continued:

> Whether this persistence in ignoring capable blacks who could be of invaluable assistance to you stems from sheer resistance to the idea, or a kind of blind loyalty to Mr. Doty, I do not know. I do know that what could have been a meaningful signal of change in the unwritten policies of our Establishment museums has all the earmarks of the kind of paternalism we have come to expect. You certainly have no right to expect that it will go unchallenged.[118]

Baur's resistance to the suggestion of teaming Robert Doty with a guest curator was clearly motivated by something other than institutional policy, as he claimed, because just a few months after *Contemporary Black Artists in America* closed, on November 16, 1971, the Whitney opened the exhibition *Two Hundred Years of North*

American Indian Art, organized by guest curator Norman Feder, who worked at the Denver Art Museum.

Correspondence between Ghent and Baur continued through May 1970, and in the end Ghent played the only card he had left: he informed Baur that he did not want his name listed in the catalogue as an exhibition consultant. In a letter dated April 21, 1970, he asked that the museum "refrain from using my name in connection with the show because I have very serious reservations which will not allow me to give sanction to something sight unseen."[119] This letter, sent a full year before the show opened, was the first step in what would ultimately become an artists' boycott.

During this time, the first major contemporary African American art exhibition organized by an African American curator opened in Boston. Organized by art historian Edmund Barry Gaither, *Afro American Artists: New York and Boston* presented over 160 works by seventy artists at the Boston Museum of Fine Arts (MFA). A group of Boston artists had been pressing director Perry Rathbone to develop programs with African and African American content. With his joint appointment as curator at the MFA and the National Museum of Afro-American Art, Gaither was charged with fulfilling this goal. Though his mission was not overtly expressed in such terms, Gaither said he was asked to take on the project to "ameliorate the anger against the museum being generated by the artists."[120] He would have preferred at least a year of lead time, but the MFA said it needed the show sooner. Artists were pressuring the museum to take action. Later, Gaither learned that the artists themselves were concerned that the more time that passed, the more likely it was that the museum would drop its commitment.[121] Time constraints led Gaither to decide that the show would focus only on New York and Boston.

Most of the work had been made within the previous two years, but even within its strict geographic and chronological parameters the exhibition was vast. Its scope included artists ranging in age from such senior figures as Romare Bearden, Lois Mailou Jones, Norman Lewis, and Hale Woodruff to a younger generation that included Emma Amos, Malcolm Bailey (only twenty-three at the time), Emilio Cruz, and Raymond Saunders. And the roster included artists working in a wide range of styles. Beyond this breadth, Gaither's catalogue made the project into a groundbreaking statement. His essay provided history and concepts that put the phenomenon of the "black art" show in context:

> At its simplest, a "black show" is an exhibition of work produced by artists whose skins are black. The term seldom connotes the presence of properties or qualities intrinsic in the work and therefore it does not act as an art historical

definition. A "black show" does not belong to the same order as a "cubist show." The "black show" is a yoking together of a variety of works which are, for social and political reasons, presented under the labels "black" or "Afro-American." Such a show is thus a response to pressures growing out of racial stresses in America. At the same time, "black shows" attempt to introduce a body of material to a race-conscious public in order to force that public to recognize its existence and its quality.[122]

He went on to assess the strengths and weaknesses of this exhibition format, charting its history and acknowledging and critiquing shows that had come before.

Despite the clarity of the argument presented by Gaither, the *New York Times* chose to view the project only through the lens of high modernism. In a review published on May 31, 1970, Hilton Kramer first chided Gaither for producing a show in "response to pressures growing out of racial stresses in America."[123] He then went on to dismiss the work, pigeonholing all of it as social realism despite the inclusion of work by Norman Lewis, Al Loving, Alma Thomas, and other abstractionists. In his catalogue essay, Gaither had explained how realism is used by some artists in the show as a means of communication that is accessible to a broad base of art audience members, but for Kramer realism meant only one thing: "a visual language of outworn devices and established clichés."[124] In Kramer's view, realist art by definition lacked "artistic values," and only work that evidenced the "stylistic conventions of modernist esthetics" (which he referred to as "mainstream" expression) was worthy of critical consideration.

In fact, it was Kramer who was trading in outworn devices. In a response published three weeks later, Gaither called for a new criticism "sensitively attuned to the necessary dialogue between art and society." This new criticism, he said, "would distinguish between effete social realism of the Old Left and socio-political art of current nation builders."[125] In a subsequent article, Benny Andrews put it more bluntly: "Why in the hell is it so damn confusing to see the Black artist expressing his feelings about his people, his environment and life?"[126]

As arts editor of the *New York Times*, Kramer had a uniquely visible and powerful platform from which to disseminate ideas that he had inherited from the modernist art critic Clement Greenberg.[127] Like Greenberg, Kramer argued for an avant-garde "free zone" of cultural activity in which formal innovation was the only revolutionary act—the only art, that is, that qualified as "mainstream."[128]

In "The Politics of Art," published in *Artforum* in 1968 as part of the magazine's "Problems in Criticism" series (which also included an essay by Greenberg), Barbara

Rose argued that Greenberg and his followers displaced political expression from the realm of "real world" politics to the realm of aesthetics as a means of dealing with the disappointing ineffectiveness of revolutionary art and the suppression of cultural expressions associated with the Left under McCarthyism. Political issues, she contended, have been sublimated within aesthetics so that "revolutions" in form replace political revolution. Thus Greenberg, Rose reported, "in a recent discussion of Picasso's *The Charnel House* did not feel called up to mention, even in passing, that the subject was a death camp."[129] Rose's theory helps explain the suppression of political content both in Agee's *The 1930's: Painting and Sculpture in America* and in Doty's *Contemporary Black Artists in America*, as we shall see.

The dynamic Rose describes was also at work in Jack Baur's book *Revolution and Tradition in Modern American Art*, originally published in 1951, the year before Baur was hired as a curator at the Whitney, and reprinted with a new introduction in 1967.[130] In his 1967 introduction, Baur distanced himself from the aesthetic values of Gertrude Vanderbilt Whitney: "The Eight, in searching out the unconventional aspects of urban life, asserted a social liberalism as radical in its day as their styles were conservative. Our early modernists, on the other hand, were generally conventional in their choice of subject, but in style they flouted the long realist tradition in American art and fashioned a profounder revolution, which has not yet run its course."[131] The Ashcan School may have embodied humanistic social content, but for Baur, modernist abstraction was where the "real" revolution took place.

Gaither offered a fresh view of representational art, specifically figuration:

The figurative dimension was almost always misunderstood in the discussion of African American art. . . . When the African American artist discovers himself or herself as a subject, in the wake of the Civil War and at the very end of the 19th century with the real rush to come with the First World War, the first major project is the rehabilitation of the representation. And the reason that becomes so important is because parallel to the denigrating images that had been structured in theater advertising and fine arts was the hidden suggestion that some how African Americans were a little less than human.[132]

Kramer wrongly associated the representational work in Gaither's show with the social realist tradition of a different era. Kramer's vision never extended far enough to grapple with African American art in relevant and timely terms.

It is telling that in articles published in the *New York Times* on January 18 and February 8, 1970, Kramer chided the Art Workers' Coalition for failing to accomplish what the BECC had already undertaken.[133] The Art Workers' Coalition had criticized the Museum of Modern Art for changing its collecting policy. MoMA was founded primarily as a *kunsthalle*, a space for changing exhibitions, but in 1953 it established a permanent collection and became a conventional museum. Kramer proclaimed, "One can quarrel with policies of selection and presentation, with standards of judgment and the over-all reading of art history. But to deny the value of museums in principle . . . is to deny something fundamental about modern esthetic culture and the truly radical democratization of its values."[134] Kramer was well aware that the artists of the BECC had been actively questioning the criteria museums used to select and present art as they sought to broaden and reform existing institutional structures. Nonetheless, Kramer wrote, "In my opinion, the Art Workers Coalition is, at the present moment, the only professional art group in this country that is addressing itself to the fundamental social and political problems that currently afflict the visual arts both as a profession and as a cultural enterprise."[135]

Discussions about *Contemporary Black Artists in America* continued among the members of the BECC through the fall. When Doty's assistant called Benny Andrews on November 13, 1970, to schedule a studio visit, Andrews declined, saying he did not want his work included in the exhibition; he felt it was a conflict of interest to be both an advocate for the show and a participant.[136] In his journal he wrote, "After I hung up, a shudder went through me, I guess it might have been because today Friday November the 13th is my birthday, and a nut for astrology told me that the moon would be in Scorpio today, and dammit with all that, I guess I should get the willies."[137] Doty himself called three days later to try and persuade Andrews to change his mind, but Andrews replied that he didn't support Doty's organizing the show without an African American cocurator and that his mind was made up.[138]

A few weeks earlier, Andrews had had a studio visit with Henry Geldzahler, curator of contemporary art at the Metropolitan Museum of Art, and both had agreed that "all-black shows are over and the next step is to select black artists that relate to specific aims of future exhibitions, and to be more selective."[139] From October 31 to November 18, Andrews had a one-person show on view at the Acts of Art Gallery in Greenwich Village; the opening fulfilled his vision of how the arts community should function. Acts of Art had been founded in 1969 by Nigel Jackson to provide a downtown venue for African American art, but it was not separatist in its ideology. Jackson had attracted a distinguished group of "honorary board members" whose names added both breadth of vision and prestige to his operation: John

Hightower, who had been executive director at the New York State Council on the Arts when the gallery was founded and, in spring 1970, had become director of the Museum of Modern Art; James Robinson, founder of Operation Crossroads Africa, a cultural exchange program and forerunner of the Peace Corps; Edward Spriggs, director of the Studio Museum in Harlem; Marcia Tucker, associate curator at the Whitney Museum; and Barry Gaither. The night of the opening, October 30, Andrews wrote in his journal:

> My one man exhibition opened at the "Acts of Art Gallery" 31 Bedford Street, N.Y.C., Nigel Jackson, Director. The exhibition was a realization of a wish I'd had for a long time, rhetoric aside, and that was to break through to several different groups and make a point of proving that with good art work, a conscientious art dealer, (N. Jackson), a good exhibition can be put on. It does not matter that we are black, that the gallery has only 500 square feet of exhibition space, that it is hard to find, etc. What does matter at this stage of art history in general and black in particular, is "heart and soul." I was especially pleased to see black people in regular Western dress, mingling with black people in African dress, students black & white, artists black & white, collectors, friend[s], and passersby, all were happy to be there. It was more than my show, it was a place to meet, talk and relax for awhile.[140]

The Museum of Modern Art purchased two pen-and-ink drawings from the show, *Came Out Fighting* and *The Cross Bearers* (1964). Then, in January, the museum acquired a painting that curator Jennifer Licht had seen during a studio visit with Andrews in December, *No More Games* (1970). Andrews was gaining notoriety among curators and writers all over the country. He had no self-interest in Doty's project, but remained involved as an advocate and agitator for institutional change.

On December 18 four members of the BECC—Andrews, Chuck Bowers, Cliff Joseph, and Nigel Jackson—met with Grace Glueck to discuss details of their opposition to the Whitney's show. On January 31 members of the BECC and supporters Lucy Lippard, Rudolph Baranik, Jon Hendricks, Jean Toche, Bill Hudson, Ed Clark, and even Faith Ringgold, who had criticized the BECC's male chauvinism, assembled in front of the Whitney Museum (figs. 3.4–3.7). They marched in unity carrying signs that bore large-scale reproductions of Glueck's article stating that an African American curator would be hired.

Following the lead of Henri Ghent and Benny Andrews, between January 16 and April 19, 1971, twenty-four of the seventy-eight artists invited to be in the exhibition

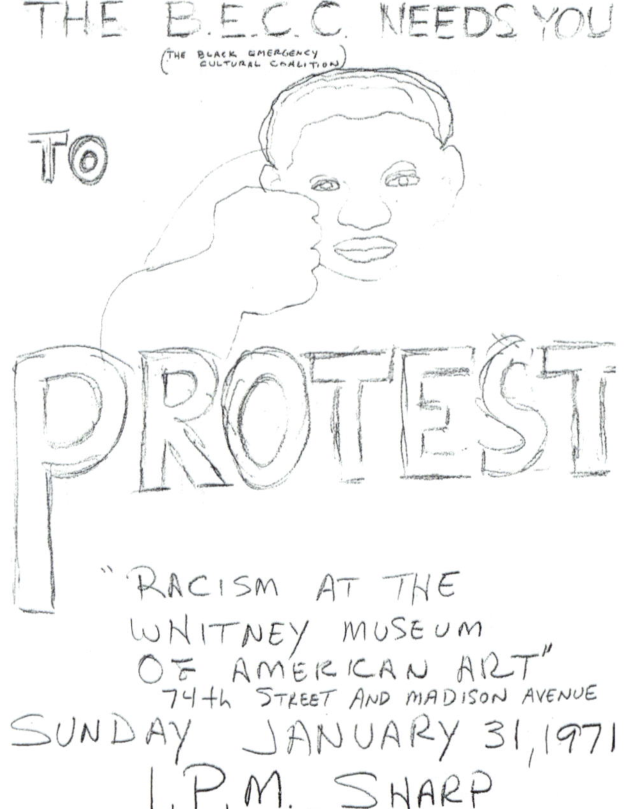

Fig. 3.4 Poster for Black Emergency Cultural Coalition protest, January 1971. Unknown artist.

decided to boycott the show.[141] Some withdrew via telephone, others with letters and telegrams.

Barbara Chase-Riboud, who was living in Paris and heard about the boycott after the show opened, sent a telegram asking that her work be removed:

> JUST READ NEWYORK PRESS HERE TERRIBLE CIRCONSTANCE RE-EXHIBT AND WITHDRAWALS STOP STORRY NOT INFORMED BEFORE STOP OBLIGED REQUEST MY SCULPTURE REMOVED AS QUICKLY AND QUIETLY POSSIBLE STOP DONNOT WANT PUBLIC WITHDRAWAL STOP PLEASE BELIEVE SCINCERE REGRETS PERSONAL SYMPATHY [sic]
> BARBARA CHASE RIBOUD[142]

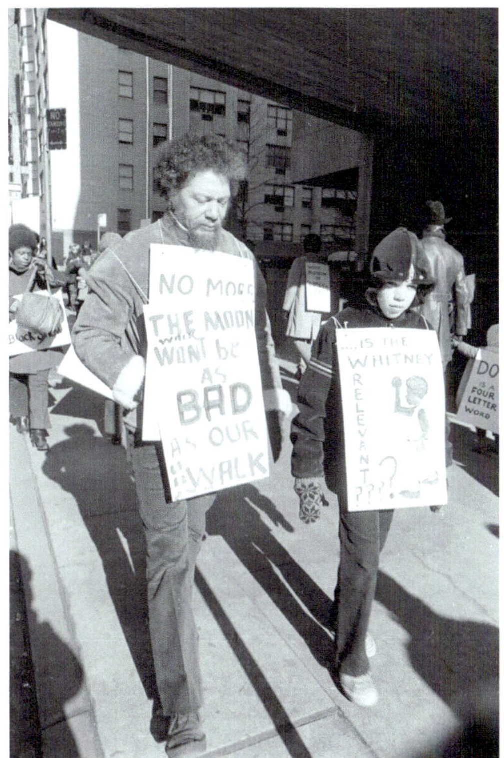

Fig. 3.5 Benny Andrews and his son protesting at the Whitney Museum of American Art, January 31, 1971. © Jan van Raay.

Fig. 3.6 Protest at the Whitney Museum of American Art, January 31, 1971, with Nigel Jackson (left) and Vivian Browne (center). © Jan van Raay.

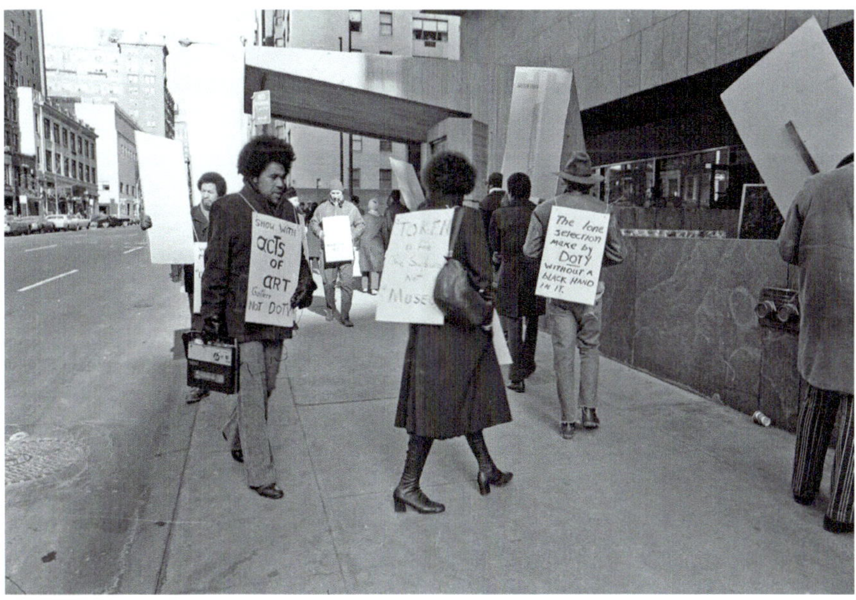

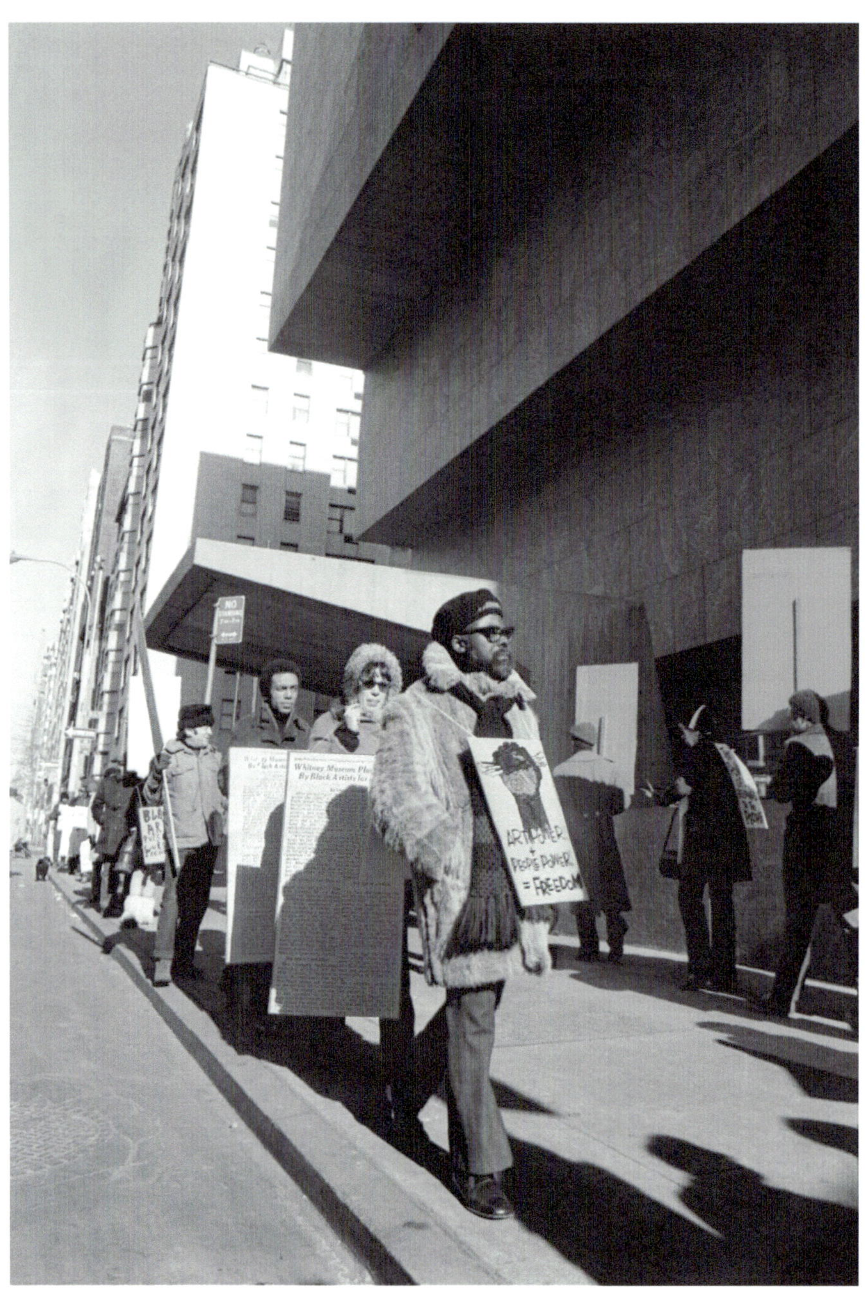

Fig. 3.7 Protest at the Whitney Museum of American Art, January 31, 1971, with Cliff Joseph in foreground. © Jan van Raay.

Eldzier Cortor, who withdrew the work *Memorabilia*, wrote:

> Dear Mr. Doty
>
> . . . I am canceling entering the painting you selected several months ago . . .
>
> Due to the fact that I feel the Whitney Museum has still not fulfilled the promises formerly made to the Black Emergency Cultural Coalition I wish not to be associated with this particular Whitney show.
>
> I cannot in full conscience enter my work in the Whitney exhibition until B.E.C.C.'s list of grievances are resolved.

Doty responded: "I am extremely disappointed that you put politics before art. . . . I am sorry that the public shall be deprived the joy of seeing it. We are all made to suffer by your actions."

John T. Scott, based in New Orleans, who withdrew three works, *A Called Meeting*, *Bishop*, and *Nobody's Flag*, sent this letter to Margaret McKellar, Doty's assistant: "The political overturns of your show 'Contemporary Black Artist in America' makes it necessary for me to withdraw. . . . The fact that the Whitney did not find it necessary to seek Black advisors caused me to believe that your museum was neither interested in, nor did not respect the opinions of the Black Emergency Cultural Coalition [*sic*]."

Romare Bearden withdrew after the show was hung, but before the official opening. At 4:15 p.m. on April 5, 1971, he sent a telegram that read:

> REQUEST ANY WORK OF MINE BE WITHDRAWN FROM CURRENT EXHIBIT NOW WITH SO MANY QUALIFIED ARTISTS NOT EXHIBITING THIS SHOW CAN NOT SERVE ORIGINAL PURPOSE
> ROMARE BEARDEN.

The painting intended to be included was in the Whitney collection, most probably *Eastern Barn* (1968), purchased in 1969. The museum posted a partial list of the artists who withdrew (fig. 3.8). The actual number was larger.

The decision to withdraw was difficult. Joe Overstreet has described being torn by artist friends on both sides of the fence. Al Loving, who stayed in the show, said to him, "Joe, it's only a painting. Don't pull out."[143] Yet he did. He along with John Dowell, Sam Gilliam, Daniel LaRue Johnson, Melvin Edwards, Richard Hunt, and William T. Williams published a collective statement in *Artforum* condemning the show's primary focus on the racial identities of the artists and only secondarily on

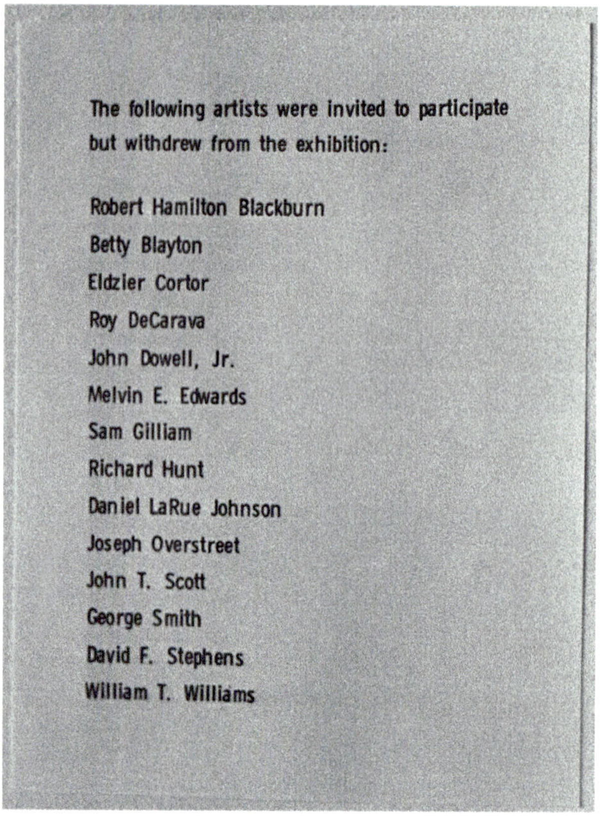

Fig. 3.8 Signage in *Contemporary Black Artists in America* exhibition at the Whitney Museum of American Art, April 6, 1971. The museum listed fourteen artists who withdrew from the show; the actual number was twenty-four. Photo: Tyrone Dukes / The New York Times / Redux.

their work.[144] Mahler Ryder remained for financial reasons: if he had withdrawn, he would have had to pay the cost of shipping his work back to Providence, Rhode Island, where he worked as a professor at the Rhode Island School of Design.

Artist Fred Eversley orchestrated his own subversive intervention. When Doty visited his studio in Venice, California, the curator also saw some work by Elyn Zimmerman, a Caucasian artist who was Eversley's assistant and a student at UCLA. Doty didn't meet Zimmerman face to face but, at Eversley's suggestion, agreed to include her work in the show. Eversley chose to remain in the exhibition (as did Zimmerman), but this action poked a hole in its race-based premise.[145]

One photographer, John Shearer, was listed in the press release and was sent a loan agreement, but he never returned it, and his work didn't appear in the galleries. Shearer, a photographer for *Look* magazine best known for his heart-wrenching photograph of John F. Kennedy Jr. saluting his father's coffin at JFK's funeral, had known Doty from the George Eastman House when he was a student at the Rochester Institute of Technology. The curator had shown an interest in the artist's work and, according to Shearer, "He made a big difference in my life. He was an older white guy who liked my work." This was unusual.[146] It's not clear whether Shearer boycotted the show or was traveling on assignment and merely neglected to return the loan form.

Most of the artists did not attend the opening, and when Barkley Hendricks came up from Philadelphia and saw the protestors marching in front of the museum, he refused to cross their picket line (fig. 3.9). He has recently said that he might have pulled his work, but he didn't know about the boycott because, being outside New York, he was out of the loop.[147]

Protestors once again staged a march at the museum. A press release from the BECC denounced the show and proclaimed that in order for the exhibition to authentically embody the concept of black experience, "it is essential that it be selected by one whose wisdom, strength and depth of sensitivity regarding blacks is drawn from the well of his own experience."[148] Despite the withdrawal of nearly one-third of the artists, *Contemporary Black Artists in America* opened as scheduled on April 6, 1971.

One can loosely trace the contours of *Contemporary Black Artists in America* by looking at Doty's ideal list of the seventy-eight artists invited to be in the show. Twenty-three of these artists had been featured in Gaither's New York/Boston exhibition.[149] Several artists were affiliated with Fisk University, including Driskell, Stephanie Pogue, and Vincent Smith. Another twelve of the artists were included in Samella Lewis and Ruth Waddy's two-volume book series, *Black Artists on Art*, including Murry DePillars, Noah Purifoy, Betye Saar, and Charles White, who remained in the show, and David Hammons and John Riddle, who withdrew.[150] There was considerable overlap with Ruder & Finn's circulating exhibition of *30 African American Artists*. From the Ruder & Finn show Doty picked up Avel de Knight, Al Hollingsworth, Tom Lloyd, Robert Reid, Raymond Saunders, and Thomas Sills, who all agreed to participate; and Benny Andrews, Romare Bearden, Betty Blayton, Melvin Edwards, Sam Gilliam, Richard Hunt, and Algernon Miller, who did not.

The version of the exhibition presented to the public featured the work of fifty-six African American artists and one Caucasian artist. The artists hailed from major cities around the country: San Francisco, Los Angeles, Chicago, Detroit, Nashville, Washington, Philadelphia, and Boston, as well as New York. Included were established figures such as Jacob Lawrence, who was forty-four years old at the time, and Charles White, who was fifty-three, as well as younger artists, such as twenty-eight-year-old Howardena Pindell and twenty-five-year-old Evelyn Terry.[151]

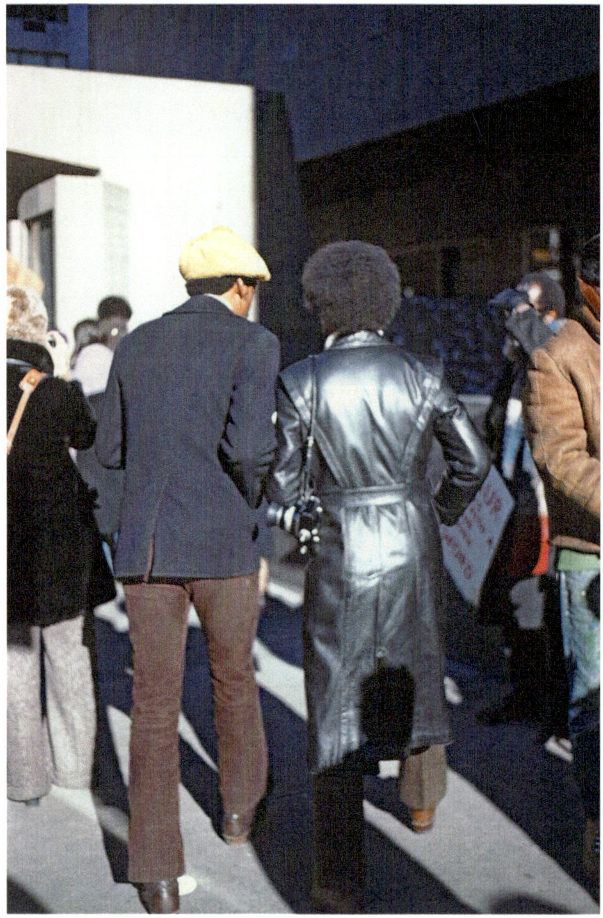

Fig. 3.9 Barkley Hendricks refusing to cross the picket line against *Contemporary Black Artists in America* in front of the Whitney Museum of American Art, April 1971. Courtesy of Barkley Hendricks.

The work was diverse. Some pieces contained figural imagery and others were abstract. A folk art strain was embodied in a work by Noah Purifoy, the assemblage artist from California. In sum, the only connecting thread appeared to be that all the artists were African American. Or so the museum thought.

Installation photographs and the floor plan of the show indicate that the layout loosely grouped works according to morphological similarity. Stepping off the elevator, visitors encountered Al Loving's wall-size *WYN . . . Time Trip I* (1971), an arrangement of brightly colored diamond-shaped canvases that look like cubes in a constant process of oscillating between concave and convex forms. In a vista to the left, the patterning in this piece is echoed in the basket-weave pattern in John E. Chandler's *Garvey's Quest* (1971) (figs. 3.10 and 3.11). To the right, the honeycomb

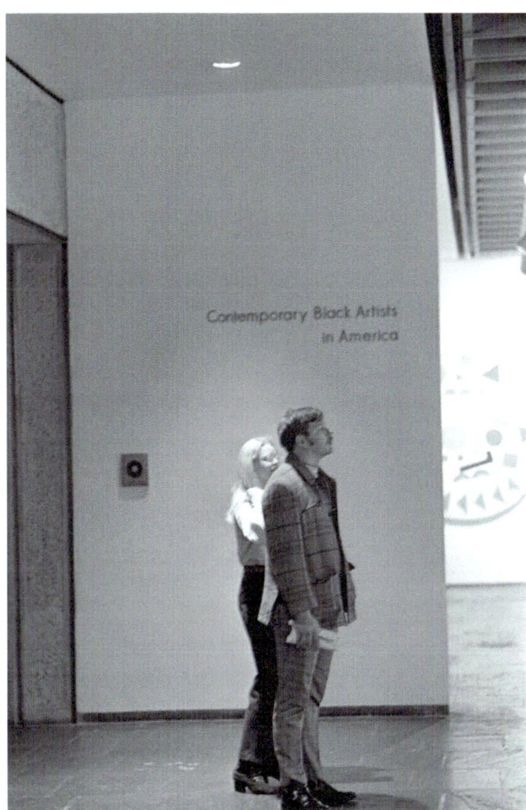

Fig. 3.10 Installation view of *Contemporary Black Artists in America* exhibition at the Whitney Museum of American Art, New York, April 6–May 16, 1971. *Rasolar* (1970) by Ernest Frazier is visible in the background. Photo: Tyrone Dukes / The New York Times / Redux.

Fig. 3.11 Installation view of *Contemporary Black Artists in America* exhibition at the Whitney Museum of American Art, New York, April 6–May 16, 1971. Left to right: Elyn Zimmerman, *#10* (1970); John E. Chandler, *Garvey's Quest* (1971); Al Loving, *WYN … Time Trip I* (1971); Walter Davis, *Black Bird Totem* (1970); Raymond Saunders, *Marie's Bill* (1970) and five drawings; James Lee, *Cleo II* (1970). Photo: Tyrone Dukes / The New York Times / Redux.

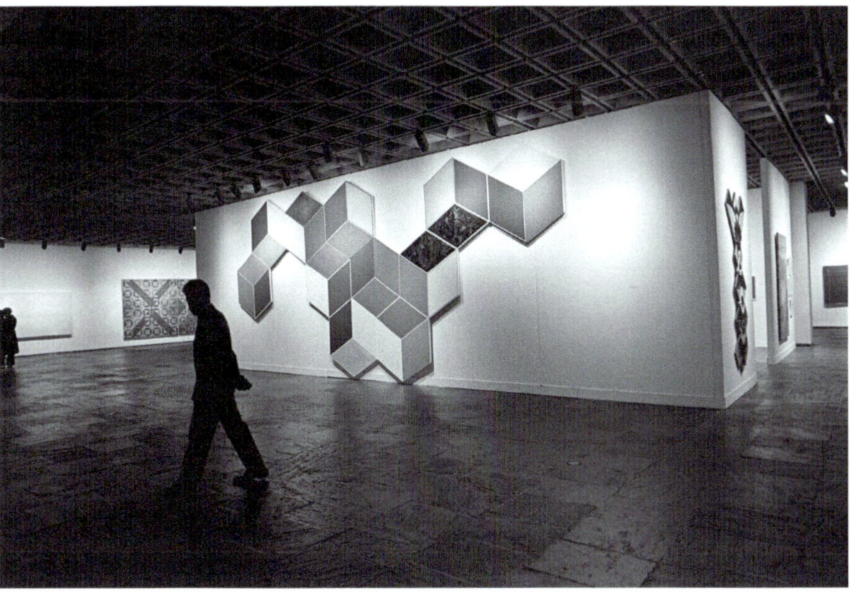

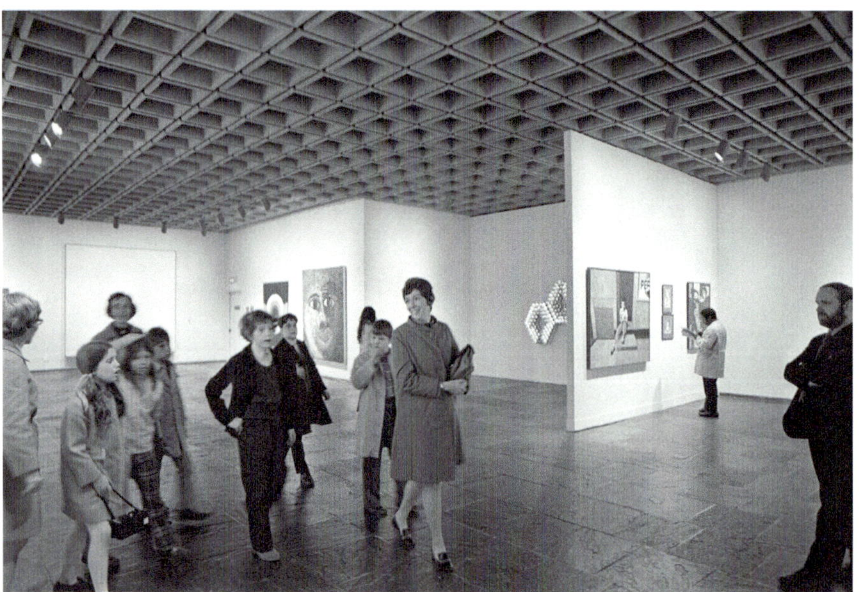

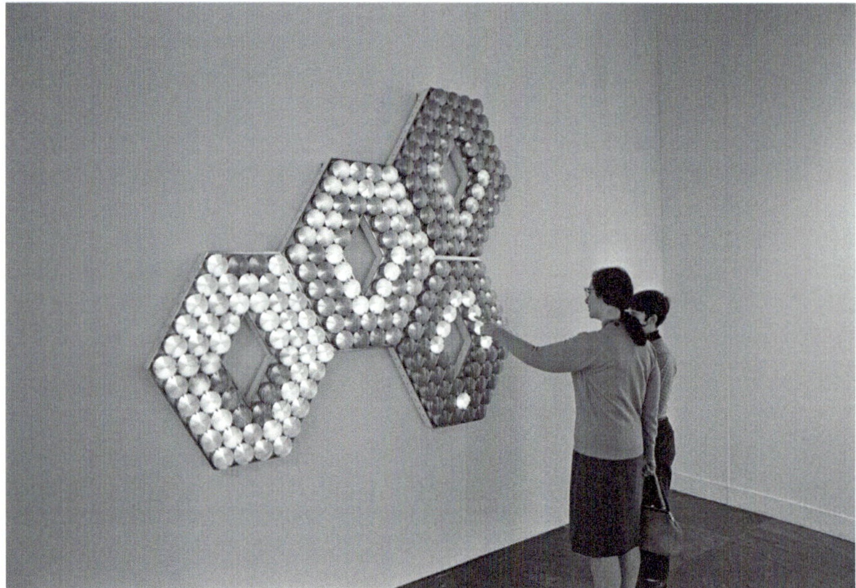

Fig. 3.12 Installation view of *Contemporary Black Artists in America* exhibition at the Whitney Museum of American Art, New York, April 6–May 16, 1971. Left to right: Marvin Brown, Untitled (1970); William Howard Henderson, *Revolution* (1970) and *The Smile* (1968); Tom Lloyd, *Moussakoo* (1968); Phillip Lindsay Mason, *Manchild in the Promised Land* (1969); Phillip Lindsay Mason, *With Everything on My Mind* (1968); Phillip Lindsay Mason, *So Many Things I Might Have Done, But Clouds Got in My Way* (1968); Charles W. McGee, *Untitled No. 1* (1969). Photo: Tyrone Dukes / The New York Times / Redux.

Fig. 3.13 Installation view of *Contemporary Black Artists in America* exhibition at the Whitney Museum of American Art, New York, April 6–May 16, 1971. Tom Lloyd, *Moussakoo* (1968). Photo: Tyrone Dukes / The New York Times / Redux.

form is reiterated in Tom Lloyd's *Moussakoo* (1968), which was composed of flashing hexagonal industrial lamps (figs. 3.12 and 3.13).

Prominently showcased in the first gallery was Frank Bowling's large and luminous painting *Where Is Lucienne?* (1970) (fig. 3.14). This piece contains veils of rich color partially concealing ghost images of maps, faces, and buildings. On the wall adjacent to Bowling's work were pieces by three women: a large untitled painting from 1970 by Howardena Pindell composed of small dots of color; a painting by Mavis Pusey; and Betye Saar's *Whitey's Way* (1969), a small mirrored case containing two rows of toy alligators and a macabre, skeletal black figurine. The alligators refer to the derogatory reference to black children as "alligator bait." The box is festooned with images of the American flag and a miniature swag.[152] These three works were presented along with two drawings by Roland Ayers. Across from this alcove hung Walter Davis's *Blackbird Totem* (1970).

The next gallery contained Charles McGhee's *Untitled No. 1* (1969) and Phillip Lindsay Mason's *Manchild in the Promised Land* (1969), a painting that borrows its name from Claude Brown's 1965 book about growing up in Harlem. The two works share a graphic quality (fig. 3.15).

Raymond Saunders's *Marie's Bill* (1970) was hung with five of the artist's drawings (fig. 3.16). Past this wall and around to the left, a long narrow gallery contained primarily abstract works, including Marvin Brown's large untitled painting, James Lee's *Cleo II* (1970), and a resin sculpture by Fred Eversley.[153] Further along were two biomorphic sculptures, including Henry Rollins's *Blue Totem*, which was reminiscent of a fetish object, and *Kate* by John Torres in carved alabaster, along with several representational paintings and drawings (fig. 3.17). At the end of this corridor were two figural pieces: a carved wooden sculpture by John Rhoden titled *Blue Eyes (Indonesian Legend)* (1965) and Charles Searles's large figure painting *News* (1970) (fig. 3.18).

Inside a gallery situated in the inner core of the space were works by eighteen artists. Flanking the south doorway was Barkley Hendricks's self-portrait and a large work by Hughie Lee-Smith depicting a white man standing on his head while a black man watches him from behind in the far distance. Also included in this gallery was a print by Frank Sharpe entitled *Man: Amnesty* (1970) and Jacob Lawrence's *Pool Game* (1970) (fig. 3.19). Benny Andrews has contended that the more politically explicit works were clustered by Doty in this inner gallery to minimize their visibility and impact. It's true that this area contained some provocative works, such as Murry DePillar's *Aunt Jemima* (1968), a send-up of the pancake mix icon as a militant revolutionary based on Delacroix's *Liberty Leading the People*, wielding

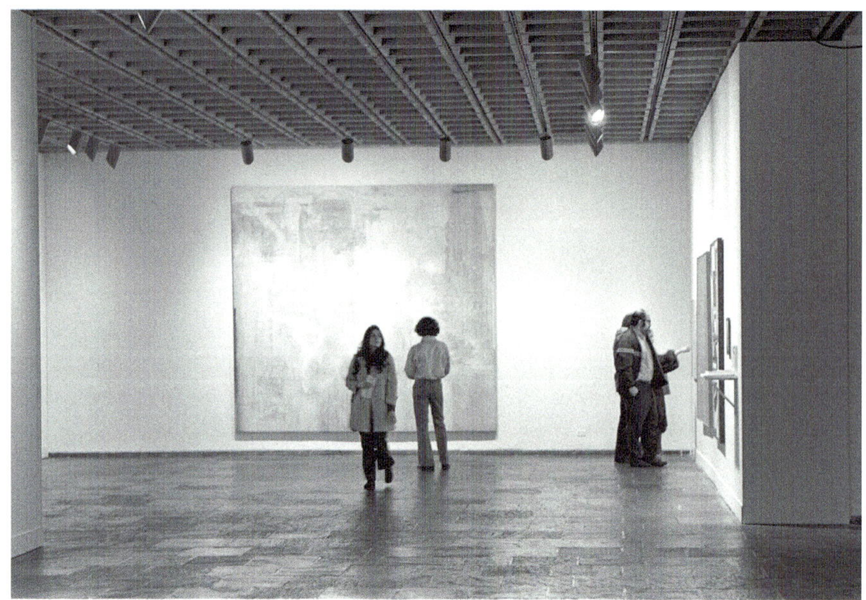

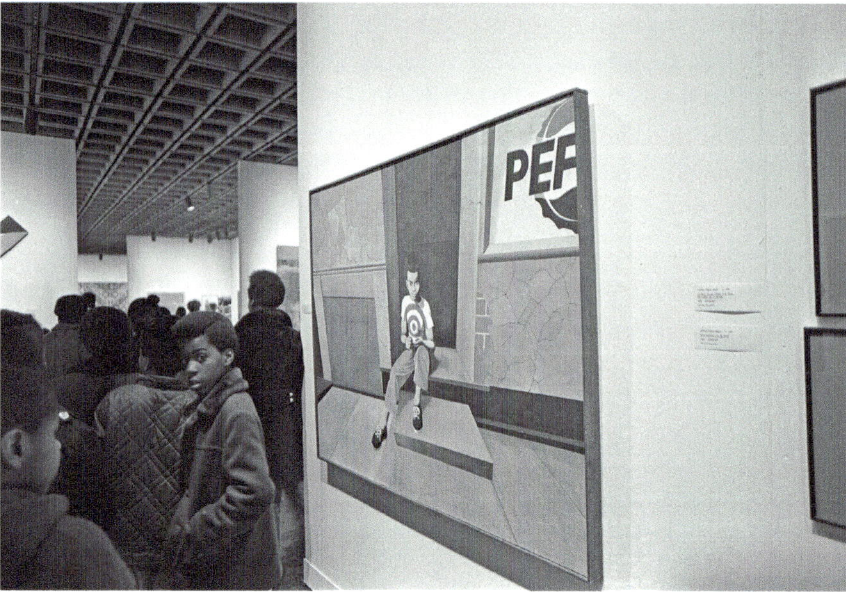

Fig. 3.14 Installation view of *Contemporary Black Artists in America* exhibition at the Whitney Museum of American Art, New York, April 6–May 16, 1971. Left to right: Frank Bowling, *Where Is Lucienne?* (1970); Roland Ayers, *The Creation* (1970) and *Atlantis Rising, II* (1969); Howardena Pindell, Untitled (1970); Mavis Pusey, *Dejyqea* (1970); Betye Saar, *Whitey's Way* (1970) and *Time* (1970). Photo: Tyrone Dukes / The New York Times / Redux.

Fig. 3.15 Installation view of *Contemporary Black Artists in America* exhibition at the Whitney Museum of American Art, New York, April 6–May 16, 1971. Phillip Lindsay Mason, *Manchild in the Promised Land* (1969). Photo: Tyrone Dukes / The New York Times / Redux.

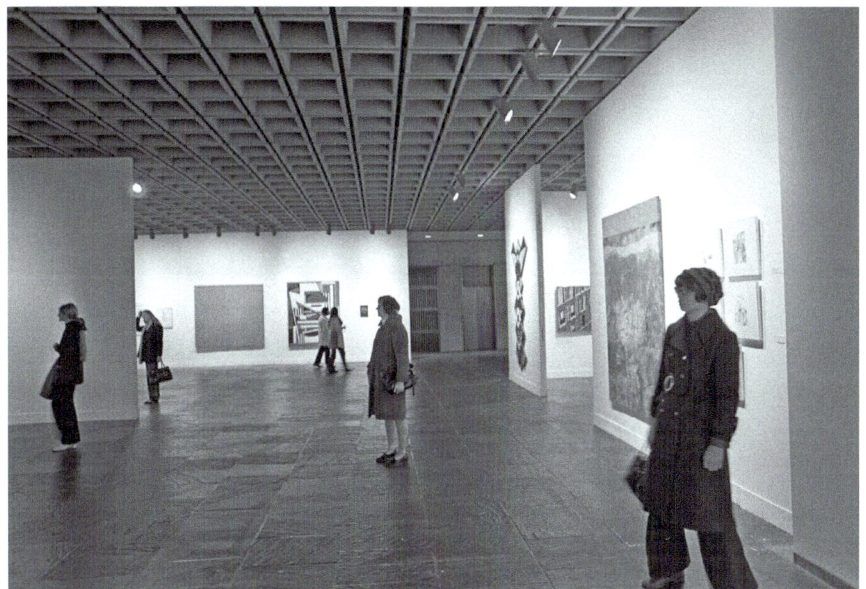

her spatula with a gloved fist as if she were Tommie Smith with a bayonet.[154] But works with similarly charged content were also interspersed throughout the exhibition. In the first gallery was Betye Saar's *Whitey's Way*. About two-thirds of the way through the exhibition was Mahler Ryder's ink drawing *The Great American Bus* (1969), which depicts the fallen figure of "Lady Liberty" lying on the floor of a bus. And the last gallery contained Charles White's *Wanted Poster #6* (1969), a work from a series based on pre–Civil War posters advertising slave auctions and rewards for runaways. In these works White's naturalistic figures appear as if incorporated into folded fabric, often intermingled with motifs taken from the American flag. Here White uses the Confederate flag. It is difficult to discern a coherent logic to the installation design, owing no doubt in part to the fact that so many artists withdrew from the show.

One of the most interesting juxtapositions was a pairing of works by William Howard (Mike) Henderson, *The Smile* (1968) and *Revolution* (1970) (fig. 3.20). The

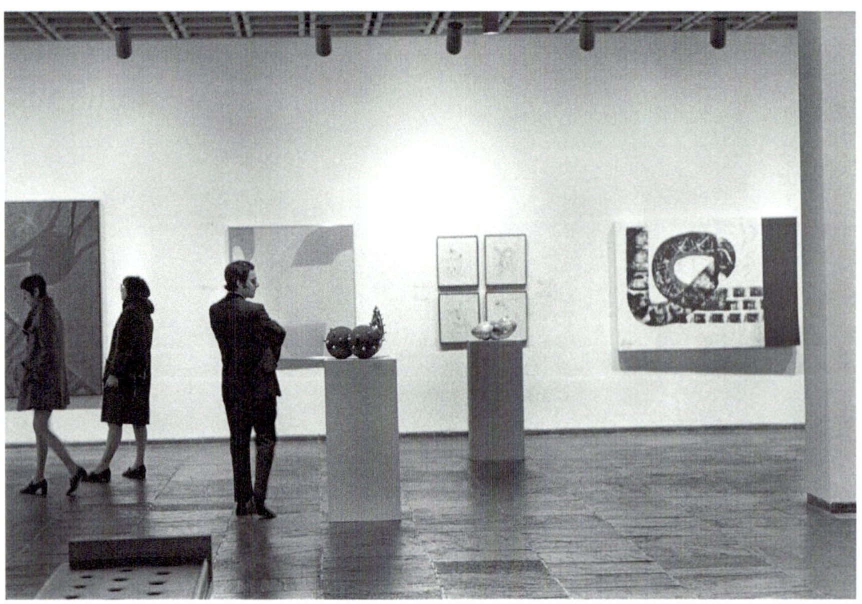

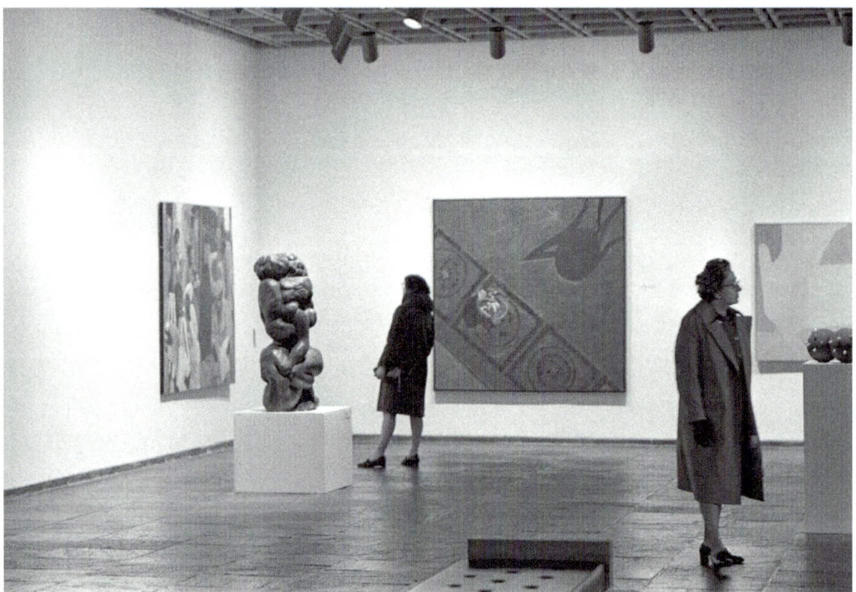

Fig. 3.17 Installation view of *Contemporary Black Artists in America* exhibition at the Whitney Museum of American Art, New York, April 6–May 16, 1971. Left to right: Franklin A. White Jr., *The Red Cap* (1970); Thomas Sills, *Return* (1970); Henry Rollins, *Blue Totem* (1970); Lloyd G. McNeil Jr., four untitled drawings (1970); John Torres, *Kate* (1970); Nathaniel Knight, *Rhythm of My People, II* (1970). Photo: Tyrone Dukes / The New York Times / Redux.

Fig. 3.18 Installation view of *Contemporary Black Artists in America* exhibition at the Whitney Museum of American Art, April 6, 1971. Left to right: Charles Searles, *News* (1970); John Rhoden, *Blue Eyes (Indonesian Legend)* (1965); Franklin A. White Jr., *The Red Cap* (1970); Thomas Sills, *Return* (1970); Henry Rollins, *Blue Totem* (1970). Photo: Tyrone Dukes / The New York Times / Redux.

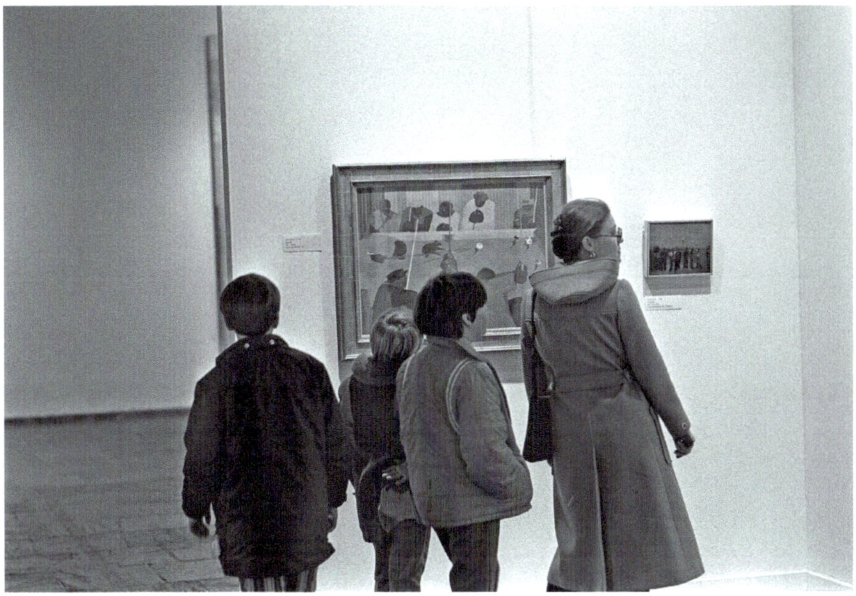

Fig. 3.19 Installation view of *Contemporary Black Artists in America*
exhibition at the Whitney Museum of American Art, April 6, 1971.
Left to right: Jacob Lawrence, *Pool Game* (1970); James Brantley,
The Informer (1970). Photo: Tyrone Dukes / The New York Times / Redux.

earlier work is a gestural painting of a smiling face. The later piece is abstract, but suggestive of a disc, target, or the concentric circles of an eye. The juxtaposition marks a pivotal change in the artist's style. Henderson's works of the late 1960s were figural and often contained harrowing subject matter, including violent assaults of whites on African Americans. Why did Doty select *The Smile* and not one of these earlier pieces? Does the title of *Revolution* reflect the sublimation of social and political content in this abstract work? Did the curator intend to link these paintings with respect to their content, or their form? Or did he simply place them side by side because they highlight the contrast between abstraction and representation that is at the heart of Doty's project?

In his catalogue essay Doty wrote, "The exhibition is devoted to American artists who are Black—creative individuals, with widely disparate intentions, ideas, and goals; artists whose works are categorized as 'Black Art,' or 'African American art,' despite the fact that diversity is their universal trait."[155] However, the essay didn't actually endorse this range of African American art; the critical framework glorified abstraction as a universal artistic language.[156] Doty acknowledged the

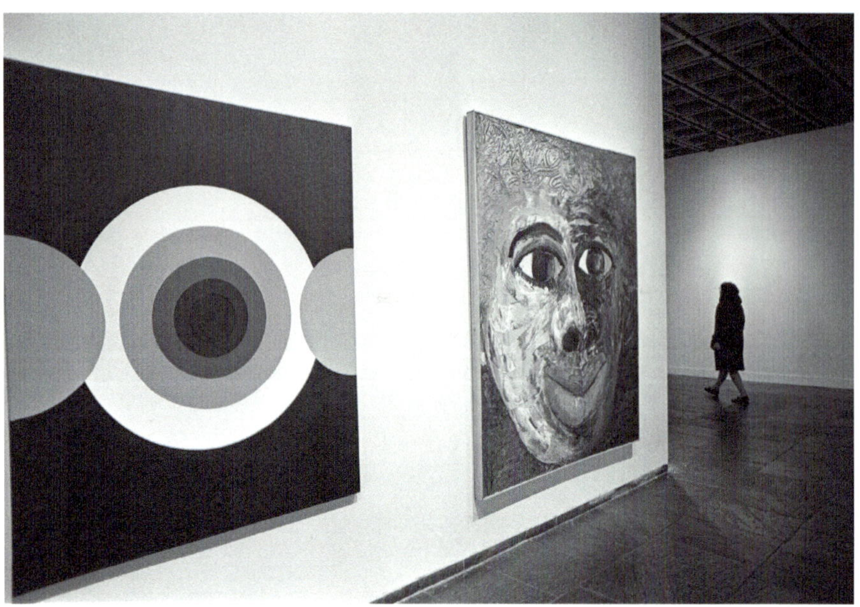

 Installation view of *Contemporary Black Artists in America* exhibition at the Whitney Museum of American Art, April 6, 1971. Left to right: William Howard Henderson, *Revolution* (1970) and *The Smile* (1968). Photo: Tyrone Dukes / The New York Times / Redux.

interest of some black artists in African traditions and gave a brief nod to the concept of culture as a site of revolutionary struggle by quoting artist and graphic designer Emory Douglas; he referred to Douglas not by name but merely by his title, minister of culture for the Black Panther Party. Ultimately, however, Doty reported that "extremist exhortations are categorically dismissed by many Black artists who refuse to believe that art should be subjected to the necessity of conveying a political message."[157]

Doty conceded that the important black art of the 1920s, '30s, and '40s was primarily figural, but he stereotyped the work of Archibald Motley Jr., Aaron Douglas, Jacob Lawrence, Romare Bearden, and Charles White as using realism and representation to communicate the "conflict, stress, and tragedy" of "the Negro artist" as well as the "role of the hero" in the life of black people. By the 1970s, he wrote, black artists had evolved and were reacting to the "ideas and techniques of the current mode, sensing and assimilating new directions of thought and vision." Abstract art, he proposed, represented a more advanced stage of development for black art beyond "mere depiction." He enlisted several artists to substantiate this point.

He cited Richard Hunt and Barbara Chase-Riboud's transitions from figural work to abstraction and Daniel LaRue Johnson's move from assemblage to a "preoccupation with problems of color, form and space." He asserted that Melvin Edwards had repudiated the historical references in his *Lynch Fragment Series* in favor of work that "demonstrates a coalescence of static and flexible states, rather than racial tragedy." Revealingly, Hunt, Chase, and Edwards had all withdrawn their work from the exhibition, suggesting that Doty was not a reliable expert on their work. "Ultimately," Doty concluded, "the Black artist and his audience must respond to 'the authority of the created thing,' that unique quality which originates only with the creative individual, and which flourishes only under a spirit of free inquiry."[158] Was this thesis, that progress in art was the movement from representation to abstraction, the rationale for hanging Henderson's two works side by side? In succinct shorthand, this juxtaposition encapsulated the dichotomy set up by the show.

Abstract art, for Doty, represented freedom from the constraints of social and political circumstance and freedom from the burden of history, the triumph of "aesthetics" over "politics," yet the show was predicated on the idea of "black identity," a distinctly nonaesthetic premise. Despite Doty's repudiation of a racially or culturally specific interpretative rubric for the show, the fact that these artists were selected on the basis of race belied a fundamental contradiction in the exhibition itself. *Contemporary Black Artists in America*, like many of the accommodations of the 1960s, "held a cloudy mirror up to its antagonists, reflecting their demands . . . in a distorted fashion."[159] Even overtly militant work was defanged, purged of its politics through the lens of high modernism.

The denial of the museum as a politicized space affected all artists. On the very day that *Contemporary Black Artists in America* opened, Thomas Messer, director of the Solomon R. Guggenheim Museum, announced the cancellation of a major exhibition of the work of Hans Haacke. The catalyst for the cancellation was Haacke's desire to exhibit a new work, *Shapolsky Real Estate Holdings* (1971), which traced the ownership of dozens of tenement buildings in New York City to one owner, Harold Shapolsky. No one associated with the Guggenheim was named in the piece, but the work exposed with vivid specificity how capitalism enabled the few to amass fortunes by exploiting the many. The subversive work hit close enough to home that Messer cancelled the show in order to "protect" the museum's supposed political neutrality.[160]

One topic that Doty addressed in his essay that held powerful potential to redefine the history of modern art was his association of African American artists with the modernist interest in African tribal art. Drawing a connection between the interest in African art during the Harlem Renaissance and the Afrocentrism of the

1960s and early '70s, Doty explains in the beginning of his essay: "Now, as a means of arousing greater knowledge and a desire for cultural heritage among their people, many Black artists art turning to the tribal arts of Africa as a source, taking as their subject matter folklore, religious and political stories and myths, animal and other symbols, illustrations of the people, and the vivid colors and rhythmic forms of tribal artifacts."[161] The omission of African American artists from the canonical histories of modernism has only recently begun to be redressed, and had Doty linked his exhibition with this major theme in the history of modern art, his show would have been a discursive breakthrough.[162] His broad conception of the influence of African art—one that involved subject matter and political content, not just form—would have radically redefined the dominant art historical formulation as expressed in Robert Goldwater's 1938 book *Primitivism in Modern Painting*, which had been updated and issued in a new edition in 1967 reflecting current interest in the subject.[163] But this visionary redefinition of modernism as encompassing the work of African Americans was beyond the curator's capacity. Unable to radically reimagine the history of twentieth-century art, Doty fell back on a received formalist paradigm that segregated and simplified.

Whether the abstract work to which Doty was attracted actually embodied the universalist notions that he claimed is questionable. The title of Ernest Frazier's *Rasolar* references the work of Sun Ra, the eponymous leader of the Afro-futurist musical group whose works were informed by numerology, Egyptology, astrology, biblical texts, and a visionary approach to electronic jazz music.[164] Howardena Pindell's use of circles was based on her memory of drinking from the root beer mugs with red circles on the bottom designated for people of color. "I see that as the reason I have been obsessed with the circle, using it in a way that would be positive instead of negative."[165] In contrast to Doty's view of abstraction, Kellie Jones has pointed out that often the seemingly abstract visual vocabularies used by African American artists had symbolic or associative meanings that were simply inaccessible to white art critics.[166] Writing about the 1970 Lobby exhibition of work by Melvin Edwards, Jones points out that the artist's installation made of chains and barbed wire "integrated his artistic practice with political thought."[167] His earlier *Lynch Fragment* series had explicitly referenced racist violence. His statement in the exhibition brochure, Jones says, did so obliquely:

> *How long is a chain?*
> *How long is a change?*
> *How heavy is a chain?*
> *How heavy is a change?*[168]

Ironically, among the artists who were most vocal in their opposition to the show and voiced the most penetrating criticism were some who worked abstractly, even some whom Doty had cited in his essay as exemplifying his thesis. The artists' statement published in *Artforum* exhorted that an exhibition that attempts to create a definitive survey of African American artists must be a "model of its kind, and try to deal with the complex issues (social and esthetic) justly." In their joint statement, John Dowell, Sam Gilliam, Daniel LaRue Johnson, Joe Overstreet, Melvin Edwards, Richard Hunt, and William T. Williams wrote: "The Whitney Museum has anti-curated its survey which results in misrepresenting and discrediting the complex and varied cultural and visual history of the African American. The museum thus acts as a falsifier of history and minimizes the value of our works and therefore ourselves."[169]

In the curatorial discourse of the late 1960s and early '70s exhibition context became an increasingly decisive factor in the production of meaning. Thus William T. Williams may have envisioned his work in relation to myriad historical and contemporary contexts, including the work of Frank Stella and Kenneth Noland, but by contextualizing his paintings in a "black art show," Doty was forcing them to perform the work of racial uplift regardless of the artist's intentions. Underscoring this point is the fact that while the *Contemporary Black Artists in America* show was going on upstairs, Williams was showing his work downstairs in the *Structure of Color* exhibition alongside Frank Stella, Kenneth Noland, and a host of others, including Josef Albers, Hans Hoffmann, and Ellsworth Kelly. Had Williams allowed his work to be shown in *Contemporary Black Artists in America*, viewers would have been able to judge for themselves which context brought out the most compelling dimensions.

Doty's glorification of abstraction was particularly out of character. He had been trained as a photography historian. His major exhibitions at the Whitney immediately preceding and following *Contemporary Black Artists in America* were shows featuring figural art. These shows included a group show entitled *Human Concern/Personal Torment: The Grotesque in American Art*, held in 1969, and *Extraordinary Realities*, in 1973.[170] In the catalogue for the former, Doty wrote: "A sense of duty continues to sustain the humanist art of our time. . . . Such artists are no longer concerned with vague theories of 'social realism,' but rather dedicated to communicating directly their intense contempt, disillusionment and disgust for a political and social structure which continually permits, if not actually encourages, conflict and suffering."[171]

Yet in *Contemporary Black Artists in America* art that addressed political and social structures, such as the history of slavery, through figuration was demeaned and dismissed. Doty's ambivalence toward much of the work in the show reflects the tension between the socially motivated response to external pressures to be inclusive and the inability to get beyond the paradigm of formalism at a time when the Whitney was striving for mainstream acceptance and authoritative status.

Paradoxically, Doty's curatorial viewpoint in *Contemporary Black Artists in America* echoed William Agee's curatorial interests in *The 1930's: Painting and Sculpture in America* even though the former focused on African American artists and the latter did not feature any. Agee had said, "The 1930s as a period had been misunderstood, distorted, and over generalized. Because the political, social and intellectual currents of the time were both then and now dominated by the [Great Depression] psychology, we have assumed that the painting was almost exclusively an art of social realism. However, at least three or four other currents prevailed during the time, which produced art of high quality and lasting importance."[172] Both curators formulated curatorial statements that elevated abstraction above representation.

One of Doty's more outrageous claims was that the "deficiencies" of representational art were the result of African American artists' feeling compelled to address their "blackness." The black artist, he wrote, "must answer to his own cultural loyalties and the community, both of which insist that he create art that expresses blackness."[173] This statement implies that if African American artists simply stopped thinking of themselves as African American, a place in the art world would open up for them and their history of exclusion would become a thing of the past. But that sentiment disregards the layers of racialization in the various discursive contexts of the art world. Deeply entrenched stereotypes contaminated not only the museum field but also much art criticism of the time. For example, in his *New York Times* review of the exhibition John Canaday wrote that it "is not very black and not very good."[174] In a subsequent article he called it "vanilla pudding."[175] And finally, Canaday selected Charles Searles's painting *News* as "the best as well as the blackest painting" because "rather than idealizing or sentimentalizing members of his race, he has shown them as brutalized creatures whose explosion into violence would be vicious and unreasoning within the society responsible for their brutalization."[176] For African American artists this seemed to be a no-win situation. The use of abstraction, hailed by mainstream critics and curators as the most laudatory art, was considered a repudiation of black cultural identity, and the use of figuration was considered an expression of torment and anguish. Many critics had difficulty seeing artwork by African American artists as conveying anything other than a social group agenda.

Shortly after *Contemporary Black Artists in America* opened, David Driskell wrote Doty a letter of support:

I am sure that there will be a number of criticisms directed towards those of us who would not listen to the nonsense of the people who are so much concerned with politics and not art, but I feel certain that it was much more important to stand by your convictions and have the show than give in to some of the demands that were made. It has always been our policy to be concerned with quality of art first, and I am certain that we are all aware of the fact that there have been injustices and there will continue to be some regarding the display of artist works just as there are injustices in the whole sociological pattern of our lives here in the United States. But the optimistic person is one who looks forward to the time when these things will be cleared up. We have gone on record, many many years ago here at Fisk University, trying to promote an atmosphere which encourages a professional attitude toward the arts without being political. We have taken the position that it is our basic responsibility, being a Black institution, to promote works of art that have been done by Blacks, but this is always based on quality, not on what the populace says.[177]

Being situated at Fisk University, a historically black institution, Driskell had a less fraught path when it came to exhibiting the work of African American artists; he did not have to contend with an institutional history of African American exclusion.

Flora Biddle, Gertrude Vanderbilt Whitney's granddaughter who was a trustee of the museum at the time and would become its president in 1977, wrote to Doty in sympathy and solidarity:

The Whitney Museum is being confronted. This has happened in the past, and will surely in the future; the measure of our contemporaneousness is our willingness to deal with the people and problems pressing us in a creative and spirited fashion.

In this case—so much talking, so much reflection, and such a heartfelt desire to help went into the final compromise reached with the BECC and it's natural to feel resentful of what appears to be a betrayal by them. I believe that their actions in no way change the validity of our original decision.

The use of our show by the BECC to make a point is probably equally valid in terms of what they wish to accomplish; they will perhaps reach wider exposure, have a stronger impact upon those whom they hope to reach or awaken. What they say is basically true; the black artist *has* been discriminated against as unjustly as any black person. This can be emphasized in different ways—they have chosen the political path, and the Whitney has chosen *its* only means of expression to say exactly the same thing. I'm convinced that having this exhibition is right and timely, and will be of value in the long run.

. . . Those artists who have felt they must choose between their roles, as black men or women, and as artists, will *suffer* because this is a terrible choice to have to make today. For them we can only express sympathy and a hope that they may find a way to combine the two as non-destructively as possible.[178] (emphasis original)

One might find this expression of sympathy condescending, but more insidious—and pervasive in the art world—was the inability of whites to see African Americans as artists.

On April 5, the day before the Whitney show opened, the BECC held a press conference at the Studio Museum in Harlem to publicly denounce the Whitney show and announce a rebuttal exhibition, which opened the following day at the Acts of Art Gallery. Billed as a "Group Show of Representative Works by Black Artists," the rebuttal exhibition contained works by an eclectic group of painters, sculptors, photographers, and printmakers from all over the country (fig. 3.21). The show included two artists who had withdrawn from the Whitney show, Betty Blayton and Richard Mayhew, in addition to Hale Woodruff and Reginald Gammon, former members of the Spiral group (along with Mayhew); BECC leaders Benny Andrews and Cliff Joseph; Ademola Olugebefola, a leader of the Weusi group; Vivian Browne and Art Coppedge; Junius Redwood, who had shown at the Museum of Modern Art in 1943 in an exhibition featuring Viktor Lowenfeld's students from the Hampton Institute; the late Bob Thompson; dozens of lesser known and younger artists; and Jackson himself. Jackson wryly turned the "quality debate" against the Whitney Museum and said, "I'm showing the real stuff and they're showing a watered down standard."[179]

Installed in the center of the gallery, anchoring the exhibition, was a sculpture by Ed Wilson depicting a grim circle of ten skeletal figures with sunken chests, hunched over a table with a mirrored surface. The title, *Board of Directors*, evokes the image of gaunt, heartless power brokers in the exercise of their institutional authority narcissistically seeing no one but themselves. In this exhibition context the work serves as a sardonic evocation of the authorities at the Whitney Museum. The Acts of Art Gallery produced a small catalogue after the exhibition opened, with images of all the works, two short essays, and a reprint of a favorable review published in a local newspaper.[180]

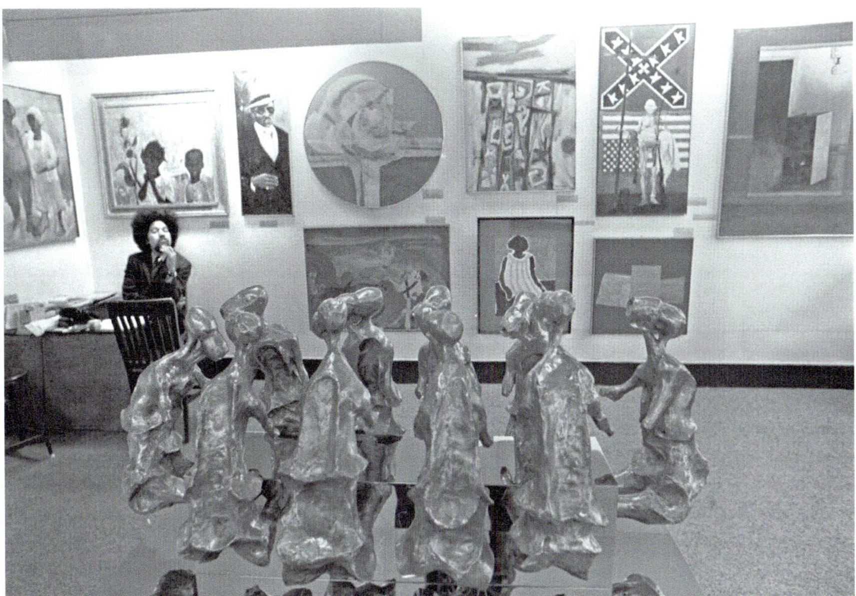

Fig. 3.21 Installation view of *Rebuttal to Whitney Museum Exhibition* at
Acts of Art Gallery, April 1971, with director Nigel Jackson. Foreground:
Ed Wilson, *Board of Directors*. Background from left to right: Ann Tanksley,
Atlantic City; Walter Williams, *Summer Song*; Robert Threadgill, *The Player*;
Betty Blayton, *Iconograph* (top); Bob Thompson, Untitled (bottom); Hale
Woodruff, *Celestial Gate* (top); James Denmark, *Woman with Yellow Dress*
(bottom); Cliff Joseph, *The Superman* (top); Lynn Brooks, Untitled (bottom);
Russ Thompson, *Harlem River Room*. Photo: Tyrone Dukes / The New York
Times / Redux.

When Betsy Jones, a curator at MoMA, visited the rebuttal show, she had the occasion to meet Jackson. They discussed MoMA's purchase of Andrews's drawings
from his show at Acts of Art the previous fall, as well as the purchase of the painting *No More Games* directly from the artist after a studio visit by MoMA curator Jennifer Licht. "After a rather long conversation," Jones wrote in a memo to Licht, "he
complained—gently—that the Museum should have bought the Andrews [paint-
ing] from him since he had given Andrews a show. . . . I expressed some surprise
& said that I had clearly understood that Andrews did not have a dealer. . . . He admitted he did not have a contract with Andrews, nor indeed with anyone else, but
there was a reiterated, though vague, threat that he was soon going to expose this
behaviour of the Museum—he kept saying 'this will all come out soon.' "[181] The incident caused John Hightower to resign from the Acts of Art board on October 11,

1971.[182] Marcia Tucker, from the Whitney, had already resigned before the opening of the rebuttal exhibition.

Shifting alliances and fractured loyalties were commonplace, as stakes were high and sensitivities keenly attuned. Tom Lloyd chose to participate in the *Contemporary Black Artists in America* exhibition, but when he read the catalogue essay, he was incensed. Instead of withdrawing, as other artists had, he edited and produced a small book condemning Doty's publication. In his introduction, he characterized the project as a "counterstatement" to the *Contemporary Black Artists in America* catalogue and an "affirmation of Black Art philosophy as interpreted by eight Black artists."[183] The booklet contained five short pieces: three reprints of previously published material, Lloyd's introduction, and Doty's catalogue essay reprinted as an appendix.

The contributors to *Black Art Notes*, some associated with the Black Arts movement, included Melvin Dixon, Imamu Amiri Baraka (LeRoi Jones), Jeff Donaldson, Bing Davis, Ray Elkins, Francis and Val Gray Ward, Babatunde Folayemi (Tony Northern), and Lloyd himself. The book opened with a group of short quotations, including this statement by poet Adam David Miller: "I would like to see the idea of 'universal' laid to rest, along with such outmoded usages as civilization, as applied to the West; Social protest, as applied to Afro literature; Pagan and fetish, when applied to non-Christian religions; Primitive, barbarian, and folk, as applied to lifestyles or as judgments of culture; and jungle, as applied to African space. These terms are too-heavily weighted European culture judgments to be of much use."[184]

Together the quotations and essays advocated black self-definition and self-determination. They addressed the roles of art in everyday life and in black liberation and condemned the assimilationist premises of Doty's essay.

Ray Elkins, for example, wrote, "The Curator [Doty] has chosen to rap on a subject that no European can rap on. Black art is something that only a Black man can express. Racism in America has made it impossible for Blacks to do their own thing. Now we have people like him running around talking and writing on the subject of Black art and making use of the same old tricks, uncle tom's [sic] and black artists who paint things that have no real meaning to the life and death struggle of Black people."[185]

Amiri Baraka's essay refuted the concept of universalism: "True integration in the world would be as a varied projection of special experiences each one refined to be hopefully beneficial in some way to the world."[186] But in a move typical of his writings of the time, he also points fingers, not only at whites but also at what he called "white artists in Black face": "To paint white colored and call it black is the white man's reaction to the movement of the Black Artist for Self-Determination, which is the only 'artistic freedom.' A Black Art show full of white artists in Black face, soul pimps, pathological niggers who love white flesh, is the white man's idea of what a black art show is all about."[187]

In particular, Baraka cited Richard Hunt and Barbara Chase-Riboud as being "in the tradition of white art, black face or not."[188] These artists are featured in Doty's essay and described as having moved from figural to abstract work, but both had dropped out of the Whitney show, a fact that Baraka appears not to have known. Indeed, the major flaw of this publication is that most of the authors had not seen the exhibition and took Doty's essay at face value, failing to differentiate between the artists' work and Doty's characterization of it.

What was the legacy of this period of ferment at the Whitney Museum? The tactics of the BECC, particularly its willingness to picket the museums it aimed to penetrate, were not necessarily the most effective for achieving their goals. For all his foibles and fumbling with the *Harlem on My Mind* exhibition, Allon Schoener made a good point in an interview with cultural historian Laurin Raiken in 1971. When asked if perhaps the artists who were protesting museums were trying to draw attention to themselves in order to advance their careers, he said no. Protesting was not an effective career booster:

> If you wanted to go into careerism, you would have cultivated [art dealer] Leo Castelli; you would have cultivated [curator] Henry Geldzahler; you would have cultivated one of the lower echelon curators at the Whitney Museum or the Museum of Modern Art who could have enhanced your opportunities to develop, according to the art profession, a name for yourself. To develop a name for yourself with the Artists Protest Movement may generate a certain amount of support with the group of artists who are involved in the Artists Protest Movement. It hasn't generated any support or recognition for anybody within the art establishment.[189]

Reginald Gammon, who was asked to participate in *Contemporary Black Artists in America* but declined, has said, "There are some things you lose because you want to gain certain things."[190] However, participating in *Contemporary Black Artists in America* was not a career booster either. Marvin Brown recalls feeling ambivalent about the exhibition when he talked with Doty, then crestfallen when he saw the result.[191] Benny Andrews empathized with the artists who were ambivalent about participating: "All of us are struggling so hard to be in museums and, of course, the Whitney is one of the museums that we would all want to be in. So it was a very hard thing to do, not to be in the show. And by the same token, to be in it—it was a very painful thing for all of us."[192] In the end, it is impossible to determine whether being in the show or dropping out was a better career strategy. David Hammons dropped out of the show and has become internationally acclaimed, while many other artists allowed their work to be shown and have been all but forgotten. Benny Andrews refused to participate and went on to a prolific career as both an artist and an arts administrator, exhibiting widely and running the Visual Arts Program at the NEA in the early 1980s, but he would never have an exhibition at the Whitney.[193]

The BECC's interaction with the Whitney produced a public debate about the critical function of curatorial viewpoint. Benny Andrews and other artists saw the limitations of mere inclusion. The power to select, frame a point of view, and contextualize an object to produce meaning was just as important in influencing how that work would be read as the inherent qualities of the work itself. It's not that artists and curators were unaware of this issue previously, but the events of *Contemporary Black Artists in America* underscored the emergence of new value systems in the established art world, a heteroglossia of voices and subject positions that included artists of color. The conflicts broke open a dialogue that laid bare the subjectivity of the museum's voice, the impossibility of the neutral voice boldly and shamelessly claimed by those in positions of institutional authority—a theme that would be pursued as a critical strategy in the decades that followed, most powerfully by artist Fred Wilson, starting with his 1987 installation *Rooms with a View: The Struggle between Culture, Content, and Context in Art* and continuing in his best-known work, *Mining the Museum* (1992).[194]

The artists in *Contemporary Black Artists in America* were used in the Whitney's own struggle to jockey for position in the art world as it transitioned from a family run operation into a national institution. Ultimately, the most important questions raised by the exhibition, ones that have become increasingly meaningful in the age of museum marketing and branding, are these: How can museums evolve responsibly in the stories they tell themselves about who they are and why they exist? Are museums willing to defect, and in the words of art historian Leo Steinberg, "depart into strange territories leaving the old stand-by criteria" behind?[195] How does the project of creating institutional identities square with the writing of art's histories in all their complexity and range?

Romare Bearden: *The Prevalence of Ritual* and *The Sculpture of Richard Hunt* at the Museum of Modern Art

On February 24, 1970, William S. Rubin, curator of painting and sculpture at the Museum of Modern Art, wrote to Arthur Drexler, curator of architecture and design: "It would be interesting to have—as the Art Workers Coalition originally suggested—an exhibition on the relationship of African and other ethnic and indigenous arts to the tradition of modern painting and sculpture. This would make a fascinating exhibition—even though that contribution is, I believe, less marked than some people believe—and could also provide the basis for a most useful publication."[1]

Fourteen years later, in 1984, the idea would come to fruition in the infamous exhibition *"Primitivism" in 20th Century Art: Affinity of the Tribal and the Modern*.[2] As with so many art museums' responses to cultural activism in the late 1960s and early '70s, Rubin's *"Primitivism"* exhibition held up a distorted mirror to the artists' demand. Rather than acknowledge modern European artists' indebtedness to African and other indigenous arts or explore cross-cultural influences, the exhibition followed a well-trodden path. "Art" was defined as the creation of white European and European American artists. People of color were ignored both as makers of the ceremonial and functional objects on display and as modern artists in their own right. The show perpetuated the exclusion of black subjectivity from modernity. In Rubin's view, only two African Americans warranted inclusion: Romare Bearden and Martin Puryear. Their works were illustrated in the last few pages of the two-volume catalogue with little or no explanation as to how they fit into the exhibition as a whole.

The exhibition and its catalogue focused on two themes: first, *influences*, beginning with artists who either retraced the paths of European colonizers, such as Gauguin traveling in the Marquesas, or looked to the trophies of conquest for inspiration, such as Picasso, who famously visited the Trocadero Museum; second, *affinities*, inexplicable visual resemblances independent of any known instance of contact between the modern artist and the tribal work. Rubin meticulously reconstructed European and European American artists' contact with objects transported from French, Belgian, German, and British colonies into European museums and private collections while omitting information about the indigenous cultural contexts of the objects, which he insisted was irrelevant.[3] He elevated the European artist who appropriated tribal art to the role of "liberator," writing in the "*Primitivism*" catalog: "We owe to the voyagers, colonials, and ethnologists the arrival of these objects in the West. But we owe primarily to the convictions of the pioneer modern artists their promotion from the rank of curiosities and artifacts to that of major art, indeed, to the status of art at all."[4]

Rubin examined in minute detail works by European artists—sixty-seven pages are devoted to Picasso's *Les Demoiselles d'Avignon*—but ignored major events in the history of twentieth-century art, including, most notably, the Black Arts movement of the 1960s and '70s. In his critique of "*Primitivism*" Rasheed Araeen observed: "Those who have been seen as 'primitives' are in fact part of today's society, and to ignore their actual position in this respect is to indulge again in imperialist fantasies."[5]

What had the Art Workers' Coalition (AWC) actually proposed? The AWC was a group of arts activists who came together between 1969 and 1972 to change the art system. They wanted free public access and sought to make museums more democratic and accountable, particularly to the artists on whose work their very existence depended.[6] Spurred on by a leftist ethos of laborers' rights, artists such as Nancy Spero, Carl Andre, and Hans Haacke extended this critique to labor relations in the art world.[7] As the term "art worker" implies, the AWC was, according to Raphael Montañez Ortiz, "a union [to] protect the artist from cultural institutions that want to exploit the artist and neglect the artist once they profit from the artist. . . . [We] wanted some respect for [our] process and some control, the kind of control that labor was struggling for in the structure of factory and manufacturing. That was basically the discussion. What does the artist have in common with the laborer? And what kinds of protections does the laborer have that the artist doesn't have? And how could the artist acquire some of that protection?"[8] For Ortiz, exploitation of any worker, including the artist or "artworker," was tantamount to the abuse suffered by indigenous people under colonial rule or the subjugation of African Americans under slavery. Ortiz and artists Faith Ringgold, Tom Lloyd, Jon Hendricks, and others in the group placed particular emphasis on integrating museums.[9]

Various versions of the AWC manifesto were devised throughout 1969 and 1970. In early 1970 the roster of demands included an "exhibit showing the impact that the artists of African [*sic*] and South America have had upon the twentieth century western cultural revolution in painting, sculpture, music and dance."[10] This manifesto also demanded that MoMA create a black and Puerto Rican advisory board, and hold more exhibitions and acquire more work by black and Puerto Rican artists. Most importantly, it called for the creation of a new wing devoted to African American and Puerto Rican art. The artists wanted full enfranchisement in the institution that defined modernism. The document was signed "Art Workers' Coalition Black and Puerto Rican Committee and other Black and Puerto Rican Groups," followed by the names of artists Tom Lloyd, Faith Ringgold, Ralph Ortiz, Bob Carter, Todd Williams, Jack Hunte, Adrian Garcia and James Sepyo, Martin Rubio, Armando Soto, and Joan Barnes.[11]

The AWC's perspective parallels the view expressed in a series of articles published in 1969 in *Muhammad Speaks*, the newspaper of Elijah Muhammad's Nation of Islam. Cultural appropriation, author Bill Quinn explained, was an outgrowth of colonialism and an analogue to human exploitation and the mining of natural resources: "Casting about fitfully for inspiration, the impoverished artistic showmen of the Western world discovered the rich heritage of Africa's last 2,000 years. So bountiful was this new source that, where Europeans had produced no new schools of painting since the Renaissance, they were able to produce at least a dozen between 1880 and 1940."[12]

In one of his articles, Quinn actually named MoMA as a culprit in this biased cultural hierarchy:

> In New York City, the Western world's grandest center of art and culture, there is a Museum of Primitive Art. The museum's name would imply that its contents are "rough, crude, simple"—"even uncivilized." . . . Yet, housed there is a good cross section of the most sophisticated artworks of Africa, Polynesia and the pre-Columbian Americas.
>
> Nearby is the Museum of Modern Art. Housed there, as its name would imply, are many of the proudest, most sophisticated achievements of 20th century Europe and white America.
>
> The rub is, that the contents of the Museum of Modern Art are directly derived from—and, in some cases; stone-cold copies of—the works displayed in the Museum of "Primitive" Art.[13]

Each article was illustrated with side-by-side comparisons of African and European sculptures (fig. 4.1). Ironically, MoMA's ubiquitous advertisements for the "*Primitivism*" exhibition would contain just such juxtapositions (fig. 4.2).

In a sense, the "*Primitivism*" exhibition was a grand refusal of the political and cultural changes brought about by the social movements of the 1960s. It continued, and was perhaps intended as the last word in, a debate with a generation of artists and activists that had challenged the authority of museums, their power

Trace Culture of White World to African Aesthetic and Artistic Base

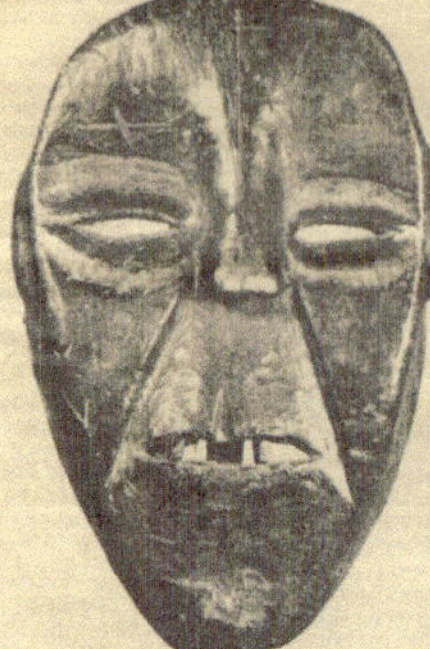

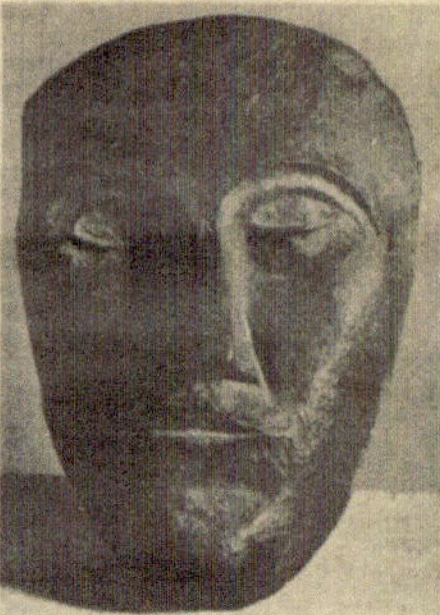

"PRIMITIVE" MASTERPIECE is the work of an African artist of the Belgian, Congo—probably of the Azande nation. Pablo Picasso effort at right, entitled "Head of a Woman (1907)," shows obvious origins of his work. Prior to study of African art, Picasso art was hung up in European pseudo-photographic tradition.

(Continued from page 27)

blown racial civil war. The U.S. as a nation is doomed, in any case, to break up into a series of regional and racial ministates, and such a civil war "would merely accelerate the process."

IN THIS SPACE, we are concerned with the wasting away of the white man's artistic dynamic, which, as was glimpsed in an earlier column (Muhammad Speaks, March 14), was experiencing its last Greco-Roman gasps at the end of the 19th Century. Casting about fitfully for inspiration, the impoverished artistic showmen of the Western world discovered the rich heritage of Africa's last 2,000 years. So bountiful was this new source that, where Europeans had produced no new schools of painting since the Renaissance, they were able to produce at least a dozen between 1880 and 1940. European sculpture, which was conceptually static between the creation of the Venus de Milo (ca. 150 B.C.) and Edgar Degas' Little Dancer of Fourteen Years (1880 A.D.), flowered into as many different interpretations as there were sculptors, with the European "discovery" of African sculpture.

Not a new wellspring of inspiration, but inspiration itself had come to white artists. They certainly could appreciate, if they couldn't originate, the relationships of rhythmic tension between the various plastic surfaces, the interplay of forms and colors and textures, and all the other charactersistics of this vital aesthetic. This appreciation was rapidly translated into imitation.

ONE OF THE most famous white artist of the 20th century is Pablo Picasso. This Spanish-born collector of artistic styles has lived through virtually the entire span of so-called "modern" art. He is most noted for his paintings which, though they demonstrate it less obviously than his sculpture, owe the deepest gratitude to the African view of form. He is an eclectic, a practitioner of any style which his abilities allow him to duplicate. He is, however, seldom credited with being an originator, even by his white admirers.

Cubism, his most famous contribution to Western art, was initiated in conjunction with French painter Georges Braque in 1907. Prior to this time, Picasso had collected a group of African masks, chiefly of Congolese origin, which he kept in his summer studio in Estaque, France. They were both a source of uneasiness and stimulation to his artistic outlook. He began to see the fantastic array of geometric forms, which were the elemental components of these masks. For many months, he worked on a large canvas, entitled The Young Maidens of Avignon, in which he tried to introduce into contemporary figure composition those characteristics of the sphere, cone and cube which he saw in the African models. Braque, Picasso's close friend, saw the painting hanging in the Spaniard's studio, and it stimulated him to do a series of landscapes utilizing the forms which had motivated Picasso. These landscapes were later exhibited in Paris galleries (1908-09). When he saw them, one French critic exclaimed. "What bizarre cubiques!" Thus was born one of the foremost moments of the Western world's hour of "modern" art. On its heels followed Picasso's disclaimer of any inspiration from "primitive" African sources. However, as if his paintings weren't evidence enough to the contrary, the Spaniard's attempts at sculpture often look as if they had been poured into molds made by the now anonymoust West and Central African old masters.

IT IS OFTEN said that art forecasts history. If this is so, since we can see abundant evidence of the dominance of the Black aesthetic in Western culture, can the dominance of the remainder of the Black experience be far behind?

GRACEFUL CURVES and lines of African sculpture on simple utensils, such as this pulley from the Ivory Coast (above), illustrated sensitivity and conceptualization of Black craftsmen. Picasso work, "Head of Woman (1951)," attempts to recreate strength and beauty of treasures such as that seen on common African tool above. Unlike many of his European contemporaries, Picasso has openly acknowledged his debt to African art while the white Western press has attempted to play it down.

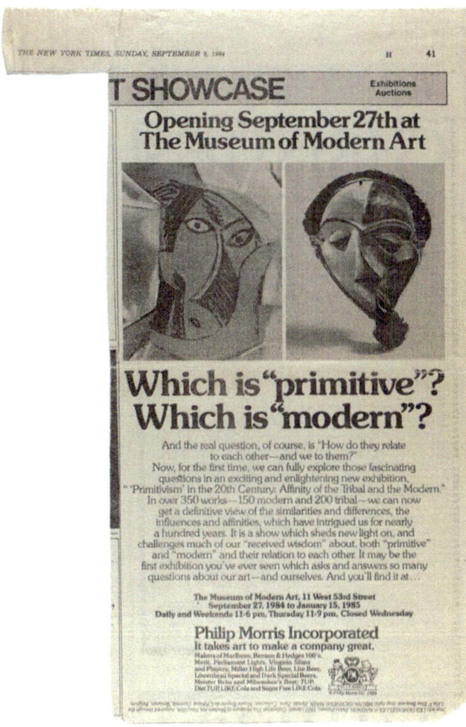

Fig. 4.2 Advertisement for the Museum of Modern Art's exhibition *"Primitivism" in 20th Century Art: Affinity of the Tribal and the Modern* published in the *New York Times*, September 9, 1984. Public Information Records, II.A.1041. The Museum of Modern Art Archives, New York. Digital Image © The Museum of Modern Art / Licensed by SCALA / Art Resource, New York.

to write artists in and out of history and to shape that history in accordance with hegemonic beliefs and interests.[14] As if suspended in the past, *"Primitivism" in 20th Century Art: Affinity of the Tribal and the Modern* rehashed a colonial narrative of modern art history on an epic scale.

MoMA wasn't the AWC's only target, but it was their main one. AWC member Lucy Lippard wrote in June 1970 that the group took on MoMA because of "its rank in the world, its Rockefeller-studded Board of Trustees with all the attendant political and economic sins attached to such a group. Its propagation of the star system and consequent dependence on galleries and collectors, its maintenance of a safe, blue-chip collection, and particularly, its lack of contact with the art community and recent art."[15]

Many of the AWC's initiatives to change the art system would come to pass, in time. By the early 1970s most American museums had free admission at least one day a week. In 1978 the U.S. government passed legislation giving artists copyright over their work, thus preventing profiteering through the sale of unauthorized reproductions. Even demands that weren't achieved institutionally were advanced in other ways, especially through subversive works of art that used exhibition contexts to launch institutional critiques, such as Hans Haacke's *MoMA Poll*, shown in MoMA's *Information* show in the summer of 1970. The participatory piece asked visitors to cast ballots indicating whether or not they approved of New York governor Nelson Rockefeller's position on the Vietnam War. Rockefeller's mother, Abby Aldrich Rockefeller, had been a founder of the museum, and family members had always held leadership roles on the board of trustees. At the time the work was shown, the governor was considering a run for the presidency. The piece harnessed the museum as a vehicle for public debate.

More difficult to achieve was the demand for inclusion of artists of color. Unlike the Black Emergency Cultural Coalition's protests at the Metropolitan Museum of Art and the Whitney Museum of American Art, where the dominant issues were those of equity and integration, the agendas and priorities of the AWC were diffuse. According to Lippard, membership was loosely defined as anyone who showed up for a demonstration or came to one of its weekly meetings at a downtown art space called "Museum." Issues and actions were discussed; debate and dissension were common, but resolutions were rarely voted on. The membership itself was diverse. The group included self-identified Marxists who eschewed the commodification of art and others who felt that if art was to be a commodity, artists should get a larger piece of the pie. Some thought museums and the whole art system were moribund. Carl Andre, for instance, advocated that "all artists should withdraw instantly from all commercial connections, gallery and otherwise. . . . No cooperation with museums. . . . Museums will never be right: they are owned by the wrong people, controlled by the wrong people and staffed by the wrong people."[16] There were those who rejected this assessment. Writer Michele Wallace has stated that she and her mother, artist Faith Ringgold, were not aligned with fellow AWC members in their hostile posture toward museums and galleries:

> Faith and I did not share [the] view that the art world and the art establishment were moribund and that the principal purpose of art production at this point would be to rail against American capitalism, corporatism, and hypocrisy. The whites in the Art Workers' Coalition and Art Strike who took their inclusion in the culture arrangements of the dominant culture for granted might be excused for feeling as though conventional forms of art making would be too much of a compromise with the status quo, but such assumptions could have little relevance for African American artists who had

had little opportunity by then to be included in the art world, nationally or internationally.[17]

Ironically, Andre claimed that "elimination of the art world" would also eliminate disparities between opportunities afforded African American and white artists. "Black artists [would] simply become part of the community of artists."[18] But there was no basis to support this claim. Uneven levels of awareness and understanding of racial discourse thwarted unity around the practice of antiracism. For example, Alex Gross, a visible and vocal AWC member, published an article in the *East Village Other* in which he referred to artists as the most "niggerized breed on the face of the earth." Co-opting the most derogatory of racial slurs to portray all artists, including whites, as victims, he implicitly denied differences in access to power such as those that enabled him to make this claim in print.[19]

The word "racism" appears often in AWC demands, the names of its offshoot groups, and the titles of its actions, such as the "New York Art Strike Against Racism, War, and Repression," but parsing the antiracist work from the antiracist rhetoric requires close examination of the activities of a handful of AWC members. Many chronicles of the AWC's activities distort this history. For example, one source describes the AWC, which came into existence in 1969, as "crucial in leading to the founding of such neighborhood museums as the Studio Museum in Harlem, El Museo del Barrio, and the Bronx Museum of the Arts."[20] Planning for the Studio Museum had actually started in 1965, and the museum opened in 1968 prior to the founding of the AWC. El Museo del Barrio grew out of the demands of African American and Puerto Rican parents and activists in Central Harlem and East Harlem that their children be educated about their ancestral cultures. Raphael Ortiz, a teacher in New York City's High School of Music and Art, was tapped as its director by the superintendent of school district 4 independent of his involvement in the AWC. Ortiz and Faith Ringgold were both educators and activists long before the AWC coalesced as a group; they, along with Tom Lloyd, used the AWC as an umbrella and a brand for their antiracist activities, enlisting members for actions they conceived and spearheaded.

Tom Lloyd was a sculptor born in Jamaica, Queens, in 1929 whose work in the 1960s consisted of electronic constructions made of lights. He had studied art at the Pratt Institute in Brooklyn and the Brooklyn Museum. His one-person exhibition had inaugurated the Studio Museum in Harlem in 1968, and his visibility had earned him a seat at the symposium on black art organized by the Metropolitan Museum of Art, with artists Romare Bearden, Sam Gilliam, Richard Hunt,

Jacob Lawrence, William T. Williams, and Hale Woodruff, which was published in the January 1969 issue of the Met's *Bulletin* to coincide with the opening of the exhibition *Harlem on My Mind*. Despite Lloyd's insistence during the symposium that, as an African American artist, he was marginalized by the mainstream art world, his record indicates otherwise.[21] Lloyd's sculptures had been included in a broad range of exhibitions: *Art Turned On* at the Institute of Contemporary Art in Boston (1965); *Light as a Creative Medium* at the Carpenter Center at Harvard University (1965); *Light in Art* at the Contemporary Arts Museum in Houston (1966); *Art Electric* at the Sonnabend Gallery in Paris (1966); and a solo exhibition at the Wadsworth Atheneum (1966). He showed in *Counterpoints* (1967) at the Lever House, and its subsequent venues when versions of the exhibition traveled.[22] After the Studio Museum show, he was offered an exhibition at the Howard Wise Gallery, a venue that focused on electronic art.[23] He would also be prominently featured in the Whitney Museum's 1971 exhibition *Contemporary Black Artists in America*.

Before joining the AWC, Lloyd had tried to find a place within the Black Emergency Cultural Coalition. On November 29, 1968, he had attended a meeting at Jack Whitten's studio along with Benny Andrews, Daniel LaRue Johnson, Jack White, and others. The point of the meeting, as recorded in Andrews's journal, was to "chart a course for us as young artists unencumbered by the past to move into a new area as far as blacks and the arts are concerned."[24] Andrews noted that Lloyd's brand of racial politics was incompatible with that of the other artists: "Tom Lloyd alienated everyone" with his militant social change agenda, particularly his insistence on racial discrimination as the focal point; "the others to a man felt the number one aim must be artistic integrity, blackness and everything else must be left to others."[25] The BECC sought inclusion as a matter of ethics, favoring negotiation and peaceful protest over confrontation. Lloyd left the group and found a more sympathetic community among the artists in the Art Workers' Coalition (fig. 4.3).

Faith Ringgold came to the AWC through Lloyd. The two had met at the demonstration against the Whitney Museum's *1930's: Painting and Sculpture in America* exhibition in November 1968. Ringgold has recalled that when Lloyd drew her into the group he had "an interesting relationship to the AWC; as its only black artist, he functioned like a separate committee."[26] Ringgold, trained at the City College of New York, was painting by night and teaching art by day at New York City's Brandeis High School Annex. Born and raised in Harlem, she had traveled to Europe and toured the great museums of Paris, Florence, and Rome. Bold and confident, she had made a spectacular solo debut at the Spectrum Gallery in December 1967 with her *American People* series, which included her landmark work, *The*

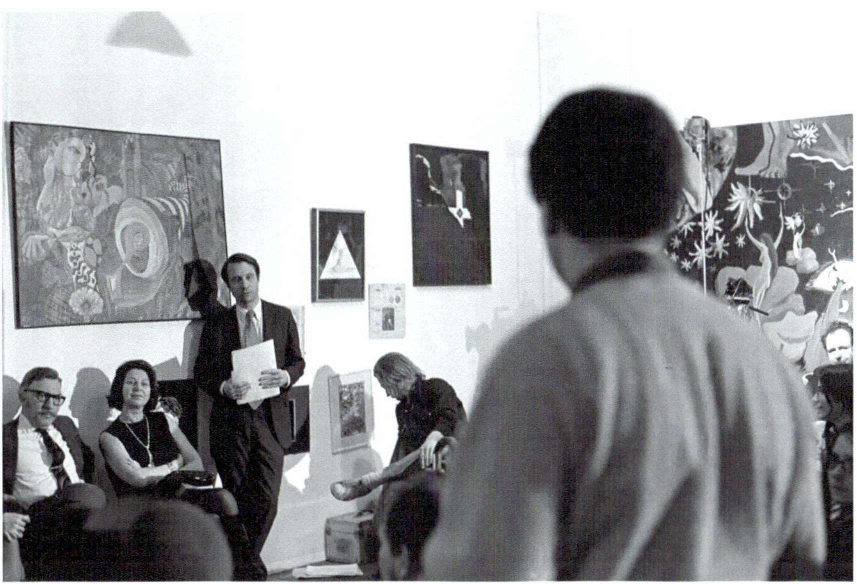

Flag Is Bleeding (1967), in which three figures, white and black, arms interlocked, are melded with an image of the American flag (fig. 4.4), and *Die*, which was inspired by Picasso's *Guernica* (fig. 4.5). Like Lloyd, she had been included in the *Counterpoints* show, where *The Flag Is Bleeding* received wide visibility because it was exhibited in the window of the exhibition's venue, Lever House, facing Park Avenue at Fifty-Fourth Street. At the time she became involved with the AWC, Ringgold was focusing on her *Black Light* series, which, in response to the July 1969 moon landing, included a searing, critical commentary on national priorities titled *Flag for the Moon: Die Nigger*.[27] Ringgold would become a stalwart in the activist movement, using confrontation and persuasion to integrate the Museum of Modern Art (fig. 4.6).

Raphael Montañez Ortiz had been raised on the Lower East Side of New York City in a predominantly Jewish Orthodox community. His mother had moved to New York City from Puerto Rico in 1932, and Ortiz was born two years later. He learned to draw from his uncle, a sign painter, who had developed a technique for painting images on glass in reverse that fascinated Ortiz; the technique was designed for painting bodega windows. As a child, he took a mail-order art course and became the "school artist," drawing pictures on the blackboard for the holidays.

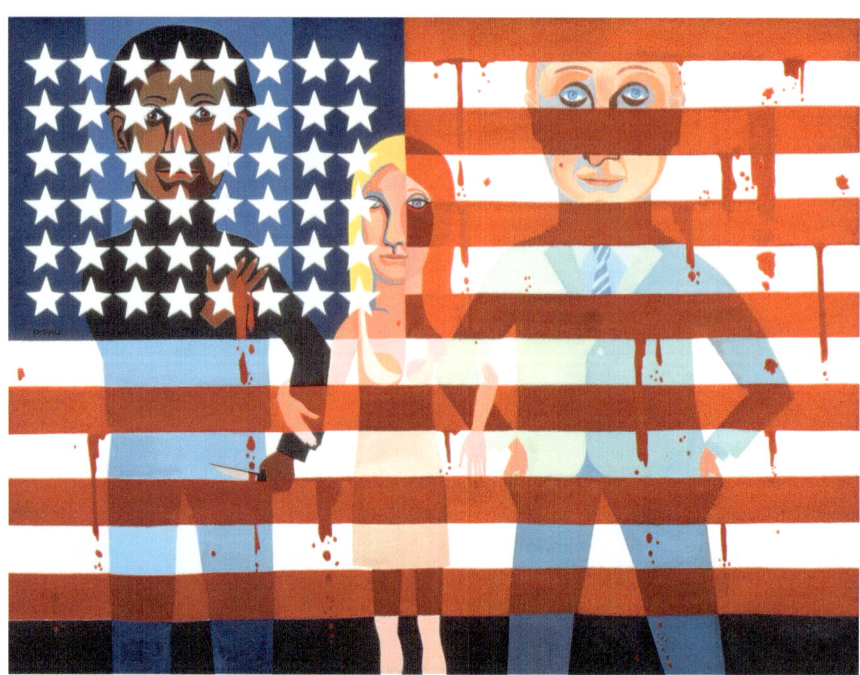

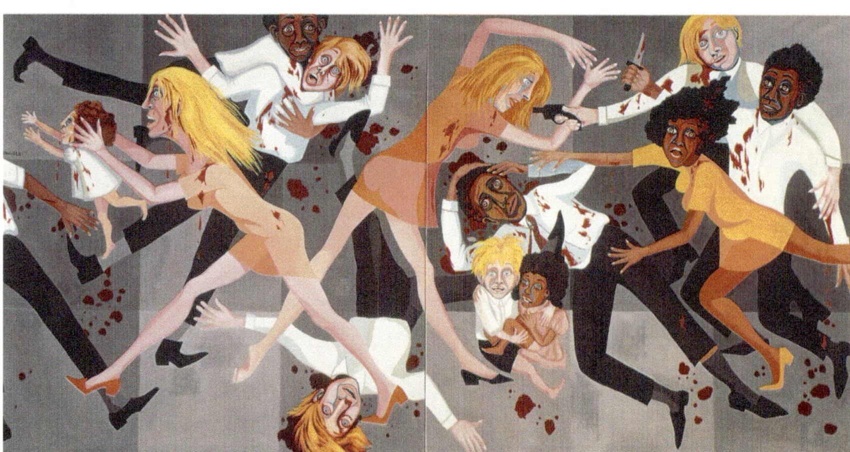

Fig. 4.4 Faith Ringgold, *American People Series #18: The Flag Is Bleeding*, 1967, oil on canvas, 72×96 ins. © Faith Ringgold.

Fig. 4.5 Faith Ringgold, *American People Series #20: Die*, 1967, oil on canvas, 72×144 ins. © Faith Ringgold.

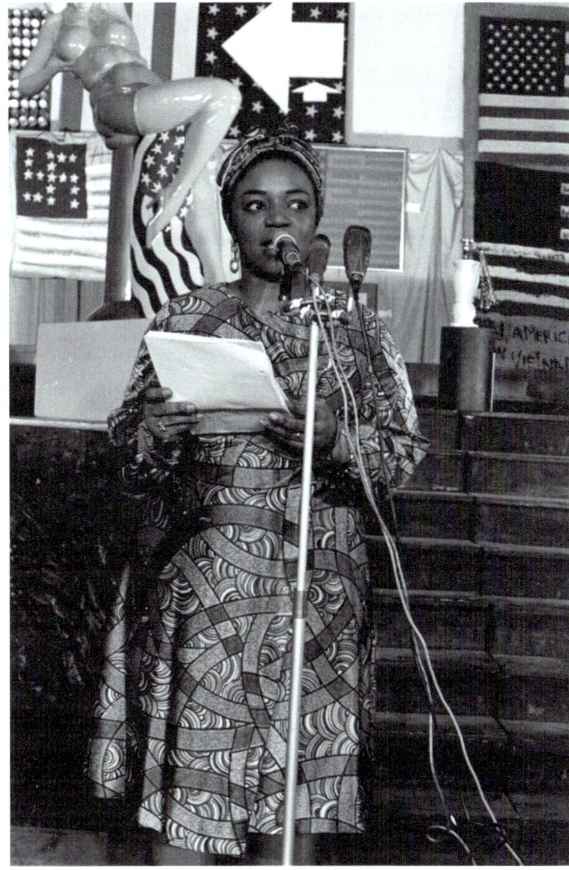

Fig. 4.6 Faith Ringgold, artist, educator, and activist, at the *People's Flag Show*, Judson Memorial Church, November 9, 1970. © Jan van Raay.

Like Lloyd, he had attended the Pratt Institute in Brooklyn, completing both bachelor's and master's degrees. He came to the AWC through his friendship with artists Jean Toche and Jon Hendricks, who spearheaded the AWC affiliate group, the Guerrilla Art Action Group (fig. 4.7). Ortiz had met Toche at the Destruction in Art Symposium in London in 1966, and Toche in turn introduced him to Hendricks. At the time, Hendricks was the director of the art gallery located in the basement of the Judson Memorial Church, a venue for innovative multimedia, performance-based work started in 1962 by a group of artists including Yvonne Rainer, founder of a resident dance company. It was a job Hendricks had created for himself in 1964 to satisfy his community service requirement as a conscientious objector to the war in Vietnam.[28] In October 1967 Ortiz performed at the church as part of the performance series 12 *Evenings of Manipulations*, and in April 1968 he and Hendricks collaborated on the DIAS USA event.[29]

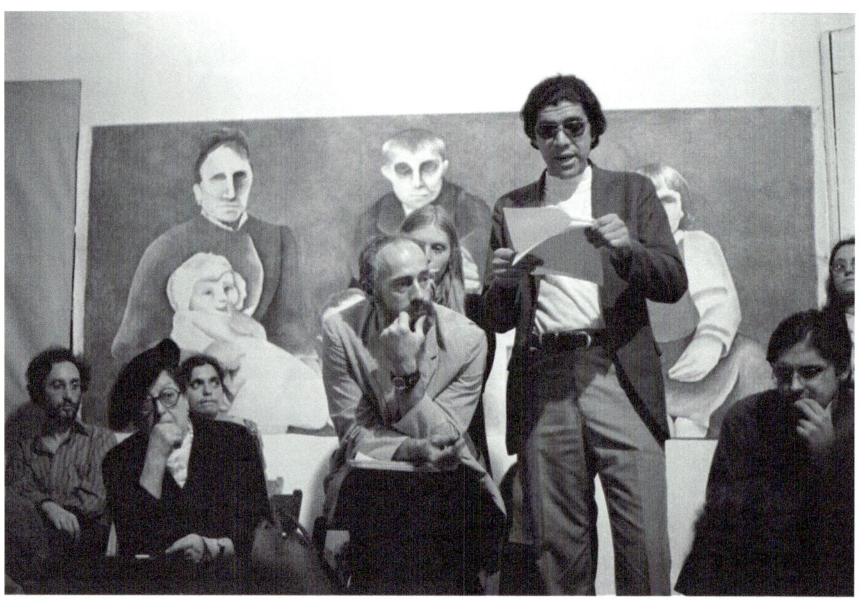

Fig. 4.7 Raphael Montañez Ortiz, artist, educator, and activist, at an Art Strike meeting (Robert Morris on left), May 20, 1970. © Jan van Raay.

When the AWC was founded, Ortiz was pursuing a doctorate in education at Columbia University and teaching at the High School of Music and Art. In the summer of 1969 he founded El Museo del Barrio. He also built a bridge between the AWC and the Puerto Rican Artists Union, which he described as a cultural version of the Young Lords, a Latino political group that had modeled itself on the Black Panthers. Other Puerto Rican artists who participated in the AWC included Marcos Dimas, Adrian Garcia, Manuel Otero, and Armando Soto, who would cofound Taller Boricua in 1970, initially as a printmaking studio to produce posters for demonstrations and events. Younger than Ortiz, these artists were students who had begun to organize Puerto Rican exhibitions in colleges and community centers in New York.[30]

In their April 1969 pamphlet publicizing a rally they intended to hold at MoMA, Lloyd, Ringgold, and Ortiz presented their mission:

Although we are all members of the same human family, our experience as a people has helped to make us different from other groups, just as our individual experiences make us as individuals different from one another. That differentness is a right: it makes us who and what we are, and that differentness has a right to be respected and preserved. The differentness of other Americans is recorded and preserved in the art of their group; their children and our children see it, and this fosters identification and a sense of worthwhileness. Our children and we ourselves are entitled to this same identification, respect, and sense of worthwhileness enjoyed by others. The public vehicle for helping to sustain and encourage all of this is the museum. For people alive, developing and contributing today, the foremost vehicle in the world for telling the story of cultural contribution is the Museum of Modern Art.[31]

MoMA had been founded in 1929 as the first museum to begin charting the terrain of modern art, and its authority arose, in part, from its involvement in art movements as they were happening. The museum's founders conceived of a collection that would always remain contemporary by "shedding its skin." After a certain period of time, when specific pieces had gained the stature of "classics," their ownership would be transferred to the Metropolitan Museum of Art.[32] The ambition was to have a collection that was perpetually current, with a "fixed scope but changing contents."[33] This policy would be redacted in 1953, and by the 1960s the commitment to living artists appeared to be waning. The AWC wanted to reinvigorate this mission because they believed the museum had a moral responsibility to support artists, not build a canon of masterworks or stockpile artworks as if financial assets. Hans Haacke pointed out that the sale of even one major artwork by an established master could support the museum's engagement with many living artists.[34]

It is no mistake of grammar that the Museum of Modern Art came to be known as "the Modern Museum." Founding director Alfred Barr's aspiration was not only to exhibit modern art, but to create a modern institution. Its collection was designed to synthesize all the arts, including new forms, such as film, that had not yet been accepted as art. The museum's purview was to include painting, sculpture, prints, drawings, film, design, architecture, theater arts, and dance. (The latter two would ultimately be dropped and photography added.) Barr's frequent research trips to Europe had introduced him to the work of the Bauhaus as early as 1927, and he was impressed by the idea of having all the arts holistically brought together, from furniture and fountain pens to paintings and propaganda posters.[35]

Barr's inaugural exhibition in November 1929, *Cézanne, Gauguin, Seurat, and van Gogh*, featured four artists who were already accepted by the art intelligentsia, including the museum's founders and trustees, but within a few years, Barr had mounted an eclectic range of groundbreaking projects: *Modern Architecture: International Exhibition* (1932); *Persian Fresco Painting* (1932); and *American Folk Art: The Art of the Common Man in America, 1750–1900* (1932–33).[36] Barr cherished both the mainstream of art and the creeks and eddies. He was curious about the unfamiliar and the connections between different forms of human creativity.

In 1934 Barr proclaimed, "The truth is that modern art cannot be defined with any degree of finality either in time or in character and any attempt to do so implies a blind faith, insufficient knowledge, or an academic lack of realism."[37] Nevertheless, there were tendencies in art that attracted Barr more than others, and primary among them was abstraction. "Sometimes in the history of art," he wrote in 1936, "it is possible to describe a period or a generation of artists as having been obsessed with a particular problem."[38] Whereas earlier artists sought verisimilitude to nature, "in the early twentieth century the dominant interest was almost exactly the opposite. . . . By a common and powerful impulse they were driven to abandon the imitation of natural appearance."[39]

Barr's interest in art that rejected verisimilitude led to explorations of what he called "Art of the past which seems 'Modern.'" In a 1933 prospectus for the museum's exhibition program Barr laid out an ambitious global, transhistorical program:

> For the past 500 years Europeans have been more or less retrospective in their appreciation of art, choosing certain phases of past art for special admiration. The last hundred years have seen a great increase in variety, and a great acceleration of change in taste. Artists, collectors, critics have ransacked the past not only of Europe but of the whole world, for styles and forms which are sympathetic to contemporary taste. A lively and conscious interaction has been established between modern art and whatever resembles it in Medieval or Baroque, Egyptian or Cretan, Chinese or Mayan, Benin or Papuan.
>
> It is the function of our Museum to exhibit these discoveries and resurrections of the "Modern" art of the past.[40]

As we shall see, Barr's interest in a holistic, global, transhistorical curatorial program would be funneled into the more narrow concept that came to be called "primitivism."

Barr proposed that the museum have three collections: one consisting of what we now conventionally think of as "modern art," the "advanced" or "difficult" art of the present; and two supplementary educational collections, one containing "fine paintings representing those phases of the older European traditions which seem most significant *at present*" (emphasis original).[41] The other would be composed of "non-European works of art, Coptic textiles, Scythian bronzes, Japanese prints, Chinese painting, and African and pre-Columbian objects" because of their importance to such movements as Post-Impressionism, Cubism, Fauvism, German Expressionism, and other art of the late nineteenth and early twentieth centuries.[42] The intent behind showing these objects was to "destroy and weaken the prejudice of the undereducated against non-naturalistic kinds of art."[43]

Barr would never realize his aspiration to create these supplementary collections, but he worked this concept into a ten-year exhibition program that supplemented presentations of nineteenth- and twentieth-century European art with exhibitions of objects that represented its various influences and parallels from other cultures and times.[44] The museum's earliest foray in this direction was the exhibition *American Sources of Modern Art (Aztec, Mayan, Incan)*, organized in 1933 by Holger Cahill, who would shortly go on to become the national director of the Federal Art Project of the WPA.[45] The show juxtaposed ancient New World sculptures with works by William Zorach, Max Weber, and other contemporary artists in the United States. This show was the first manifestation in the Museum of Modern Art of what Bill Rubin would later, in this 1984 *"Primitivism"* exhibition, call "affinities." Holger explained: "There is no intention here to insist that ancient American art is a major source of modern art. Nor is it intended to suggest that American artists should turn to it as the source of native expression. It is intended, simply, to show the high quality of ancient American art, and to indicate that its influence is present in modern art in the work of painters and sculptors some of whom have been unconscious of its influence, while others have accepted or sought it quite consciously."[46] Subsequent exhibitions in this series included *African Negro Art* (1935); *Prehistoric Rock Pictures in Europe and Africa* (1937); and three shows organized by Barr's successor as the museum's director, René d'Harnoncourt: *Twenty Centuries of Mexican Art* (1940); *Indian Art of the United States* (1941); and *Arts of the South Seas* (1946). These shows would be followed by *Ancient Arts of the Andes* (1954).[47]

The museum's 1935 show *African Negro Art* was perhaps the most influential exhibition in the series. Organized by art historian James Johnson Sweeney, the show featured 603 works of African art from over fifty private collections and fifteen museums around the world. African art had been juxtaposed with modern art on previous occasions, such as in Alfred Stieglitz's 291 Gallery in 1914 and a 1923 show at the Brooklyn Museum. At MoMA, the presentation of African art took on greater weight and authority by virtue of the scale of the exhibition, the stature of its lenders, and the show's ancillary components. Walker Evans was commissioned by art historian Robert Goldwater, who was then a professor at the Institute of Fine Arts at New York University, to photograph all of the objects for the catalogue illustrations as well as a series of posters that traveled to historically black colleges and universities around the country. In all, the project consisted of five components: the exhibition, the catalogue, the portfolio of photographs, the traveling exhibition of selected photographs, and a smaller circulating exhibition of sculptures from the show.[48] Sweeney's press release read: "The art of the primitive negro in its mastery of aesthetic forms, sensitiveness to materials, freedom of naturalistic imitation and boldness of imagination parallels many of the ideals of modern art."[49]

Like Cahill in his assessment of indigenous art of the Americas, Sweeney questioned the existence of direct influential relationships. He wrote in the catalogue introduction:

> Whether or not African Negro art has made any fundamental contribution to the general European tradition through the interest shown in it by artists during the last thirty years is a broadly debatable point. . . . When we occasionally come across something in contemporary work that looks as if it might have grown out of a genuine plastic assimilation of the Negro approach, on closer examination we almost invariably find that it can as fairly be attributed to another influence closer to home. Cézanne's researches in the analysis of form, to take an obvious example, not only laid the foundation for subsequent developments in European art but also played an important part in opening European eyes to the qualities of African art.[50]

Despite the tenuous connection drawn between "modern" and "African" art, the museum consistently framed the latter as ancillary background material. Rubin would echo this sentiment in his text for the "*Primitivism*" show.[51]

African Negro Art was MoMA's prelude to the *Cubism and Abstract Art* show of 1936, one of the exhibitions that would come to define Alfred Barr's career. The exhibition was intrinsically educational in its aspiration to help viewers decipher the language of abstraction. On the jacket cover of the exhibition catalogue Barr showcased what was to become his famous flowchart mapping the many influences that produced modern abstract art (fig. 4.8). Modern movements were indicated in black and influences in red, including "Japanese prints," "Near Eastern Art," "African Negro Sculpture," and "Machine Esthetic."[52]

African Negro Art resonated with African American artists and scholars in New York City. Charles C. Seifert, who ran the Ethiopian School of Research History at 313 West 137th Street, was an educator who had amassed a large library of books on

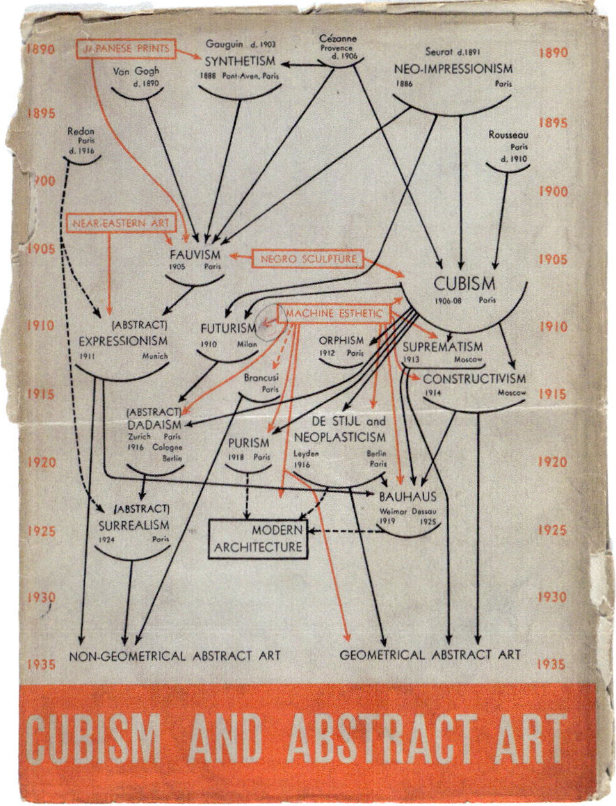

Fig. 4.8 Cover of the exhibition catalogue *Cubism and Abstract Art*, New York, the Museum of Modern Art, 1936. Offset, printed in color, 7¾×10¼ ins. Digital Image © The Museum of Modern Art / Licensed by SCALA / Art Resource, New York.

African and African American history, maps, manuscripts, and a collection of African sculpture and artifacts that he opened to the Harlem community for study.[53] Seifert brought young artists to see the MoMA exhibition, including Jacob Lawrence, who was then eighteen years old, and Romare Bearden, who was twenty-four.[54] A drawing by Norman Lewis from 1935 indicates that he too saw the exhibition or photographs of the objects in it (figs. 4.9 and 4.10).

Alain Locke, who had been writing about the relationship between contemporary African American art and African art for over a decade, also took great interest in the show. He sought and received permission from the museum to photograph the works specifically to illustrate his essay "African Art: Classical Style," published in the *American Magazine of Art* in 1935.[55] In this essay Locke praised the museum for showing "African art in its own context" and proving "the existence of a 'grand style,' with corresponding heroic proportion and simplicity."[56]

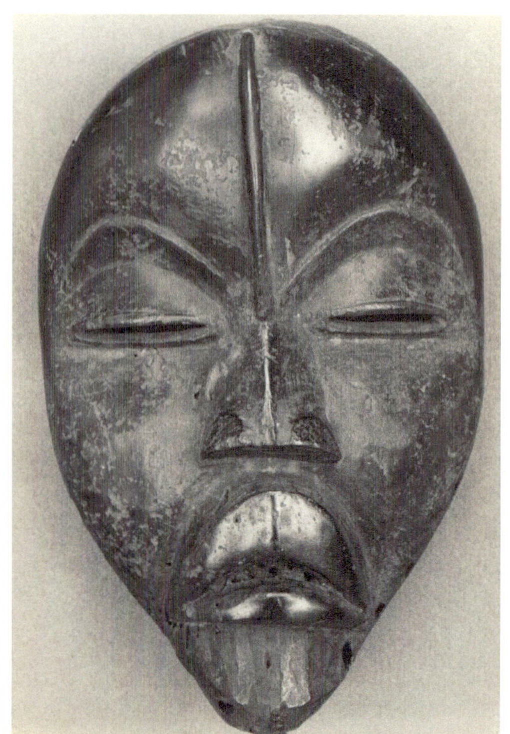

Fig. 4.9 Walker Evans, *Mask*, 1935, gelatin silver print, photograph 9 ½ × 6 ½ ins. The Michael C. Rockefeller Memorial Collection Gift of Robert Goldwater, 1961 and 1962. From a portfolio of photographs based on the exhibition *African Negro Art*, New York, the Museum of Modern Art, 1935. © Walker Evans Archive, The Metropolitan Museum of Art. Image source: Art Resource, New York.

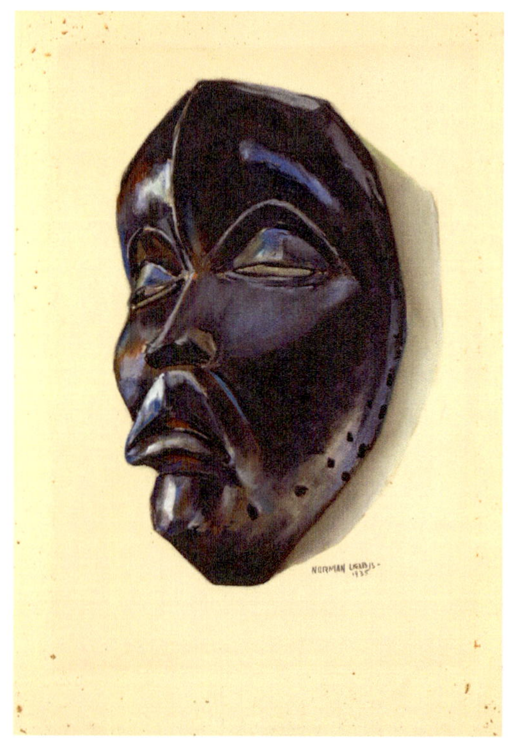

Fig. 4.10 Norman Lewis, *Dan Mask*, 1935, pastel on sandpaper, 18 × 12½ ins. © Estate of Norman Lewis. Courtesy of Michael Rosenfeld Gallery, LLC, New York, NY.

Ten years earlier Locke had been urging African American artists to consider their own relationship to African art: "Since African art has had such a vitalizing influence in modern European painting, sculpture, poetry, and music, it becomes finally a natural and important question as to what artistic and cultural effect it can or will have upon the life of the American Negro."[57]

Locke overcame the fact that African art had been introduced via European art by positing an unconscious, almost biologistic identification for African American artists: "Because of our Europeanized conventions, the key to the proper understanding and appreciation of it [African art] will in all probability first come from an appreciation of its influence upon contemporary French art, but we must believe that there still slumbers in the blood something which once stirred will react with peculiar emotional intensity toward it."[58] In 1927, he claimed a more sociohistorical connection: "In importing African art to America we are bringing over cultural baggage of the American Negro that was crowded out of the slave ship."[59]

The relevance of African art for African Americans was a point of debate between Alain Locke and art historian James Porter. Porter had completed his undergraduate work at Howard University in 1927 and went on to earn his MA in art history in 1937 at New York University's Institute of Fine Arts under the tutelage of art historian Robert Goldwater. Porter's master's thesis on the work of African American artists from 1724 to 1900 would lay the foundation for his book *Modern Negro Art*, published in 1943, which focused on twentieth-century art. In the book Porter discouraged artists from looking to Africa because "the admonition to imitate the ancestral arts could only foster academicism and tended moreover to confuse the special geometric forms of African sculpture with African feeling."[60] The fact that European artists such as Picasso and Brancusi also borrowed formal attributes from African art should have been sufficient, in Porter's view, to demonstrate the fallacy that such borrowing was based on cultural identification. While he admired "the powerful forms and religious message" of some African art, he admonished "any American artist" who would choose to make art that is "unintelligible" through "primitive" allusions.[61]

Porter's disdain for "primitivism" is surprising given that Goldwater, the reigning authority on "primitivism" in modern art, was his thesis adviser at the Institute of Fine Arts. Goldwater's influential book *Primitivism in Modern Painting* (1938) proposed a taxonomy for the study of this subject, positing four categories: romanticization of the exotic; a visual code for expressing emotional content; a source of formal languages; and a sign for a primordial human essence thought to be found in the work of untrained artists and children. Goldwater called this last type "primitivism

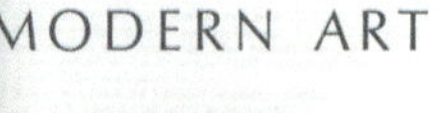
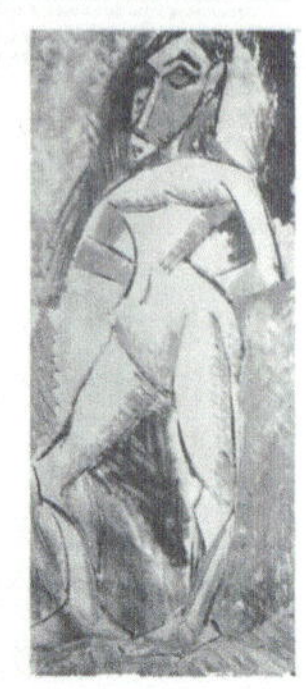
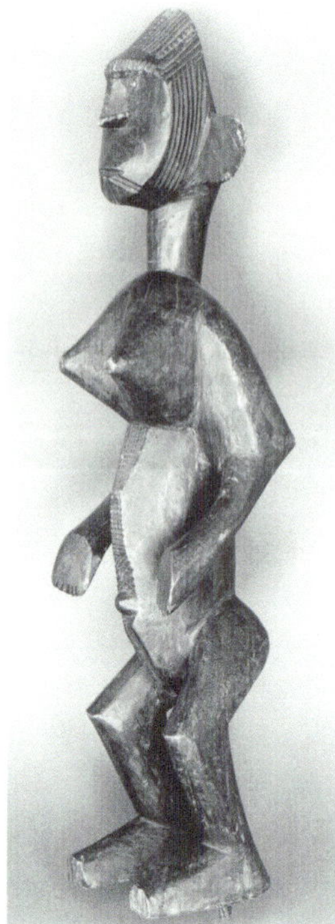

Fig. 4.11 Frontispiece of *Primitivism in Modern Art* by Robert Goldwater, 1967 (revised edition), featuring Walker Evans's photograph of a Senufo figure exhibited in *African Negro Art* at the Museum of Modern Art in 1935, and Pablo Picasso, *Nude (Study for Les Demoiselles d'Avignon)*, 1907.

Fig. 4.12 Walker Evans, *Statuette*, 1935, gelatin silver print, 3⅝ × 1½ ins. New York University, Institute of Fine Arts, Visual Resources Collection. From a portfolio of photographs based on the exhibition *African Negro Art*, New York, the Museum of Modern Art, 1935. © Walker Evans Archive, The Metropolitan Museum of Art. Image source: Art Resource, New York.

of the subconscious."[62] Notably, neither the 1938 edition of *Primitivism in Modern Painting*, which contained two images from Walker Evans's portfolio from *African Negro Art* juxtaposed with works by Picasso, nor the revised and enlarged 1967 edition, *Primitivism in Modern Art*, which promoted one of these comparisons to the frontispiece (figs. 4.11 and 4.12), included any work by African Americans, even though Goldwater was aware of relevant examples, suggesting perhaps that Porter had influenced his teacher. In these discussions we encounter conflicting concepts of primitivism: Locke saw African art as having a direct connection with African American artists, whereas Porter saw primitivism as a European construct.

Like Porter, Romare Bearden eschewed the theory that African American artists should seek connection to African art. In 1942 he wrote to a friend, the artist Walter Quirt, "To try and carry on in America where African sculpture left off would be to start on a false basis—the gap of years, the environment, and ideology, is too great."[63] Bearden saw twentieth-century African American artists as cocontributors to modernism by virtue of their modern subjectivity regardless of their interest in African art.

By the early 1940s, perhaps earlier, Barr had developed some familiarity with African American art through his association with Porter. In the preface to his 1943 book, *Modern Negro Art*, Porter not only thanked Goldwater but also "acknowledge[d] with thanks the many comments and suggestions offered by Mr. Alfred H. Barr, Jr. and Miss Dorothy Miller, of the Museum of Modern Art [Barr's assistant, who later became the museum's first curator], who read with care the galley proofs of this book."[64] Given these associations, which were both personal and professional— Barr and his wife Marga were friends with Goldwater and his wife, the artist Louise Bourgeois—Barr's decision to exclude African American artists' work from his Cubism exhibition is noteworthy and, despite Barr's progressiveness in so many ways, indicates a blind spot in his omnivorous curatorial vision.

Barr continued his program of exhibitions covering "the Primitive arts" with *Prehistoric Rock Pictures in Europe and Africa* (1937), a show that consisted of objects borrowed from the collection of the Institute for the Study of the Morphology of Civilization in Frankfurt directed by anthropologist Dr. Leo Frobenius.[65] The exhibition filled three floors of the museum and featured 150 facsimiles of rock paintings and engravings from "parts of the earth as remote from each other as the North Cape of Norway and the Cape of Good Hope."[66] The facsimiles were painted by expeditions of European artists and were exhibited with photographs showing the actual rocks on which the prehistoric pictures were found. A third component of the exhibition was a series of reproductions of Native American rock paintings in California produced by artists employed in the Federal Art Project.[67] Finally, in keeping with Barr's drive to seek cross-cultural parallels, he installed a selection of paintings described as "bear[ing] a certain similarity to the pictures painted and engraved by prehistoric man."[68] Included in this selection were works by Miró, Arp, Klee, and Masson, among others.

In 1939 Barr acquired Picasso's *Les Desmoiselles d'Avignon* (1906–7) for MoMA, capping his first decade at the museum with a work that seemed to embody his vision of a transhistorical aesthetic. Many art historians have identified the influence of African and Iberian art, repeatedly citing the artist's storied encounter with African art at the Trocadero Museum, which allegedly triggered the completion of the masklike faces on the figures in the painting in 1907. But Suzanne P. Blier has made a compelling argument that Picasso's source material may have included photographs reproduced in a series of volumes published by Carl Heinrich Stratz titled *Die Rassenschönheit des Weibes* (*The Racial Beauty of Woman*) starting in 1901, and Leo Frobenius's 1898 volume on African masks, which featured black-and-white and color illustrations.[69] Frobenius studied the interaction of cultures and wrote about the need to understand cultural interpenetration as a requisite to understanding human history.[70]

Barr's second career-defining exhibition was *Fantastic Art, Dada, Surrealism* (1936), a sweeping survey of 694 objects highlighting similarities between modern art and all manner of bizarre, eccentric, and uncanny images and objects dating from the fifteenth century through the 1930s from a dizzying array of sources. Underlying the exhibition was Goldwater's concept of "primitivism of the subconscious." The show included not only the work of Dali, de Chirico, Ernst, Kandinsky, Klee, Picasso, and other twentieth-century artists, but also Hieronymus Bosch's grotesque landscapes; Giuseppe Arcimboldo's heads depicted as composites of fruits and vegetables; and William Blake's visionary dreamscapes. There were objects from popular culture, such as a Walt Disney drawing of a wolf inside an elaborate torture chamber; children's drawings; art of the "insane"; folk art; commercial art; and "miscellaneous objects and pictures with a Surrealistic character" that included a "spoon found in a condemned man's cell" that had been severed into four parts, turning it into a functionless collection of abstract forms. The show also featured a section on architecture and a film series. With breathtaking diversity the exhibition contextualized Dada and Surrealism within a world of fantastical imagery, both high art and vernacular culture.[71]

Many other MoMA shows explored a diverse array of "primitive" tendencies in contemporary art in such projects as *Children's Work* (1938); *Masters of Popular Painting: Modern Primitives of Europe and America* (1938); *American Folk Art* (1938); and *Modern Primitives: Artists of the People* (1941).[72] The press release for the *Modern Primitives* exhibition captured Barr's humanistic vision:

> 20th century primitives belong to no movement or "ism." They work in no tradition either technical or esthetic. All of them earn or earned their living as ordinary men, pjstmen [*sic*], milkmen, house painters, circus performers, customs officials, fishermen, farmers, printers, ditch diggers or mill hands. Yet they are not ordinary men, for they love painting and taught themselves to paint with little or no instruction without the fellowship of other artists, often without even the sympathy of their friends. . . .
>
> The Modern Primitives, though each developed in personal isolation, seem international in character even more than their professionally trained

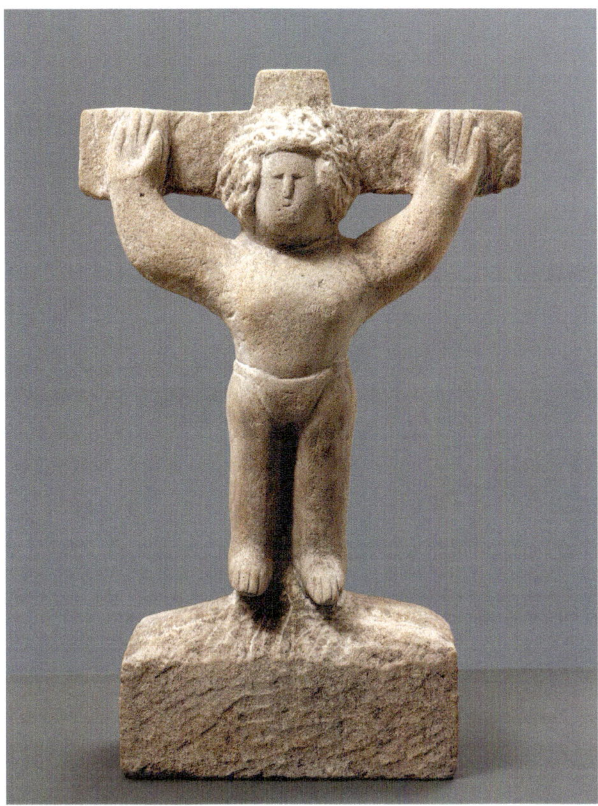

Fig. 4.13 *Crucifix of Carved Stone*, attributed to William Edmondson, Nashville, TN, probably 1932–37, limestone. Image courtesy the Colonial Williamsburg Foundation. Museum Purchase.

colleagues. It is hard to tell a French primitive from an American. All share the common denominator of Western culture at its most democratic level and all express the straightforward, innocent and convincing vision of the common man, ignorant of art or unaffected by it.[73]

This inquisitive and populist mindset led Barr to the work of William Edmondson, the first African American to be shown at the museum. The show, *Sculpture by William Edmondson*, was held in 1937 as part of this series on modern primitives.[74] Clearly Edmondson's art (fig. 4.13) resembled the chunky, simple yet monumental feel of Brancusi's work, but Edmondson was not a member of the museum's inner circle. Rather, his description in the museum's press release for the show states he had "no art training and very little education, and has probably never seen a piece of sculpture except his own. He works at his home in the Negro section of Nashville where his yard is littered with uncut tombstones."[75] Bridget Cooks has criticized the museum's characterization of Edmondson, noting that "the release seems more like an argument against the exhibition than a promotional text for it."[76] Yet condescending undertones are difficult to ascribe to racial motivations, since Edmondson's exhibition was part of the larger project of showcasing a wide array of "modern primitives," all of whom were described as being outside the institutional and social world of what was in the process of being defined as modern art. Indeed, the category of the "primitive"—in all its various forms—was a productive concept for the discourse of modernism because it was associated with the breakdown of representation.

In the 1940s MoMA began to engage with African American artists who fit more snugly into the world of high art. The museum held a series of exhibitions by trained African American artists, perhaps influenced by Barr's exposure to Porter's groundbreaking book, or as a result of the higher visibility of African American artists and increased opportunities made available through the WPA arts projects. Perhaps Barr was spurred on by an African American art show at the Baltimore Museum of Art in 1939, and he may have been inspired by the annual exhibitions of work by African American artists initiated by Hale Woodruff at Atlanta University in 1942. Barr was probably aware of Woodruff's work, since Abby Aldrich Rockefeller had bought watercolors by Woodruff in 1929 from Edith Halpert's Downtown Gallery.[77]

Whatever the impetus, in 1942 the museum made its first acquisition of a work by an African American artist, Jacob Lawrence's *Migration of the Negro* series (1940–41). The work had been shown at the Downtown Gallery in 1941 in conjunction with a group exhibition of African American art put together with the help of Alain Locke.[78] The exhibition received rave reviews, and Lawrence's acceptance by the art world and the public was confirmed when twenty-six of the panels were reproduced in *Fortune* magazine in November 1941.[79] *Migration of the Negro* was sought after by two museums, MoMA and the Phillips Collection in Washington. Lawrence had intended for the sixty panels to remain intact, but he agreed to divide the work between two museums, with the even numbers going to MoMA and the odd numbers to the Phillips Collection in order to preserve the narrative structure in each part. Despite his disdain for primitivism in the work of other African American artists, James Porter described Lawrence as "promising" in *Modern Negro Art*. In Lawrence, Porter saw not an artist reaching back to Africa, but someone searching for a language embodying a universal humanism.[80]

After its acquisition, the *Migration* series was sent in its entirety on a national tour that culminated with a showing at MoMA from October 10 to November 5,

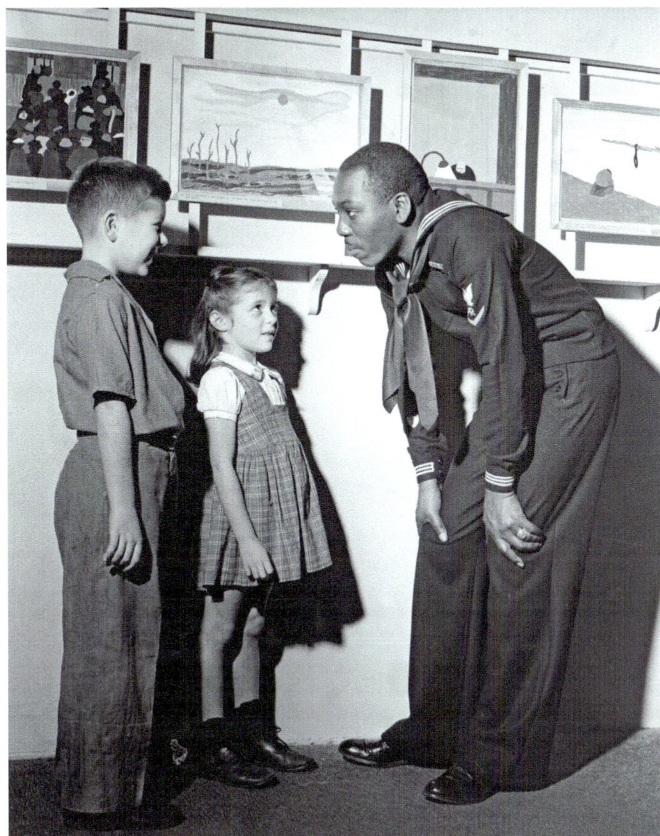

1944. In the interim, on October 20, 1943, Lawrence was drafted into the U.S. Coast Guard. When the piece was finally shown at MoMA, it was accompanied by eight sketches created by the artist while in the service (fig. 4.14).

The museum's inexperience with African American art is evident in the racially charged use of language in some of the texts accompanying the Lawrence show. The exhibition press release, for example, originally read: "Jacob A. Lawrence, Steward's mate, First Class, USCGR, has painted at least 17 sketches of life aboard ship while on duty with the USS Sea Cloud. The eight shown here reflect the sincerity and sensibilities common to his race." Before the release went out, Lawrence's rank was corrected to "Specialist Third Class," and the description of his work was changed to read: "The eight [sketches] shown here record, in his strong original style, typical Coast Guard Activities."[81]

When the work was shown at MoMA, the reviews were generally positive and demonstrated a breadth of responses. In her review in the *New York World-Telegram and Sun*, Emily Genauer admired its formal qualities, particularly its "deftly handled spatial design and constructively used color" and "tonal subtlety."[82] Elizabeth Catlett, writing in the *People's Voice*, highlighted the social content: "One cannot look at these seemingly simple portraits of the startling lack of the bare necessities of life, the frustration and complexities of daily struggle, and the determined mass movement towards democratic equality, of these Negroes without a decided self-examination."[83]

In 1943 MoMA exhibited the work of other African Americans, college students from the Hampton Institute in Virginia, one of the oldest schools dedicated to the education of African Americans and Native Americans.[84] The seven men and one woman featured in the show were current and former students of Viktor Lowenfeld, an art educator who had been living in Vienna and fled the Nazis to come to the United States in 1938. The artists included Annabelle Baker, John Bean, John Thomas Biggers, Joseph Mack, Alfred James Martin, Junius Redwood, George Spencer, and Frank Steward. The show was not given center stage; it was held in the Young People's Gallery rather than in the main galleries. But the museum did acquire one piece from the exhibition, a drawing by Junius Redwood.[85] The acquisition was celebrated in an article in the *Bainbridge Mainsheet*, the paper of the U.S. Naval Training Station in Bainbridge, Maryland. The writer proclaimed, "To an artist that's the same as hitting a home run with bases loaded during a World Series."[86] Unmentioned in the museum's exhibition materials, or in the press, was that Elizabeth Catlett and Charles White were also teaching at the Hampton Institute at the time. White had been commissioned to paint a mural depicting historic African American leaders, and both artists lived in Virginia and worked for Lowenfeld while White executed the work.[87] The artists traveled to New York City for the opening and met with Alfred Barr (fig. 4.15). MoMA would acquire its first pieces by White in 1970, two prints from the *Wanted Poster Series*; not until 1988 would the museum obtain a piece by Catlett, also a print, *Malcolm X Speaks for Us*.

In December 1942 Barr's far-reaching aesthetic interests led him to display a shoeshine stand designed by Joe Milone, which he compared to "a lavish wedding cake, a baroque shrine, or a super-juke box."[88] Trustee Stephen Clark, who was then both president and chairman of the board, was a man of conservative tastes who enjoyed the pleasantness of Matisse but thought Barr's openness and inclusivity was, according to art historian Russell Lynes, "a felonious assault on taste and on the dignity of the Museum."[89] Clark rallied the board against Barr, ultimately

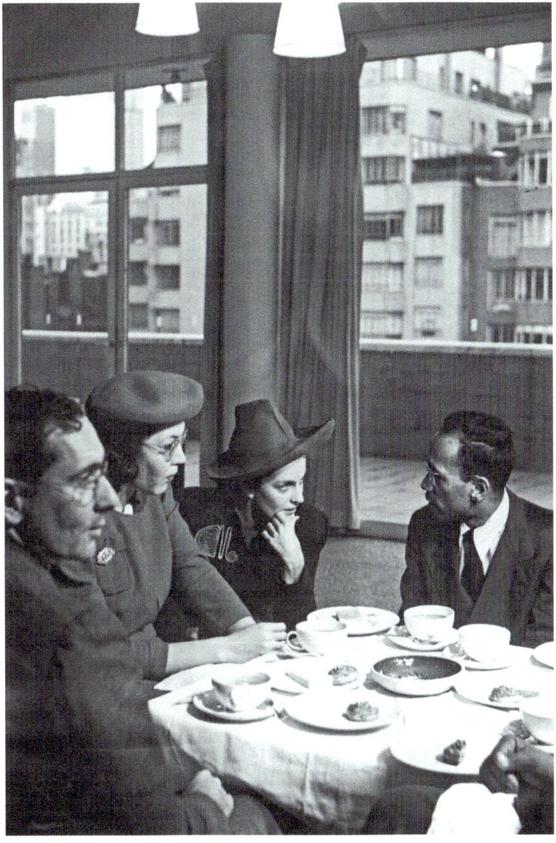

Fig. 4.15 Left to right: Alfred H. Barr Jr., Elizabeth Catlett, Dorothy Miller, and Charles White, at the private tea that opened the exhibition *Young Negro Art* (work of the students at Hampton Institute), October 26–November 28, 1943, at the Museum of Modern Art, New York. Digital Image © The Museum of Modern Art / Licensed by SCALA / Art Resource, New York.

succeeding in removing him as director in 1943. Eventually Barr settled into the role of curator of the museum collections, a painful demotion, but one in which he could take solace knowing that he was "writing" the history of modern art through his acquisitions for the museum. With Barr's removal as director, MoMA's involvement with African American art tapered off.

In the 1940s the trustees turned their attention to the war effort and to Latin America, using the museum as a cultural ambassador and propaganda arm for the U.S. government. From 1940 to 1946 Nelson Rockefeller ran the federal government's Office of Inter-American Affairs, which had been created to check the growing influence of the Nazis in Latin America and promote support for the economic and political aims of the United States.[90] In an amazing spurt of activity MoMA held nine shows of Latin American art between 1940 and 1944, kicked off with a festival of Brazilian music and the monumental exhibition *Twenty Centuries of Mexican Art* (1940). In all, there were three shows of Brazilian art and architecture, one exhibition of Cuban paintings, one exhibition of Mexican costumes by Carlos Merida, a show of Latin American works from the museum's own collection, and the acquisition and display of the *May-Day Sketchbook* of Diego Rivera. Rockefeller also enlisted MoMA's Circulating Exhibitions Department to send exhibitions of American art to Latin America.[91]

René d'Harnoncourt was a key member of Rockefeller's team both in the Office of Inter-American Affairs and later at MoMA. In 1943 he was asked to become acting director of art projects in Rockefeller's office. The following year he joined the staff of the Museum of Modern Art as vice president in charge of foreign activities and director of the Department of Manual Industries (later called "Design").[92] In 1949 he was appointed as MoMA's second director.[93]

The end of Barr's leadership at MoMA brought the end of his dream of building parallel collections of modern art and "art of the past which seems modern." D'Harnoncourt would organize two more shows as part of the program of "primitive" art, *Art of the South Seas* (1946) and *Ancient Art of the Andes* (1954). But d'Harnoncourt would also institutionalize physically and discursively the separation of "modern" and "primitive" by helping Rockefeller create the Museum of Primitive Art in 1957 to house his collection of African and Oceanic art, with Robert Goldwater as its director.[94] Located on Fifty-Fourth Street, the Rockefeller collection remained in dialogue with the program at MoMA, but the conversation would be short-lived. In 1969 Rockefeller donated the entire collection to the Metropolitan Museum of Art and helped raise funds for a new wing to house the works, the Michael C. Rockefeller Wing. This was undertaken as part of the Met's Master Plan.

During d'Harnoncourt's tenure many of the museum's other early experiments would end. In 1953 the board of trustees voided an agreement that had been established with the Metropolitan Museum of Art to deaccession works older than fifty years, and MoMA became a collecting museum and in many ways a period museum: as MoMA curator Kirk Varnedoe has written, the museum "froze" the concept of modernism.[95]

Several shows of the 1950s featured work from Japan, implicitly touching on the theme of reconciliation after World War II, including *Japanese Household Objects* (1951), *Japanese Pottery* (1954), *Japanese Exhibition House* (1954–55), and *Japanese Calligraphy* (1954). These exhibitions implicitly treated the museum as a cultural meeting ground encouraging contact with a former enemy. The concept of global unity after the war was also expressed in *The Family of Man* (1955), which presented photographs of rituals and social practices from around the world.

Despite its international scope, the museum's record of working with African American artists and other artists of color in the United States was slim. None of its group exhibitions of American art organized between 1929 and 1963, neither those that traveled nor those held at the museum, included a single African American, except for two works: one by William Edmondson in the show *American Art 1609–1938* organized to travel to the Jeu de Paume in Paris in 1938, and one by Philadelphia portrait painter Samuel Brown lent by the WPA Art Program for a 1940 series of traveling exhibitions of American art organized by the Circulating Exhibitions Department.[96] No African Americans were included among the 113 artists featured in the exhibition *Modern Art in the United States* (1956), composed of works from MoMA's collection.[97]

Barr's new role as curator of the museum's collection enabled him to continue to play a vital role in the museum's acquisitions throughout the 1950s and '60s, both behind the scenes by lobbying key staff and trustees and in the field. His research files show that he followed new developments in art, including the increasingly visible public presence of African and African American art.[98] In 1964 he was asked to join the board of consultants for the Center for Cross-Cultural Communication, which would later become the National Museum of African Art. The project was designed to strengthen relations between Africans and Americans and between African Americans and whites. The director, Warren M. Robbins, wrote to Barr: "Under political impetus, international and domestic racial barriers are breaking down with progressively increasing speed. The need, consequently, becomes immediate in the United States for an understanding of the Negro's roots and for the gradual diffusion of historically accurate and honest information regarding his antecedent culture."[99] Barr wrote back to say that he "very much approves" of the center and offered to lend his name to the list of advisers, but he did not have the time to be a working member.

Through his role in acquiring individual works of art for the museum, Barr would continue to manifest an ecumenical approach to modernism. In 1962 he acquired *Archeological Find, 3* (1961) by Raphael Montañez Ortiz (fig. 4.16). Like Barr, Ortiz was a curatorial omnivore with an interest in both folk traditions and high art, as Ortiz would later demonstrate in his program for El Museo del Barrio, which emphasized a wide range of Puerto Rican traditions in music, theater, dance, painting, and popular arts and handcrafts.[100]

At the time they met, Ortiz was associated with the neo-Dadaist "Destructionists," and his work may have appealed to Barr because it evoked the visceral, emotional, and antirational qualities of Dada and Surrealism. While in art school at the Pratt Institute in the early 1950s Ortiz had experimented with creating works made

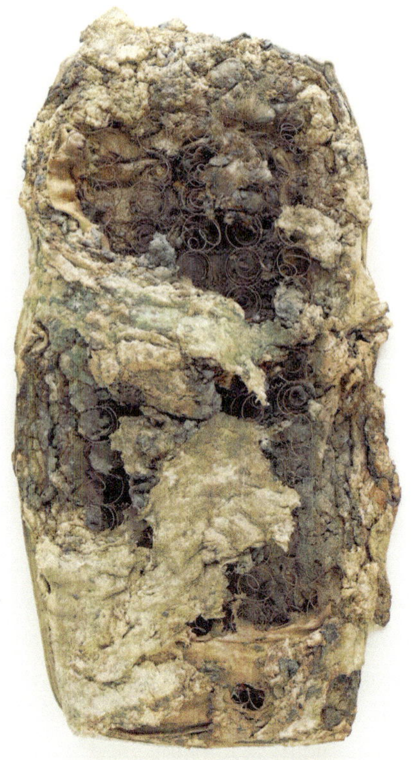

by processes of burning found objects. He would find pieces of discarded furniture, wrap them in chicken wire, and set them on fire. He began experimenting with peyote and looking into Celtic and druid rituals. He was trying to understand the Dada aesthetic, which had appropriated aboriginal aesthetics.[101]

For Ortiz, turning to ritual was not the same as the "primitivist" romanticization of the "native." Instead, by "examining the aboriginal culture, trying to move beyond the Eurocentric focus, even of Dada . . . I wanted to go to the source. I wasn't interested in Modernism as an aesthetic as such, but where Modernism came from. Where did it appropriate from?"[102] More pointedly, "I saw all Modernism as essentially Eurocentrism's struggle to recapture its indigenousness."[103] Ortiz was a member of the postwar avant-garde who combined a neo-Dada aesthetic of transgression with a resistance to institutional modernism from a postcolonial perspective.

Despite Barr's efforts to keep the museum current and engaged with new art and artists, MoMA was in the process of consolidating and institutionalizing a narrow view of modernism. By the late 1960s, the museum was reprising its own past discoveries and the history of its own innovations. In 1967 alone, MoMA held three Picasso exhibitions.[104] Artists, staff members, and even trustees felt the museum was stuck in a rut and challenged the need for yet another exhibition of work by an artist who had been championed by the museum decades earlier. Longtime trustee Beth Straus said, "The Museum is imitating itself."[105] Russell Lynes, in his 1973 history of the museum, wrote: "[MoMA] had taken to collecting its own past; it was reviving its own revivals. It was rediscovering its discoveries—Art Nouveau, Dada and Surrealism; good old reliable in retrospect—Picasso, Matisse, Calder, even Walker Evans for the third time; good old movies and good old architecture—Mies van der Rohe, Le Corbusier, Frank Lloyd Wright."[106]

Hans Haacke said, "The 'masterwork' approach," set in motion when the museum instituted a permanent collection, "has resulted in timidity, conservatism, arrogance and a systematic mythologyzation [*sic*] of modern art."[107] Activist Alex Gross wrote that the museum "might eke out the rest of the century as a hobbling old crone, its image of yore never to be recaptured."[108] Even the museum's exhibition design, which seemed fresh and new in the museum's early years, was criticized in the late 1960s: "The very arrangement of sleek white partitions and walls, which not long ago seemed the ultimate definition of tasteful austerity and quiet with-it-ness, now looks monotonous and institutional, unimaginative and pedantic."[109] Just at the point in global history when independence movements were fracturing European cultural hegemony, MoMA was solidifying the European canon of nineteenth- and twentieth-century art.

There were some cross-currents in the museum's program, modest projects that engaged current civic issues. Arthur Drexler, director of the museum's Department of Architecture, mounted *The New City: Architecture and Urban Renewal*, an exhibition held in 1967 in which the museum commissioned four teams of architects to devise solutions to issues such as "How can new housing be built without the jarring social effects of relocation?" and "How can a monotonous grid plan be modified to improve circulation and create new neighborhoods?"[110] Moreover, some members of the Junior Council got involved in setting up the Studio Museum in Harlem and the Children's Art Carnival, an educational program started by MoMA educator Victor D'Amico that moved to Harlem in 1969 under the directorship of Betty Blayton. But the overwhelming majority of activities, for the first time in the history of the museum, now centered on constructing a master narrative of modernism. When d'Harnoncourt made his last staff appointment before retiring from the museum in 1967, he set this process in motion: he hired William S. Rubin as curator of painting and sculpture.[111]

A professor of art history at Sarah Lawrence College, Rubin had gotten involved with the museum in 1966 as guest curator of the exhibition *Dada, Surrealism, and Their Heritage*, which opened in March 1968. Whereas Barr's 1936 show, *Fantastic Art, Dada, Surrealism*, had presented works made just a year or two earlier, Rubin's show was primarily historical.[112] And whereas Barr's show had juxtaposed a disparate array of objects and images, Rubin's featured strictly high art. And, finally, while Barr's show had embodied the playful spirit of Dada and Surrealism, Rubin's show vapidly analyzed iconographic and formal influences.[113]

Dada, Surrealism and Their Heritage became a target for artists who objected to the "museumification" of this once radical work, anticipating the performative protests of the Guerrilla Art Action Group (GAAG), which would begin the following year. Gene Swenson, a critic who had been guest curator of a show at MoMA in 1966, *The Other Tradition*, but subsequently had a falling-out with the museum, took out a series of ads in the *Village Voice* that read, "Dedicated to the lost but not forgotten spirit of Dada and Surrealism."[114] As Scott Rothkopf has written, "Rather than applaud his beloved Surrealism's ascent into the ivory tower, Swenson railed against the museum alongside other critics . . . who lamented the art's symbolic castration at the hands of a formalist curator more concerned with his subject's stylistic taxonomy than its seditious sex appeal."[115] Swenson invited anyone who wished to gather outside what he referred to as the "Mausoleum of Modern Art" on the night of the opening, March 25, 1968. Hundreds of protestors showed up, including art critics Gregory Battcock and John Perrault.

Inside the museum, Jon Hendricks and Raphael Ortiz staged a protest of their own. Hendricks had obtained an invitation to the private opening by calling the museum and presenting himself as director of a gallery that represented an artist in MoMA's exhibition. This was almost true; the Judson Memorial Church had been the site of Claes Oldenburg's performance *The Street* in 1960 four years before Hendricks arrived there.[116] The ruse worked and Hendricks received an invitation for two. While Swenson's protest proceeded outside, Hendricks and Ortiz smuggled live chickens into the building, putting them inside the sleeves of their overcoats and carrying their coats swung over their arms. They found the exhibition galleries containing Duchamp's work, then waited, expecting the artist to make an appearance, at which point they planned to release the chickens.

Duchamp never arrived, and Hendricks recalls: "Finally we said, look he's not going to show, and so we . . . let go of the feet of the chickens, who were upside down, and they slid down the sleeves of the jackets and landed on the floor, and we kept walking. We didn't turn around so we didn't know if anything was happening and immediately the chickens squatted and shat right there—this was in Duchamp's room. So, that was good."[117]

An article in the *New York Times* the next day reported that three hundred "hippies" had protested at the Dada preview.[118] The article also revealed that Duchamp had spent the evening in the museum's sixth-floor penthouse drinking and dining. According to the article, the menu was, uncannily, "chicken à la Ritz."

Succeeding René d'Harnoncourt as director was Bates Lowry, an art historian and chairman of the art history department at Brown University in Providence, Rhode Island. Lowry was appointed in May 1967 and arrived at MoMA on a full-time basis a year later. In 1967 and 1968 several long-serving staff members retired.[119] These changes alone would have been a monumental transition, but added to this was d'Harnoncourt's sudden death: six weeks after Lowry took over the directorship, d'Harnoncourt was killed in a car accident.

Between the time Lowry was appointed director in spring 1967 and his full transition in the summer of 1968, the political climate in the United States had become much more polarized. Racial conflict exploded in on ongoing torrent of violent confrontations in the summer of 1967. Martin Luther King Jr. had been assassinated on April 4, 1968, and Robert Kennedy had been killed on June 5. The world that existed when Bates Lowry accepted the position of director in 1967 was gone.[120]

The fall of 1968 was a season of art protests for which Lowry was unprepared. On November 17, 1968, artists protested against the exclusion of African Americans from the Whitney Museum's 1930's: *Painting and Sculpture in America* show organized by Bill Agee. (Agee had left the Whitney just before the show opened and was now working at MoMA.) Five days after this, on November 22, the Harlem Cultural Council withdrew its support for the Met's *Harlem on My Mind* exhibition. On the same day, Charles Inniss resigned as director of the Studio Museum in Harlem in the face of calls for local control. In fall 1968 MoMA would also get its first taste of African American artists' power.

In September 1968 Carroll Janis, son of the art dealer Sidney Janis, approached the museum about hosting a gathering of poets and writers for an evening of programming commemorating Martin Luther King Jr. The program took place on Sunday, November 3, and featured James Baldwin, Allen Ginsberg, Ralph Ellison, and Robert Penn Warren. Accompanying the event was a benefit exhibition, the proceeds of which would be donated to the Southern Christian Leadership Conference.[121] The original jury for this exhibition was composed of Bill Rubin from MoMA; Edward Fry, associate curator at the Guggenheim Museum; Henry Geldzahler, curator of contemporary art at the Metropolitan Museum of Art; and John Gordon, curator at the Whitney. Though the event was intended to support civil rights, the organizers neglected to involve a single African American as juror or artist, stunning the community of artists who were working toward integration. Once this incongruity was pointed out, the exhibition's jury was expanded to include Henri Ghent, director of the Community Gallery at the Brooklyn Museum and a leader in the BECC; Carroll Greene Jr., curator of the Afro-American Art Collection at the Frederick Douglass Institute in Washington, DC; Charles Inniss, director of the Studio Museum in Harlem; and Ed Taylor, executive director of the Harlem Cultural Council. These individuals were listed as consultants to the project.

Ghent, Greene, Inniss, and Taylor expanded the artists list by adding Charles Alston, Benny Andrews, Romare Bearden, Peter Bradley, Vivian Browne, Beauford Delaney, Sam Gilliam, Felrath Hines, Richard Hunt, Daniel LaRue Johnson, Jacob Lawrence, Norman Lewis, Tom Lloyd, William Majors, Richard Mayhew, Faith Ringgold, Betye Saar, Raymond Saunders, Thomas Sills, Hughie Lee-Smith, Bob Thompson, Charles White, Jack White, and Jack Whitten. Ultimately, twenty-four of the show's eighty-one artists were African American, and the exhibition provided a rare opportunity to see the work of African American artists alongside that of their peers. But photo-documentation of the installation indicates that most of the African American artists were clustered in a single room (fig. 4.17). A few appear to have been shown in galleries with both African American and white artists, including Betye Saar, whose assemblage *Black Phrenology Man* (1966) was placed near works by Joseph Cornell, Saul Steinberg, and Fairfield Porter (fig. 4.18). Daniel LaRue Johnson and Bearden were placed in proximity to Claes Oldenburg and H. C. Westermann (fig. 4.19).[122] But the episode reveals a conflict between the

Fig. 4.17 Installation view of the benefit exhibition *In Honor of Martin Luther King, Jr.* at the Museum of Modern Art, New York, October 31–November 3, 1968. From left to right: Jacob Lawrence, *Builders #1* (1968), gouache, $2,700; Benny Andrews, *A Soul* (1968), oil and collage on canvas, $2,600; Vivian Browne, *Two Men* (1968), etching and aquatint, $85; Charles White, *Birmingham Totem* (1966), Chinese ink painting, $2,200; Hughie Lee-Smith, *Man in a Boat* (1967), oil on canvas, $1,200; Richard Hunt, *Natural Form* (1968), welded steel, $1,800; Jack Whitten, *Painting for Martin Luther King, Jr.* (1968), oil on canvas, $1,500. Photographer: James Matthews. Digital Image © The Museum of Modern Art / Licensed by SCALA / Art Resource, New York.

Fig. 4.18 Installation view of the benefit exhibition *In Honor of Martin Luther King, Jr.* at the Museum of Modern Art, New York, October 31–November 3, 1968. From left to right: Saul Steinberg, *Inventory* (1967), mixed media, $2,500; (top) Betye Saar, *Black Phrenology Man* (1966), etching and assemblage, $500; Joseph Cornell, *Time Transfixed* (ca. 1964), collage, $1,500; Fairfield Porter, *Queen Anne's Lace-Evening* (1961), oil on canvas, $900. Photographer: James Matthews. Digital Image © The Museum of Modern Art / Licensed by SCALA / Art Resource, New York.

Fig. 4.19 Installation view of the benefit exhibition *In Honor of Martin Luther King, Jr.* at the Museum of Modern Art, New York, October 31–November 3, 1968. From left to right: Daniel LaRue Johnson, *Homage to Rene d'Harnoncourt* (1968), painted wood, $6,000; Charles Hinman, *Katydid* (1967), acrylic/shaped canvas, price unknown; Claes Oldenburg, *Model-Colossal Monument and Drain* (1967), wood/Liquitex, $6,500; H. C. Westermann, *A Human Condition* (1964), pine, $3,000; Romare Bearden, *Soul Three* (1968), $2,500; Tom Wesselmann, *Great American Nude #97* (1968), NFS; Andy Warhol, *Marilyn Monroe* (n.d.), four silkscreens, $200 each. Photographer: James Matthews. Digital Image © The Museum of Modern Art / Licensed by SCALA / Art Resource, New York.

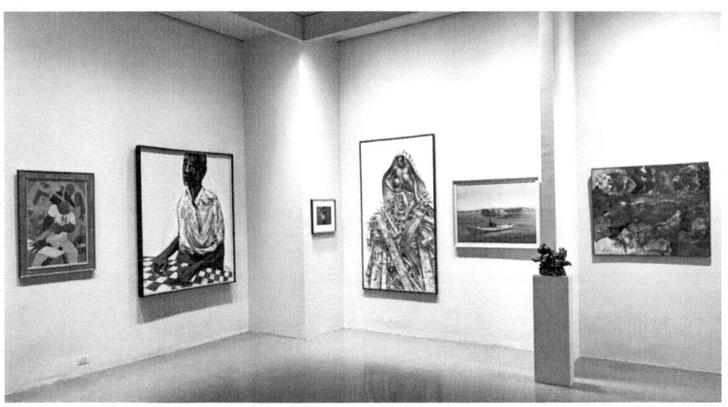

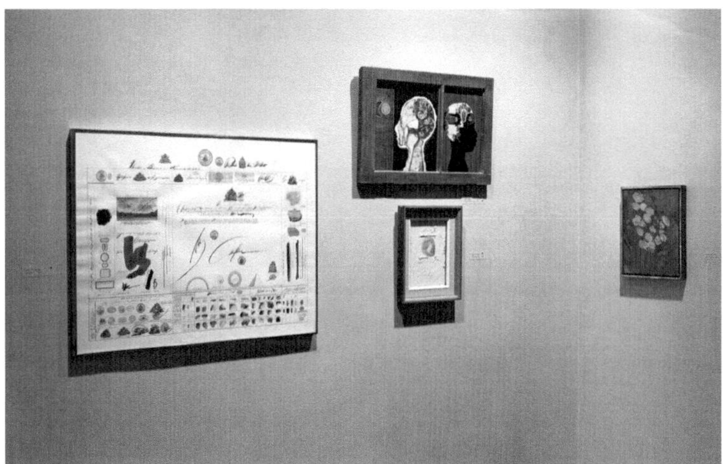

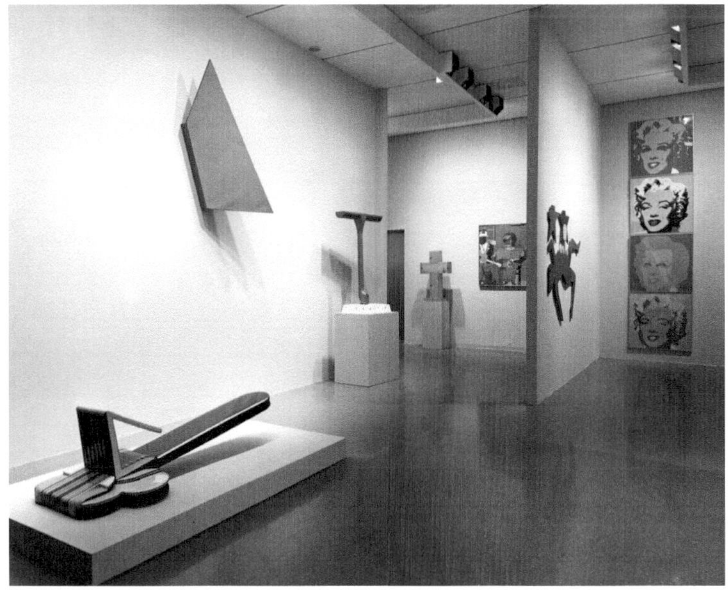

liberal intention to declare solidarity with the civil rights movement and a lack of awareness of what this might entail.

Two months later Lowry experienced what is widely considered to be the founding event of the Art Workers' Coalition, the removal by the artist Takis (Takis Vassilakis) of his work from the exhibition *The Work of Art in the Mechanical Age* on January 3, 1969. The artist removed the work *Tele-sculpture* (1966) to protest the curatorial decision to include the piece over his personal objections.

Immediately after the January 3 action, the artists demanded a meeting with Lowry to discuss the relationship of artists to the museum. The director agreed, but when the AWC sent a list of twelve artists who planned to attend, Lowry complained that that would be too many people for a discussion, and limited the number to six. Twelve showed up on the appointed day, January 24, 1969, and were turned away. The meeting was rescheduled for January 28. This time seven artists arrived, including Tom Lloyd, who was not on the original list but had joined the ranks of Gregory Battcock, Hans Haacke, John Perreault, Willoughby Sharp, Takis, and Wen-Ying Tsai. Bates agreed to receive them.[123] Representing the museum, in addition to Lowry, were curatorial staff members Arthur Drexler, Wilder Green, Bill Lieberman, and John Szarkowski, and public relations director Liz Shaw. The full arc of the AWC's negotiations with MoMA would proceed over a three-year period in three phases, the first with Bates Lowry as director, the second with an interregnum leadership committee, and the third with director John Hightower.

The first iterations of the AWC demands had not included any antiracist agenda items. The artists' primary demand was a public hearing on the general topic "The Museum's Relationship to Artists and to Society."[124] But at the January 28 meeting with Lowry, after Lloyd had joined the group, the thirteen demands included "a section of the Museum, under the direction of black artists . . . devoted to showing the accomplishments of black artists" and that "the Museum's activities should be extended into the Black, Spanish and other communities. It should also encourage exhibits with which these groups can identify."[125]

Over the next few weeks, communication between Lowry and the artists would become a game of one-upmanship in which the artists would give the director ultimatums and deadlines, and he would come back with bureaucratic stalling tactics. For example, Lowry tried to dodge the artists' demand for a public hearing by telling them that he was setting up a "Special Committee on Artist Relations" to study the issues.[126] The artists were not swayed by this gesture, which would prove to be empty, and ramped up their activities with guerilla actions and protests. On March 22 the artists held a "preview demonstration" in which fake free passes were distributed to visitors; if the museum refused to agree to their demand for free admission, the artists would take matters into their own hands.

On March 30, 1969, they staged a demonstration in which three hundred people gathered in the Sculpture Garden to protest and proclaim the inadequacy of the museum's representation of African American artists. On that day, Lowry was prepared. He had had his staff produce a four-page handout to distribute to visitors, again invoking the special committee. It began: "I hope that your visit today will not be inconvenienced by the artists' demonstration about the Museum's policies and programs. For some time we have been discussing the relationship of museums and artist and the responsibilities of the museum to the community and society. To continue these on a broader basis we will announce very shortly the composition of a Special Committee made up of people who are independent of the Museum."

The flyer went on in the form of a Q&A, asking and answering a series of questions that culminated with pointed rebuttals to issues raised by the AWC:

IN SELECTING WORKS OF ART FOR INCLUSION IN AN EXHIBITION OR THE COLLECTION DOES THE MUSEUM CONSIDER THE SEX, NATIONALITY, RELIGION, POLITICS, RACE OF AN ARTIST?

No.

WHAT CRITERIA DOES THE MUSEUM APPLY?

Quality; historical significance; significance of the moment.[127]

"Quality" and "significance": the museum employed the terms as if their meaning were self-evident, as if the social and political pressures raging throughout American culture about structural inequality had no relation to the museum's role. The claim of "historical significance" and most especially "significance of the moment" may have reflected MoMA's limited sense of its own institutional identity as a museum with a newly articulated dual mission—collecting and exhibiting—but this characterization demonstrated a pronounced insularity and blindness to the changing social and political order going on *outside* the museum.

Not to be stopped by Lowry's resistance, the AWC held their own Open Hearing at the School of Visual Arts on April 10, attended by about 250 artists, writers, and other "art workers." The hearing touched on many issues, but the wing for African American and Puerto Rican artists turned out to be the most contentious. Grace Glueck reported in the *New York Times* that one speaker denounced the idea of a "darkies wing" and mocked the concept of cultural specificity itself: "How about a wing for women? WASPs over 30? Jewish Heterosexual Magic Realists?"[128] Although just one of the AWC's demands at the time and, in fact, not the most important to some members, the demand for racial inclusion emerged as the most controversial.[129]

Within a few days, Faith Ringgold and Tom Lloyd took off their boxing gloves. They asserted that a section of the museum under the control of African American and Puerto Rican leaders would be called the Martin Luther King, Jr. Wing for Black and Puerto Rican art. (The name was later expanded to the Martin Luther King, Jr.– Pedro Albizu Campos Center. Campos was a champion of Puerto Rican independence who spent much of his life imprisoned for subversive activities and had died in 1965.) Ringgold and Lloyd planned a community meeting in which two hundred African American and Puerto Rican students were invited to assemble in the museum's auditorium on Sunday, April 13, to discuss the museum's "obligation to portray the cultural contributions of black and Puerto Rican artists." A flyer announcing the event called the absence of African Americans and Puerto Ricans "cultural genocide" and went on to say, "The Museum maintains wings for the exhibition of Dutch, Russian, Italian, Austro-Germanic, and other ethnic and national cultural contributions," referring to the organization of works in the museum's galleries according to movements: *Russian* Constructivism, *Italian* Futurism, and *German* Expressionism.[130] As Ringgold wrote in a pamphlet announcing the April 13 event:

> We have been 34 years [*sic*] at the Museum waiting to be free without being separate, and there have been no retrospectives for Jacob Lawrence or Romare Bearden, no publications devoted to their work, no group shows for our younger artists. If our art is not to be mixed with the art of whites, well, so be it! Give us our own wing, where we can show our Black and Puerto Rican artists, where we can proclaim to the world our statement of what constitutes value and truth and the spirit of our people! Give it to us, or tell us that we have no place at all in your museums, just as we have no place in your churches and clubs and cooperatives! Can the Museum of Modern Art at least be that honest about it?[131]

When Ringgold and Lloyd informed Lowry of their impending meeting, he denied them access to the auditorium or any other space to congregate in the museum and once again raised the specter of quality:

> As in all museums, the works in our galleries are selected for their quality as works of art; they are grouped according to stylistic affinities without regards to the artist's religions, race, political affiliation or the country in which he was born. For the convenience of our visitors, the galleries are arranged in

rough chronological sequence according to historic styles or movements in 20th-century art.

Thus, for example, the School of Paris galleries contain works by artists from varying political views and whose native countries range from Spain to Russia. The German Expressionist galleries contain works by artists of different religious beliefs. The so-called New York School includes work by artists born in many different sections of this country.[132]

The letter demonstrated that Lowry didn't grasp the essential difference between exhibiting an array of European and European American artists and admitting American artists of color. Reflecting back on that experience recently, Ringgold has said that her ideas were "completely foreign to him, totally foreign. It was like you were talking to yourself."[133] Like his fellow directors at other museums, Lowry claimed to be "color blind." On April 13, when Ringgold, her daughter Michele Wallace, and others defied the museum's attempt to thwart their action and toured the museum under the watchful eye of the staff, they found only two works by artists of color: panels from Jacob Lawrence's *Migration of the Negro* series upstairs and, on the ground floor, Wifredo Lam's *The Jungle* (1943).[134]

Word spread about the demand for desegregation at the museum, prompting a backlash, as suggested in this letter of concern to Gardner Cowles, vice chairman of the museum, whose son Charles was a member of MoMA's Junior Council and had been a founding trustee of the Studio Museum in Harlem:

April 20, 1969

Dear Mr. Cowles—Have received your letter requesting an increase in our annual subscription. Ordinarily I might give it to you, but at this time, I wish to see how the museum reacts to the ridiculous suggestions of militant blacks. I am all for showing the work of black artists, who merit a show, on the same basis as white artists. I am not for a black show, just because they want it—or any special treatment. It is my opinion that MAMA [*sic*] should try to remain a 1st class museum and leader in contemporary art movements.

A placating reply from Margaret ("Meg") Potter, an associate curator in the Department of Painting and Sculpture, assured the letter writer that no show of work by black artists would be held at the museum.

Dear Mrs. Field:

Your letter to Gardner Cowles in reply to his membership request has come to this department for reply to your comments on the museum. In regard to the demands of black artists and other who have protested against the museum's policies, I think you would be pleased by the museum's careful handling of this matter. Protest against authority or "established" institutions seemed to have reached a stage of national contagion, and the sad experiences of other institutions have provided us with some cautionary lessons in treating explosive situations. A committee on artists relations is being formed to consider the relationship of the museum to the contemporary artist and to determine what injustice, if any, exists in the relationship. Staff members are also discussing the issues informally with the artists whom they know, and you will be glad to know that the matter is subsiding. Certainly the museum is not considering a show of black artists. We do not, of course, note the race of an artist on any of the museum records, nor is race ever an issue in choosing works for an exhibition.[135]

Bates Lowry was fired on May 15, 1969. The reasons may have included the difficulty of the transition after d'Harnoncourt's death, the presence of a large budget deficit, and the perception among staff members and trustees that Lowry had too heavy a hand in curatorial affairs. The director's inability to deal effectively with artists who were disrupting museum operations may have also been a factor. The artists had correctly interpreted Lowry's promise to convene a special committee to study artists' relations as a stalling tactic. Four months after this promise, the time Lowry left, the committee still had not materialized.

After Lowry's ouster, while the museum undertook the search for a new director, the institution was run by Walter Bareiss, one of the trustees, serving as chair of an interregnum executive committee that included Wilder Green, director of the exhibition program, and Richard Koch, director of administration. The Art Workers' Coalition pushed on, finding a more sympathetic reception by the museum's senior staff, who, under the leadership of Arthur Drexler, agreed to a series of meetings with the AWC.

The first meeting was held in September 1969 with Drexler presiding and many senior staff members in attendance, including Bill Lieberman, Bill Agee, Kynaston McShine, Jenny Licht, Willard Van Dyke, John Szarkowski, and Bill Rubin from the curatorial departments; Bob Carter from Publications; Liz Shaw, head of Public Relations; Wilder Green and Dick Koch, from the executive team; Waldo Rasmussen, in charge of circulating exhibitions; and Charlie Hesse from Development. In addition to the artists in the AWC, the museum invited others who had long-standing relationships with the museum, including Robert Motherwell, George

Segal, and Robert Rauschenberg. Some of these artists were sympathetic to the AWC's positions, some not.

The museum staff had reviewed the AWC's thirteen demands and came prepared with responses clustered under themes: the museum's relationship to artists; the museum's relationship to racially and ethnically diverse audiences; hours and admission; artists' rights; pending copyright legislation; an artists' registry; outdoor works; technology-based works; and artists' grievances. Each theme was addressed with a brief response.

This first meeting was long—and not very productive. Michele Wallace, seventeen years old at the time, reminded the staff of the Martin Luther King Jr. exhibition the previous year and criticized the museum for segregating the artists.[136] Arthur Drexler denied the charge, but Wallace insisted, saying, "I was there. I saw it. I was right there in the middle." Rubin jumped in to say, "I installed it and I can show you my photographs." With utter disregard for Rubin's authority and position, Wallace retorted, "My dear, you installed a segregated show."[137]

Indeed, Rubin's record regarding African American artists was poor and his knowledge thin. On October 23, 1968, just one week before the opening of the King exhibition, Rubin's secretary, Cintra Lofting, sent a memo to Wilder Green, director of exhibitions, informing him that she had received a list of artists and works which were "unknowns to us."[138] Identified as "unknowns" were all but five—Charles Alston, Richard Hunt, Tom Lloyd, Richard Mayhew, and Thomas Sills—of the twenty-four African American artists presented in the exhibition, including Jacob Lawrence.[139]

The overarching message delivered to the artists at the meeting was unambiguous:

> BILL RUBIN: We are not going to recommend having a black or Puerto Rican wing. Since we don't believe in them, we wouldn't administer them in any case. . . .
>
> TOM LLOYD: So your answer to the black wing is no? Period?
>
> ARTHUR DREXLER: You're correct in making that assumption, Mr. Lloyd. That is true.[140]

On October 31, 1969, while the museum was still between directors, Jon Hendricks and Jean Toche, the core members of GAAG, famously removed Malevich's *White on White* and replaced it with the AWC's most current thirteen-point program.[141] After this action, it became clear that the activists had gotten under the museum's skin, and in a memo to the members of the staff executive committee dated November 3, 1969, PR director Liz Shaw wrote, "I feel more and more strongly that we must do something about black artists."[142] It is noteworthy that at MoMA, as at other museums at the time, responses to activists were often managed by the museum's public relations staff, suggesting that public image trumped other concerns.

At Shaw's urging, a second meeting between the senior staff and the artists took place on November 25, 1969. Once again, the museum invited additional artists to attend.[143] The best-known accomplishment of this meeting was the curators' agreement to collaborate on what would become the famous "And Babies?" poster, featuring John Haeberle's photograph of a path in the Song My village in South Vietnam strewn with the dead bodies of civilians who had been killed by American armed forces as part of a massacre in My Lai in March 1968.[144] Exposure of the bloodbath had hit the news just two weeks prior, in mid-November 1969. When the staff ran the poster by MoMA president Bill Paley, he insisted that the museum withdraw its support and sever its association with the project. This resistance only strengthened the artists' resolve to have the poster seen as widely as possible. One of the most memorable images of this time is the photograph of an AWC guerrilla action called the "Memorial Service for Dead Babies," staged in the museum's galleries in front of Picasso's *Guernica* on January 3, 1970, exactly one year after Takis's removal of his work from the *Machine Art* show.[145] The photograph prominently features Tom Lloyd holding the poster (fig. 4.20) and was published on the cover of *Studio International* magazine.[146]

When the staff members had agreed to collaborate on the poster at the November 25 meeting, they did not foresee controversy. They were quite sympathetic to many of the artists' positions. At the end of the meeting, subcommittees were created to follow up on some of the projects discussed, including a subcommittee on black and Puerto Rican artists.[147] This group met twice between November 1969 and February 1970 and developed ideas for educational programming that included textbooks and audiovisual materials on black and Puerto Rican art; in-service training for public school teachers by black and Puerto Rican artists; a program of busing children from predominantly black and Puerto Rican neighborhoods to the museum; and concerts of "rhythm and blues" and "Puerto Rican folklore" in the museum's sculpture garden. These programs were designed for all, not just African American and Puerto Rican audiences, and would have meant a radical recalibration of the museum's definition of "modernism." Indeed, just as Barr's ten-year program of "primitive" exhibitions defined an approach to modernism in the 1930s and '40s, this programmatic initiative might have ushered in a new, postcolonial vision of modernism.

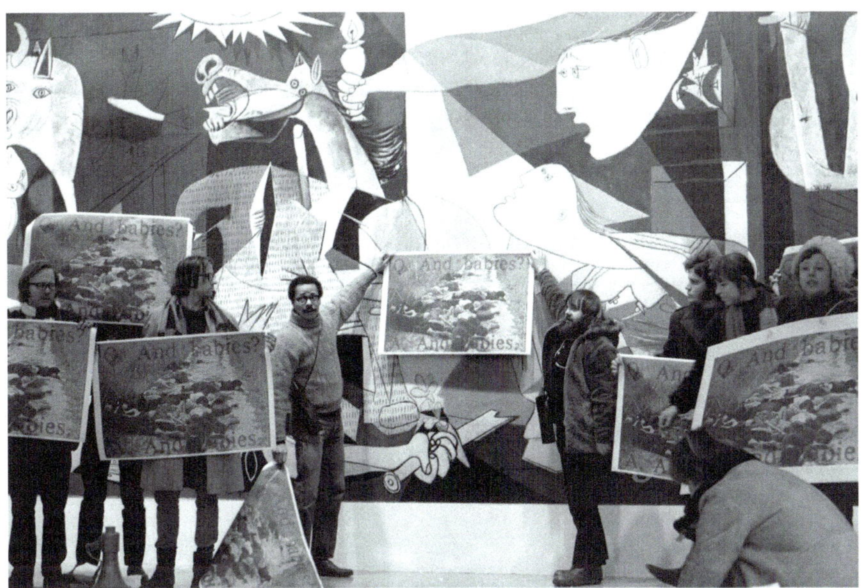

Fig. 4.20 Art Workers' Coalition and Guerrilla Art Action Group protest in front of Picasso's *Guernica* at the Museum of Modern Art, with the AWC's "And Babies?" poster, January 3, 1970. © Jan van Raay.

For Ringgold, Lloyd, and Ortiz the most important proposal remained the creation of the Martin Luther King, Jr. Wing. Despite their initial opposition, the museum staff seemed to warm to this idea and explored it with other artists. On December 10, 1969, Benny Andrews received a phone call from Arthur Drexler inviting him and other leaders of the BECC to meet with him and museum representatives Bill Rubin and Bill Agee to discuss the King initiative. The meeting took place a few days later. Was the staff seriously considering the proposal or looking for reasons to reject it? According to Andrews, the BECC told the staff that they rejected the idea of a separate wing for artists of color, though they wholeheartedly supported integration.[148]

It is hard to imagine what the board of trustees was expecting when they appointed John Hightower as the museum's next director in late 1970. As executive director of the New York State Council on the Arts from 1964 to 1970, Hightower had championed a democratic philosophy of art. He had seen that funding was distributed to arts organizations serving a wide range of constituencies, from poetry readings throughout the State University of New York system to experimental programs at Judson Memorial Church, where Jon Hendricks ran the gallery. He had channeled seed money into the creation of new organizations, such as El Museo del Barrio, and organized a three-day conference on neighborhood arts organizations and the social role of museums in communities. He had gone out on a limb with the NYSCA-sponsored *Harlem on My Mind* exhibition. And he had just recently helped organize a partnership between NYSCA, the Metropolitan Museum of Art, and Tom Lloyd in which NYSCA granted $8,500 for Lloyd and other members of the AWC to conduct surveys about prospective arts initiatives in predominantly African American and Puerto Rican neighborhoods in New York City.[149] Through his highly visible activities as executive director of NYSCA, Hightower had laid his cards on the table, but the trustees didn't pay attention to his record. Hightower believes "they didn't know what they were getting. And I wasn't trying to be particularly coy. I told them everything I knew and showed them things I'd written."[150] Hightower was brought in under the protective cloak of Nelson Rockefeller, his boss at NYSCA, who handpicked him for the job. His appointment was not challenged by the other MoMA trustees.

But in fact, Hightower hadn't been their first choice. The trustees had offered the job to Sherman Lee, director of the Cleveland Museum of Art, a conservative and vocal museum director, who had turned it down. Hightower and Lee couldn't have been further apart in vision and goals. While Hightower viewed "art" and "life" as nearly synonymous, Lee regarded museums as art's resting places: "If today is, at least, in part, made up of yesterday, how can the museum fail to discharge its given role of mausoleum, of conservator of the past for today and tomorrow?"[151] In a speech given at the Dayton Art Institute on February 26, 1969, Lee had described two projects, Christo's wrapping of the Museum of Contemporary Art in Chicago and the Met's *Harlem on My Mind* show, as projects that cheapened the museum and reduced it to a "used-car lot."[152]

Hightower plunged into action immediately. The time seemed ripe to reassess the museum's vision and programs. According to artist Faith Ringgold, "Hightower, he was a good guy. He was not so entrenched in tradition. He seemed to [be] willing to break tradition and open things up to a new way of thinking."[153] The new challenges being posed by artists and arts activists aligned with Hightower's progressive vision of the late twentieth-century museum. If artists were turning to political subjects and calling for institutional change, Hightower thought MoMA should heed their call.[154] In MoMA's November 1970 newsletter he wrote, "Artists have traditionally been the most conscientious and, at times, the most provocative critics of society, and our obligation, as a museum, is to reflect the concern and work of the artist."[155] Under Hightower's leadership the museum became, as it had been in its early years under Barr, an energetic place, responsive to artists, potentially permeable with multiple agendas emanating from inside and penetrating from without. He did not see this as being at odds with the museum's mission to collect.

Hightower's tenure at the Museum of Modern Art would be short-lived—eighteen months—but his efforts to bring about institutional change were dramatic. He welcomed dissenting and diverse voices and enjoyed mediating debates about the museum's role and character. In Hightower, the Art Workers' Coalition found an ally, who, like them, viewed the museum as a political site. On March 2, 1970, before he had officially assumed his post but after his appointment had been announced, Hightower met with 150 members of the Art Workers' Coalition at their weekly meeting at "Museum" to discuss reforms at MoMA.[156] He may have overestimated his ability to broker change. Grace Glueck has recalled: "It was pretty unprecedented for the director of the Museum to come to one of those things, but they asked him to come and he did. And he said, as I remember, a lot of foolish things, making foolish promises to them and making concessions which he had no right to do, on the part of the Modern."[157]

These concessions, however, did not prevent the artists from putting Hightower through trial by fire. Hightower has recalled, "The first day on the job, May 1, 1970, there was a sit-in in my office. . . . The group included Faith Ringgold . . . and Ralph Ortiz and Tom Lloyd—oh my god—who had a nasty habit of calling at 2 o'clock in the morning."[158]

The next day, May 2, the Guerrilla Art Action Group staged an action outside the museum, the only GAAG action in which Ortiz took part, and it blended guerrilla street theater with elements of the artist's earlier work, such as chicken and blood—in this case fake blood made of tomato juice.[159] The performance began with what appeared to be a routine protest, a common sight at the time (fig. 4.21). Then, a sleek black limousine pulled up in front of the museum. Out came three well-heeled passengers: Jon Hendricks playing "the director," Jean Toche "the trustee," and Cynthia Lindquist "the secretary." "The director," dressed in black tie, emerged from the limo and regarded the protest in horror. He beckoned "the trustee," who gave an order to "the director," who gave the order to "the secretary," who gave the order to "the guards" (played by other artists already on the scene) to build a barricade to protect the museum. (The barricade was built out of chicken wire.) Gradually the conflict escalated (figs. 4.22 and 4.23). "The guards" then brought out the rest of the props—toy rifles, cap guns, smoke bombs, and tomato juice—and a melee ensued while the artists rallied behind a large Puerto Rican

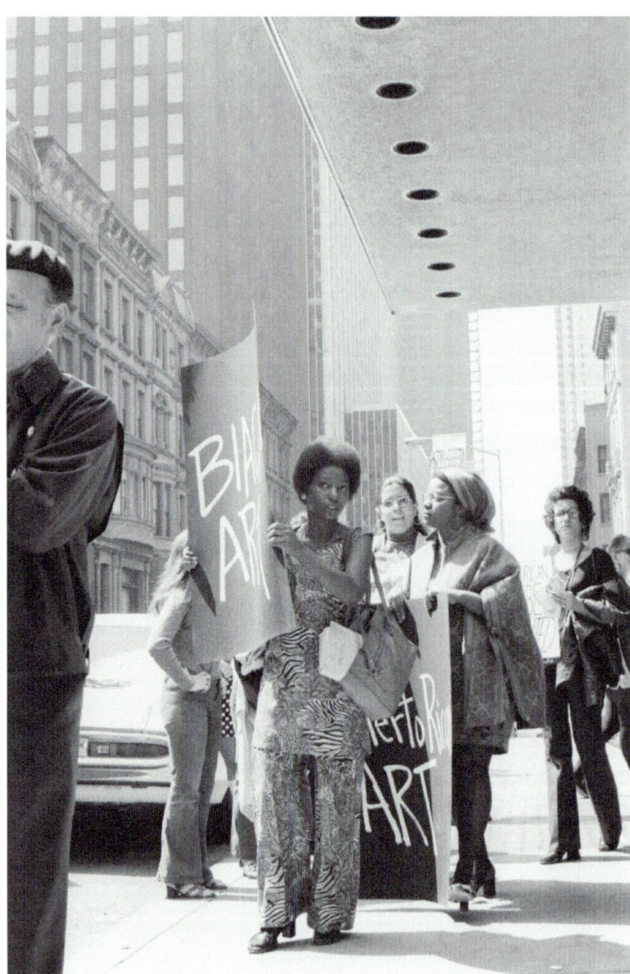

Fig. 4.21 Michele Wallace (center) and Faith Ringgold (second from right) at the Guerrilla Art Action Group protest at the Museum of Modern Art, May 2, 1970. © Jan van Raay.

flag unfurled by Adrian Garcia. Ortiz dragged "the trustee" into the center of the demonstration and tore at his fancy clothes. A smoke bomb went off, and Toche and Hendricks climbed back into the limo and raced off just as police cars drove up. The aim of the action was "to do an irrational, visceral, classist visualization of the racist mental attitudes of the controlling forces of the Museum of Modern Art, and to point out through the action the myths, fears, and their protective fantasies, that have historically exploited and excluded the art and life-styles of Puerto Rican and black people."[160] Using parody and street theater, the artists attempted to represent relations of power both within the institution and between the institution and artists.

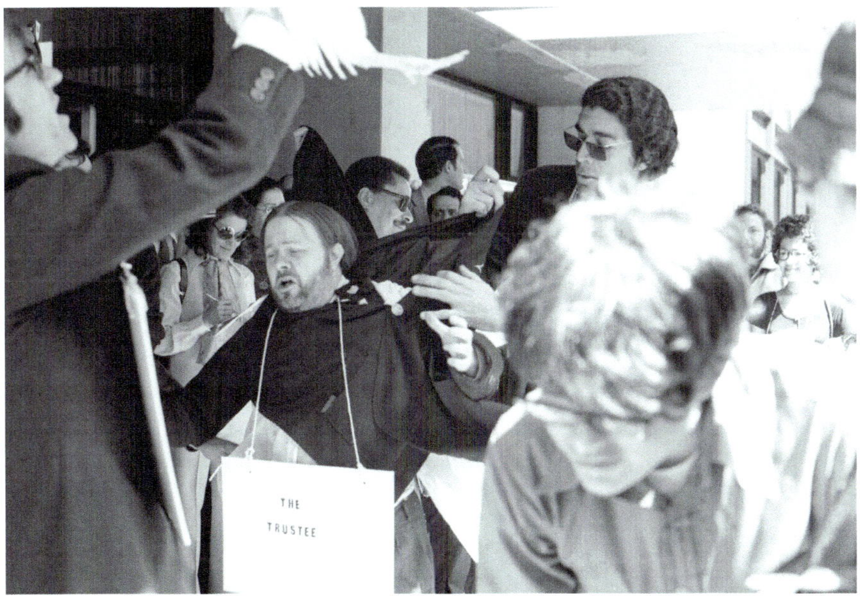

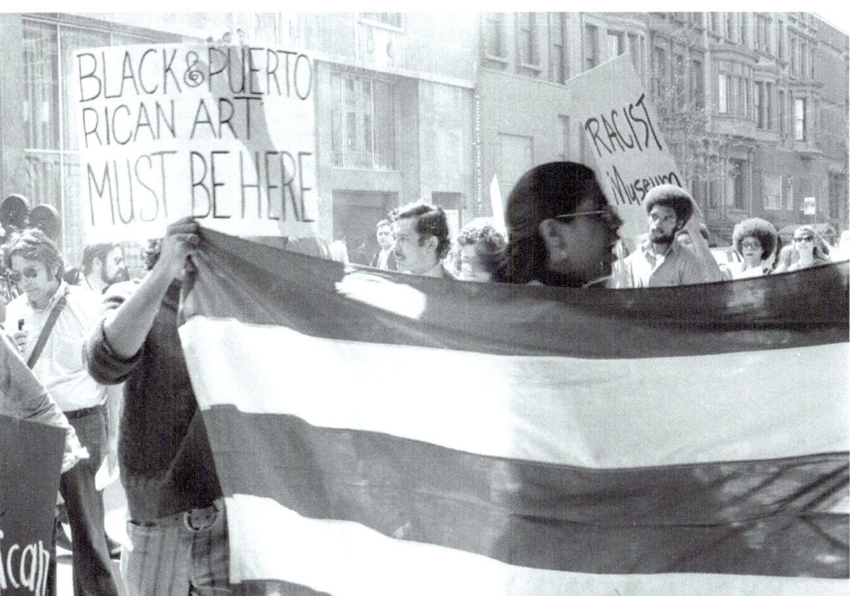

Fig. 4.22 Guerrilla Art Action Group protest at the Museum of Modern Art, May 2, 1970. Jon Hendricks holding chicken (left); Jean Toche wearing sign that reads "The Trustee"; Tom Lloyd (in background); and Raphael Montañez Ortiz unfurling flag. © Jan van Raay.

Fig. 4.23 Guerrilla Art Action Group protest at the Museum of Modern Art, May 2, 1970. © Jan van Raay.

Handouts distributed at the May 2 action called for "rearranging of institutional patterns" at the museum. The artists demanded the hiring of a coordinator for a Martin Luther King, Jr.–Pedro Albizu Campos Study Center—the "study center" was considered a stepping-stone to a full-fledged "wing"—and immediate action on the development of a black and Puerto Rican advisory board; acquisition of no less than one hundred works of art by black and Puerto Rican artists; a series of exhibitions that ran the gamut from African and South American art to posters by black and Puerto Rican artists; a retrospective for Romare Bearden; and a mural program.[161]

Unlike Bates Lowry, who had been flummoxed by such demands, Hightower wasted no time responding to the artists' call for action. He conferred with Faith Ringgold and other AWC members, and on May 4, 1970, he wrote to curator Carroll Greene to explore the possibility of working at the museum: "Faith Ringgold, whom I believe you know, suggested that I get in touch with you regarding some of the plans for the Museum of Modern Art. I would like very much to meet you and wonder if you are going to be in New York City any time soon. If so, I would very much appreciate having the chance to meet you."[162]

On June 15 Hightower conferred with Benny Andrews and the executive committee of the BECC to further discuss the idea of the Martin Luther King, Jr.–Pedro Albizu Campos Study Center. He had already identified Raphael Ortiz and Carroll Greene as potential directors. The BECC agreed to the center, in principle, but reserved the right to voice disagreements over final plans, including its leadership. BECC members did not want to undermine an effort to give black artists more opportunities, but privately they voiced misgivings about a strategy that separated artists of color from the rest of MoMA's collection and exhibitions. They wanted the legitimacy of full inclusion.[163] Tellingly, none of the BECC members had participated in the demonstration on May 2, 1970, when the AWC made its biggest public push for the center.

While these discussions ensued with the artists, Hightower swiftly convinced the board of trustees to elect its first African American members: Clifton Wharton Jr., president of Michigan State University; and Dr. Mamie Phipps Clark. A specialist in child development, Clark was head of the Northside Center for Child Development in Harlem. She was married to Kenneth B. Clark and had served as a consultant for HARYOU, and she was on the advisory board of the Children's Art Carnival in Harlem. Both accepted the invitation.[164]

Just six weeks into his post, on June 17, 1970, Hightower introduced into the agenda of a trustees' meeting the issues of the museum's inclusion of artists of color. Hightower proposed hiring Carroll Greene to conduct a study to determine how the museum might address the concerns raised by Ringgold, Lloyd, and Ortiz.

Bill Paley responded by buying time. He said the subject was too important to be handled without discussion by the Executive Committee, which, he said, would come back to the full board of trustees with a resolution. The next day, James Thrall Soby, who had served variously as a staff member and trustee of the museum since 1940, wrote a private note to Paley and David Rockefeller. His reflections provide a rare glimpse into the often hidden world of power and privilege:

Dear David and Bill:

I was awake for a long time last night brooding about the very serious problem with which our Museum is faced regarding protests from ethnic and biological groups. It seems to me that I've been exposed to this problem forever, since as long ago as 1932 or 1933 when I was on the staff of the Wadsworth Atheneum in Hartford, the huge Negro population of that city threatened to break every window in the building if we showed the great Griffith film, *Birth of a Nation*. In the end we did show the film, but only after many meetings with the Negro community.

Our own museum now seems to be threatened primarily by two groups: a minority group, the Negroes; and a majority group, the women (at least statistics seem to show that there are more women than men in America, God help us). These are the groups most consistently urged on us by the Artists Coalition [*sic*], the organization which I assume is giving poor John Hightower the most trouble.

Before we take any action whatever, one way or another, I should think all the members of the Executive Committee and the Board of Trustees should be made aware that we cannot show or buy more works of art by Negro or female artists without letting down our standards. This is sad but completely true. There are at present simply not enough first-rate Negro artists to compete on a numerically equal basis in our loan shows or our purchases. . . . Our museum has long since owned works by outstanding Negro artists such as Jacob Lawrence and Romare Bearden. And we have given a one-man (excuse the phrase) to Georgia O'Keeffe and included large groups of pictures by women artists in our loan shows. I think it would be worthwhile for the Trustees to have a list of women and Negro artists we have shown and/or bought before we accept the Coalition's charge of total neglect. . . .

Finally, I have the greatest sympathy for John Hightower's uncomfortable position at the moment. I don't, however, think, that there should be an outside chairman, whether female, green, black or purple on any committee appointed to study this serious matter. Let's keep all authority on our own premises and do the best we can. Maybe a show of Black artists would help. I tend to doubt it because the good ones want to be judged by our own strict standards which have nothing to do with race, color or creed.[165]

On June 25, executive officers David Rockefeller, Paley, Henry Allen Moe, Bliss Parkinson, Blanchette Rockefeller, and Soby, several other trustees, and eight staff members met to discuss the museum's "involvement in minority concerns," as Paley put it.[166] Hightower reported that he had discussed the issue with members of the staff and with several African American artists and, based on these conversations, recommended that the museum hire an outside consultant to conduct and compile a report "which would define what a black arts study program is and could be at the Museum." He had no idea that Soby had preloaded this discussion in private correspondence with Paley and David Rockefeller. He described Carroll Greene Jr. as "an expert in the field of Black arts" with an orientation that was "international rather than concerned with community issues." He explained, "Mr. Greene does not want a community gallery on the order of what is being done in Brooklyn [by Henri Ghent at the Brooklyn Museum], but wants to see black artists represented in the Museum under existing standards." He further reported that some of the artists with whom he spoke are concerned that there not be separation, but rather more integration in the museum's regular activities.[167]

Hightower stressed the importance of having an African American provide leadership, citing lessons to be learned from the protests against the Whitney's *Contemporary Black Artists in America* show and the Met's *Harlem on My Mind* exhibition, which were both directed by whites. He pointed out that the artists' demands were a result of the exclusion of African American artists from the Martin Luther King Jr. memorial exhibition, which he described as the "spark" for the request for a Martin Luther King, Jr. Wing.

Mamie Clark endorsed Greene for the job as someone she knew and respected, but the senior trustees insisted on keeping their own hands on the reins. As David Rockefeller put it, he was reluctant to place the project in the hands of an "outside person" because of the "danger" that the resulting study might not be kept private. Rockefeller suggested that a committee of the trustees be formed to explore "the issues," and another trustee suggested that Greene be asked to serve as a consultant to the committee. Curator Bill Lieberman opined that MoMA had "more works by Black artists than any museum in the country" and suggested that the study "determine if in fact there is a 'black art.'"[168]

By the end of the meeting, a committee was formed to respond to the charges that the museum had a legacy of neglect regarding artists of color. The committee's charge was "to study the role of the Museum of Modern Art with respect to the works of various ethnic groups and to recommend to the Board of Trustees any changes in the operations of the Museum which it may find appropriate and desirable in order to increase its usefulness in this area."[169]

The Committee to Study Afro-American, Hispanic, and Other Ethnic Art was chaired by J. Frederic Byers III, a newly appointed trustee and Paley's son-in-law, who also had been a Junior Council member and a founding trustee of the Studio Museum in Harlem. Thirty-one years old, like Hightower he had graduated from Yale College and was the financial backer and partner of the Bykert Gallery, which showed contemporary artists. Carroll Greene was engaged as a consultant. Blanchette Rockefeller was appointed head of the Subcommittee on Collections and Exhibitions. Beth Strauss led the Subcommittee on International Programs. And Dr. Mamie Clark rounded out the team as leader of the Subcommittee on Community Programs.

The day after this meeting Soby wrote to Alfred Barr:

I went in for the Executive Committee meeting yesterday. Thank God they seem to have abandoned the idea of having an outside, Negro chairman of the new committee to deal with the Artists Coalition [*sic*], which I think would have been a serious mistake, as I'd written to David R. and Paley, with copy to you. Instead they appointed young Briggs, the new Trustee, who seems bright and has the time to spend. I can't remember the full committee but it seems like a good one and has that extremely intelligent new Negress Trustee, Mrs. Clark on it. . . . I managed to get them to agree that many of our Trustees should have a list to inform them what we've already done for female and Black artists; most of them seem to assume that we've never done anything, which is absurd. And Liz Shaw reminded them of the large African Negro sculpture show of years ago; if that ain't a major part of the modern Black artist's heritage, I don't know what is. It was a short meeting but pleasant (for me anyway) because it was decided to keep authority to reply and act within the Museum. They did appoint a Negro, Carter X (I just can't remember his last name, though I've got it written down somewhere) whom many people there knew and approved) [*sic*] as a consultant to the new ethnic committee.[170]

Soby's disdain for the institution's process of introspection is suggested by his flippant disregard for proper names; the man Soby refers to as "Briggs" was committee chair Frederic Byers. "Carter X," perhaps an allusion to Malcolm X, he substitutes for Carroll Greene.

Howardena Pindell, then an assistant curator in the department of Prints and Illustrated Books—one of the few African Americans in a curatorial position in any museum at the time—asked Hightower if she could serve as one of several staff members on the committee.[171] He agreed. Pindell had also wanted to participate in some of the artists' protests but was afraid she would have lost her job.[172] Later she picketed in favor of the formation of the MoMA's union, the Professional and Administrative Staff Association of the Museum of Modern Art.

In a memo to Mamie Clark dated October 23, 1970, Pindell suggested several ideas for making the museum more accessible, including expanding the museum's press list:

> Members of the Black and Puerto Rican Press should be added to our regular mailing list and press review list in order that they may be more fully informed of the activities of the Museum. I feel that is somewhat patronizing to notify them only of events that we feel may be of some interest to them. . . . The International Sub-Committee has touched on this point in a discussion concerning the publicity program necessary for the African textiles and Decorative Arts exhibition in the fall of 1972. We do not need to wait that long to let the public know that we are accessible.[173]

Pindell also suggested instituting Spanish-language gallery talks and expanding outreach programs for children based on the model of the Children's Art Carnival.

One of Pindell's most prescient projects was a review of artists in the museum's print collection. She identified 1,633 artists and compiled national tallies: "American—597; Australian—5; Austrian—12," and so on. "Puerto Rican" artists—there were 10—were broken out from "American."[174] Pindell would apply this practice more broadly in the art world in the 1980s, monitoring the demographics of exhibitions at New York museums and commercial galleries.[175]

Besides working behind the scenes with the trustees, Hightower generated visible new projects almost immediately. The first week of May 1970 was a violent one for the nation and for the world. On May 1 the Kent State antiwar protests began, culminating in the Ohio National Guard opening fire on students on May 4 and killing four. In the ensuing days, colleges and universities across the country shut down as thousands of students protested. Four days later, police opened fire on a student rally at Jackson State College in Mississippi, killing two students and wounding twelve. Tens of thousands converged in New Haven as jury selection began in the

trial of nine Black Panthers accused of murdering a fellow Panther thought to be an
FBI informant. The courthouse was located just a block from the Yale University
campus, and having attended Yale College, Hightower may have been particularly
moved by this event. On May 5, American forces bombed a Cambodian village that
had been held by the North Vietnamese. No North Vietnamese soldiers were found,
only the bodies of four Cambodian civilians. On May 9 protestors gathered in Washington, DC, to demonstrate their opposition to the incursion and to call for the
withdrawal of U.S. military forces from Vietnam and other Southeast Asian nations.
"The whole thing just kept exploding," Hightower has recalled.[176]

On May 5, 1970, an AWC offshoot led by Robert Morris and Poppy Johnson, Art
Strike, called for the closing of all museums to protest the bombing of Cambodia
and the Kent State killings. Hightower refused and instead led the museum on
a bold path. He kept the museum open, waived the admission fee, and issued this
statement:

> WE PROTEST THE KILLING OF FOUR STUDENTS AT KENT STATE
> UNIVERSITY IN OHIO AND THE WOUNDING OF OTHERS. WE PRO-
> TEST SENSELESS REACTION TO DISSENT FROM THOSE FOR WHOM
> ORDER IS THE HIGHER PRIORITY THAN FREE DISCUSSION AND OPEN
> DEMONSTRATION.
>
> WE ALSO OPPOSE THE CLOSING OF THOSE INSTITUTIONS WHICH
> IN SOME WAY NURTURE FREDOM [sic]—SO ESSENTIAL AND FRAG-
> ILE A PART OF THE ARTS—AND WHICH PROVIDE ALL OF US WITH
> A FORM OF INTENSELY HUMAN COMMUNICATION. WERE IT TO BE
> OTHERWISE, THE ARTS WOULD BE USED TO COMPOUND RATHER
> THAN DISPEL THE INHUMANITY THAT SEEMS SO INTENSELY TO
> PERVADE OUR SOCIETY.
>
> CONSEQUENTLY THE MUSEUM OF MODERN ART WILL BE OPEN
> FREE TO THE PUBLIC TODAY.
>
> JOHN B. HIGHTOWER
> DIRECTOR

Later that month, Art Strike—now the New York Art Strike against War, Repression, Racism, and Sexism—called for all museums and galleries to close again on
May 22, 1970, a "one day stoppage . . . of business-as-usual."[177] With the exception
of an exhibition of work by Frank Stella, who requested that his show be closed,
the Museum of Modern Art remained open, this time not only waiving the admission fee but using the occasion to present an exhibition that would reflect back to

the public the events of the prior month. John Szarkowski, the museum's curator of photography, culled a group of fifty-seven photos by eleven photographers depicting events that had taken place just two weeks earlier. The pictures in this exhibition, entitled *May 2–May 9*, presented antiwar marches in Washington and New York City and the New Haven demonstration in support of the Black Panthers (figs. 4.24 and 4.25).[178] "The idea [was] to take that moment and not just have the museum ignore it, but to provide some kind of visual condensation of it," Hightower said.[179] The exhibition ran from May 23 through June 2, 1970. The museum also handed out pamphlets provided by various activist groups at an information table staffed by museum personnel (figs. 4.26 and 4.27).

This exhibition may have sown the seeds of a much larger endeavor, a group show of works drawn from the museum's collection that addressed war, violence, social injustice, and other themes that resonated with the current social and political situation. The idea originated with curator Kynaston McShine, but the show would ultimately be seen to fruition in the summer of 1971 by Betsy Jones, associate curator in the Department of Painting and Sculpture.[180] In a memo to Jones dated July 21, 1970, Bill Lieberman noted that such an exhibition would provide the opportunity to show José Clemente Orozco's *Dive Bomber and Tank*, Diego Rivera's *Agrarian Leader Zapata*, and Jacob Lawrence's *Migration of the Negro* series, all works by artists of color, as well as Picasso's *Guernica* studies. Various titles were considered, including "Modern Artists and the Human Predicament" and "The Modern Artist and the Human Condition."[181] Finally, the museum settled on "The Artist as Adversary"—an interesting and perhaps telling choice, given the sometimes adversarial relationship between the museum and the artist/activists advocating change.

Reflecting McShine's engagement with younger artists who were questioning the politics of the art system itself, when asked to suggest themes for the show, the curator sardonically suggested a gallery devoted to works "which have enriched our collection as a result of Hitler's *Entartete Kunst* campaign," the confiscation and auctioning of thousands of modern artworks to raise money for the Nazis' war effort.[182] Such institutional self-reflexivity was anathema to the museum's trustees. Not surprisingly, his suggestion was refused.

The nimbleness of the staff's response to social events as they were unfolding was remarkable, particularly in light of internal resistance. This intense level of activity was so unprecedented that it escaped the notice of some arts activists, including Women Artists in Revolution (WAR), an affiliate of the Art Workers' Coalition that would conduct their own negotiations with the Brooklyn Museum the following year and spearhead feminist protests at other major museums,

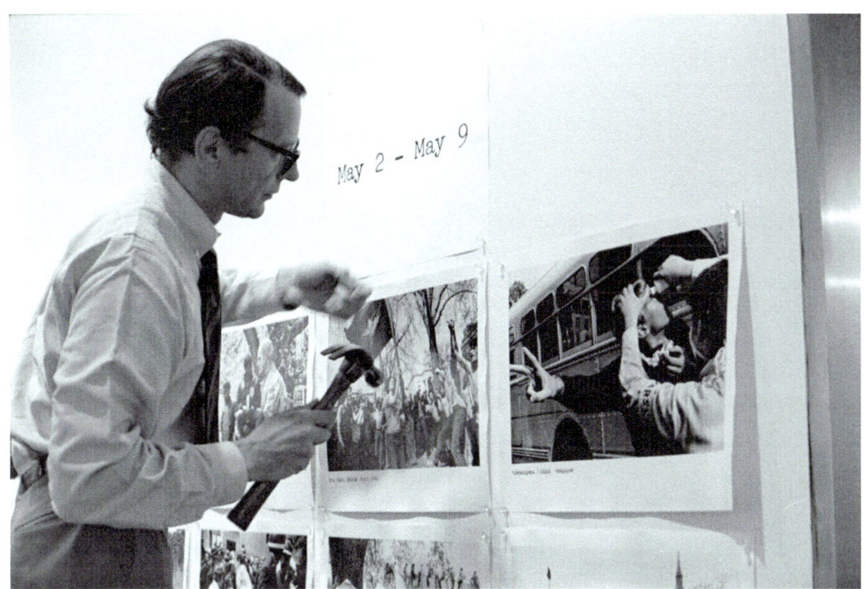

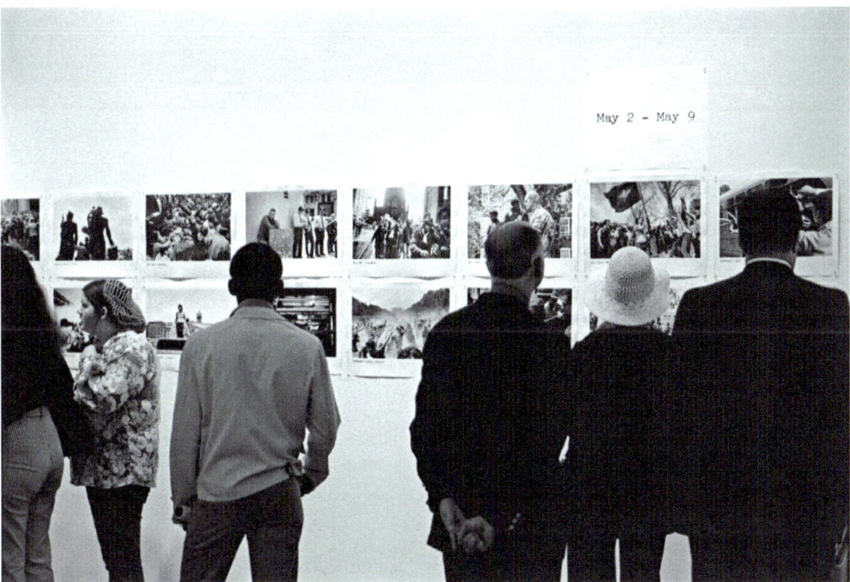

Fig. 4.24 John Szarkowski, curator, installing *May 2–May 9* photography exhibition during New York Art Strike, May 22, 1970. Photographed by Susan Bernstein. Digital Image © The Museum of Modern Art / Licensed by SCALA / Art Resource, New York.

Fig. 4.25 Visitors viewing *May 2–May 9* photography exhibition during New York Art Strike, May 22, 1970. Photographed by Susan Bernstein. Digital Image © The Museum of Modern Art / Licensed by SCALA / Art Resource, New York.

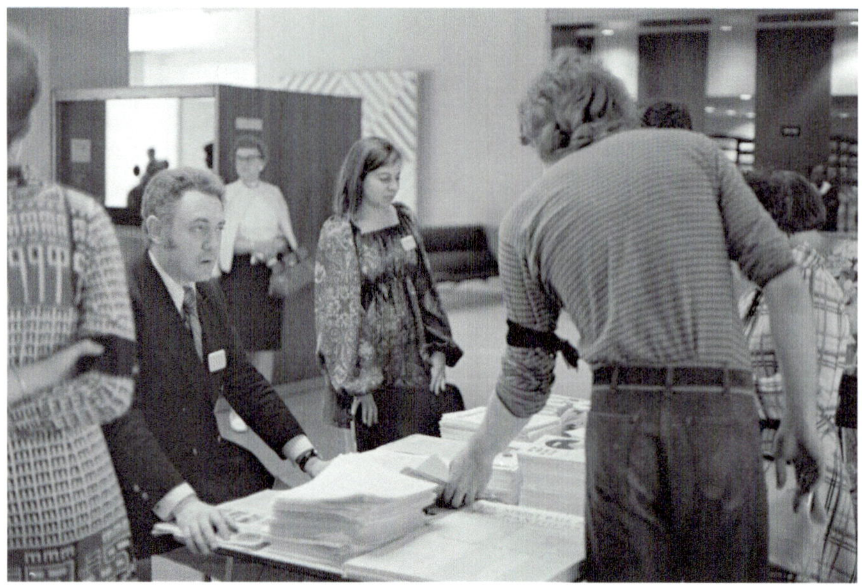

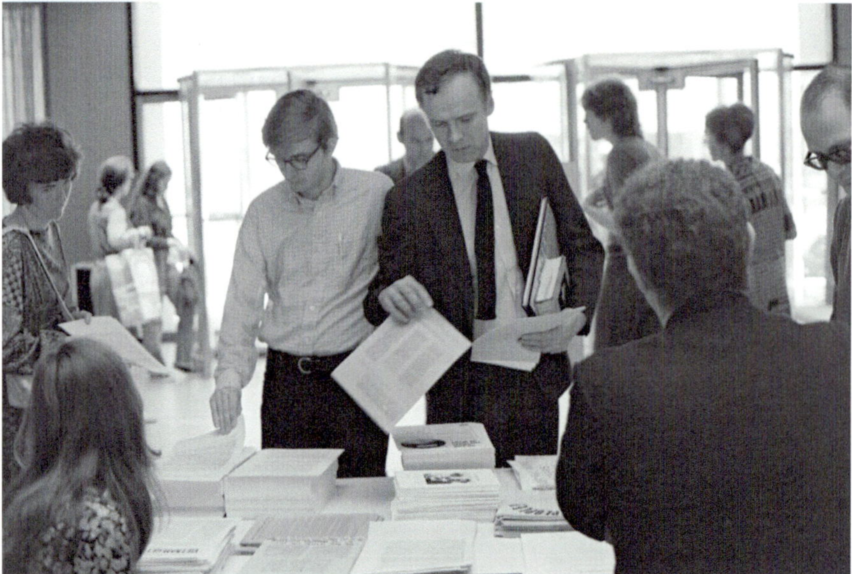

 William S. Rubin, curator, seated at pamphlet table in the Museum of Modern Art lobby during New York Art Strike, May 22, 1970. Digital Image © The Museum of Modern Art / Licensed by SCALA / Art Resource, New York.

 Visitors at pamphlet table in the Museum of Modern Art lobby during New York Art Strike, May 22, 1970. Digital Image © The Museum of Modern Art / Licensed by SCALA / Art Resource, New York.

including the Whitney. In a letter dated June 1, 1970, members of WAR condemned Hightower:

> MR. HIGHTOWER:
>
> THERE ARE EVENTS IN HISTORY THAT HAVE TO BE TAKEN INTO ACCOUNT.
>
> YOU CAN NOT LET "BUSINESS AS USUAL" DOMINATE THE SCENE WHEN DRASTIC CHANGES IN LIFE AND POLITICS ARE TAKING PLACE.
>
> YOU CAN NOT SMUGLY COMPROMISE IMPASSIONED AND PEACEFUL PLEAS FOR ACTION.
>
> WE REPRESENT W.A.R., WOMEN ARTISTS IN REVOLUTION. WE HELPED CLOSE THE METROPOLITAN MUSEUM, FRIDAY, MAY 22, AS AN EXPRESSION OF OUR DESPAIR AND ANGER OVER WAR AND RACISM. THIS ACTION WAS TO CONDEMN THE COVETOUS AND POWERFUL—THE ACQUISITIVE AND THE "ELITE" OF OUR SOCIETY.
>
> W.A.R. CONDEMNS YOUR ACTIONS AND YOUR STATEMENTS OF THAT DAY.
>
> IT WAS ANOTHER ELITIST*CHAUVINISTIC MISTAKE: A COMPLETE MISREADING OF THE MOTIVATIONS OF THE ART COMMUNITY. YOU HAVE MORE TO FEAR FROM THE MILITARISM OF THE WHITE HOUSE AND THE PENTAGON THAN YOU DO FROM ARTISTS. WE DEMAND THAT YOU MAKE A PUBLIC STATEMENT, AN ACT OF COMMITMENT AGAINST WAR, RACISM, SEXISM, AND REPRESSION.
>
> FOR W.A.R.,
>
> Doloris Holmes 442-3784   Corinne Robins 477-1353
>
> Sara Saporta 254-1758   Nancy Spero 873-8662[183]

In his written reply Hightower not only refuted the group's accusation—"Had you been here that day you would have realized that the Museum was attempting to react positively to the request of the arts community to make a commitment against war, racism, sexism and repression"—he also enclosed the text of a presentation he had given that very day, May 22, at the annual conference of the American

Association of Museums. Art Strike had disrupted the conference by insisting that one of its members, Raphael Ortiz, address the audience directly following the keynote address by Nancy Hanks, chair of the National Endowment for the Arts. At an evening panel designed to respond to Art Strike, Hightower opened a discussion on the topic of "Racism, Sexism, Repression, and War" by asserting:

> The specter of death in America touches everything we do and everything we think and everything we accept. The status quo has become intolerable, indeed maddening. "Business as usual" is impossible particularly from the standpoint of conscience.
>
> American troops invade Cambodia. The ABM anti-ballistic system is increased. One hundred billion dollars a year goes into the machinery of war and death. The stranglehold of this staggering amount of money on the economy is so pervasive it cannot even be detected. And yet the instruments of our society reflect life—churches, universities, museums, the symbolic barometers of human concern—are threatened more than ever with questions of relevance, immediacy, community, and human identity.
>
> This evening's panel discussion is not a panel discussion in any conceivable traditional sense. The statements tonight will be presented in the form of recommendations to museums throughout the country through the American Association of Museums for specific ways in which museums can help correct the hopelessness we feel so intensely these days about the issues uppermost in all our minds: Racism, Sexism, Repression, and War.[184]

While the women of WAR attacked Hightower from one side, the trustees began to voice disapproval from the other. Bill Paley was angered by Hightower's sympathetic stance toward Art Strike on May 22, and Walter Bareiss, the longtime museum insider and trustee who had headed the interregnum committee before Hightower's appointment, later claimed to have saved Hightower's job by protecting him from Paley's wrath. Bareiss claims to have told Paley, "He's new and he didn't understand quite what your instructions were as far as declaring solidarity with the black artists."[185] In fact, Hightower did understand; he just disagreed.

Still new on the job, he remained undaunted. On July 27, 1970, in a personal letter to Alex Gross, an AWC member, Hightower wrote: "Things are fairly quiet here in the Big Apple. Tom Lloyd has managed to alienate just about everybody who he hadn't already alienated and has accused the Art Strike Committee of being racist. MOMA is thoroughly confused and unsettled by me. At least, they are addressing themselves to questions they should have asked five or six years ago. Hopefully the 'agonizing reappraisal' will continue indefinitely to the point where this place is a little less arrogant and precious."[186]

Hightower was serious about taking steps toward greater representation of artists of color at MoMA. Throughout the spring and summer of 1970 he continued meeting with Lloyd, Ringgold, and Ortiz to discuss the King Center. Ringgold has described how Hightower would visit her at home, sit at her kitchen table, and talk about institutional change: "John Hightower was fabulous and we were about to get something happening."[187] He formed an advisory board that included, in addition to Lloyd and Ringgold, Vinnette Carroll, his former colleague at the New York State Council on the Arts and author of the off-Broadway musical *Your Arm's Too Short to Box with God*, as well as two trustees. As Ringgold documented in her biography: "Things were beginning to take shape as the Martin Luther King, Jr. Study Center project was now presented as a proposal to the museum for funding. The qualifications and responsibilities of the director of the center were outlined, and the program's educational and cultural guidelines had been worked out."[188]

Hightower and Ringgold formed an unprecedented alliance. Through these conversations, Lloyd, Ringgold, and Hightower also hammered out a plan for the museum to mount an exhibition of the work of Romare Bearden with Carroll Greene as curatorial consultant. Ringgold hoped that this position could grow into a permanent spot on the curatorial staff and, eventually, head of the Martin Luther King, Jr. Study Center.[189]

Ultimately, Hightower did not want to proceed with the center without solid commitment from all the African American artists he had consulted. He himself harbored misgivings about segregating artists of color in a separate wing. And the most powerful trustees on the board were against it. But Ringgold was persistent. She tried to reach Coretta Scott King to ask for her support, but King's widow did not respond. Her response was merely a letter to Hightower commending him on selecting Carroll Greene to work on the Romare Bearden exhibition, which did not mention the Martin Luther King, Jr. Study Center.[190]

Despite protestations that race was not a consideration in the museum's selection of artists, in fall 1970 the curatorial staff began to plan exhibitions specifically featuring African Americans. Under consideration for retrospectives were Jacob Lawrence, Romare Bearden, Archibald Motley, William H. Johnson, and Bob Thompson. Richard Hunt was added to this list at the suggestion of Bill Lieberman.[191] Artists being considered for either one-person or group shows included Richard Mayhew, Bernie Casey, Barbara Chase-Riboud, Russ Thompson, Felrath Hines, Jack White, Melvin Edwards, Sam Gilliam, Noah Purifoy, Alvin Loving Jr., Daniel

LaRue Johnson, Hayward Oubre, Fred Eversley, Lloyd McNeill, John Rhoden, William Majors, Norma Morgan, and Norman Lewis. In a separate category labeled "Social Commentary and/or Protest" were Jacob Lawrence, Charles White, Faith Ringgold, Phillip Lindsay Mason, Benny Andrews, and Al Hollingsworth.[192]

By October 1970 the museum had settled on two concurrent exhibitions, one presenting the work of Romare Bearden, and the other, Richard Hunt.[193] The shows opened simultaneously and were promoted as a pair (fig. 4.28). According to John Hightower, the shows were one-person exhibitions by artists "who happened to be black," rather than black artists' shows. This positioning enabled the museum to avoid "the paternalistic patina of excusing itself for putting on a black artists' exhibition."[194] Some of the other artists who had been considered would later be included in group exhibitions, such as *The Artist as Adversary*. Sam Gilliam would be featured in the museum's Projects series in a show that ran from November 9 to December 8, 1971, organized by Kynaston McShine. The Projects series, which McShine originated, presented small shows of new art in a gallery near the museum's lobby.

When the museum offered Bearden this major exhibition, he was fifty-nine years old and widely considered a senior figure. The museum had already purchased two of his works, an oil painting entitled *The Silent Valley of Sunrise* (1959) in 1960 and *Patchwork Quilt* (1970), a collage made of cloth, paper, and paint acquired the year it was made (fig. 4.29). Thirty-five-year-old Richard Hunt had been born in Chicago and earned a degree at the School of the Art Institute of Chicago in the late 1950s. He was best known for his sculptures in welded metal (fig. 4.30), including several large outdoor commissions for public sites and college campuses throughout the country. By 1970 he had already joined the art establishment and was a member of the National Council on the Arts, an advisory group to the chair of the NEA. As Faith Ringgold had suggested, the Bearden show was organized by Carroll Greene. The Hunt show was pulled together by in-house curator Bill Lieberman.

Bearden had been a working artist for over thirty years. He had studied art at Boston University, New York University, and the Arts Students League. He'd been an active member of the Harlem Artists Guild and had studied in Paris under the GI Bill. He had been a founder of the Spiral group and had helped establish the Studio Museum in Harlem. His work had illustrated the covers of *Time* magazine and the *New York Times Magazine*. He'd been showing in galleries since 1945.[195] His work had made appearances in the Whitney Museum's Painting Annuals since 1945, and in 1965 his *Projections* had been featured at the Corcoran Gallery in Washington, DC. By 1971 he had had over 120 solo and group exhibitions. Bearden was clearly

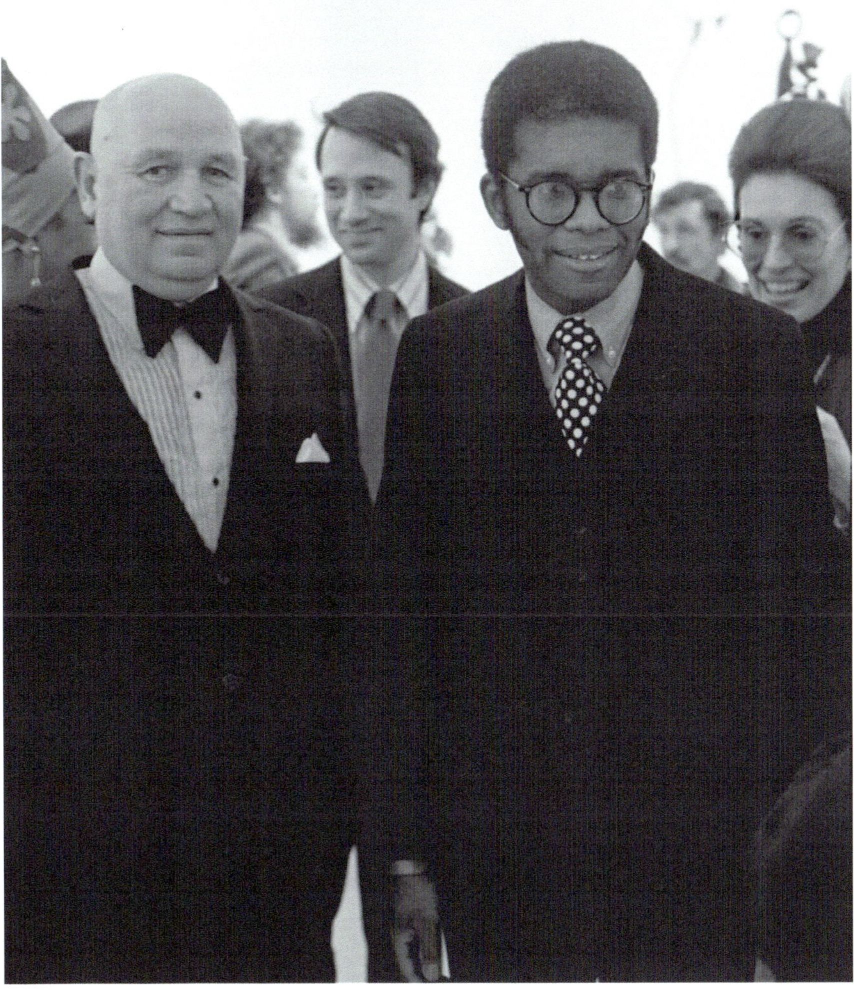

Fig. 4.28 From left, Romare Bearden, John B. Hightower (background center), and Richard Hunt at the openings of *Romare Bearden: The Prevalence of Ritual*, March 25–June 7, 1971, and *The Sculpture of Richard Hunt*, March 25–June 9, 1971. Digital Image © The Museum of Modern Art / Licensed by SCALA / Art Resource, New York.

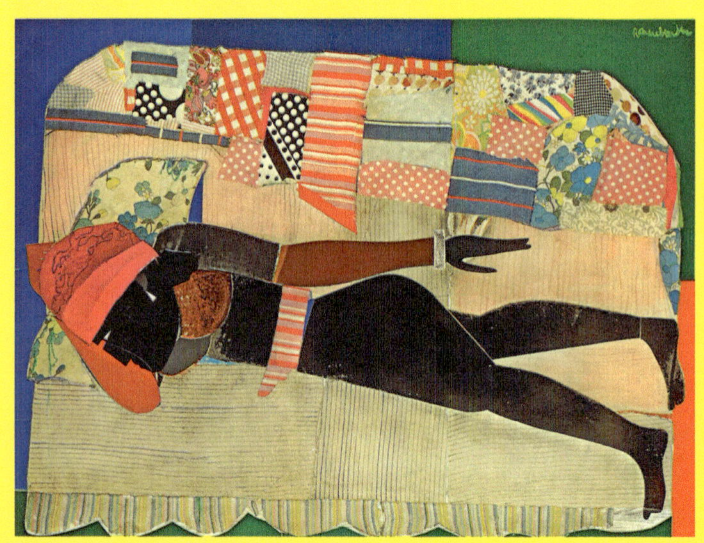

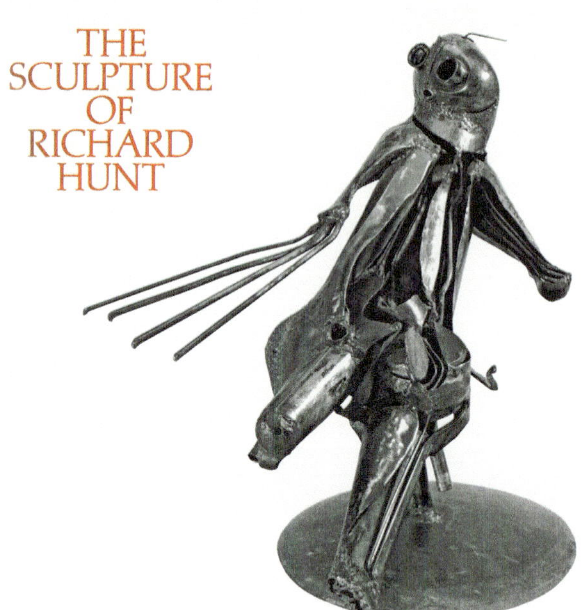

Fig. 4.29 Catalogue for *Romare Bearden: The Prevalence of Ritual* (New York: Museum of Modern Art, 1971). Digital Image © The Museum of Modern Art, New York.

Fig. 4.30 Catalogue for *The Sculpture of Richard Hunt* (New York: Museum of Modern Art, 1971). Digital Image © The Museum of Modern Art, New York.

overdue for recognition, and the opening of the exhibition had an air of jubilation as artists young and old united in celebrating the artist and his work (figs. 4.31 and 4.32). Norman Lewis, Benny Andrews, and William T. Williams all attended, though Faith Ringgold has said, "I was not invited to the opening, because it was thought that I would still be angry and maybe do something."[196]

Carroll Greene pointed out in his essay for the booklet accompanying the show that Bearden had absorbed influences from a wide range of sources: Byzantine, Dutch, African, and modern European. "His goal," Greene says, "consistently has been to create a universal art in a contemporary medium while remaining true to his particular cultural heritage and experience."[197] This breadth situated Bearden's work squarely within Alfred Barr's global, transhistorical notion of modernism without negating its individuality and specificity. All of this was communicated without overblown rhetoric or sweeping generalizations about the state of black art.

At the entrance to the exhibition visitors encountered the artist's work *Folk Musicians* (1941–42) (figs. 4.33 and 4.34), and the show also included *Three Folk Musicians* (1967), a piece that reprises the same subject matter in collage (fig. 4.35). Both works reference one of the icons in MoMA's collection, *Three Musicians* (1921) by Pablo Picasso (fig. 4.36). Moreover, Bearden's collage technique evokes the visual syntax of Synthetic Cubism, which grew out of Picasso's own experiments in collage. Thus the exhibition of Bearden's work seemed to evolve naturally from the museum's past commitment to Picasso's work and to Cubism, as well as reflecting the important influence of Cubism on Bearden's art.[198] Would Bearden have been given a show if his work had not complemented MoMA's canon so well?

Richard Hunt was only thirty-five years old, but his exhibition was referred to by its curator, Bill Lieberman, as a retrospective.[199] The press release for the show outlined the various phases of Hunt's oeuvre: "from the early 'found-object' pieces, through the more linear 'drawings-in-space,' to the denser, more monolithic, enclosed forms of late 1960's and . . . studies for a recent architectural commission."[200] But even Lieberman conceded that Hunt's career was "astonishingly short."[201] Indeed, Hunt's rise in the art world had been meteoric. He had earned his BAE from the School of the Art Institute of Chicago in 1957 and immediately started showing at the Allan Gallery in New York, which was also handling Jacob Lawrence at the time. He was included in the 1958, 1962, 1964, 1966, and 1970 Whitney Sculpture Annuals; the 1958 and 1961 Carnegie International exhibitions; and the Festival Mondial des Arts Nègres '66 exhibition, *Ten Negro Artists from the United States*, which also included senior artists Lawrence, Charles Alston, Bearden, and Norma Morgan. He had previously shown at MoMA three times: in *Recent*

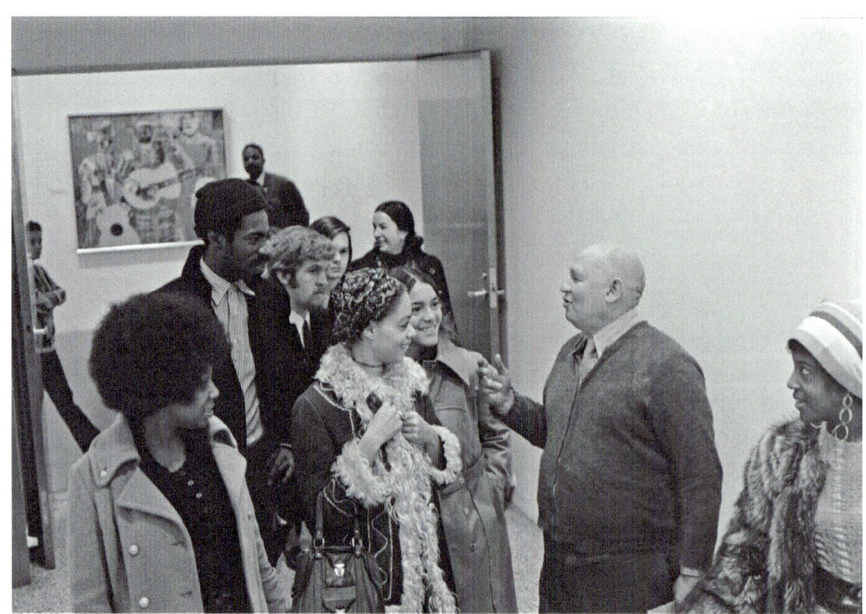

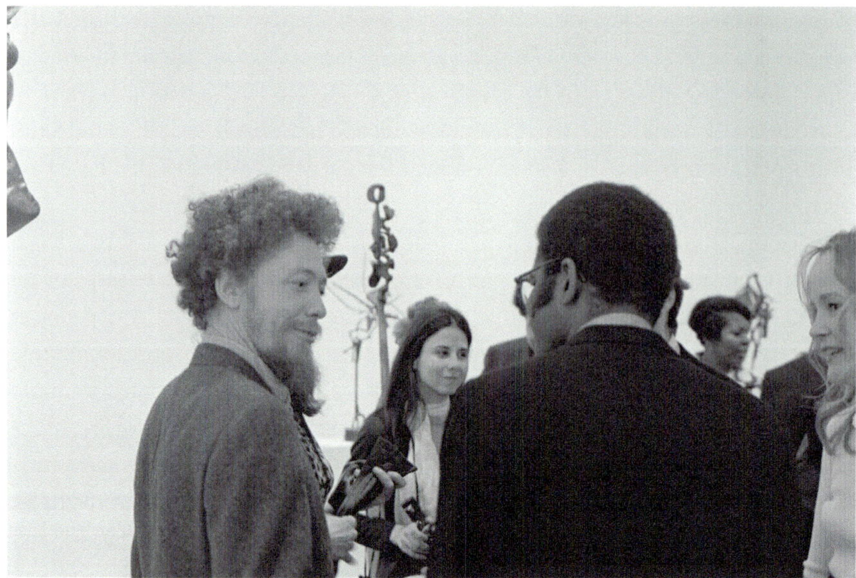

Fig. 4.31 Romare Bearden speaking with guests at the opening of *Romare Bearden: The Prevalence of Ritual*, March 25–June 7, 1971. Digital Image © The Museum of Modern Art / Licensed by SCALA / Art Resource, New York.

Fig. 4.32 Benny Andrews (left) and Richard Hunt at the opening of *The Sculpture of Richard Hunt*, March 25–June 9, 1971. Digital Image © The Museum of Modern Art / Licensed by SCALA / Art Resource, New York.

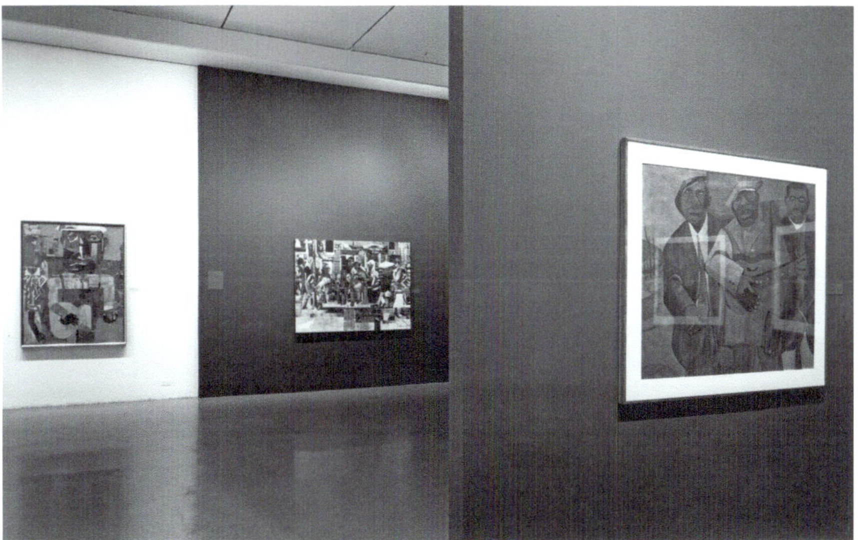

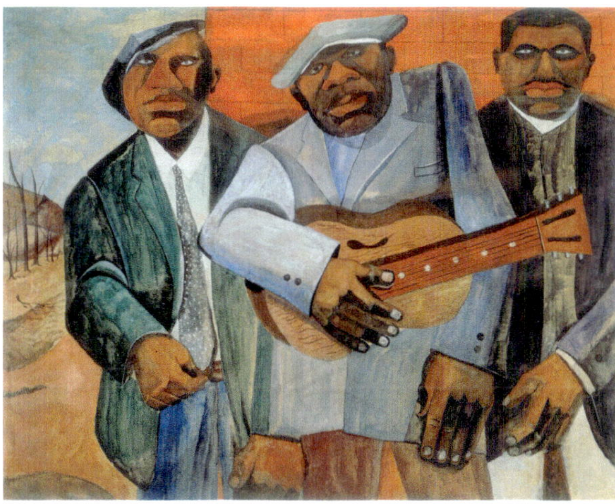

Fig. 4.33 Installation view of *Romare Bearden: The Prevalence of Ritual*, March 25–June 7, 1971, the Museum of Modern Art. Art © Romare Bearden Foundation / Licensed by VAGA, New York. Digital Image © The Museum of Modern Art / Licensed by SCALA / Art Resource, New York.

Fig. 4.34 Romare Bearden, *Folk Musicians*, 1941–42, gouache with ink and graphite on brown paper. © Romare Bearden Foundation / Licensed by VAGA, New York, NY.

Sculpture U.S.A. (1959); the 1968 benefit exhibition honoring Martin Luther King Jr.; and a show of prints from Tamarind in 1969. In 1962, five years after graduating from college, he had been awarded a Guggenheim Fellowship, and in 1968 he had been appointed to the National Council on the Arts. Prior to the exhibition, the museum had acquired one sculpture, *Arachne* (1956), and eight of his prints.[202] After the show, it purchased two more prints, *Prometheus* (1956) and *Crucifix Figure* (1957), and a drawing, *Untitled* (1964).

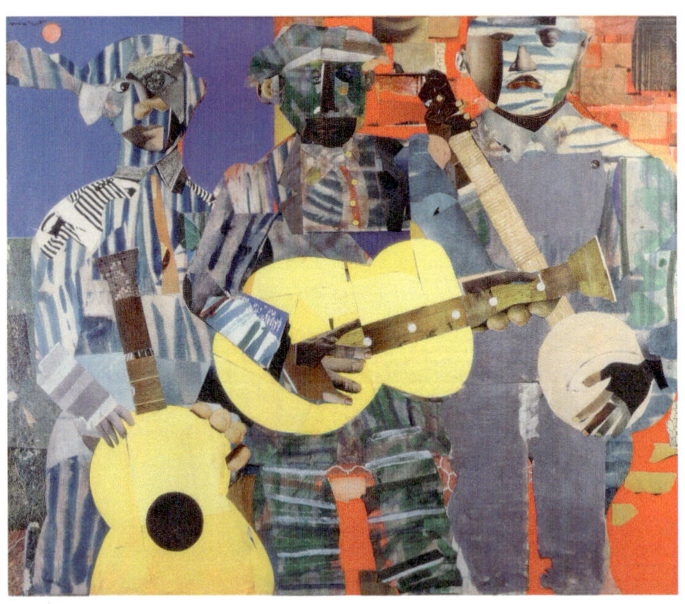

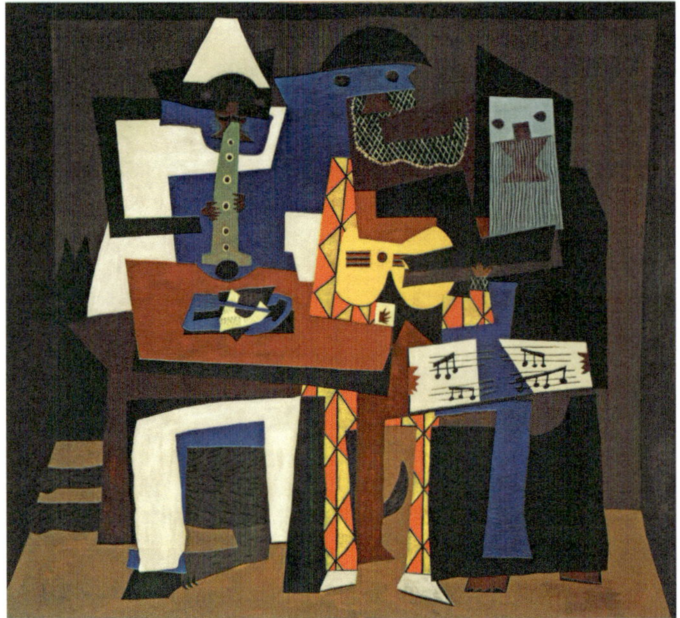

Fig. 4.35 Romare Bearden, *Three Folk Musicians*, 1967, collage of various papers with paint and graphite on canvas, 50⅛×60 ins. © Romare Bearden Foundation / Licensed by VAGA, New York, NY.

Fig. 4.36 Pablo Picasso, *Three Musicians*, 1921, oil on canvas, 6 ft. 7 ins.×7 ft. 3¾ ins., the Museum of Modern Art, New York. © 2014 Estate of Pablo Picasso / Artists Rights Society (ARS), New York. Digital Image © The Museum of Modern Art / Licensed by SCALA / Art Resource, New York.

By pairing Bearden with Hunt the Museum of Modern Art hedged its bets. The two artists not only came from different generations but also worked in different styles. Hunt was an abstract sculptor, while Bearden's work was representational and depicted scenes of both the rural South and the urban North. An exhibition review in *Art in America* put it this way: the artists were "poles apart in their esthetic philosophy. . . . Hunt's totally abstract welded-steel sculpture bears no reference to the 'black experience,' while Bearden's 'montage-paintings' of Negroes going about their daily lives attempt to confront it directly."[203] While such tidy categories may not have captured the full dimension of the artists' bodies of work, the statement shows that the museum's gambit to demonstrate diversity in its approach to African American artists paid off.

Clearly, MoMA had been following the various debates about "purity" and "politicization" in art. The Hunt exhibition's research files contain newspaper articles in which Hilton Kramer and Edmund Barry Gaither, curator of the exhibition *Afro-American Artists: New York and Boston*, debated whether art with socially meaningful subject matter disqualified it from "critical discriminations based on purely artistic values."[204] In a gesture clearly demonstrating on which side of the debate Lieberman fell, the curator quoted Kramer in his exhibition essay: "The most perceptive critic of Hunt's work has been Hilton Kramer. . . . Mr. Kramer observes that Hunt's many forms 'suggest highly agitated emotions, without specific representational references,' and as early as 1963 wrote: 'I think that Hunt is one of the most gifted and assured artists working in the direct-metal, open-form medium—and I mean not only in his own country and generation, but anywhere in the world.' "[205]

Today, including excerpts of an art critic's review in an exhibition catalogue would be almost unthinkable. It conjures up the notion that the art world is an insiders' game of collusion. But in 1971 Lieberman did not hesitate to align his show with Kramer's opinion. If Kramer himself had selected an artist to show at MoMA, it might very well have been Richard Hunt. Not surprisingly, Kramer wrote two glowing articles about the show in the *New York Times*, one when it opened and a second comparing the Hunt show with a concurrent exhibition of work by Tony Smith.[206] In the second piece Kramer lavished even more praise on Hunt: "In terms of chronological age, he [Hunt] is still a 'young' artist, yet in terms of the history of his career and accomplishment, he is an established figure distinctly senior to Mr. Smith, who is 59."[207]

African American artists turned out in droves to attend the exhibitions' openings, and after its run at MoMA the Bearden show toured to museums throughout the United States, ending in New York at the Studio Museum in Harlem.[208] The Hunt show was presented at one additional venue, the Art Institute of Chicago.[209]

Did this balancing act work? There were no public demonstrations against the shows, but the artists who had been working hardest to bring about change at MoMA denounced the decision to show Hunt. When the pairing had been announced in the fall of 1970, Faith Ringgold was incensed. Citing Hunt's comments at the Metropolitan Museum of Art's symposium "The Black Artist in America," Ringgold wrote to Hightower:

> In the name of Black Determination, Richard Hunt cannot have a retrospective at MOMA. . . . It was Black Determination which got a retrospective in the first place. Surely a man like Mr. Hunt, who dares deny the existence of such a force, should not be the one to first sample the fruits of it. Mr. Hunt is an establishment artist who feels very unoppressed and satisfied that he is known to whites, although he remains totally unknown to the black community.
>
> . . . We were the ones who were able to get MOMA to listen. Mr. Hunt will not benefit from our blackness. Let him bring us something for our youth to give us strength and to help us to build a black cultural consciousness. Black women and students will protest his retrospective at the Museum of Modern Art. We consider this a WHITE ESTABLISHMENT BLACK TRICK, and an insult to the black community. We will not allow it to go uncontested.
>
> Mr. Hightower, you do need the advise [sic] of the artists who are concerned and involved enough to act in protest. Obviously, the ones with which you are in contact agree with you; but then Uncle Tom always agrees with "whitey."
>
> Yours in Peace and Progress?
>
> Faith Ringgold[210]

Attached to the letter were pages copied from the symposium transcript that had been published in the January 1969 issue of the Met's *Bulletin*, with several of Hunt's statements underlined, especially the heated exchanges with Tom Lloyd:

> Well, "the aesthetics of Black art" is a problem I really don't address myself to, in either my work or my thinking. The problem of the Negro in terms of the contemporary situation in art—showing in museums and galleries and all those things—seems to be more or less tied up with the prevailing currents in art itself. For instance an artist working in kinetic, light, or minimal things [perhaps a gibe at Lloyd, whose works incorporated lights] might have a better chance of breaking into the scene than somebody who's paint-

ing figuratively. . . . I feel lucky that I was born in Chicago and haven't had to contend with the sort of problems that exist here [in New York]. . . . I don't see how a Negro in America, even with segregated situations, can escape having influences that come from his family, from his background in the ghetto or whatever he happens to be, from his formal education, from his exposure to the arts. The thing gets pretty much mixed up, and the idea of separating out these experiences, good or bad, Black or not, seems sometimes rather useless and sometimes rather tiresome. (emphasis original)

During the Metropolitan's symposium Lloyd had retorted: "Well, I don't think so. You know what I think, Mr. Hunt, is that you are a conditioned Black man. I think you are oblivious to what's happening. . . . To me you don't seem like a man concerned with Black people, with Black kids, with Black culture. I don't think that enters your feelings. And that bothers me, that bothers the hell out of me."[211]

Ringgold was not the only critic of the show. Charles Allen wrote in the *New York Times*, "The exhibition of the works of two Black artists does not make a nonracist policy, although it could well mark the beginning. . . . The walls haven't come tumbling down any more than they did when New York City got its first Black bus driver."[212]

Hightower never intended these exhibitions to be isolated events. In his response to Ringgold dated November 4, 1970, he had written, "I would hate to think of it being the only exhibition of the work of Black artists that was to be put on by the Museum."[213] Had he remained director, perhaps this would have been the start of regular and sustained inclusion of artists of color in the museum's program. But after his departure it would be twenty-five years before MoMA would organize another major one-person show of work by an African American artist. In 1996 MoMA held a retrospective of the work of Roy DeCarava.[214] Its first show of work by an African American woman, Lorna Simpson, would take place in 1990 as part of the museum's Projects series of small shows.[215]

In June 1971 the Byers Committee, which had been formed a year earlier, presented to MoMA's full board its report on the museum's role with respect to "Afro-American, Hispanic, and other ethnic art." Encouragingly, the report began with a "statement of the problem" that included a section written by Carroll Greene worth quoting at length because of the richness and subtlety with which he frames the issues for the committee:

The term "ethnic art" generally implies those artistic expressions—styles, techniques, forms—which are broadly characteristic of a religious, racial, national, or cultural group.

In a modern technological society, however, especially a multi-racial, pluralistic culture such as that of the United States, individual artists of a particular ethnic group may or may not create art which is broadly—or even narrowly—characteristic of that ethnic group.

This fact has prevented certain artists from participating in the dominant cultural and institutional life of the United States. The American melting pot has been especially inhospitable to black Americans, Hispanic Americans, American Indians and other groups who have been unassimilated, either by insistence or through choice.

The tendency of the majority of "assimilated" white Americans to assign the term "the ethnics" to certain other groups of Americans is misleading and often derogatory because it implies that the so-called "ethnics" are somehow less American than themselves.

In recent years more and more racial, national and cultural groups have begun to reassert their distinctiveness. Virtually none have wished to withdraw from the national culture.

Instead, they have opted for a more responsible and visible role in the culture. When their demands are resisted or ignored, they answer with cries of Reform or Revolution. Cesar Chavez, the Mexican-American labor leader, says, "The system works well for whites, but it doesn't work for us." Chavez's words and those of many Black and Puerto Rican leaders have thus far reflected a desire to be partners in the American System.

But the fact remains that the integration of minorities into the mainstream of American life is still the option of the white majority. When that majority seriously makes the decision to integrate, then our American institutions will reflect it.

The current separatist wave among minorities is an historic reaction of people whose rejection by the majority (witting or unwitting) has left them no self-respecting alternative. ("Since you don't want me, I don't want you.")

The need of blacks and other minorities to build their own social institutions within their own communities should not be construed as unhealthy. Rather it is a call for responsible leadership on the part of minorities themselves. Nor should this development be used to delay the integration of our major institutions. These two concurrent developments will probably in the long run strengthen rather than weaken the American social fabric. At this time each segment—the majority and the minorities—have important, even if sometimes separate, tasks to accomplish.[216]

The rest of the report contained research on the museum's history of inclusivity and recommendations for the future.

The Subcommittee on Acquisitions and Exhibitions wrote that it began its work by "assessing the validity of the charge" that the museum "concentrated on white Western, largely Europe-derived, art to the exclusion of non-European minority artists."[217] After reviewing lists of projects and acquisitions, the members of the subcommittee concluded that there was "substance to the charge of ethnocentricity," but that it was not a conscious bias and that the museum "has not wholly overlooked ethnic art in developing its acquisitions and exhibitions policy." "Early in The Museum of Modern Art's history," the report stated, "the Museum pioneered in this field," though the committee admitted that the museum "has not, however, been sufficiently attentive in recent years to minority artists."[218] The committee found that although the museum's acquisitions policy was not consciously ethnocentric, selections of the collection were based primarily on "white experience," and the report recommended that a special fund be created for the acquisition of work by artists of color, as well as curatorial travel and research. The amount suggested was $25,000, with one-fourth to be donated by the trustees and the remainder to be raised from outside sources. The report stressed that any apparent ethnocentric decisions were completely unwitting.[219]

The Subcommittee on International Programs concluded that the charge that MoMA's International Program was too concerned with "Western cultures" was "groundless." The subcommittee cited the activities of the museum in Latin America, though it neglected to mention that these activities were in the service of Nelson Rockefeller's agenda as head of the Office of Inter-American Affairs, a federal agency established in 1940 to suppress German and Italian economic activity in Latin America and increase the political influence of the United States.[220] The report acknowledged that the museum had had little contact with other museums or educational institutions in Africa, a "deficiency" that may be alleviated, it said, by the touring show *Twenty-Five Contemporary American Painters and Sculptors as Printmakers*, which had been circulating "in Africa" for three years, as well as a forthcoming exhibition at the museum of African textiles and jewelry.[221] The print show toured to eleven cities, including several venues in Abidjan, Côte d'Ivoire; the Centre for Arts and Culture in Accra, Ghana; and the National Museum in Mogadishu, Somalia.

The museum's "success" in its international programs, though cited as evidence of the museum's inclusivity, raises a critical problem: the displacement of concerns about the representation of American artists of color by engagement with artists outside the United States. As cultural theorist Chon Noriega has observed, "To go 'global' suggests that one has undone the myth of a single American cultural identity. But, if one has not done that, if the myth remains, then the international arena merely provides a chance to place that myth in a broader context."[222]

Finally, the Subcommittee on Community Programs painted a complex picture of the museum's relationships to the racially and ethnically diverse constituencies of New York City. The findings were informed by interviews with dozens of people, including artist and BECC leader Benny Andrews; Courtney Callender, commissioner of the Department of Cultural Affairs in the New York City Department of Parks; Vinnette Carroll, the artistic director of the Urban Arts Corps and formerly the head of the Ghetto Arts Program at NYSCA; curator Edmund Barry Gaither; Don Harper, an audio producer who had worked on the *Harlem on My Mind* exhibition; Frank Donnelly, a social worker and founding trustee of the Studio Museum in Harlem; and cultural historian and community organizer Laurin Raiken. The subcommittee lauded the museum for its projects and events for minority constituents, such as its sponsorship of the Children's Art Carnival in Harlem, but criticized the museum for the fact that most of its projects were "white-sponsored and white-directed" and its publications on artists of color were almost all authored by whites. While many of the museum's past and present efforts may have appealed to diverse ethnic groups, the panel's advisers observed that they remained largely unknown because they were inadequately promoted in the relevant communities.[223] The advisers strongly suggested that future MoMA "ethnic projects" be directed, or at least influenced, by the people they are designed to serve and that the museum's contacts with minority communities be greatly improved. This section of the report concluded with the assessment that the museum's past activities "were valuable chiefly as an indication that the spirit was willing; the flesh still requires strengthening."[224] In conclusion, the subcommittee recommended that the museum design programs to engage minorities educationally; set up committees that include minority participants; and undertake exhibitions to explore the cultural identities of these groups. A detailed attachment noted: "There was considerable discussion of satellite museums which appear to be seen by the community as segregated outposts, patronizing and paternalistic. Moreover, as one participant said, 'every time we get to the big leagues they change the rules.' No form of physical separation was considered as either building good will in the non-white community or extracting the interest and support of the larger community."[225]

On the surface, the report stressed the museum's eagerness to address the problems and suggestions voiced by the AWC, and to reflect the reactions and concerns of those people whose advice the museum had sought. But the committee's ultimate conclusion suggests utter complacency. Answering the question of the committee's original charge, the museum's responsibility to "Afro-American, Hispanic, and other ethnic art," the report concluded: "*It is significant that fulfilling this role requires no substantive change in the Museum's present policy. Most of the revisions suggested by the subcommittees, and herewith recommended by the Committee, simply seek to modify existing programs*" (emphasis original).[226]

Reading deeper into the report, one can see that the conclusion reached by the committee was not necessarily based on the empirical research it had commissioned. For example, curator Mildred Constantine reviewed the exhibition program from 1929 to 1970 and found: "If we analyze the exhibitions which the Museum has shown during the last decade, it is obvious that the program illustrates a narrowing point of view; a concern with Western cultures, and a report of established art movements."[227]

In some cases the conclusions were in direct contradiction to its subcommittees' recommendations. For example, the Subcommittee on Community Programs recommended that the museum "recruit, train, and *employ more minority group staff members on every level of its operation*" (emphasis original).[228] The final report, however, recommended that any new program be incorporated into the museum's existing structure and implemented "as much as possible by the present staff."[229] The results made John Hightower aware that "there really was a strong sense of not wanting to change, of considering what change might consist of and then deciding . . . we really don't want to be on the cutting edge."[230]

From the trustees' perspective Hightower had taken them out too far on a limb. As David Rockefeller wrote in his memoir:

[John Hightower] believed that museums had an obligation to help society resolve its problems. Since Vietnam was one of the principal societal problems of the day, John thought MoMA should participate in the national debate. Before long the museum's lobby resembled an antiwar protest headquarters. He allowed the bookshop to sell a poster of the infamous My Lai massacre, with the caption "And babies too . . ." and "The Museum of Modern Art" emblazoned in bold letters along the bottom. When President Nixon's invasion of Cambodia provoked widespread unrest on the nation's college campuses, Hightower dropped the museum's admission fee, ran continuous showings of antiwar films, and permitted MoMA staff members to stand outside distributing antiwar pamphlets.[231]

Hightower was fired on January 2, 1972. Rather than refreshing the museum's mission, the dynamic disorder of this period culminated in an abrupt retrenchment and an official reaffirmation by the board of trustees that the museum was doing just fine and need not concern itself with art and issues of the day.

What stopped change? Raphael Ortiz has hypothesized that MoMA's trustees "were acculturated in such a manner as to not serve the best interests of culture. Perhaps the cultural institution from their view, but not the larger meaning of a cultural institution within the culture of a nation."[232] According to Bob Malone, the exhibition designer of *Harlem on My Mind* who had worked with Hightower at NYSCA, "The trustees at MoMA saw Hightower as another Roosevelt, a turncoat. They saw him as a kind of elegant young man that looked like Ivy League, but in his head they suspected that he had been turned. He had been brainwashed into approving of this sort of thing, and therefore, he had to go. They were protecting their own value structure and their own control and their own sense of morality."[233]

Richard Oldenburg, a large, congenial man who had been running the museum's Publications Department since 1969, succeeded Hightower as director. On November 8, 1972, he stood before the board of trustees and summed up the state of the institution:

> The year had been a difficult one for the Museum, with a change in Directorship, a number of unusual labor problems [unionization of the staff], and the necessity of instituting a cost reduction program. Yet, difficult though the year had been, and with all the Museum's affairs being attentively watched and reported by the press, it was during this period that a number of major acquisitions were made, some important and very successful exhibitions were held, and very substantial support received from government, business, and individual friends. . . . This record of success in the face of adversity is eloquent testimony to the basic strength of the institution and a tribute to all who have supported it so steadfastly during this difficult period.[234]

Essentially, Oldenburg reassured the board that it was back to business as usual.

In 1973 Oldenburg promoted Bill Rubin to the position of director of the Department of Painting and Sculpture. Rubin was now the most powerful figure on the staff. In the ensuing years, the Museum of Modern Art would become increasingly haphazard in its engagement with African American artists and other artists of color, and its approach to modernism would narrow.[235] Rubin's four signature exhibitions—*Cézanne: The Late Work* (1977); *Picasso: A Retrospective* (1980);

"*Primitivism*" *in 20th Century Art* (1984); and *Picasso and Braque: Pioneering Cubism* (1989)—demonstrate the narrow range of his main interests, primarily Cubism and its antecedents. The museum's program would become increasingly insular, an airtight narrative that ran from Cézanne and Picasso to Piet Mondrian, Jackson Pollock, and Jasper Johns. Rubin pinpointed the birth of modernism in the School of Paris generally, and the personage of Pablo Picasso specifically. Indeed, judging from his texts in the "*Primitivism*" catalogue Rubin believed that the entire history of modern art hinged on one work, *Les Demoiselles d'Avignon*, a painting, he contended, that triggered an entirely new approach to art.[236] Rubin's vision would drive both the museum's exhibition program and its acquisitions until his retirement in 1988. During this period, even the museum's modest advancements in racial and ethnic diversity were all but forgotten.[237]

In 1984 the museum published the first major catalogue of its collection in conjunction with the opening of its newly renovated and expanded building designed by Cesar Pelli.[238] On the book's cover, the museum chose to reproduce Matisse's *Memory of Oceania* (1953), a large collage with gouache and charcoal that dates from the same year MoMA established its permanent collection (fig. 4.37). In many ways the piece is a likely choice for the cover of a coffee-table book, with its bright colors, its decorative quality, and the artist's name recognition. To those more knowledgeable the selection also suggests the themes of primitivism and posits the centrality of French art. Yet there is another aspect of this selection detectable only to the museum's inner circle: the piece was Bill Rubin's first major acquisition for the museum. With this single gesture, the museum symbolically handed authorship of the collection to him.

In an interview with art historian Barbara Rose in 1984, just before the opening of the "*Primitivism*" exhibition, Rubin claimed that Alfred Barr had handpicked him as his successor: "Alfred Barr made me his choice for the job of curating the collection he had formed."[239] Walter Bareiss disputed this. In a 1991 interview for MoMA's archives Bareiss declared, "I spoke to Mrs. Barr about this also because I was curious: what exactly did Alfred Barr have in mind? He was most disappointed in Bill Rubin because he was trying to change the Museum, and that's what I was afraid of, too, that Bill Rubin was going to change the Museum."[240]

Rubin changed it indeed.[241] Throughout its history, the Museum of Modern Art had probed and experimented with exhibitions exploring various cultural manifestations of modernity. Barr's early experimental exhibitions of art from around the globe demonstrated openness to the concepts of both cultural specificity and universal humanism. Even toward the end of his career at MoMA Barr encouraged debate

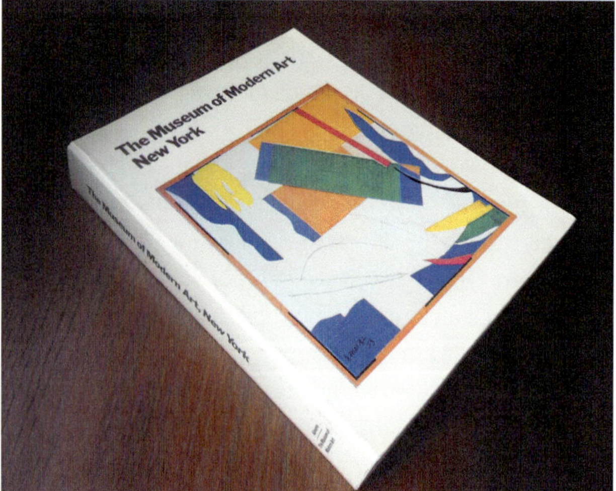

Fig. 4.37 *The Museum of Modern Art, New York: The History and the Collection*, 1984. Cover image: Henri Matisse, *Memory of Oceania*, 1952–53, gouache and crayon on cut-and-pasted paper over canvas, 9 ft. 4 ins.×9 ft. 4⅞ ins. © The Museum of Modern Art, New York. Photo by author.

and responsiveness to the constant evolution of art. In a letter to the editor of the *New York Times* published in 1960 he refused to be labeled "the most powerful taste-maker in American art today" by critic John Canaday. He insisted that "we must show the disparate, even contradictory, yet significant kinds of art our complex civilization has produced."[242]

Rubin's vision, by contrast, was teleological, not panoramic. John Elderfield has said that Rubin "was the one who really brought to it [the collection] the historical positivistic sense of order, and the notion of the great unrolling of the modern movement."[243] As curator Betsy Jones has explained, "When he [Rubin] became director of the Museum collections, he really just began filling gaps. . . . He'd go back and fill in one month in the work of Picasso because we didn't have anything in June but we had August and July."[244] Rubin called these gaps "lacunae." Walter Bareiss recalled: "I never particularly liked this idea of filling in when we don't have a Picasso or Matisse or, for that matter, a Juan Gris from the year 1924, we only have one from 1923."[245]

According to Robert Storr, a curator at MoMA from 1990 to 2002, "Barr was interested in art and he knew, at least for his own purposes and from his own position, who the great ones were and who the less great ones were, and who may be the minor but interesting ones, but he was actually interested in all of it."[246] By contrast, Storr has described Rubin's curatorial method as canon building: "The impulse is to align acknowledged greatness of one with acknowledged greatness of another and produce this idea that there's an absolutely direct, unpolluted bloodstream from one to the next, to the next, to the next and nothing else matters unless it becomes an interesting cousin. . . . He [Rubin] was very concerned with the certainty of things, not with the spark of things."[247]

Rubin not only suppressed the museum's exploratory dimension; he also downgraded its involvement with contemporary art. The Projects series of work by emerging artists started by Kynaston McShine in 1971, which was the main venue for artists of color at MoMA, was suspended from 1981 to 1986. In the interview with Rose, Rubin said, "We don't have the space to show new art in depth because the museum's collection covers one hundred years of art. Since the 'outer edge' is, after all, covered widely by hundreds of galleries in this city and by other museums, I can't quite see taking down the Picassos, Kandinskys, the Pollocks and the Johnses to show very new art in depth."[248] Walter Bareiss lamented the museum's lapsed engagement with contemporary art: "The Museum of Modern Art should be a museum of modern art and modern art does not end in the year 2000 anymore than it ended in the year 1980 or something, nor will it end in the year 2010. If the Museum survives, it will be The Museum of Modern Art and, as such, has the responsibility to show and collect whatever happens to be going on."[249]

Rubin's reactionary impulse would find its fullest manifestation in the exhibition *"Primitivism" in 20th Century Art* (fig. 4.38), which resurrected a narrative that Barr first pursued in the 1930s, but neglected to account for the social and political changes of the intervening decades: the debates between art historians Alain Locke and James Porter about the importance of African art to African American artists; the inspiration of the African independence movements of the 1950s and '60s; and the engagement with the concept of ancestral legacy that inspired so many African American artists, curators, and critics to explore the idea of a black aesthetic in the 1960s and after.[250] Rubin also ignored African American artists' travels to Africa in the 1960s, '70s, and '80s, which provided firsthand experience of African art and culture.[251]

In one of the many debates surrounding the *"Primitivism"* show, cocurator Kirk Varnedoe stated that the show aimed to be "studying the ways people may be alike, rather than just emphasizing the ways they're different."[252] But in the global search for likeness, where were the American and European artists of color? How do we account for the absence of African American artists who looked to African art as a prime source of inspiration: Aaron Douglas, John Biggers, Lois Mailou Jones, Palmer Hayden, and the entire Black Arts movement? Where was William Edmondson, who had been given a one-person exhibition at the museum in 1937 and whose work the museum had described as "modern primitive"?[253] How is it that Jacob Epstein (fig. 4.39) warranted nine pages in the catalogue, but Sargent Claude Johnson

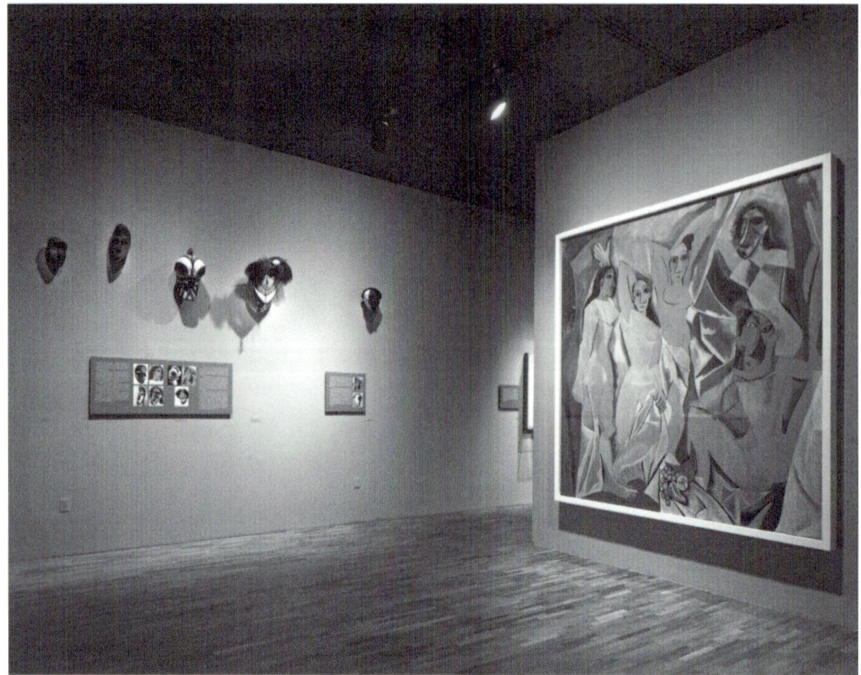

(fig. 4.40) was left out? Henry Moore's sculptures (fig. 4.41) were also in, but Elizabeth Catlett's out (figs. 4.42 and 4.43). Why was the 1970s represented almost entirely by documentation of earthworks? And why did Paul Klee, A. R. Penck, and Keith Haring's "pictographs" warrant inclusion (fig. 4.44), but not Ben Jones's patterned figures (fig. 4.45)?[254]

Gail Levin, who wrote the essay on American art for the *"Primitivism"* catalogue, had included in her initial draft a discussion of the Harlem Renaissance, especially the work of Palmer Hayden and Aaron Douglas. Indeed, her article on "primitivism" in the American literary tradition published in the November 1984 issue of *Arts* magazine (concurrent with the *"Primitivism"* exhibition) evidences this research.[255] Levin, an Americanist who had persuaded Rubin to expand his inclusion of American art beyond Abstract Expressionism, tried to interest him in the Harlem Renaissance, but he "simply couldn't go there aesthetically," she has said.[256] Older, more powerful, and unrestrained in the exercise of his authority, he ordered her

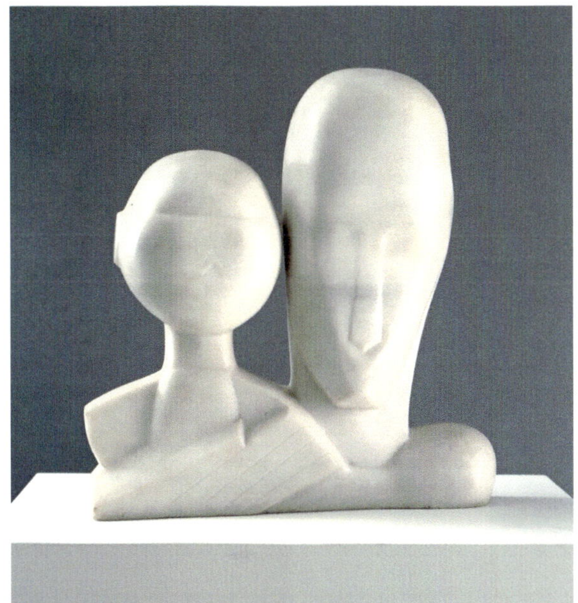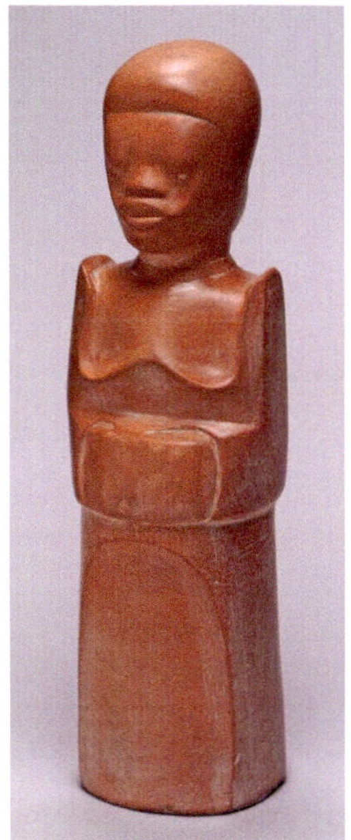

to remove the material. "I felt quite demolished," Levin has recalled, "but I wasn't looking to make an enemy. . . . What can I say? I could not stand up to Rubin. It was his show."[257]

Looking back, Faith Ringgold has said, "I don't think artists really understand that things do get worse and not better unless you do something. They don't get better naturally."[258] Yet some things did get better. The reaction against "*Primitivism*" inspired new approaches to the history of modern art and, in the words of Kobena Mercer, to "cosmopolitan modernisms," that is, how modernist "attitudes took shape in different national and cultural environments."[259] As art historian Jack Flam has pointed out, "Rubin and Varnedoe had conceived their exhibition in one cultural climate and in doing so helped to provoke the overt manifestation of another."[260] Since the 1990s art historians and curators have produced a growing

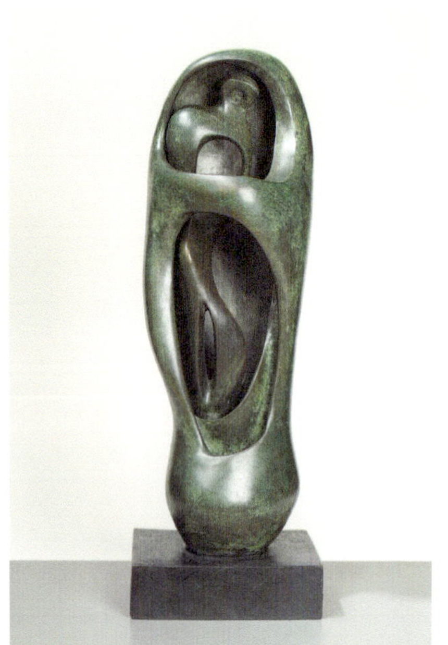

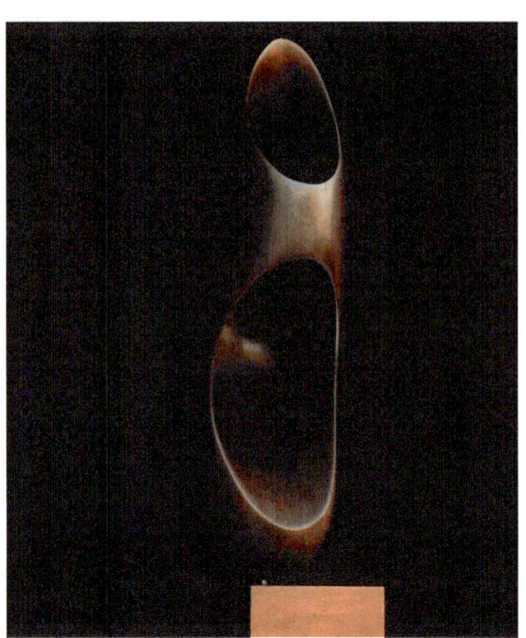

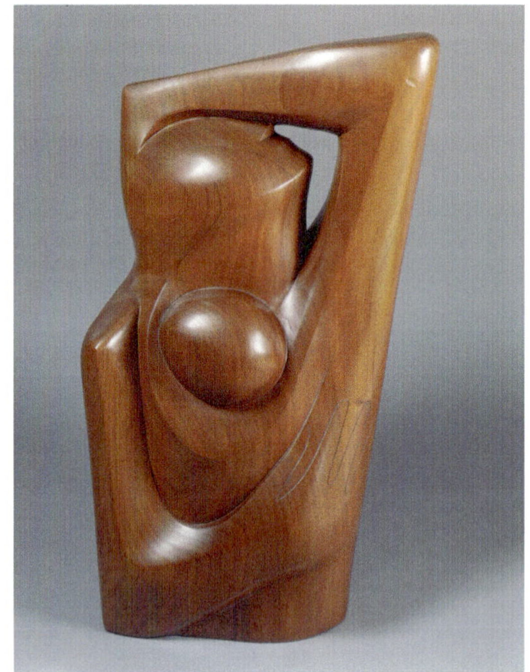

Fig. 4.41 (*above left*) Henry Moore, *Working Model for Upright Internal and External Forms*, 1951, bronze, 25 ³⁄₁₆ × 8½ × 8 ins. Collection of the Art Gallery of Ontario. Reproduced by permission of the Henry Moore Foundation. © The Henry Moore Foundation. All Rights Reserved, DACS 2015 / www.henry-moore.org.

Fig. 4.42 (*above right*) Elizabeth Catlett, *Mask*, 1972, tropical wood, 11 ins. high. © Estate of Elizabeth Catlett / Licensed by VAGA, New York, NY.

Fig. 4.43 (*right*) Elizabeth Catlett, *Mother and Child*, 1971, carved cedar, 26½ × 17 × 9 ins. Collection of Kalamazoo Institute of Arts, Kalamazoo, MI; Courtesy of Michael Rosenfeld Gallery LLC, New York, NY. © Estate of Elizabeth Catlett / Licensed by VAGA, New York, NY.

dissolving level the sense of community with immemorial rhythms of natural order and human tradition. These latter conditions seem laudable enough, and yet they are virtually the same terms Albert Speer had in mind in his design for the ceremonial zeppelin fields and parade grounds of the Third Reich. Indeed, one of the German monuments most admired by the Nazis was a great circle of monoliths consciously modeled on Stonehenge, intentionally kept devoid of independent sculpted figures and slated for use especially on solstice festivals, where the alienating atomism of modern society would be dissolved in a reaffirming merger of *Blut und Boden*, of the folk with the cycle of the seasons and the soil.[19]

While total art and totalitarian art may start out from very different places, they share enemies and can wind up approaching each other. To the extent that primitivism presents itself—as many of its recent advocates have presented it—as the righteous foe of the modern, it falls into perilous fellowship with other such foes and begs unflattering comparisons. If we want an unhappy answer to why a modern Stonehenge, this is at least in the vicinity.

However, it is richer and more in keeping with everything this book has been about to see primitivism, modern or postmodern, not only as a symptom of cultural disaffection but as a sign of life. Only in its least creative moments and only for the conventionally minded or uninformed can the twentieth-century fascination with the tribal be seen as a wholly negative—or wholly affirmative—response to modernity. It has been, as primitivist thought has always been, a dialogue of self-projection, discovery, and self-criticism, in which modern life provides both the need for alternatives and the means for uncovering and understanding them. Daumier and folk prints gave Gauguin his points of affinity with Hokusai and the Marquesans, and they in turn reinvigorated Giotto for him (p. 185). Gauguin then, with Cézanne, led Picasso toward his crucial connection with tribal sculpture, and that helped him elevate to greater effect his admiration for Rousseau and his own caricatural power.[20] Amid all that is familiar in the latest neoprimitivist painting, both in the nationalist rhetoric that boosts it and in the revivalist look (e.g., A. R. Penck), what is most happily recognized is the restatement, however slight, of this kind of dialogue, in the new infatuation with graffiti

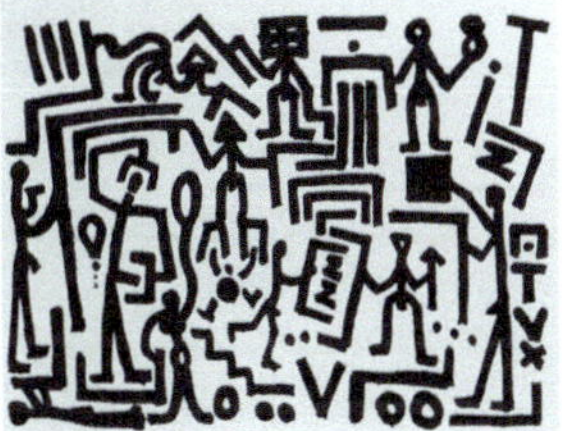

A. R. Penck. *Défense*. 1983. Resin on linen, 8'1½" x 11'4½" (247.6 x 346.7 cm). Mary Boone Gallery/Michael Werner Gallery

682   VARNEDOE

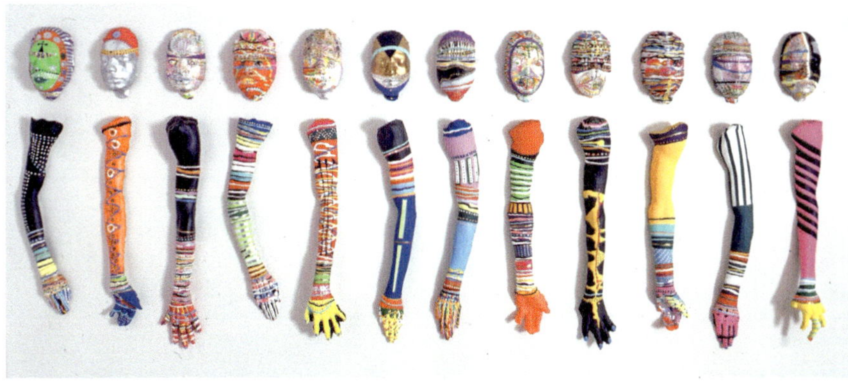

Keith Haring. Untitled (Totem). 1983. Enamel on wood, 9' x 43" (262 x 109.2 cm). Collection of the artist

Here the sophisticated devices of modern international signage blend with cartoon conventions and streetwise inventions in alternatively upbeat and ominous subterranean pictographs of modern life (e.g., Keith Haring). Communication theory and cave painting meet in the South Bronx. More deeply and richly, this essential interchange is manifest in the best of the art we have been discussing. Minimalism, structuralism, and modern technology have not simply provided the antitheses from which recent primitivism has fled, nor only encouraged the bookish smothering of instinctual originality. They have opened up as well new ways of access to Primitive thought and society, new levels of affinity that in turn reform and redirect our art and point to the recovery of neglected inspirations among our own resources.

The idea of primitivism as flight from civilization, or of Primitive art as a wholly "outsider" challenge, is an offshoot of the Romantic notion that true progress, true revolution, indeed truth in its most irreducible sense is only accessible when we step outside the enchaining confines of culture.[21] Modern ideas of the mind and of the constraints of language suggest that this fantasy of escape is never to be realized. Yet this need not mean that the power of primitivism lies only in delusion, or that we are prisoners of conventions that bar us from contact with anything beyond our ken, or kin. Modern thought and style are not only blinders but also powerful lenses. The history of modernist primitivism and the character of its best recent examples speak directly to the point. This is a process of revolution that begins and ends in modern culture, and because of that—not in spite of it—can continually expand and deepen our contact with that which is remote and different from us, and continually threaten, challenge, and reform our sense of self.

Fig. 4.44 Page from catalogue for *"Primitivism" in 20th Century Art: Affinity of the Tribal and the Modern*, featuring images of works by A. R. Penck and Keith Haring. © The Museum of Modern Art, New York.

Fig. 4.45 Ben Jones, *Black Face and Art Unit*, 1971, twelve life-size painted plaster casts, dimensions variable. Collection of the New Jersey State Museum. Museum Purchase. FA1984.92. Reproduced with permission. © Ben Jones.

body of scholarship that has reshaped understanding of twentieth-century art.[261] Inadvertently, the *"Primitivism"* show led to the shattering of the very premises on which it was based. Even with this advancement in scholarship, though, exhibitions embracing global modernity in major museums are still few and far between.[262]

Who is responsible for MoMA's retrenchment? Was it Bill Rubin? Was it the board of trustees? Was Rubin a culprit and Hightower a tragic hero, or were both just part of a system that "naturally" reproduces itself and resists change? Imani Perry has pointed out that even within systems of structural racism individuals do play a role in advancing or denying equality: "Juries choose whom to convict, producers choose which news stories to run."[263] Agency does exist in the choice of whether to maintain the status quo or work toward change—and what kind of change one wants to be part of.

In the late 1960s and early '70s the front door to the art world cracked open a bit. The demand for integration challenged museums' hiring practices, acquisition priorities, and overall institutional identities. By 1972 there had been enough exhibitions of work by African American artists that no credible curator could claim that such art didn't exist. But in the major museums the inclusion of African American artists was undertaken as a supplement to existing programs, thus confirming rather than challenging hegemonic art historical narratives. In the years that followed, a new pattern emerged.

First, specific physical spaces were set aside within museums for exhibitions by "emerging" artists, a category that often included artists of color of all ages who were perceived as always emerging, but rarely having arrived. The Whitney Museum of American Art established a Lobby Gallery on the ground floor that featured a larger proportion of artists of color than the museum showed in its regular galleries. Between 1971 and 1975 this space presented exhibitions by twelve artists of color.[1] Likewise, in 1971 the Museum of Modern Art inaugurated its Projects series in a gallery devoted to small shows of relatively short duration. Sam Gilliam was featured in the fourth show in the series; later in the 1970s four other U.S.-based artists of color were exhibited: Liliana Porter, Rafael Ferrer, Nam June Paik, and Shikego Kubato.[2] And in 1989 the museum presented work by Houston Conwill.[3] After the Bearden and Hunt shows of 1971, a twenty-five-year hiatus ensued before the next major one-person exhibition of work by an African American artist, Roy DeCarava in 1996.[4]

Along with these legitimate, albeit marginal spaces, many museums created what Benny Andrews acidly termed "kitchen galleries," that is, spaces located outside the formal galleries, often in the museums' restaurants. The Community Gallery at the Metropolitan Museum, for example, was situated in the Junior Museum Snack Bar, a cafeteria typically used by visiting school groups as a place to eat brown-bag lunches. The "members lounge" of the Penthouse Restaurant at the Museum of Modern Art served as a gallery for works from the museum's Art Lending Service and featured artists Romare Bearden, Alvin Smith, Jack Whitten, and Bob Thompson, making this the only place at MoMA where works by African

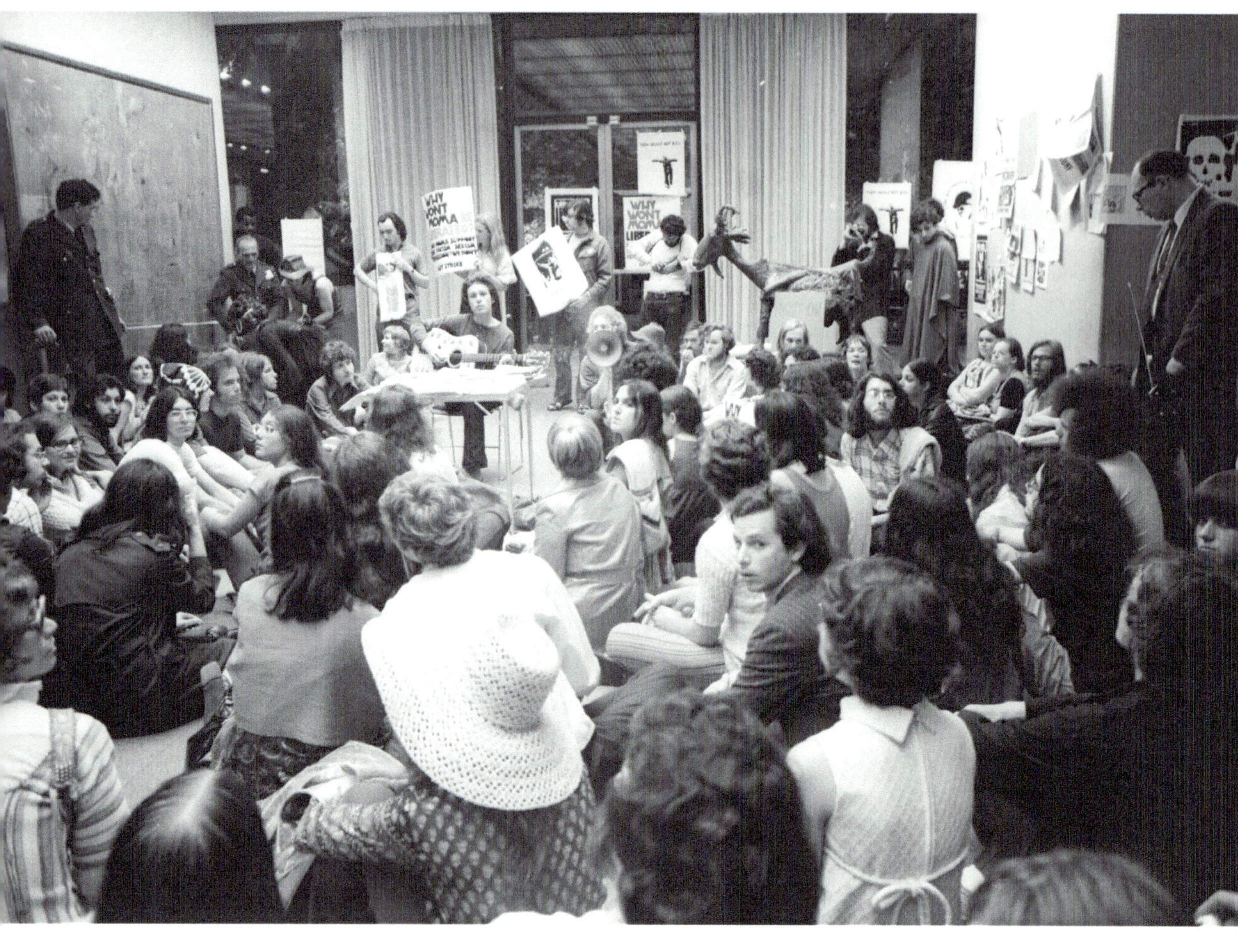

Fig. E.1 Lobby of the Museum of Modern Art with installation of Wifredo Lam, *The Jungle* (1943), on left-hand wall, day of New York Art Strike, May 22, 1970. Country Joe McDonald was scheduled to perform at Jazz in the Garden but instead joined the protestors in the museum's lobby. © Jan van Raay.

American artists could be seen on a consistent basis.[5] This physical segregation that began in the 1970s continued for decades, as John Yau described in his essay on the placement of Wifredo Lam's 1943 painting *The Jungle* in the hallway leading from MoMA's lobby to its coatroom. In 1988 Yau wrote, "The artist has been allowed into the museum's lobby but, like a delivery boy, has been made to wait in an inconspicuous passageway near the front door."[6] Photos of the New York Art Strike protest on May 22, 1970, reveal that the lobby was the location of choice for this piece for at least a generation (fig. E.1).

These developments physicalized the hierarchy that privileged European and Euro-American artists over artists of color and embedded new structures of inequality within the institutions themselves. Artists of color continued to be denied access to main gallery spaces, along with the ancillary benefits that came with such shows: exhibition catalogues, press openings, and larger audiences. One might ask, "Weren't these marginal exhibition venues stepping-stones to bigger and better opportunities?" The historical record shows that, sadly, they were not. Instead, these spaces drew an invisible color line within the museums themselves.

In a second and more widespread development, demands for cultural equity and accessibility were reframed as issues of audience development: museums devised education programs as the vehicles for sustained interaction with communities of color. In 1970 the American Association of Museums received requests from over fifty museums from around the country asking for advice on how to reach "minority groups" (a term used in this case to refer to African Americans and Latinos, poor and working class) through retooled or expanded education programs and what were called "outreach" programs for "underserved constituencies"—a phrase that replaced the more odious label that was popular in the 1960s, "culturally deprived."[7] The focus on audience development echoed the civil rights movement goal of overcoming Jim Crow by desegregating shared public spaces, including public recreational facilities, such as swimming pools.[8] Undeniably, eradicating this dehumanizing manifestation of racism was part of the critical work of the civil rights movement. But when museum administrators applied this strategy in their own institutions, it became an unspoken alibi for neglecting significant biases in other parts of the museum's operations and in their underlying conceptions of art. The museum establishment accepted African Americans' right to consume art along with whites, but not to qualify for the same recognition as artists or as writers of art history in the roles of curator, director, and trustee, with very few exceptions. Initiatives that had been established in the early 1970s to enhance the collection and exhibition of works by artists of color were quietly curtailed.

Nonetheless, one result of the creation of education programs specifically conceived for "minorities" was the hiring of people of color to staff them. At the Metropolitan Museum of Art, the Community Programs Department appointed the museum's first African American and Puerto Rican staff members, beyond custodial staff. These included Ted Gunn, who had served as acting director of the Studio Museum in Harlem in 1968 and '69 during the hiatus between directors Charles Inniss and Ed Spriggs; Irvine R. MacManus Jr., a recent graduate of Hunter College in political science who had volunteered on several political campaigns in New York City and had family ties to Puerto Rico; Catherine Chance, a journalist and art critic for the *Amsterdam News*, who had covered the *Harlem on My Mind* exhibition and controversy; and later, in 1972, art historian Lowery Stokes Sims.

The Community Programs Department at the Met was both a gateway and a buffer between the museum and its various new constituencies. Its activities ranged in scale from a modest series of "borough evenings" for residents of Brooklyn, Staten Island, Queens, and the Bronx to the full-scale establishment of new museums. Among the Community Programs Department's offerings was Eye-Opener, a bus containing a portable exhibition modeled after the Harlem Cultural Council's Jazzmobile and Dancemobile that drove around the city and stopped in different neighborhoods to do on-the-spot art workshops. Slide lectures on topics in the history of art were offered at senior citizen centers by retired teachers who were, according to Sims, not considered "classy enough" for the museum's regular volunteer program.[9] The Community Programs Department facilitated loan exhibitions from the Met's collection and shared technical expertise with small organizations.

By the end of 1971, the Met had worked with over one hundred neighborhood arts programs, educational organizations, government agencies, and not-for-profit groups, from Big Brothers Inc. to the New York City Board of Education; from the Children's Art Carnival in Harlem to the Office of Economic Opportunity. Many of these programs consisted of art workshops taught by museum staff members, the results of which were hung in the Junior Museum Snack Bar gallery and in a small space near the coat-check room called the Eighty-First Street Gallery. The exhibitions included *Salute to Senior Citizens*, organized with the New York City Office for the Aging; *A View from the Gut*, consisting of work by recovering drug addicts from Phoenix House; and *None beyond Help*, which presented art by clients of the Association for Mentally Ill Children. All of these groups were amalgamated under the term "community."[10]

As late as 1976, Cathy Chance, who had been promoted to the position of director of the Met's Community Programs Department in 1973, said she was "still hoping for a 'real gallery' for her department."[11] Her hopes were in vain. In 1978 Philippe de Montebello succeeded Tom Hoving as the museum's director; the galleries housing the Temple of Dendur were completed and opened to the public; and as the last page turned in this chapter of the museum's history, the Community Programs Department was disbanded. In retrospect it is hard not to see the museum's outreach activities as a tactic devised to appease critics of the museum's expansion projects—its Master Plan—which outlived its usefulness in the board's eyes once those plans were realized.

Beyond the walls of the major museums, artists, curators, and educators created their own spaces, new types of arts organizations that have been called "culturally specific," "culturally grounded," or "community based."[12] These new galleries, museums, and collectives showcased the art of groups that had been excluded from major institutions and, most importantly, that defined their sense of community themselves. Places like the American Indian Community House (1969), El Museo del Barrio (1969), Taller Boricua (1970), and the Asian American Arts Centre (1974) emerged from the belief that only through separate organizations could groups of people who had been neglected or dismissed by the major cultural institutions assert their own cultural narratives. For the artists and communities they served, these arts organizations stood as living monuments to the power of self-determination and resistance to white hegemony. As Michele Wallace and Faith Ringgold put it after their activism had been chronically thwarted by the major museums, artists asserted that the museum establishment was "not supposed to get in there and save us. No. We're here. We do that."[13] The goal was not inclusion, but expansion—expanding the system of opportunities for artists to show their work and for audiences to see it.

The Studio Museum in Harlem had blazed the trail in 1968, and by the early 1970s such organizations were mushrooming all over the country, each with its own genesis and structure, but all seeking to attract and unite communities around common cultural values and artistic concerns. In New York City alone, dozens of museums and arts organizations were started in the 1970s whose programs brought into public view works by artists who were known within their own circles, but not more broadly. This enabled new conversations and exchanges not only within specific communities but also between them.[14] Those organizations that obtained not-for-profit status often received financial support from the New York State Council on the Arts. The federal government encouraged this activity with the creation in 1970 of a funding program called Expansion Arts that supported organizations rooted in urban, rural, and tribal communities that were not reflected in major cultural institutions.

Looking back from the perspective of the late 1980s, Rasheed Araeen pointed out a dark side to this development. He suggested that ethnically based community arts programs were insidiously introduced as systematic forms of cultural management of the "desires, aspirations and demands of black people for equal status in society. . . . This, in turn, would help disenfranchise black people in terms of their demands for equal power within the dominant culture or mainstream as they would be turned into *minority* cultural entities" (emphasis original).[15] Araeen was talking about the British context, but the same concern can be voiced about New York City, where a parallel system of cultural organizations was institutionalized in the 1970s.

While we may celebrate the importance of these organizations, there is also no denying that they emerged from a new convergence of interests. They served not only the interests of their constituencies but also those of the major museums. Every new project at the major museums had engendered a new controversy. This was in part because fundamental change is not easy, but also because the museums' actions were often concessions and appeasements, not deep, sincere engagements. Deep engagement would have required new collecting strategies and different kinds of exhibitions and programs, and it would have demanded self-examination. As these museums racked up controversy after controversy, they no doubt felt they had dodged a bullet when this new solution presented itself, one that didn't involve them directly. In the culturally grounded museum, the agendas of separatists and the cultural establishment found a stable equilibrium.

In New York City, the Metropolitan Museum of Art was particularly active in helping to establish community-based museums. To encourage support for its Master Plan for expansion, the museum had agreed to assist each of the boroughs of New York City in developing its own local museum.[16] The Bronx Museum of the Arts started with an exhibition in the Rotunda of the Bronx County Courthouse in 1971 organized in collaboration with the Bronx Council on the Arts. Later, the museum opened in its own building on 170th Street and the Grand Concourse in what was once a Jewish enclave and had become a predominantly Latino neighborhood.[17] The seeds of the Queens Museum were sown in the winter of 1971–72 when the Met lent paintings to the Queens Borough President's Office and organized ten small exhibitions in the borough's branch libraries. In New York City's most culturally and linguistically diverse borough, the Queens Center for Art and Culture opened in 1972 in the New York City Pavilion from the 1939 World's Fair in Flushing Meadow.[18] On Staten Island, in 1976, a dilapidated home for retired merchant seamen was refurbished and rechristened as the Snug Harbor Cultural Center.

The Met was also active in helping artist Tom Lloyd establish the Store-Front Museum in Jamaica, Queens, a neighborhood cultural center with an Afrocentric

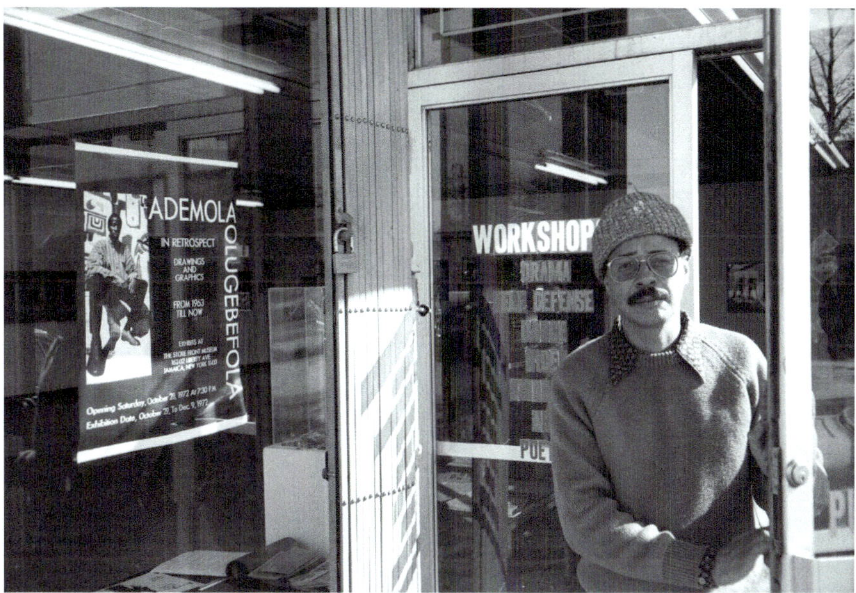

Fig. E.2 Tom Lloyd, director, in front of the Store-Front Museum, Jamaica, Queens, November 3, 1972. Photo: Ari L. Goldman / The New York Times / Redux.

philosophy (fig. E.2). The Met began working with Lloyd in May 1970 as he and a planning group, mostly artists associated with the Art Workers' Coalition, polled members of various communities around New York City to develop interest in establishing community arts centers. Lloyd received a grant from the New York State Council on the Arts just as John Hightower was transitioning from his position as director of NYSCA to director of MoMA. Hightower worked with Tom Hoving, director of the Met, to arrange to have the Met serve as Lloyd's fiscal receiver until his group obtained its not-for-profit status. With legal services provided by the Met's general counsel, the Store-Front Museum was soon chartered as a 501(c)3 charitable organization, and on June 15, 1971, Lloyd opened his museum in a one-story building owned by the City of New York.[19] The inaugural exhibition, *African Images*, featured West African ceremonial costumes and sculptures, on loan from the Tribal Arts Gallery in Manhattan.[20] The museum continued until 1988.

One of the Met's most ambitious projects was a collaboration with El Museo del Barrio, the exhibition *The Art Heritage of Puerto Rico: Pre-Columbian to Present* (1973), co-organized by Marta Moreno Vega, who succeeded Raphael Montañez Ortiz as El Museo's director, and Irvine R. MacManus Jr., a staff member in the Met's

Community Programs Department.[21] Vega had seen the *Harlem on My Mind* exhibition and approached the Met's vice director for education, Harry Parker, about investing in a Puerto Rican project. When Vega threatened to have "artists come to your doorstep and protest," she was introduced to MacManus and Lowery Stokes Sims, who, she says, "were brought around to sort of calm me."[22] Through a strategic alliance that served the interests of both institutions, Vega and MacManus collaborated on several projects. Vega wanted to mount an exhibition of Taino art, and with MacManus's help and the imprimatur of the Met she was able to secure loans from the American Indian Museum at 155th Street and Broadway. Using display cases and lights borrowed from the Met, a show of roughly thirty pieces opened in 1972. This was a prelude to Vega and MacManus's largest collaboration, *The Art Heritage of Puerto Rico*, a major exhibition encompassing works borrowed from museums in Puerto Rico, the United States, and abroad. By this time, El Museo occupied a series of storefronts owned by the New York City Board of Education on Third Avenue between 106th and 107th Streets. The Met had the buildings renovated and outfitted for display. The exhibition opened first in the storefronts, then traveled to the Met—a mere twenty-five blocks away, but miles apart in the public imagination.

To buttress these community and culturally grounded museums, the Rockefeller Foundation created a program designed to train "minority groups" for positions as educators and leaders in these museums.[23] Fellowships were offered at four institutions: the Metropolitan Museum of Art in New York, the de Young Museum and Neighborhood Arts Program in San Francisco, the Walker Art Center in Minneapolis, and the Dallas Museum of Fine Arts. According to a Metropolitan Museum report, the idea was to develop a generation of museum administrators to address the "growing pressure on art museums to respond to the needs of the 'new audience' that, though unschooled in the traditions of connoisseurship or high art, were nevertheless clamoring at its doors."[24] Launched in December 1972, the program aimed to "provide personnel for these emerging institutions and for the programs which grew out of the enlarging social concerns of traditional museums."[25]

Beyond the condescending and self-congratulatory tone of this description, the program had a central flaw: the notion that people of color were only suited to lead other people of color. The program's mandate was specifically to train participants to work in education programs and with "minority" populations. This limitation reflected the state of liberal discourse at the time. For while it is true that the arts leaders who joined the Rockefeller program may have benefited from their association with an art world power center, undergirding the program was the persistent pull of segregation—a continuation of the order of things, as philosopher Michel Foucault put it in 1967, the grouping together of certain things and the distinguishing between other things on the basis of differences that are construed as real but are actually constructed: in this case, an imaginary restriction on human agency held in place by a perverse collision of black power and white supremacy.[26]

The focus on educating "new audiences"—a code word for people of color—also had a fouler implication. On the surface it seemed to embody a benign, even admirable goal: making education equally accessible to all. Indeed, this was one of the major goals of the civil rights movement achieved with the *Brown vs. Board of Education* Supreme Court decision of 1954. But the myopic focus on education, which has become permanently installed as a fixture in the museum field since the 1970s, was a substitute for radical transformation of curatorial practices and a placeholder for egalitarian hiring. The idea that audiences who had been discriminated against and excluded would now be invited inside under carefully managed and monitored conditions—as subjects of the museum's tutelage, under the watchful eye of museum officials—suggests a form of social management rooted in ignorance and fear.[27]

Yet, as problematic as this originating conceptual framework may have been, the fact remains that the Rockefeller program and similar initiatives trained a generation of arts leaders who changed the art world. Among those who participated in the program at the Met were Linda Goode Bryant, who went on to work as an educator at the Studio Museum in Harlem, then started the Just Above Midtown gallery, the first major New York City gallery to focus on artists of color.[28] At her interview for the Rockefeller Fellowship, Goode Bryant had worn army fatigues and shouted that the Met was "a racist institution" and that she wanted to "burn the motherfucker down!" Still, even more than burning down the Metropolitan Museum, she wanted to "figure out how to be subversive in this environment."[29] For Goode Bryant, the experience was most useful once she started to see "the connection between the museum and the critics and the art historians and the galleries and . . . just how all of that conspires to create a market."[30] She opened Just Above Midtown on November 18, 1974, at 51 West Fifty-Seventh Street, the heart of the blue-chip art market, showing the work of a broad range of artists, including Senga Nengudi, Houston Conwill, Maren Hassinger, and David Hammons (including Hammons's first show in New York City). Goode Bryant believed that "something has more value, if it is in the place of the oppressor."[31] In addition to being a meeting place for artists and art lovers, her gallery was an intervention in the epicenter of the commercial art capital of the world.

As new arts organizations emerged outside the Met's official outreach programs, many members of the Community Programs Department staff expanded and redefined their roles. They began to serve as resources for these new institutions.

According to Lowery Sims, "We had the official Community Programs and then we had the renegade community programs where we felt that as employees of the Met we were there to help everybody on our own time and to scrounge materials wherever we could."[32] Eventually, Sims herself felt limited in her position in the Met's Community Programs Department, an office that bore a marginal relationship to what the museum considered its core work. In 1975 she was able to move from Community Programs into the Twentieth-Century Art Department as an assistant curator, and gradually she rose through the ranks. Looking back, she has said, "I was trying to figure out how I could maximize my position at the Met to really make a change, a lasting change. And I finally figured out that being a curator was it because you do affect a collection. The collection is forever, more or less, so that's really what I wanted to do."[33]

Sims's credentials were as strong as those of any other young curator who had preceded her at the Met, and she had the added advantage of a breadth of knowledge and active involvement in artistic circles that enabled her to bring distinct contributions to the work of her department. Yet her path was more challenging than earlier generations of young, white men who had come before her, who had been taken under the wing of powerful mentors to be groomed for leadership positions. As a junior staff member and a woman of color, she did not have the clout to exercise substantial influence, and throughout the late 1970s and '80s she was only allowed to do what she has characterized as "penny ante stuff."[34] Her colleagues in the museum world contended—indeed, told her to her face—that she'd only gotten the job because she was black, while some of the African American artists who had fought for access to the Met wondered "why [she] wasn't mounting all the shows."[35] Sims's challenge was steep. She proposed various projects, including a show of European art from 1940 to 1970, which would have expanded the conversation started by a popular exhibition covering the same period in American art mounted by her boss, curator Henry Geldzahler, in 1969. Had Sims been permitted to do the show, one can imagine her including not only artists whose work was already well known but also figures like Barbara Chase-Riboud, the African American expatriate sculptor and writer who settled in Paris in the 1960s and whose monumental metal and fiber sculptures possess a commanding presence; or Bob Thompson, a painter who moved to Europe in 1961, then made a home in Ibiza, and whose sensual landscape and figure paintings use striking color, texture, and composition to boldly interpret traditional subjects.[36] But Sims was hampered. Her first exhibition at the Met, *Stuart Davis, American Painter*, opened in 1991, sixteen years after she had joined the museum's curatorial staff.

While the Davis show was a triumph, considerably expanding understanding of the artist's place in the history of twentieth-century art, Sims's accolades would come mainly from her work outside the Met. The vibrant, expanding contemporary art scene in New York provided her with opportunities to write, speak, and organize exhibitions. After being invited to write her first freelance essay, a piece on the Uruguayan artist Joaquín Torres-Garcia, she realized how she could make her impact: "I knew that I had to have a total outside career from the Met if I was going to develop. That was a very conscious decision."[37] Sims remained in her position but accomplished dozens of projects with other institutions, including publishing important essays on the work of Elizabeth Catlett, Robert Colescott, Howardena Pindell, and Wifredo Lam. In 2000 she left the Met to become executive director and president of the Studio Museum in Harlem, posts she held until 2007.[38]

Affirming the rightful place of African American art in the canon of American art became the central focus of the Studio Museum in the late 1970s and '80s. But in the turbulent context of New York City's fiscal crisis, the pathway to this goal was loaded with challenges. Ed Spriggs, the museum's director since 1969, had resigned his position in 1975 to teach at Howard University, and Courtney Callender was appointed as his successor. Callender had formerly served as a community relations officer for the New York City Parks Department in 1966 under Tom Hoving, and later as New York City's deputy cultural commissioner from 1969 to 1972. Callender knew the city well and cared deeply about its well-being, particularly the relationship between its physical infrastructure and the social lives of its residents.

By this point the museum had outgrown its original home at 2033 Fifth Avenue between 125th and 126th Streets, and the staff and board began discussing a move to a new space. Board chair Richard V. Clarke advocated relocating south to Fifth Avenue and 104th Street, closer to the string of museums running north on the Upper East Side from the Museum of Modern Art on Fifty-Third Street to the Museum of the City of New York at 103rd. Callender disagreed. He felt the museum should remain in central Harlem, "the political and cultural center of the black Western world," as he put it.[39] Against the backdrop of New York City's financial collapse of 1977, during which poor neighborhoods, including Harlem, were hit the hardest, Clarke contended that "no one wants to come up there." "The place is dying," he said. Indeed, between 1970 and 1980, Harlem's population fell by 33 percent; the neighborhood suffered from neglect and abuse; its streets were scarred with buildings that had been abandoned or burnt out.[40] Clarke felt the museum needed to "move forward" by attracting what he called "the three B's—the beautiful black bourgeoisie."[41] Callender rejected this idea, which he saw as a repudiation of the museum's own past, the turning of its back on its own neighborhood. He insisted that the museum contribute to "keeping this community intact."[42] This public rift caused Callender and the museum to part ways. At this point Betty Blayton, whose entrée into the New York art world in the early 1960s had been aided by Clarke and who had sparked the idea of the Studio Museum during her work with the HARYOU-ACT program in the mid-1960s, resigned her position on the board.

Stepping into this fraught situation was Mary Schmidt Campbell, a twenty-nine-year-old newly minted PhD who had written her dissertation on Romare Bearden and had been working at the Everson Museum in Syracuse, New York. As director, Campbell asserted that the Studio Museum had a central role in the fields of art and art history. Her challenge and her goal was to acquire the resources to ground the museum in the neighborhood, the city, the nation, and the world.[43] With the museum's subject matter established—African American culture—and a program of exhibitions, artists' residencies, and workshops, Campbell energetically pursued permanence: "In '77 the idea was to take this wonderful set of programs that's in a loft over a liquor store and a Kentucky Fried Chicken, and lift it to the next stage, which was a formal museum with a collection, accreditation, traveling exhibitions, a body of literature, and a more thorough participation in the discourse on American art."[44]

After searching for several years, the museum acquired a building at 144 West 125th Street, donated by the New York Bank for Savings, which held the mortgage but could not find a buyer. By then, Richard Clarke, still the board chair, had come around to supporting the museum's remaining in central Harlem, and together the staff and board raised the funds to renovate and relocate to the place where the museum stands today.[45] The new building opened in 1982 with three major exhibitions: surveys of work by Charles White and James VanDerZee, and a large group show of work by nineteenth- and twentieth-century artists entitled *Ritual and Myth: A Survey of African American Art*. While many of the arts organizations founded in the 1970s have closed, typically for financial reasons, the Studio Museum has become an established institution. Campbell believes that the turning point came when the museum acquired real estate and made the decision to collect.[46]

With the establishment of a permanent home and collection came the need for capital and acquisition funds and bigger operating budgets. "And so," explains Campbell, "we began to be more assertive about fundraising." The Studio Museum sought philanthropic support from corporations, foundations, and especially government sources. And they were successful: funding for the museum's new building came from the National Endowment for the Arts, the New York State Council on the Arts, the City of New York, private foundations, and the Exxon Corporation;

the museum also earned revenue by leasing the top floors of its building. That is not to say it was an easy path. Back in its early days the museum had held a certain cachet for New York's liberal art and culture power brokers, people who wanted to be seen in Harlem, such as Carter Burden when he was running for city council and Tom Hoving as he drummed up support for the Met's Master Plan. By contrast, in the 1980s Kinshasha Holman Conwill, Campbell's deputy and then her successor as director, recalls working with white representatives of major foundations who would not set foot in Harlem, even to see an exhibition they had funded, out of fear and discomfort.[47] This has, no doubt, changed yet again as Harlem has once again become a fashionable destination in the 2000s.

Like the ever evolving story of race relations in the United States, the trajectory of museums is neither straight nor steady. During the late 1980s the climate in the art world changed again. The generation that had grown up in the 1960s took up the mantle of a previous generation of artists and activists. Major museums renewed their receptivity to showing works by artists of color. Collaborations produced exhibitions offering multiple perspectives, such as *The Decade Show: Frameworks of Identity in the 1980s*, an exhibition of 140 artists collaboratively organized in 1990 by the Museum of Contemporary Hispanic Art, the New Museum of Contemporary Art, and the Studio Museum in Harlem. Artists who made work that used exhibition contexts to critique institutional racism, such as Carrie Mae Weems, Fred Wilson, James Luna, Guillermo Gomez-Peña, and Coco Fusco, were invited into major museums to create projects that exposed and subverted cultural hierarchies. Museum professionals debated anew how to achieve "excellence and equity," the name given to a report by a task force of the American Association of Museums, first published in 1992 and now in its third edition.

But as soon as artists of color neared the center of power, this new period ended. The crest of the wave came in 1993 with the Whitney Museum's first substantially diverse biennial: about half of the show's eighty-four artists were people of color.[48] The critical response was vitriolic. Art writers maligned much of the work as "hectoring" and "didactic." The epithet "victim art" was used to demean works that addressed social problems.[49] Though many of the artists included in that show have since been recognized as the defining artistic voices of their generation, they were nonetheless narrowly and pejoratively pigeonholed as doggedly addressing the topic of identity. And as demonstrated in the substance and the subtitle of the *Excellence and Equity* report—*Education and the Public Dimension of Museums*—and its publication in second and third editions in virtually unchanged form (most recently in 2008), the primary strategy devised for including people of color in the major museums was the creation of education programs. This is still the primary strategy many decades later.[50] This is not to say that nothing at all has changed, but that the theoretical frameworks of institutions have not changed. The reins of power have not been shared. Without culturally specific museums, that is to say, museums that declare their points of view and the criteria they use to select and prioritize art, the situation would be much worse.

Significantly, a second wave of museums with explicitly expansive missions has emerged in the past twenty years. This time, the institutions are larger, less like community centers and more like major museums.[51] The federal government has stepped up and created a suite of museums within the Smithsonian Institution that offer a chorus of voices: the National Museum of the American Indian, with branches in New York City and Washington, DC; the National Museum of African American History and Culture; and, currently under discussion, a museum of Latino culture.[52] Would these institutions have been founded if those running the major museums in the late 1960s and 1970s had reimagined their institutions as places that encompassed the full spectrum of art, or through multiple lenses that allowed for the articulation of more complicated art histories or divergent notions of beauty? It is impossible to know. Places like the Studio Museum, whose mission is to serve as a "nexus for artists of African descent . . . and for work that has been inspired and influenced by black culture," now provide constant opportunities for artists of color and for audiences who want to see works by artists of color; in addition, they do the heavy lifting of scouting and researching for curators in major museums who want to show a broad spectrum of work but may not have the support, confidence, or commitment to seek out artists of color before they've been validated by the marketplace, the critics, or another institution. And, significantly, these newer museums make a place for any artist whose work is consistent with their missions. In the case of the Studio Museum, virtually any artist in the world, and certainly every artist in the United States, would qualify for consideration.

The tendency to view whiteness as normative persists in the major museums, and even though it may be expressed in ways that are more subtle now than in the 1960s, the result is a similar kind of bigotry: in the assessment of a museum director that an African American candidate for a curatorial position is not the right choice because she's too "narrow" in her focus, based on the assumption that her only interest is African American art and, even if this were the case, that art by African American artists does not speak about the fullness of human experience; in the perception of a funder that white curators are the most objective evaluators of art because they don't favor a particular cultural group (except perhaps their own, which is not seen as favoritism); in the steady rhythm of the token exhibition. The greatest legacy of this period was not a profound change within the major museums, but a restructuring of the museum system as a whole. The path that was opened by the Studio Museum in Harlem in 1968 has grown to be a large, complicated, variegated landscape of organizations that define their subject matter and constituents in many different ways.

As the United States moves toward a minority majority population, institutions that deny vast horizons of human experience will find themselves no longer "major." What, after all, is the purpose of art if not to communicate through visual, visceral, intellectual, and emotional means the range and complexity of what it is to be human—to give form to both the strange and the intimate; what we fear and what attracts us; our shame, desire, sorrow; what teases at our memories and challenges us to become our future selves? No single group has a monopoly on the ability to produce forms with meanings that echo with the deepest secrets of human experience, and any museum that claims to be universal yet offers only a sliver of human expression denies not only the artists who are excluded or tokenized, but also the public for whom museums claim to exist.

ABBREVIATIONS

AAA	Archives of American Art, Smithsonian Institution, Washington, DC
BHA	Camille Billops and James V. Hatch Archives, Emory University, Atlanta, GA
EBA	The Estate of Benny Andrews, Brooklyn, NY
MMAA	The Metropolitan Museum of Art Archives, New York, NY
MoMA Archives, NY	The Museum of Modern Art Archives, New York, NY
SCRBC	Schomburg Center for Research in Black Culture, New York Public Library, New York, NY
WMAA Archives	Whitney Museum of American Art, Francis Mulhall Achilles Library, Archives, New York, NY
WUFMA	Washington University, Film and Media Archive, St. Louis, MO

INTRODUCTION

Epigraph: Benny Andrews, interview by author, Litchfield, CT, July 14, 1999.

1. See Steinberg, "The Liberal Retreat from Race during the Post–Civil Rights Era," 14.

2. Pindell, *The Heart of the Question*, 18.

3. See, for example, Anderson, *Reinventing the Museum*.

4. The museums jointly purchased the piece then divided the panels; even numbers went to the Museum of Modern Art and odd numbers to the Phillips Collection.

5. The piece was included in the show *The Artist as Adversary*, held at the Museum of Modern Art, July 1–September 27, 1971.

6. The exhibitions were *Jacob Lawrence: The Migration Series* (Museum of Modern Art, Exh. #1701, January 12–April 11, 1995) and *One-Way Ticket: Jacob Lawrence's Migration Series and Other Works* (April 3–September 7, 2015). The portion of the work owned by MoMA, not the entire work, was shown in MoMA's exhibition *Art of the Forties*, February 20–April 30, 1991.

7. Als et al., "Roundtable Discussion," 74.

8. Wallace, "For Whom the Bell Tolls: Why Americans Can't Deal with Black Feminist Intellectuals," in *Dark Designs and Visual Culture*, 151.

9. Calo, *Distinction and Denial*, 91.

10. Bearden and Henderson, *A History of African-American Artists from 1792 to the Present*, 178.

11. Bearden and Henderson, *A History of African-American Artists from 1792 to the Present*, 234. See also Calo, *Distinction and Denial*, 87–88. The Harlem Art Workshop and Studio started in 1933 as a joint venture of the Harmon Foundation and the Harlem branch of the New York Public Library. Charles Alston joined the project in 1934 and quickly became its director. He and the artist Henry W. Bannarn moved the studio in 1934 to 306 West 141st Street, where it became known simply as "306."

12. See Powell and Reynolds, *To Conserve a Legacy*.

13. Hills, *Painting Harlem Modern*, 98–99.

14. See Reynolds and Wright, *Against the Odds*. When the Harmon Foundation disbanded in 1967, its collections were dispersed and donated to various institutions.

15. Bearden, "The Negro Artist and Modern Art."

16. Guild members also objected to the Harmon Foundation presentation of "Negro art from the sociological standpoint rather than from the aesthetic." "Harlem Artists' Guild: A Statement," in Calo, *Distinction and Denial*, 96.

17. Raphael Montañez Ortiz, interview by author, Highland Park, NJ, January 8, 2011.

18. Perry, *More Beautiful and More Terrible*, 35.

19. Perry, *More Beautiful and More Terrible*, 37.

20. Each of these terms has had its advantages and limitations at different points in the recent history of race relations.

21. *Harlem on My Mind* promotional brochure, n.d.

22. James VanDerZee, now recognized as a great African American photographer, was not described in artistic terms by the exhibition's curator.

23. Foucault, *The Order of Things*, xx–xxiii.

24. These shows were held respectively at Kenwood Reters furniture store located at 144 West 125th Street, future home of the Studio Museum in Harlem, with sponsorship from the Harlem Cultural Council and the National Center of Afro-American Artists in Boston.

25. See Meyer, *What Was Contemporary Art?*

26. Mercer, *Cosmopolitan Modernisms.*

27. For discussions of art worlds in other cities in the United States, see Jones, *Now Dig This;* Collins and Crawford, *New Thoughts on the Black Arts Movement.*

28. While he was the governor of New York State, Nelson Rockefeller was vividly and frequently reminded of artists' concern with larger social justice issues. After the uprising at the Attica Correctional Facility that resulted in over forty deaths, the vast majority of them inmates, dozens of artists protested at MoMA carrying signs calling for Rockefeller's resignation as governor and labelling him the "Butcher of Attica."

29. Campbell, *Tradition and Conflict* exhibition (1985) and catalogue.

30. The Hatch-Billops Collection has been deposited at Emory University.

31. See Ringgold, *We Flew over the Bridge;* and Wallace, "American People, Black Light," *Black Macho and the Myth of the Superwoman, Invisibility Blues,* and *Dark Designs and Visual Culture.*

32. Willis-Braithwaite, *VanDerZee, Photographer 1886–1983;* Dubin, *Displays of Power;* Lennon, "A Question of Relevancy"; Cahan, "Performing Identity and Persuading a Public"; Cooks, *Exhibiting Blackness;* and Olin, *Touching Photographs.*

33. Bearden and Henderson, *A History of African American Artists;* Calo, *Distinction and Denial;* Gibson, *Abstract Expressionism;* Hills, *Painting Harlem Modern;* and Gaines and Lord, *The Theater of Refusal.*

34. For example, see Rosati and Staniszewski, *Alternative Histories.*

35. A particularly egregious example is Thomas Crow's *The Rise of the Sixties.* Crow ignores the struggle to integrate museums in the 1960s and includes only one work by an African American artist—a 1967 assemblage by Betye Saar entitled *Omen.* He acknowledges the civil rights movement by including a timeline of milestones such as the March on Washington (1963), the formation of Black Panthers (1966), and the appointment of Thurgood Marshall as the first black Supreme Court justice (1967), and even illustrates his introduction with a photograph of the 1956 bus boycott in Montgomery, Alabama. But ultimately he views these "countless displays of extraordinary and anonymous courage on the part of black protestors with their handful of white allies" as mere parallels to the revolutionary work produced by white artists, such as Allan Kaprow and Claes Oldenburg. Crow writes, "The dissenting experiments of artists . . . found an energizing congruence with the most exciting and successful forms of dissenting politics" (11).

36. Dávila, *Culture Works;* Dávila and Laó-Montes, *Mambo Montage;* Yasmín Ramírez's interview with Raphael Montañez Ortiz in *Unmaking;* and Yasmín Ramírez, "The Activist Legacy of Puerto Rican Artists in New York."

37. These exceptions include the exhibitions *Rhapsodies in Black: Art of the Harlem Renaissance,* organized by the Hayward Gallery in London in 1997 with a tour to several venues in the United Kingdom and the United States; *Back to Black: Art, Cinema and the Racial Imaginary,* organized by Whitechapel in London in 2005; and *Now Dig This! Art and Black Los Angeles, 1960–1980,* organized by the Hammer Museum in Los Angeles in 2011.

38. Banks, "Approaches to Multicultural Curriculum Reform."

1. THE STUDIO MUSEUM IN HARLEM

1. Grace Glueck, "Harlem Initiates First Art Museum," *New York Times*, September 25, 1968.

2. Charles Inniss, quoted in Grace Glueck, "A Very Own Thing in Harlem," *New York Times*, September 15, 1968.

3. Ed Spriggs, presentation at the seminar "Planning and Operation of Neighborhood Museums," sponsored by the New York State Council on the Arts and the New York City Department of Cultural Affairs, November 20–22, 1969, transcript p. 39, Oral History Program, AAA.

4. Ogbar, *Black Power*, 3.

5. Wahneemah Lubiano, "Black Nationalism and Black Common Sense: Policing Ourselves and Others," in *The House That Race Built*. Wahneemah Lubiano's definition of black nationalism describes the values ushered in by the new regime at the Studio Museum in Harlem:

> One way to understand it [black nationalism] is to consider the way it functions: (1) It functions as a narrative of political history—a way to narrate a past in relation to that past's and the present's politics. (2) It functions as an articulation: it gives language to, and joins together, things that have no necessary belonging in such a way that the joining makes the connection seem inevitable. (3) It functions as an articulation explaining what is good and beautiful, as style. (4) It functions as a utopian narrative—a rallying cry, an expression of desire. (5) It functions as a critical analysis—an ongoing, ever-renewed critique of black existence against white racial domination as well as an evaluation of black existence within the group. (233)

6. Blayton continued taking classes at the Art Students League through 1964.

7. See Clark and Hopkins's introduction to *A Relevant War against Poverty*.

8. Clark and Hopkins, *A Relevant War against Poverty*, 4–5.

9. In addition to Yeargens and Lewis, the group included Charles Alston, Emma Amos, Romare Bearden, Calvin Douglass, Perry Ferguson, Reginald Gammon, Felrath Hines, Alvin Hollingsworth, William Majors, Richard Mayhew, Earl Miller, Merton D. Simpson, and Hale Woodruff. For more on the Spiral group's perspective on the civil rights movement, see Romare Bearden, interview by Henri Ghent, New York, June 29, 1968, transcript p. 7, Oral History Program, AAA.

10. Betty Blayton, interview by author, New York, NY, June 29, 2011.

11. See Clark, *Dark Ghetto*.

12. Clark and Hopkins, *A Relevant War against Poverty*, 5.

13. Clark, *Dark Ghetto*, 53. See also Clark, "HARYOU: An Experiment," in Clarke, *Harlem*, 210–13. This essay is based on a speech delivered by Kenneth B. Clark at the Award Lunch of the Association for the Improvement of Mental Health, Saturday, May 11, 1963.

14. Clark, "HARYOU: An Experiment," 210–13.

15. Cazenave, *Impossible Democracy*, 216n83.

16. The project was conducted for the Stern Family Fund.

17. Janet Henry, interview by author, Jamaica, NY, March 19, 2013.

18. Other participants included Danny Goodman, Bob Saunders, Edwin Smith, John Steptoe, and Stephen Lowry. See Blayton-Taylor, "When That Time Came Rolling Down: Panel 1," 145.

19. Henry, interview.

20. Betty Blayton, interview by Camille Billops, tape recording, January 20, 1976, New York City, BHA.

21. Henry, interview.

22. Blayton, interview by Billops.

23. Lynes, *Good Old Modern*, 380.

24. Barbara Jakobson, interview by Sharon Zane, October 29, 1997, New York City, Oral History Project, The Museum of Modern Art Archives, New York, NY. Lynes devotes four pages (380–83) to the projects of the Junior Council in his history of MoMA, *Good Old Modern*, though he does not mention the Studio Museum in Harlem.

25. Blayton, interview by Billops.

26. In the 1960s the term "community-based" was used almost interchangeably with the term "culturally specific." Community control was a concept that implied a transfer of power from a centralized, dominant authority to a local group and entailed self-determination and the freedom to make decisions and allocate resources in ways that were resolved to be in the group's own best interest. The term "community" referred to a group of people who lived in geographic proximity. Because of de facto segregation, this term also implied shared racial or ethnic characteristics. I am grateful to Marta Moreno Vega for discussing this issue with me and advocating use of the term "culturally grounded."

27. Henry, interview.

28. Jakobson, interview.

29. Marilyn Bender, "The Socially Prominent Candidate in East Harlem," *New York Times*, May 25, 1969.

30. Don Henahan, "Negroes Sought for Arts Boards," *New York Times*, August 28, 1968. Born in Trinidad, McShine had come to the United States in 1954 to attend Dartmouth College.

31. James Ray Francis, Louis Draper, Herman Howard, Earl James, and Calvin Mercer, all members of a collective called Group 35, met with a second group of photographers, including Herbert Randall, Albert Fennar, and James Mannas Jr. See "Kamoinge," special issue, *Nueva Luz* 7, no. 1 (2001), quoted on Kamoinge website, accessed January 26, 2015, http://www.kamoinge.com/history.htm.

32. "Kamoinge," special issue, *Nueva Luz* 7, no. 1 (2001), quoted on Kamoinge website, accessed January 26, 2015, http://www.kamoinge.com/history.htm.

33. The group rented space in 1964 and 1965 at 248 West 139th Street, where they met and held two exhibitions. DeCarava served as the leader until late 1965. Still active, the group currently has about two dozen members.

34. See Kay Brown, "The Weusi Artists" (*Harlem Magazine*) and "The Weusi Artists" (*Nka*); Ademola Olugebefola, "Weusi History."

35. This was later renamed the Weusi-Nyumba Ya Sanaa Gallery.

36. See Rosalind Jeffries, *An Historical Perspective on the Work of Ademola for a 20-Year Celebration Program Journal*, 1982, Ademola Olugebefola Papers, reel 1, box 1, folder 1, p. 2, SCRBC.

37. The Harlem Cultural Council was the first broad arts association in New York City, followed by the Brooklyn Arts and Culture Association and the Queens Council (1966), the Bronx

Council (1967), the Cultural Council of Staten Island (1968), and the Richmond County Cultural League (1969).

38. The officers were artists Bruce Nugent and Inge Hardison, and Frederick O'Neal, president of Actors Equity.

39. The store was previously named Reter Furniture. Kenneth Sherwood purchased the store in 1965 and renamed it Kenwood.

40. Ryder, "When That Time Came," 153.

41. Ryder, "When That Time Came," 153.

42. Ryder, "When That Time Came," 153.

43. "Broker's Plan for Harlem Scored by CORE official," *New York Times*, July 27, 1968. See also Bell, *In the Black*, 76–81.

44. The branch would later become First Harlem Securities, the second black-owned member firm of the New York Stock Exchange, as a correspondent broker of Shearson Hammill, and would fulfill this promise. See "Taking Stock on Wall Street."

45. Spriggs, presentation at "Planning and Operation of Neighborhood Museum."

46. Blayton, interview by Billops.

47. Henry, interview.

48. Blayton, interview by Billops.

49. William T. Williams, interview by Camille Billops, transcript, 39, New York City, February 18–March 3, 1976, BHA.

50. Williams, "When That Time Came," 162.

51. Rheet Taylor, interview by Camille Billops, tape recording, New York City, January 20, 1976, BHA.

52. Ryder, "When That Time Came," 155.

53. Ryder, "When That Time Came," 155.

54. Ryder, "When That Time Came," 155.

55. *Art Turned On* at the Institute of Contemporary Art in Boston (1965), *Light as a Creative Medium* at the Carpenter Center at Harvard University (1965), *Light in Art* at the Contemporary Arts Museum in Houston (1966), and *Art Electric* at the Sonnabend Gallery in Paris (1966).

56. *In Honor of Martin Luther King, Jr.*

57. Blayton, interview by Billops.

58. Spriggs, "Field Notes," 74.

59. Spriggs, "Field Notes," 74.

60. Glueck, "Harlem Initiates First Art Museum"; Grillo, "The Studio Museum in Harlem," 48.

61. Benny Andrews, interview by author, Litchfield, CT, July 14, 1999.

62. Williams, interview by Billops, 44.

63. Blayton, interview by Billops.

64. Blayton, interview by Billops.

65. Theodore Gunn quoted in Grace Glueck, "Harlem Initiates First Art Museum."

66. Gunn, "When That Time Came," 158.

67. Williams, interview by Billops, 45.

68. Betty Blayton went on to become director of the Children's Art Carnival, a program that had been developed at the Museum of Modern Art by educator Victor D'Amico.

69. Gunn, *Harlem Artists 69*, 5.

70. See Watts, *Amiri Baraka*, 178–79.

71. See Hatch, "From Hansberry to Shange."

72. See Spriggs, "Field Notes." The appointment of Dr. Mary Schmidt Campbell, an art historian and leading scholar of the work of Romare Bearden, as director in 1977 is widely seen as a turning point in the museum's history as it shifted from a primarily "community-based" mission to one that was more conventionally museological.

73. Spriggs, presentation at "Planning and Operation of Neighborhood Museum," 42.

74. Mary Schmidt Campbell, interview by author, New York, NY, February 26, 2000.

75. Ryder, "When That Time Came," 154.

76. Ryder, "When That Time Came," 154.

2. THE METROPOLITAN MUSEUM OF ART

Epigraph: Robert Malone, interview by author, New York, NY, August 25, 2013.

1. Lowery Stokes Sims, interview by author, New York, NY, February 27, 2001.

2. In 1905 Alfred Stieglitz had opened "291," the first gallery to present photography in an art context located on lower Fifth Avenue in New York City. In fact, it was Stieglitz who first donated photographs to the Metropolitan Museum of Art, sowing the seeds of the museum's curatorial department of photography, which was formally established in 1992.

3. Benny Andrews, interview by author, Litchfield, CT, July 14, 1999.

4. See Benjamin, "The Work of Art in the Age of Mechanical Reproduction." See also Schoener, "Art without Pedestals"; Allon Schoener, interview by author, Grafton, VT, December 17, 1998.

5. Allon Schoener, foreword to Schoener, *Harlem on My Mind*, n.p.

6. Harry S. Parker III, interview by author, San Francisco, CA, July 19, 1999.

7. The Met's history of engagement with modern art was tentative until the museum established a Contemporary Art Department in 1967, later renamed Twentieth Century Art and now called Modern and Contemporary Art. In fact, the museum formally renounced its role in the field of modern art in 1947 when it entered into the "Three Museums Agreement" with the Whitney Museum of American Art and the Museum of Modern Art. Under this agreement each institution fixed its focus on a specific area: the Whitney on American art; MoMA on modern, predominantly European art; and the Met on the "classics." The agreement included the provision that MoMA sell to the Metropolitan works that no longer fell within the purview of "modern art." The agreement expired in 1952. See Art Workers' Coalition, *Documents / Open Hearing*, n.p.; Tompkins, *Merchants and Masterpieces*, 303–13; Lynes, *Good Old Modern*, 288–92.

8. See Tompkins, *Merchants and Masterpieces*, 37. The phrase "men of fortune" is used by Tompkins in chapter 7 to describe the museum's trustees.

9. Rita Reif, "A Birthday Cake of a Room," *New York Times*, November 22, 1969.

10. Duncan, *Civilizing Rituals*, 59–62.

11. For a discussion of the formation and evolution of the Metropolitan Museum of Art and a full record of its trustees from 1870 to 1970, see Tompkins, *Merchants and Masterpieces*, 363–65.

12. This trustee was Roland Redmond.

13. Parker, interview.

14. Though located several miles from the museum, The Cloisters was never conceived as a form of public "outreach" intended to bring culture to the "people." Rather, The Cloisters was sequestered on a fifty-six-acre site owned by Rockefeller precisely to set it apart from urban life.

15. Parker, interview.

16. Parker, interview.

17. Parker, interview.

18. Arthur Rosenblatt, interview by author, New York, NY, February 27, 2000.

19. Thomas P. F. Hoving, letter to author, February 29, 2001.

20. Hoving, *Making the Mummies Dance*, 164.

21. See Schoener, "Television in the Art Museums," 70–86.

22. Schoener, interview.

23. Schoener, *Portal to America*.

24. Another touchstone for the use of newspapers may have been the short pieces based on the day's headlines performed at the Lafayette Theater located at 132nd Street and Seventh Avenue. Opened in 1912, the Lafayette was the first New York theater to desegregate by allowing African Americans to sit in the orchestra. During the 1930 Federal Art Project one of the units based there was the "Living Newspaper," a troupe that performed sketches drawn from news stories of the day. See "Editor of the People," *New York Times*, February 13, 1938.

25. Allon Schoener, introduction to *Harlem on My Mind*, n.p.

26. Tompkins, *Merchants and Masterpieces*, 237.

27. For the essay and a related discussion, see Marable and Mullings, *Let Nobody Turn Us Around*, 290–95.

28. The only traveling component of the exhibition realized was a series of twenty photographs and texts mounted on aluminum panels made available for loan to schools through a grant from the Rockefeller Family Foundation.

29. Schoener, interview.

30. For the legislation establishing the council as a permanent agency of the state of New York, see *New York State Council on the Arts Annual Report 1966–67*, 79–82.

31. Hoving, letter to author.

32. James Ridgeway, "Columbia's Real Estate Ventures," *New Republic*, May 18, 1968, cited in the chapter titled "Columbia University, 1968: A School under Siege" in Cannato, *The Ungovernable City*, 233.

33. Hoving, cited in Cannato, *The Ungovernable City*, 234.

34. Hoving also appointed New York City's first African American official in Parks, Courtney Callender, as a community relations officer overseeing the inclusion of neighborhood residents in park decisions. Callender would later become the director of the Studio Museum in Harlem, from 1975 to 1977.

35. Thomas P. F. Hoving, preface to *Harlem on My Mind*, n.p.

36. Taylor's projects included visitor amenities, such as a restaurant and the Grace Rainey Rogers Auditorium for lectures and concerts. See Tompkins, *Merchants and Masterpieces*, 289–94, 314–25.

37. Parker, interview.

38. The Metropolitan Museum of Art competed with several museums that proposed putting the temple near a river to simulate its original location on the Nile: the Boston Museum of Fine Arts, on the Charles River; the Philadelphia Museum, on the Schuykill River; a museum in Cairo, Illinois, on the Mississippi River; and the Brooklyn Museum, which proposed to site the structure on the sands of Coney Island. See "Johnson Gives Egyptian Temple to Metropolitan Museum of Art," *New York Times*, April 30, 1967.

39. Located in Central Park, the Met's 2-million-square-foot main building is owned by the city, which pays for heat, light, and power, as well as funding a portion of the costs of maintenance and security. The trustees bear responsibility for a share of maintenance and security, plus the costs of acquisitions, conservation, special exhibitions, scholarly publications, and educational programs.

40. Robert Makla, letter to the editor, *New York Times*, November 23, 1967.

41. "Hospital Chief Assails Budget," *New York Times*, December 16, 1967.

42. Letter to the editor, *New York Times*, November 23, 1967.

43. Thomas P. F. Hoving, quoted in Ada Louis Huxtable, "Metropolitan Museum Plans Centennial Expansion," *New York Times*, April 13, 1970, 1, 53.

44. Sargent Shriver, quoted in "How Goes the War on Poverty," *Look*, July 27, 1965, in Leach, "The Federal Role in the War on Poverty Program."

45. In 1954, African American and Puerto Rican students comprised 29 percent of the elementary school population in New York City. In 1964, students in these groups comprised 50.5 percent of the total. See Mayor's Advisory Panel on Decentralization of the New York City Schools, *Reconnection for Learning*, 2.

46. McKinney's 1967 Sessions of Law of New York, ch. 484 (1967) in Mayor's Advisory Panel on Decentralization of the New York City Schools, *Reconnection for Learning*, 2.

47. McGeorge Bundy's wife, Mary, would join the board of trustees of the Metropolitan Museum in July 1968.

48. Mayor's Advisory Panel on Decentralization of the New York City Schools, *Reconnection for Learning*, 1.

49. Carol Greitzer, "A Politico Looks at John Vleit Lindsay: What Went Wrong?," *Village Voice*, September 8, 1966.

50. In 1995 the museum merged with the Smithsonian's Center for African American History and Culture.

51. Gaither, "Hey! That's Mine," 60.

52. Ed Spriggs, presentation at "Planning and Operation of Neighborhood Museums," a seminar sponsored by the New York State Council on the Arts and the New York City Department of Cultural Affairs, November 20–22, 1969, transcript, 7, AAA.

53. Metropolitan Museum of Art, "An Integrated Program of Continuing Education at the Metropolitan Museum of Art," December 1971, Office of the Secretary Records, MMAA.

54. Rosenblatt, interview.

55. Rosenblatt, interview.

56. Louise Condit, "Community Programs: History and Philosophy," January 10, 1977, Office of the Secretary Records, MMAA.

57. Morrow, *The Henry Luce Foundation 1936–1996, Sixtieth Anniversary Report*, 54.

58. Martha R. Wallace, letter to Thomas P. F. Hoving, November 14, 1967, in the *Harlem on My Mind* exhibition records, 1966–2007, AAA. The Henry Luce Foundation's support of *Harlem on My Mind* is not mentioned in the two main publications documenting the foundation's work: Morrow, *The Henry Luce Foundation 1936–1996, Sixtieth Anniversary Report*, and Guzzardi, *The Henry Luce Foundation, a History*.

59. *New York State Council on the Arts Annual Report 1969–70*, 85.

60. Schoener was introduced to Harper through NYSCA staff member Kenneth Dewey.

61. Schoener described himself as a Marxist in an interview with the author. For a statement by John Henrik Clarke about his communist affiliations, see "Portrait of a Liberation Scholar" at http://www.nbufront.org/htm/MastersMuseums/JHClarke/ArticlesEssays/LiberationScholar.html.

62. In 1949 Andrews had been appointed librarian at the Washington Heights branch of the New York Public Library, a post she held until her retirement in 1967. Regina Andrews's husband, William T. Andrews, was an assemblyman from Harlem, and Andrews herself was a board member of the Urban League.

63. Dubin, *Displays of Power*, 29–30, 254n19.

64. Schoener, interview.

65. "Media Mix," *New York Times*, December 8, 1968.

66. Allon Schoener, letter to Edward K. Taylor, November 16, 1967, *Harlem on My Mind* exhibition records, 1966–2007, AAA.

67. The Metropolitan Museum of Art, "Harlem's Rich, Varied Sixty-Year History as Cultural Capital of Black America to Be Presented in Major Exhibition by Harlem Community at Metropolitan Museum," *Harlem on My Mind* press release, November 16, 1967.

68. Thomas P. F. Hoving, quoted in Milton Esterow, "Hoving's Metropolitan to Offer Multimedia Look at Harlem," *New York Times*, November 16, 1967.

69. *The Metropolitan Museum of Art Bulletin* 26, no. 5 (January 1968): 1.

70. Schoener, interview.

71. See Cahan, "Performing Identity and Persuading a Public."

72. Schoener, interview.

73. For the most comprehensive discussion of James VanDerZee and the *Harlem on My Mind* exhibition, see Birt, "A Life in American Photography."

74. Arthur A. Cohen, letter to Lynn Nesbitt, January 27, 1968, *Harlem on My Mind* exhibition records, 1966–2007, AAA.

75. Arthur A. Cohen, letter to Allon Schoener, March 23, 1967, *Harlem on My Mind* exhibition records, 1966–2007, AAA.

76. Allon Schoener, letter to Lynn Nesbitt, June 28, 1967, *Harlem on My Mind* exhibition records, 1966–2007, AAA.

77. H. Rap Brown's political attitudes at that time are documented in his book *Die Nigger Die!*

78. Arthur A. Cohen, letter to Lynn Nesbitt, January 22, 1968, *Harlem on My Mind* exhibition records, 1966–2007, AAA.

79. For a full discussion of this topic, see Omi and Winant, *Racial Formation in the United States from the 1960s to the 1980s*, 14–54.

80. Metropolitan Museum of Art, meeting minutes from the Exhibition Research Committee for *Harlem on My Mind*, May 1, 1968, Jean Blackwell Hutson archive, SCRBC.

81. Allon Schoener, introduction to *Harlem on My Mind*, 2nd ed., n.p.

82. In the 1970s, Clarke joined the board of the Studio Museum in Harlem, and in 1996 he became a trustee of the Metropolitan Museum of Art.

83. Betty Blayton, interview by author, New York, NY, June 29, 2011.

84. The publicity firm Ruder & Finn had a cultural program directed by Carolyn Lerner (Goldsmith) and Nina Kaiden.

85. Mahler Ryder, interview by Camille Billops, Boston, MA, May 12, 1973, BHA.

86. *The Family of Man* was one of a series of photomural exhibitions organized by Edward Steichen at the Museum of Modern Art. Others in the series included *Road to Victory* (1942) and *Airways to Peace* (1943). For other precedents, see Staniszewski, *The Power of Display*, 45–57.

87. For a discussion of the presentation of *The Family of Man* exhibition at the 1959 American National Exhibition in Moscow, see Sandeen, *Picturing an Exhibition*, 125–53.

88. Allon Schoener, editor's foreword to *Harlem on My Mind*.

89. Schoener, interview.

90. *The Work of Charles and Ray Eames: A Legacy of Invention*, brochure for circulating exhibition organized by the Interpretive Programs Office of the Library of Congress, 1999.

91. For a discussion of the Eameses's Circus project, see Neuhart, Neuhart, and Eames, *Eames Design*, 90–96.

92. The Eameses had begun using slide shows in 1945 as a way of structuring visual and verbal information. Images and sounds were assembled over many years and combined in variations.

93. Neuhart, Neuhart, and Eames, *Eames Design*, 356.

94. Neuhart, Neuhart, and Eames, *Eames Design*, 91.

95. Schoener, interview.

96. Schoener, interview.

97. Schoener, "The New Aesthetic: Process Prevails (Art & the Environments)," 42.

98. See Neuhart, Neuhart, and Eames, *Eames Design*, 238–41; Lipstadt, " 'Natural Overlap.' " George Nelson had been approached by the United States Information Agency (USIA) to create a setting for the display of American manufactured products in what would be the first cultural exchange between the two countries since the Russian Revolution. Nelson in turn asked the Eameses to produce a film on "a day in the life of the United States," which would introduce the industrial display. *The Family of Man* exhibition was also presented at the 1959 American National Exhibition in Moscow, a stop on its long global tour.

99. For a discussion of how *Glimpses of the U.S.A.* was also designed to showcase American consumer goods and demonstrate to Russian audiences a superior American standard of living, see Colomina, "Enclosed by Images."

100. Schoener, interview.

101. Powell, "Re/Birth of a Nation," 24.

102. Gates, "Harlem on Our Minds," 165.

103. *Art of the American Negro*, June 27–July 25, 1966, was organized with Jim Lowe for the Harlem Cultural Council and held at Kenwood Furniture, 144 West 125th Street. *The Evolution of Afro-American Arts: 1800–1950* was held October 16–November 15, 1967, in the Great Hall of City College, City University of New York.

104. Van Deren Coke, *The Painter and the Photograph*, 227, quoted in Ruth Fine, *The Art of Romare Bearden*, 41.

105. Minutes from the *Harlem on My Mind* Research Committee meeting, March 6, 1968, Jean Blackwell Hutson archive, SCRBC.

106. Edward K. Taylor, letter to Allon Schoener, May 16, 1968, John Henrik Clarke archive, SCRBC.

107. Taylor, letter to Allon Schoener, May 16, 1968.

108. John Henrik Clarke, letter to Allon Schoener, June 6, 1968, John Henrik Clarke archive, SCRBC.

109. Falcon suggested that he consider a bronze bust of Martin Luther King Jr. by an artist named Ali Warren that had been brought to her attention by the national president of the 369th Veteran's Regiment. Eleanor Falcon, letter to Romare Bearden, June 11, 1968, *Harlem on My Mind* exhibition records, 1966–2007, AAA.

110. Schoener, interview.

111. Susan Coppello, memo to Mr. Thomas P. F. Hoving and Mr. Joseph Noble, June 25, 1968, Jean Blackwell Hutson archive, SCRBC.

112. Coppello, memo to Mr. Thomas P. F. Hoving and Mr. Joseph Noble, June 25, 1968.

113. Romare Bearden, letter to Thomas P. F. Hoving, September 27, 1968, *Harlem on My Mind* exhibition records, 1966–2007, AAA.

114. Benny Andrews journal, pp. 58–59, entry 441, November 30, 1968, EBA.

115. Allon Schoener, letter to Alvin White, November 15, 1968, *Harlem on My Mind* exhibition records, 1966–2007, AAA.

116. Jesse Walker, "A Black Art Show Is at the Museum," *Amsterdam News*, February 8, 1968.

117. James Sneed, "Open Letter to Fellow Artists," March 10, 1969, Benny Andrews Archive, Studio Museum in Harlem, NY.

118. Andrews, interview.

119. I could find no evidence that the show was officially cancelled; it may have been quietly dropped.

120. The Metropolitan Museum of Art's education and outreach efforts are discussed in the epilogue. Since the 1990s, the museum has mounted several exhibitions of African American artists' work, and in 1999 it received a major donation of 204 prints by African American artists from Reba and Dave Williams.

121. Exhibition planning document, September 1968, *Harlem on My Mind* exhibition records, 1966–2007, AAA.

122. Unsigned memo, *Harlem on My Mind* exhibition records, 1966–2007, AAA.

123. See memo from Allon Schoener to Thomas P. F. Hoving, September 30, 1968, *Harlem on My Mind* exhibition records, 1966–2007, AAA.

124. Allon Schoener, memo to Eleanor Falcon, October 24, 1968, *Harlem on My Mind* exhibition records, 1966–2007, AAA.

125. This comment was made by Edmund Barry Gaither during the discussion portion of the symposium entitled "Race and Racism in the Museum World: Harlem on My Mind" held at the SCRBC, October 28, 1995, in conjunction with publication of the second edition of the *Harlem on My Mind* catalogue.

126. Allon Schoener, memo to Eleanor Falcon.

127. Benny Andrews journal, p. 58, entry 435, November 22, 1968, EBA.

128. Grace Glueck, "Harlem Cultural Council Drops Support for Metropolitan Show," *New York Times*, November 23, 1968.

129. John Henrik Clarke, letter to Romare Bearden, August 28, 1968, in the John Henrik Clarke archive, SCRBC.

130. Allon Schoener, letter to Thomas P. F. Hoving, November 26, 1968, *Harlem on My Mind* exhibition records, 1966–2007, AAA.

131. Schoener, letter to Thomas P. F. Hoving, November 26, 1968.

132. Schoener, letter to Thomas P. F. Hoving, November 26, 1968.

133. Cliff Joseph became the cochair of the Black Emergency Cultural with Benny Andrews. Born in Panama in 1922 and raised in Harlem, Joseph attended the Pratt Institute of Art and the Turtle Bay School of Therapy. He is a painter and coauthor of the book *Murals of the Mind*. For an interview with Joseph about the Black Emergency Cultural Coalition conducted by Doloris Holmes, see oral history interview with Cliff Joseph, 1972, AAA.

134. Black Emergency Cultural Coalition, "Soul's Been Sold Again!!!" protest flyer, January 1969, in the Benny Andrews Archive, Studio Museum in Harlem, NY.

135. Benny Andrews and Cliff Joseph, open letter, n.d., in the Benny Andrews Archive, Studio Museum in Harlem, NY.

136. According to Benny Andrews's journal, Andrews talked to several writers on the day of the press conference, including Grace Glueck from the *New York Times*; Eugene Genovese, a historian who reviewed the show for *Artforum*; and Katherine Kuh from the *Saturday Evening Review*, among others. Andrews journal, pp. 68–69, entry 484, January 14, 1969, EBA.

137. Andrews, interview.

138. Andrews, interview.

139. "Museum Pickets Assail Hoving over Coming Harlem Exhibit," *New York Times*, January 15, 1969.

140. Andrews, interview.

141. Andrews journal, pp. 69–70, entry 488, January 16, 1969, EBA. See also Cooks, *Exhibiting Blackness*, 179n62.

142. The defaced paintings were Rembrandt van Rijn, *Christ with a Pilgrim's Staff* (1661); Gerard David, *Rest on the Flight into Egypt* (ca. 1512–15); Francoise Boucher, *Sleeping Shepherdess* (1750); Francesco Guardi, *The View of the Piazza San Marco* (1750s); Pietro Longhi, *Interior Scene* (1746); Giovanni Paolo Pannini, *View of Ancient Rome* (1757); Tommaso Fiorentino, *Portrait of a Man* (1521); School of Botticelli, *Coronation of the Virgin* (late fifteenth century); Jacopo Guarana, *Crowning with Thorns* (eighteenth century); and Eugene Boudin, *Market in Brittany* (nineteenth century). See Martin Arnold, "Paintings Defaced at Metropolitan," *New York Times*, January 17, 1969.

143. *Muhammad Speaks*, February 14, 1969, 28.

144. Stowe, *Uncle Tom's Cabin*.

145. For a discussion of the Ocean Hill–Brownsville conflict, see Cannato, "Community Control and the 1968 Teachers' Strike: The Debacle at Ocean Hill–Brownsville," chapter 9 in *The Ungovernable City*, 301–51.

146. Following the school strike, Mayor Lindsay appointed the Special Committee on Racial and Religious Prejudice to evaluate the state of race relations between African Americans and Caucasians. The legacy of the Ocean Hill–Brownsville experimental district was a lingering distrust between blacks and Jews. See Report of the Special Committee on Racial and Religious Prejudice (Botein Report), January 16, 1969, quoted in Cannato, *The Ungovernable City*, 361–62, 647n23. See also "Anti-Semitism in the New York City School Controversy," A Preliminary Report of the Anti-Defamation League of B'nai B'rith, January 1969, quoted in Cannato, *The Ungovernable City*, 362, 647n24.

147. Mayor John Vleit Lindsay, press release, January 16, 1968.

148. Thomas P. F. Hoving, letter to author.

149. Parker, interview.

150. Rosenblatt, interview.

151. Anti-Defamation League press release, January 17, 1969.

152. American Jewish Congress. "The Enemy Is Silence, a Statement by the American Jewish Congress," advertisement in the *New York Times*, January 31, 1969, 21.

153. Hoving, *Making the Mummies Dance*, 169.

154. The American Jewish Committee, press release, January 16, 1969.

155. A copy of the first insert can be found in the *Harlem on My Mind* exhibition records, 1966–2007, AAA.

156. A copy of the second insert can be found in the *Harlem on My Mind* exhibition records, 1966–2007, AAA.

157. Hoving, letter to author.

158. Parker, interview.

159. Letter to Mr. R. Franklin Brown, Wells & Brown, June 14, 1969, *Harlem on My Mind* exhibition records, 1966–2007, AAA.

160. Schoener, interview.

161. Schoener, *Harlem on My Mind*.

162. Werner Kramarsky, interview by author, New York, NY, November 15, 2000.

163. Kramarsky, interview.

164. Candice Van Ellison, "Harlem: A Study in Depth," high school term paper, 19, John Henrik Clarke Papers, *Harlem on My Mind* Folders, SCRBC.

165. Candice Van Ellison, introduction to Schoener, *Harlem on My Mind*. The full sentence in the original passage by Glazer and Moynihan read: "Perhaps for many Negroes, subconsciously, a bit of anti-Jewish feeling helps make them feel more completely American, a part of the majority group." Glazer and Moynihan, *Beyond the Melting Pot*, 73.

166. Reed, "Black Particularity Reconsidered," 86.

167. Schoener, interview.

168. Morton Lawrence, "Met Catalogue Expose: Text Changed in Editing," *Park East News*, January 30, 1969.

169. Candice Van Ellison, "Harlem: A Study in Depth," high school term paper, 1, John Henrik Clarke Papers, *Harlem on My Mind* Folders, SCRBC.

170. Thomas P. F. Hoving, preface to Schoener, *Harlem on My Mind*.

171. Hoving, *Making the Mummies Dance*, 168.

172. "Museum Pickets Assail Hoving over Coming Harlem Exhibition," *New York Times*, January 15, 1969, 41.

173. Schoener, editor's foreword to *Harlem on My Mind*, 55.

174. *Harlem on My Mind* exhibition records, 1966–2007, AAA.

175. Schoener, interview.

176. Similarly, *The Family of Man* exhibition contained one color image, that of a mushroom cloud. See Sandeen, *Picturing an Exhibition*, and Staniszewksi, *The Power of Display*.

177. See Staniszewksi, *The Power of Display*, 253.

178. The poem, *Something Black* (1966), was written by Yusef Iman in response to a passage from Luke 6:27–36. Iman was a member of the Nation of Islam Organization of Afro-American Unity and the Black Arts Repertory Theater. The complete poem, "Love Your Enemy," can be found in Neal and Jones, *Black Fire*.

179. The musical numbers are not identified on the album. They appear to be generic renditions in the style of music from different periods.

180. DeCarava and Hughes, *The Sweet Flypaper of Life*.

181. In 1969 the Studio Museum in Harlem mounted the first museum exhibition of DeCarava's work, *Thru Black Eyes: Photographs by Roy DeCarava*, September 14–October 26, 1969. DeCarava has had over thirty one-person exhibitions, including a retrospective at MoMA in 1996.

182. Guggenheim Fellowship proposal reprinted in Galassi, *Roy DeCarava*, 19.

183. Sherry Turner DeCarava, "Pages from a Notebook," 55.

184. The show included approximately 550 photographs and 150 photo blowups of documents and text panels. The catalogue contained 246 photographs, some overlapping with those in the exhibition, some not.

185. James VanDerZee (1886–1983) was a commercial photographer in Harlem recognized late in life for his artistry. For an excellent account of VanDerZee's life and work, see *VanDerZee, Photographer 1886–1983*, edited by Deborah Willis-Braithwaite.

186. See Duganne, "Transcending the Fixity of Race"; "Kamoinge," special issue, *Nueva Luz* 7, no. 1 (2001); and http://www.kamoinge.com/photographers.htm.

187. "Harlem: A State of Mind."

188. Exhibition Research Committee member John Henrik Clarke was in the process of editing the book *Malcolm X, The Man and His Times* (1969). A new edition, edited and with an introduction and commentary by Clarke, was published in 1990.

189. Ryder, interview.

190. Richard d'Anjou, memo to Schoener dated February 3, 1969, *Harlem on My Mind* exhibition records, 1966–2007, AAA.

191. Allon Schoener, *Harlem on My Mind* Progress Report, February 9, 1968, *Harlem on My Mind* exhibition records, 1966–2007, AAA.

192. David Noble, "Met on My Mind," *Manhattan East*, January 24, 1969.

193. A. D. Coleman, "Latent Image," *Village Voice*, January 23, 1969, 15–16.

194. Notably, Schoener included excerpts from a wide spectrum of newspapers from mainstream publications like the *New York Times* to black papers like the *New York Age*, but he neglected to include *Muhammad Speaks*, the paper of the Nation of Islam, even though it was a primary communication vehicle for one of the show's icons, Malcolm X.

195. Hilton Kramer, "Politicalizing the Metropolitan Museum," *New York Times*, Sunday, January 26, 1969.

196. Kramer, "Politicalizing the Metropolitan Museum."

197. John Canaday, "Getting Harlem off My Mind," *New York Times*, January 12, 1969.

198. Black Emergency Cultural Coalition, January 1969, in the Benny Andrews Archive, Studio Museum in Harlem, NY.

199. Genovese, "An Historian Looks at Hoving's Harlem," 35.

200. Genovese, "An Historian Looks at Hoving's Harlem."

201. Parker, interview.

202. *New York State Council on the Arts Annual Report 1967–1968*, 34.

203. *The Metropolitan Museum of Art Bulletin* 26, no. 5 (January 1968): 193.

204. Schoener, interview. A resurgence of interest in *Harlem on My Mind* is evidenced by the 1995 and 2007 republications of the 1969 catalogue by the New Press and a symposium held on October 28, 1995, at the SCRBC entitled "Race and Racism in the Museum World: *Harlem on My Mind*." A videotape of the symposium proceedings is available for viewing at the Schomburg.

Re-creations of parts of the show were mounted at Columbia University and the I. P. Stanback Museum in 2006.

205. Grace Glueck, "Metropolitan to Study Its Role in City's Communities," *New York Times*, February 24, 1970.

206. Metropolitan Museum of Art, "An Integrated Program of Community Education at the Metropolitan Museum of Art," December 1971, p. 3, Office of the Secretary Records, MMAA.

207. Metropolitan Museum of Art, "An Integrated Program of Community Education at the Metropolitan Museum of Art," December 1971, p. 2.

208. Parker, interview.

209. Paul O'Dwyer, "To Relocate Museum Facilities," letter to the editor, *New York Times*, March 19, 1970.

210. Maurice Carroll, "For Ottinger, the Big Picture Is on TV," *New York Times*, June 5, 1970.

211. *Newsweek*, August 17, 1970, 93; Paul O'Dwyer, letter to the editor, *New York Times*, March 11, 1970; Robert Weinberg, critic-at-large for architecture and planning, WNYC, quoted in Hoving, *Making the Mummies Dance*, 219; James P. O'Shea, letter to the editor, *New York Times*, June 12, 1970.

212. Andrews, journal, p. 148, entry 920, August 11, 1970, EBA.

213. Hoving, quoted in *Newsweek*, August 17, 1970, 93.

214. The Metropolitan Museum of Art, Board meeting minutes, Office of the Secretary Records, MMAA.

215. August Heckscher, "A Statement on the Metropolitan Museum of Art issued by Parks, Recreation, and Cultural Affairs Administrator August Heckscher," January 20, 1971, 4, Office of the Secretary Records, MMAA.

216. The department was disbanded in spring 1978 when Philippe de Montebello was appointed director.

217. Heckscher, "A Statement on the Metropolitan Museum of Art issued by Parks, Recreation, and Cultural Affairs Administrator August Heckscher," 4.

218. Patricia Mainardi, conversation with the author, New York, NY, January 31, 2003.

3. THE WHITNEY MUSEUM OF AMERICAN ART

Epigraph: Ralph Burgard, New York State Council on the Arts. "Planning and Operation of Neighborhood Museums," seminar sponsored by the New York State Council on the Arts and the New York City Department of Cultural Affairs, November 20–22, 1969, sound tapes and transcript, AAA.

1. Benny Andrews, interview, in "Not a Rhyme Time."

2. These artists were Romare Bearden, Robert Blackburn, Betty Blayton, Barbara Chase-Riboud, Eldzier Corter, Roy DeCarava, John Dowell Jr., Melvin Edwards, Sam Gilliam, John Gooding, David Hammons, Richard Hunt, Daniel LaRue Johnson, Richard Mayhew, Algernon Miller, Joe Overstreet, John T. Riddle, John T. Scott, John Shearer, George Smith, Carroll Sockwell, David Stephens, and William T. Williams. Ernest Frazier originally agreed to lend one painting and two photographs. The loan agreement for the photographs was voided. The painting was purchased by the museum before the exhibition and installed in the show. This

list is drawn from the museum's exhibition signage (see fig. 3.8) and documents in the loan agreement folder for the exhibition in the Whitney Museum of American Art Archives.

3. Among these shows were 30 *Contemporary Black Artists*, organized by the Minneapolis Institute of Arts with the assistance of Ruder & Finn, Inc., in 1968, which subsequently traveled to the High Museum of Art in Atlanta, the Flint Institute of Arts in Flint, MI, the Everson Museum of Art in Syracuse, and the San Francisco Museum of Art; *Contemporary Black Artists*, held at the Museum of Art at the Rhode Island School of Design in 1969; *New Black Artists*, organized by Edward Taylor at the Brooklyn Museum in 1969; *Afro-American Artists: New York and Boston*, organized by Edmund Barry Gaither for the Museum of the National Center of Afro-American Artists and the Museum of Fine Arts, Boston, in 1970; *Dimensions of Black*, held at the La Jolla Museum of Contemporary Art in 1970; and *Blacks: USA: 1973*, organized by Benny Andrews for the New York Cultural Center in 1973.

4. Whitney Museum of American Art, press release for *Contemporary Black Artists in America*, March 18, 1971, WMAA Archives.

5. "The Black Artist in America."

6. "The Black Artist in America," 251.

7. "The Black Artist in America," 251.

8. "The Black Artist in America," 249.

9. "The Black Artist in America," 253.

10. "The Black Artist in America," 258.

11. Larry Neal, "Any Day Now: Black Art and Black Liberation," *Ebony*, August 1969, 54–55, reprinted in Atkinson, *Black Dimensions in Contemporary American Art*, 9.

12. Ron Milner, interview, in "Not a Rhyme Time."

13. August Wilson, interview, in "Not a Rhyme Time."

14. Donaldson, "AfriCOBRA Manifesto?," 80. See also "AfriCOBRA and Transatlantic Connections"; Hogu, "Inaugurating AfriCOBRA"; and Jones-Henderson, "Remembering AfriCOBRA and the Black Arts Movement in 1960s Chicago."

15. Ybarra-Frausto, "The Chicano Movement/The Movement of Chicano Art," 128.

16. Ybarra-Frausto, "The Chicano Movement/The Movement of Chicano Art," 128.

17. For a discussion of *Womanhouse*, see Wilding, *By Our Own Hands*; Arlene Raven, "Blood Sister: Female Art and Criticism," in the exhibition catalogue *Division of Labor*; and Carson, "On Discourse as Monument," 121–24.

18. *Two Centuries of African American Art*, organized by guest curator David Driskell, September 30–November 21, 1976.

19. *New Perspectives in Latin American Art, 1930–2006: Selections from a Decade of Acquisitions*, November 21, 2007–February 25, 2008.

20. See Mari Carmen Ramirez et al., *Resisting Categories*.

21. Darby English has called this "black representational space." English has pointed out that in the current context "the category 'black art' is now exposed as one among those many residual identity frameworks painstakingly constructed for use in a time whose urgencies simply are not our own." See English, *How to See a Work of Art in Total Darkness*, 27.

22. See Zabunyan, *Black Is a Color*.

23. Darby English addressed this issue in the Twenty-Sixth Annual Rebay Lecture at the Solomon R. Guggenheim Museum on January 28, 2014.

24. Gibson, *Abstract Expressionism*, 71.

25. English, lecture at the Guggenheim Museum.

26. Geldzahler, *New York Painting and Sculpture*, 17.

27. Geldzahler, *New York Painting and Sculpture*, 17.

28. Geldzahler, *New York Painting and Sculpture*, 25.

29. McKinzie, *The New Deal for Artists*.

30. With the creation of the New York State Council on the Arts and the National Endowment for the Arts, museums were, theoretically, now serving the entire public, but in practice, publicly funded arts program were also a way of managing dissent by providing "expressive outlets" for citizens who, some feared, might otherwise engage in subversive activities. For a related discussion, see also Cazenave, *Impossible Democracy*, on the use of federal government funds to support social protest–based community reform. According to Donna M. Blinkiewicz, despite its pluralistic rhetoric the NEA celebrated one particular aesthetic, high modernism, in its early years and ignored the rest well into the 1970s. See Blinkiewicz, *Federalizing the Muse*, 119–20.

31. While many African American artists were given opportunities in the WPA, only after protests were African Americans allowed to be supervisors. For a chronicle of African American artists in the WPA, see Bearden and Henderson, *A History of African-American Artists from 1792 to the Present*, 227–41.

32. This general association of artists with the Old Left was expressed by Livingston Biddle: "The arts were considered possibly dangerous ground for congress to get into. It was close enough to the McCarthy period so that artists were equated on occasion with Communism." Biddle, interview with Michael Brenson, September 4, 1998, quoted in Brenson, *Visionaries and Outcasts*, 8.

33. *Congressional Record*, February 27, 1968, 4313, quoted in Brenson, *Visionaries and Outcasts*, 82.

34. Quoted in Jacobs, "What the Federal Arts Program Really Means," 28.

35. Livingston Biddle, *Our Government and the Arts*, 35, 75.

36. Claiborne Pell, lecture presented to the National Society of Arts and Letters, New York, NY, 1965, quoted in Biddle, *Our Government and the Arts*, 75–76.

37. Touting the benefits to the middle class, while providing support for "inner-city" programs, implied that one of the NEA's subsidiary purposes was to siphon off political dissent.

38. *New York State Council on the Arts Annual Report 1969–70*, 6.

39. Hale Woodruff was one of the council's founding members.

40. Laws of New York, chapter 181, section 1, article 19–1, §526, May 13, 1965. See *New York State Council on the Arts Annual Report 1966–67*, 79.

41. *New York State Council on the Arts Annual Report 1967–68*, 83, 85.

42. *The Kerner Report: The 1968 Report of the National Advisory Commission on Civil Disorders*, 144.

43. *The Kerner Report: The 1968 Report of the National Advisory Commission on Civil Disorders*, 32.

44. See *New York State Council on the Arts Annual Report 1968–69*, 78–87.

45. The Community Gallery at the Brooklyn Museum was directed by Henri Ghent, a leader among black arts activists, who was especially active in the BECC.

46. Thomas Hoving, who served as New York City's parks commissioner in 1965 and 1966 until his appointment as director of the Metropolitan Museum of Art, openly admitted that many of his government-funded arts programs were "intended to keep the city cool." Thomas P. F. Hoving, e-mail to author, February 29, 2001.

47. The exhibition was *Masters of American Watercolor*, one of seven exhibitions sponsored by the New York State Council on the Arts in 1961–62. See Brian O'Doherty, "Art: Constructions to Control Conditioned Reflexes," *New York Times*, February 10, 1962.

48. According to her granddaughter, Flora Miller Biddle, Gertrude Vanderbilt Whitney felt constrained by her privileged upbringing. To neutralize and complement her life in "society," she created the club as an escape into the world of "bohemia." Art provided the bridge that enabled Gertrude to straddle two worlds. The Whitney Museum of American Art aimed to reflect Gertrude's personality by being "both daring and conservative." Flora Miller Biddle, *The Whitney Women and the Museum They Made*, 70.

49. See Berman, *Rebels on Eighth Street*, 101.

50. Alfred H. Barr Jr., quoted in Bee and Elligott, *Art in Our Time*, 16. Lillie P. Bliss and other early supporters of MoMA acquired a number of pieces from the Armory Show that would end up in the museum's collection. The works acquired by Bliss and later donated to the museum included *Silence* (1911) and *Roger and Angelica* (ca. 1910) by Odilon Redon. Mr. and Mrs. John Hay Whitney purchased Matisse's *Goldfish and Sculpture* (1911) and donated it to the museum in 1988. *The Red Studio* (1911) remained in the artist's collection until 1926 and was eventually purchased by MoMA in 1949.

51. Berman has reported that in 1914 or 1915, Whitney wrote an unpublished speech in which she criticized modernism as "going too far." Speaking of Post-Impressionism and Cubism she said, "These schools had their origins in France, they had big followings in other foreign countries. It is easy to observe their growth in the history of art and it has seemed to me that there is one point, interesting and true, which I deem to be the credit of America. We have never gone to the same extremes to which the French, Germans, Italians, and Russians have gone in this regard. Even those . . . exponents of the independent schools preserved some semblance of sanity in their madness." Quoted in Berman, *Rebels on Eighth Street*, 104.

52. Berman, *Rebels on Eighth Street*, 101.

53. Sloan was represented in the exhibition by *The Picnic Grounds* (1906–7), now in the collection of the Whitney.

54. The purchases were Henri's *Laughing Child* (1907), Shinn's *Revue* (1908), Lawson's *Winter on the River* (1907), and Luks's *Woman with Goose* (1907). All are now in the Whitney Museum collection. See Berman, *Rebels on Eighth Street*, 91.

55. "Whitney Museum to Be Opened Today," *New York Times*, November 17, 1931.

56. The museum's oft-cited exhibition *Abstract Painting in America* (1935) was notable for being uncharacteristic. See Jones, "It's Not Enough to Say 'Black Is Beautiful,'" 157.

57. John I. H. Baur, interview by Paul Cummings, sound recording and transcript, January 22–February 19, 1970, AAA.

58. As stated in the 1961–62 issue of the *Whitney Review*, "Since it first opened its doors to the public in November, 1931, the Museum has been a family institution, founded by Gertrude Vanderbilt Whitney, endowed by her, and operated since her death by a Board consisting principally of her children." See "The Museum's New Trustees," in Whitney Museum of American Art, *The Whitney Review*, 1961/62, n.p.

59. The Whitney had been incorporated as a nonprofit, tax-exempt institution in 1935. Its first trustees were Juliana Force, Frank Crocker, Sonny Whitney, Flora Miller Whitney, and William Adams Delano. For a discussion of the museum's finances in its early years, see Berman, *Rebels on Eighth Street*, 385–86.

60. August Heckscher, "Our National Tradition" (excerpts from a talk at the cornerstone ceremony for the new Whitney Museum of American Art, October 20, 1964), in Whitney Museum of American Art, *The Whitney Review*, 1964/65, n.p. When the Whitney opened its building at 99 Gansevoort Street in 2015, as an even more powerful symbol of national stature, First Lady Michelle Obama spoke at the dedication ceremony.

61. See Goodrich and Baur, *American Art of Our Century*.

62. Flora Miller Biddle, *The Whitney Women and the Museum They Made*, 145.

63. Over half the museums in the country increased their educational activities between 1966 and 1974 due in part to the creation of the National Endowment for the Arts (NEA), which produced a new standard of accountability for museums that received federal funds. See Newsome and Silver, *The Art Museum as Educator*, 13.

64. Baur, interview, 80.

65. Grace Glueck, "Whitney to Open Branch Museum," *New York Times*, February 21, 1967. See also Eugene Lewis, "The Art Resources Center of the Whitney Museum," *Whitney Review*, 1967/68, n.p.

66. Calo, *Distinction and Denial*, 67–104.

67. Baur, interview, 81.

68. *Whitney Review*, 1966/67, 24.

69. Baur, interview, 83.

70. Lewis, "The Art Resources Center of the Whitney Museum," n.p.

71. Baur, interview, 81.

72. David Hupert, presentation at the New York State Council on the Arts, "Planning and Operation of Neighborhood Museums," seminar sponsored by the New York State Council on the Arts and the New York City Department of Cultural Affairs, November 20–22, 1969, sound tapes and transcript, 89–90, AAA. See also Harvey and Friedberg, *A Museum for the People*.

73. The Independent Study Program, still in existence, brought college students into contact with working professionals. The youth program provided studio space and materials. By offering unstructured opportunity—no formal classes were held—the program aimed to address itself "directly to the problems of maturation in a culturally disoriented environment." See Hupert, "Education Department Report," *Whitney Review*, 1968/69, 12.

74. The work *Negro Head* (1931) by James House Jr. (acquisition number 32.73a-c) appears in the museum's current catalogue but was not included in the 1954 publication, *The Whitney Museum and Its Collection*, produced in conjunction with the museum's move to Fifty-Fourth Street. Conversely, Sills's *Green Wind* (1963) is listed as an acquisition in the museum's 1963/64 *Bulletin* but is not in the current catalogue. The following pieces were included in the museum's inaugural exhibition in the Renzo Piano building on Gansevoort Street in 2015: Barthé, *The Blackberry Woman* (1932); Pippin, *The Buffalo Hunt* (1933); several panels from Lawrence's *War Series* (1946–47); White, *The Preacher* (1952); Alston, *Family* (1955); and Hunt, *Horizontal Extending Form* (1958).

75. Lloyd's exhibition at the Studio Museum in Harlem opened on September 26, 1968. His exhibition record also included *Art Turned On* at the Institute of Contemporary Art in Boston (1965); *Light as a Creative Medium* at the Carpenter Center at Harvard University (1965); *Light in Art* at the Contemporary Arts Museum in Houston (1966); *Art Electric* at the Sonnabend Gallery in Paris (1966); a solo exhibition at the Wadsworth Atheneum (1966); and *Counterpoints* at Lever House (1967).

76. Barkley Hendricks, letter to Robert Doty in *Contemporary Black Artists in America* Exhibition File, WMAA Archives.

77. *The 1930's: Painting and Sculpture in America* ran from October 15 through December 1, 1968.

78. Mary Schmidt Campbell, interview, in "Not a Rhyme Time."

79. Romare Bearden quoted in "Blacks Talk Back to Whitney Museum," *Amsterdam News*, November 23, 1968.

80. Faith Ringgold, interview by author, Englewood, NJ, January 27, 2011.

81. In 1976 Charlene Claye Van Derzee (no relation to James VanDerZee) mounted a show of work by African American artists of the 1930s and early '40s entitled *The Black Artists in the WPA 1933–1943* at The New Muse Community Museum of Brooklyn. See New Muse Community Museum of Brooklyn, *Black Artists in the WPA 1933–1943*.

82. Pincus-Witten, "Reviews," 65. Pincus-Witten goes on to discuss *Invisible Americans* and to praise the "discovery" of Joseph Delaney.

83. Bearden and Henderson, *A History of African-American Artists*, 140. Barthé's additional accomplishments in the 1930s and early '40s included a pair of bas relief panels for the Public Works of Art Project in 1937, an exhibition of eighteen bronzes at the Arden Galleries in New York in 1939, and Guggenheim Fellowships in 1940 and 1941.

84. *The Evolution of Afro-American Artists: 1800–1950* was held October 16–November 15, 1967. The show was inspired by *Ten Afro-American Artists of the Nineteenth Century*, held in 1966 at Howard University in Washington, DC.

85. City University of New York, *The Evolution of Afro-American Artists*.

86. As I will discuss in the next chapter, the Museum of Modern Art did not hold a show of American abstract art until 1951, instead favoring European art. This orientation is exemplified in the 1936 exhibition *Cubism and Abstract Art*, which excluded Americans and featured only European art.

87. Alloway, "Art," 671.

88. Hilton Kramer, "Differences in Quality," *New York Times*, November 24, 1968.

89. Baur quoted in Bert Shanas, "Black Artists Put On Anti-Whitney Exhibit," *Sunday News*, November 24, 1968.

90. See Flagg, "The Transparency Phenomenon," 220.

91. The conclusion that purportedly race-neutral decisions are often unconsciously race-specific rests on an analysis of outcomes. As Flagg explains, "Numerous studies indicate that whites receive more favorable treatment than blacks in virtually every area of social interaction, including hiring and performance evaluations; mortgage lending, insurance redlining, and retail bargaining; psychiatric diagnoses; response to patient violence in mental institutions; and virtually every stage in the criminal law process: arrest, the decision to charge, imprisonment, and capital sentences" ("The Transparency Phenomenon," 24). Using outcomes as the litmus test in art, it is hard to maintain the assertion that representation in museums is based on race-neutral decision making.

92. Kramer, "Differences in Quality."

93. Kramer's reviews were "Revisiting the Art History of the Nineteen-Thirties," published on October 20, 1968, and "Art and Politics in the Thirties," published on October 27, 1968. The report on the artists' protest was "1930's Show at Whitney Picketed by Negro Artists Who Call It Incomplete," *New York Times*, November 18, 1968. Hilton Kramer's article on quality was "Differences in Quality," cited above. One letter to the editor was an extensive rebuttal to Kramer written by Henri Ghent and published on December 8, 1968. The other was written by Alfred Werner and appeared on November 23, 1968. Also relevant was Hilton Kramer's "Art and Politics: All the Old Questions Return," *New York Times*, September 22, 1968.

94. Kramer, "Differences in Quality."

95. Kramer, "Differences in Quality."

96. Michele Wallace, e-mail to author, January 19, 2011.

97. Benny Andrews, journal, p. 83, entry 579, April 24, 1969, EBA.

98. The scope of the BECC's activities at this time was broad. While they were negotiating with the Whitney about the *Contemporary Black Artists in America* exhibition they were also negotiating with Ruder & Finn for honoraria ($500–$1,000) for artists participating in the exhibition *30 Black Artists* and to expand the show to include more artists in its national tour. They were also advocating the placement of the Michael C. Rockefeller collection in Harlem or Bedford Stuyvesant, rather than at the Metropolitan Museum of Art.

99. According to Benny Andrews's notes from the meeting, Henri Ghent sensed that he would not be the group's first choice for this position and preemptively told the group that he would not be considered for such a role.

100. While traveling in the San Francisco area in July, Andrews met with Hayward King to discuss the possibility of involving him in the exhibition. King was one of the first African Americans to hold a prominent role in arts administration in the Bay Area and at the time was director of the Richmond Art Center. No involvement on King's part came of this conversation.

101. Benny Andrews, journal, p. 98, entry 666, September 18, 1969, EBA.

102. John I. H. Baur, letter to David Solinger, Esq., September 18, 1969, *Contemporary Black Artists in America* Exhibition File, WMAA Archives.

103. Black Emergency Cultural Coalition statement in the Benny Andrews Archive, Studio Museum in Harlem, NY.

104. Grace Glueck, "15 of 75 Black Artists Leave as Whitney Exhibition Opens," *New York Times*, April 6, 1971.

105. Al Loving (December 19, 1969–January 25, 1970); Melvin Edwards (March 3–29, 1970); Frederick Eversley (May 18–June 7, 1970); Malcolm Bailey (March 16–April 25, 1971); Frank Bowling (November 4–December 6, 1971); Alma W. Thomas (April 25–May 28, 1972); Joseph E. Yoakum (October 23–November 26, 1972); Robert Reed (March 8–April 8, 1973); Mahler Ryder (November 8–December 9, 1973); Jack Whitten (August 20–September 22, 1974); Betye Saar (March 20–April 20, 1975); and Minnie Evans (July 3–August 3, 1975). For a fuller discussion of these exhibitions, see Jones, "It's Not Enough to Say 'Black Is Beautiful,'" 154–80.

106. The tenure of director David Ross, from 1991 to 1998, marked a departure at the Whitney, in which several exhibitions featured large numbers of artists of color in a variety of contexts, including the 1993 Whitney Biennial and *Black Male: Representations of Masculinity in Contemporary American Art* (1994). Ross mentored a generation of curators who went on to assume appointments as museum directors: Thelma Golden at the Studio Museum in Harlem; Lisa Phillips at the New Museum of Contemporary Art; and Adam Weinberg, the Whitney's current director.

107. See Andrews, "The B.E.C.C."

108. The catalogues for these exhibitions were, respectively, Doty, *Photo-Secession*; Doty and Waldman, *Adolph Gottlieb*; and Doty, *Human Concern / Personal Torment*.

109. David Driskell, letter to John I. H. Baur, April 3, 1970, *Contemporary Black Artists in America* Exhibition File, WMAA Archives.

110. Samella Lewis quoted in Grace Glueck, "Black Show under Fire at Whitney," *New York Times*, January 31, 1971.

111. Vivian Browne, interview by Emma Amos, March 10, 1985, New York City, BHA.

112. Robert Doty, letter to Betty Asher, January 14, 1970, *Contemporary Black Artists in America* Exhibition File, WMAA Archives.

113. Betty Asher, letter to Robert Doty, January 19, 1970, *Contemporary Black Artists in America* Exhibition File, WMAA Archives.

114. Robert Doty, letter to Art Department, Alumni Memorial Building Galleries, Lehigh University, September 2, 1970, *Contemporary Black Artists in America* Exhibition File, WMAA Archives.

115. Doty, letter to Michael J. Singletary, November 23, 1970, *Contemporary Black Artists in America* Exhibition File, WMAA Archives.

116. BECC flyer, Benny Andrews Archive, Studio Museum in Harlem, NY.

117. Robert Doty, letter to David C. Driskell, February 28, 1972, *Contemporary Black Artists in America* Exhibition File, WMAA Archives. The exhibitions were *Recent Paintings by Alma W. Thomas: Earth and Space Series 1961–1971* at the Carl Van Vechten Gallery of Fine Arts, Fisk University, Nashville, TN, October 10–November 3, 1971, and *Alma W. Thomas* at the Whitney Museum of American Art, April 25–May 28, 1972.

118. Henri Ghent, letter to John I. H. Baur, March 31, 1970, *Contemporary Black Artists in America* Exhibition File, WMAA Archives.

119. Henri Ghent, letter to John I. H. Baur, April 21, 1970, *Contemporary Black Artists in America* Exhibition File, WMAA Archives.

120. Edmund Barry Gaither, interview by author, Boston, MA, February 22, 2006.

121. Gaither, interview.

122. Gaither, introduction to *Afro-American Artists*, n.p.

123. Hilton Kramer, "Trying to Define 'Black Art': Must We Go Back to Social Realism?," *New York Times*, May 31, 1970.

124. Kramer, "Trying to Define 'Black Art.' "

125. Edmund B. Gaither, " 'A New Criticism Is Needed,' " *New York Times*, June 21, 1970.

126. Benny Andrews, "On Understanding Black Art," *New York Times*, June 21, 1970.

127. A disillusioned Marxist, Greenberg lamented that social realism not only failed to mobilize the masses but, even worse, was adopted as the state-sanctioned style of art in the USSR under Stalin. Greenberg saw Marxism as a failed utopian theory (though he was interested in Marxism and published in Marxist journals early in his career) and its manifestation in art, social realism, as a failed art movement.

128. Kramer characterized Greenberg's writings as "art criticism of a very high order—the highest, I should say, in our time." See "A Critic on the Side of History: Notes on Clement Greenberg," in Kramer, *The Age of the Avant-Garde*, 499–506. For a discussion of the association of freedom and formal innovation, see Gibson, *Abstract Expressionism*, xxiii–xxviii.

129. Rose, "The Politics of Art," 32.

130. Baur, *Revolution and Tradition in Modern American Art*.

131. Baur, *Revolution and Tradition in Modern American Art*, 5.

132. Gaither, interview.

133. Hilton Kramer, "Do You Believe in the Principle of Museums?," *New York Times*, January 18, 1970; Hilton Kramer "About MoMA, the AWC and Political Causes," *New York Times*, February 8, 1970.

134. Kramer, "Do You Believe in the Principle of Museums?"

135. Kramer, "About MoMA, the AWC and Political Causes."

136. Benny Andrews, interview conducted by Blackside, Inc., February 6, 1998, for *I'll Make Me a World*, 19, Henry Hampton Collection, WUFMA.

137. Benny Andrews, journal, p. 166, entry 1000, November 13, 1970, EBA.

138. Benny Andrews, journal, p. 167, entry 1005, November 16, 1970, EBA.

139. Benny Andrews, journal, p. 154, entry 948, September 23, 1970, EBA.

140. Benny Andrews, journal, p. 163, entry 983, October 30, 1970, EBA.

141. See note 2 in this chapter. All correspondence is in the loan agreement folder for the exhibition, WMAA Archives.

142. Barbara Chase-Riboud is included in the catalogue because she asked that her work be removed thirteen days after the opening.

143. Joe Overstreet, interview by author, New York, NY, April 12, 2006.

144. Dowell et al., "Politics."

145. Fred Eversley, conversation with author, June 14, 2007. Zimmerman's work was also featured in the 1974 Whitney Biennial.

146. John Shearer, telephone conversation with author, March 12, 2014.

147. Schoonmaker, *Barkley L. Hendricks*, 20.

148. BECC press release, April 5, 1971, Benny Andrews Archive, Studio Museum in Harlem, NY.

149. John Chandler, John W. Rhoden, Raymond Saunders, Mahler Ryder, Hughie Lee-Smith, Marvin Brown, Frank Bowling, Vincent Smith, Al Loving, Tom Lloyd, Avel de Knight, Alvin Hollingsworth, Ellsworth Ausby, Alma Thomas, Jacob Lawrence, Thomas Sills, and Algernon Miller. Romare Bearden, Robert Blackburn, Betty Blayton, Richard Mayhew, Joe Overstreet, and Barbara Chase-Riboud had also been invited by Doty, but withdrew.

150. Volume 1 had been published in 1969. Volume 2 would be released in 1971. These artists were Betye Saar, Manuel Hughes, David Driskell, Evelyn Terry, Phillip Lindsay Mason, Norma Morgan, Murry DePillars, Noah Purifoy, Charles White, and William Henderson. David Hammons and John Riddle had also been invited, but withdrew. Lewis and Waddy, *Black Artists on Art*.

151. Terry's etching *Black Flag* was not illustrated in the catalogue, though it is listed on the checklist.

152. In an e-mail to Marjorie Van Cura forwarded to the author on September 18, 2014, Betye Saar explained that she added a new element to the work in 1996, a product label depicting a caricature of a dark-skinned baby being pursued by an alligator, an explicit reference to the racist term "alligator bait."

153. In a conversation with the author's research assistant, Mireille Bourgeois, on June 9, 2008, Marvin Brown related that the untitled work illustrated in the exhibition catalogue was damaged in transit and replaced the work shown in the installation photographs.

154. Tommie Smith was the gold medalist for the 200-meter race at the 1968 Olympics. He and bronze medalist John Carlos raised their gloved fists in a Black Power salute while at the podium receiving their medals.

155. Doty, *Contemporary Black Artists in America*, 7. Doty's catalogue essay cited eclecticism as the hallmark of the exhibition. As art historian Patricia Mainardi has pointed out, eclecticism can be an instrument used to depoliticize artwork. If all works have equal status and interest, art with political aims becomes just another category of artistic practice, not a fundamental challenge to prevailing power relations. See Mainardi, "The Political Origins of Modernism."

156. Doty's framework echoed the ideas expressed by Henry Geldzahler in his catalogue essay for *New York Painting and Sculpture*. In that essay Geldzahler too defended abstraction. What I am arguing is that the terms of the debate itself represented the limitations of the dominant discourse at that time.

157. Doty, *Contemporary Black Artists in America*, 11.

158. Doty, *Contemporary Black Artists in America*, 12.

159. Omi and Winant, *Racial Formation in the United States from the 1960s to the 1980s*, 101.

160. Wallis, *Hans Haacke*, 92–97.

161. Doty, *Contemporary Black Artists in America*, 7.

162. Exemplary exhibitions include *Explorations in the City of Light: African-American Artists in Paris, 1945–1965*, at the Studio Museum in Harlem in 1996; *Rhapsodies in Black: Art of the Harlem Renaissance*, organized by the Hayward Gallery in 1997; *Challenge of the Modern African*

American Artists, 1925–1945, at the Studio Museum in Harlem in 2003; *The Global Africa Project,* at the Museum of Art and Design in New York in 2010; and *Afro Modern: Journeys through the Black Atlantic,* at Tate Liverpool in 2010.

163. Goldwater, *Primitivism in Modern Painting* and *Primitivism in Modern Art.*

164. Conversation with Fanon Frazier, June 2008. For a discussion of Sun Ra, see Vincent, *Funk,* 138; and Szwed, *Space Is the Place.*

165. Pindell, "Artist's Statement."

166. For example, among the artists invited for *Contemporary Black Artists in America* Kellie Jones has pointed out that the intersecting geometric forms in William T. Williams's *Trane* (1969) offered a visual interpretation of the sounds of John Coltrane's saxophone. See Jones, "To the Max: Energy/Experimentation," in Jones, *Energy/Experimentation,* 17. Jack Whitten compared his work to "sheets of sound" created by jazz musicians, and Jones reports that Whitten used an Afro-comb to create striations in his canvases, as well as a saw, which Jones identifies as a tool of manual labor (Jones, *Energy/Experimentation,* 20–21). The color scheme of Joe Overstreet's *Saint Expedite A* (1971) is reminiscent of the red, black, and green colors of black liberation (Jones, *Energy/Experimentation,* 19), though she writes that when she visited Overstreet on February 24, 2006, he referred to the darkest tone as a very deep purple (33n25). Jones's catalogue essay parses the relationship between each artist's work and his or her political activism.

167. Jones, "It's Not Enough to Say 'Black Is Beautiful,' " 162.

168. Melvin Edwards, artist statement in *Melvin Edwards: Works,* February 29, 1970 (Whitney Museum of American Art), cited in Jones, "It's Not Enough to Say 'Black Is Beautiful,' " 161, 178n21.

169. Dowell et al., "Politics."

170. Doty, *Human Concern / Personal Torment;* Doty, *Extraordinary Realities.*

171. Doty, *Human Concern / Personal Torment,* n.p.

172. "Art of the 1930's in Major Exhibition at Whitney Museum of American Art," press release, October 4, 1968, *The 1930's: Painting and Sculpture in America* Exhibition File, WMAA Archives.

173. Doty, *Contemporary Black Artists in America,* 12.

174. John Canaday, "Black Artists on View in 2 Exhibitions," *New York Times,* April 7, 1971.

175. John Canaday, "That Wouldn't Be a Silver Lining, Would It?," *New York Times,* April 18, 1971.

176. Canaday, "Black Artists on View in 2 Exhibitions."

177. David C. Driskell, letter to Robert Doty, April 15, 1971, *Contemporary Black Art in America* Exhibition File, WMAA Archives.

178. Flora Miller Biddle, letter to Robert Doty, *Contemporary Black Art in America* Exhibition File, WMAA Archives.

179. Nigel Jackson, quoted in "Reviews," *Raven,* June 1, 1971.

180. *Rebuttal to Whitney Museum Exhibition: Black Artists in Rebuttal at Acts of Art Gallery, NYC,* n.p.

181. Betsy Jones, memo to Jennifer Licht, April 10, 1971. Jackson had received his 33 percent commission for the drawings purchased by MoMA (one sold for $115 and the other $210), but

Andrews was under no obligation to provide him with a commission for the painting, which he sold for $5,500. Andrews was asked, and agreed, to put this in writing for the museum. John B. Hightower Papers, II.1.10, MoMA Archives, NY.

182. John Hightower wrote in a letter to Nigel Jackson dated October 11, 1971: "In an attempt to put myself in manageable order I would like to resign as a member of your Board of Directors. Aside from the fact that I have made little commitment in time to Acts of Art and probably could not do so even if I were asked, there is an ethical awkwardness involved that argues strongly against my participation and formal affiliation with your organization." John B. Hightower Papers, II.1.10, MoMA Archives, NY.

183. Tom Lloyd, introduction to *Black Art Notes*, n.p.

184. Adam David Miller, in Lloyd, *Black Art Notes*, n.p.

185. Ray Elkins, "The People's Artist," in Lloyd, *Black Art Notes*, 17.

186. Baraka, "Counter Statement to Whitney Ritz Bros," 11.

187. Baraka, "Counter Statement to Whitney Ritz Bros," 11.

188. Baraka, "Counter Statement to Whitney Ritz Bros," 10.

189. Allon Schoener, interview by Laurin Raiken, "The Art World in Turmoil," Oral History Project, transcript, 5, AAA.

190. Gammon, interview by Camille Billops, 109.

191. Marvin Brown, conversation with author, June 9, 2008. During this conversation Brown recalled that the work reproduced in the *Contemporary Black Artists in America* exhibition catalogue was not the same piece shown in the exhibition. The piece first intended for the show was damaged in shipping.

192. Benny Andrews, interview conducted by Blackside, Inc., 21–22.

193. The Whitney owns one work by Andrews, the print *New York Café*, from an edition of 250 given to the museum in 2004.

194. Fred Wilson, *Rooms with a View: The Struggle between Culture, Content, and Context in Art*, Longwood Gallery, P.S. 39, Bronx Council for the Arts, December 1987; and *Mining the Museum: An Installation by Fred Wilson* organized by the Contemporary Art Museum in Baltimore and held at the Maryland Historical Society, April 3, 1992–February 28, 1993.

195. Leo Steinberg, lecture, Museum of Modern Art, New York, 1968, first published in "Reflections on the State of Criticism," *Artforum* (March 1972), in *Other Criteria*, 98.

4. THE MUSEUM OF MODERN ART

1. William S. Rubin, memo to Arthur Drexler, February 24, 1970, John B. Hightower Papers, III.2.15, MoMA Archives, NY.

2. *"Primitivism" in 20th Century Art: Affinity of the Tribal and the Modern*, held at the Museum of Modern Art, September 19, 1984–January 15, 1985.

3. See McEvilley, "Doctor, Lawyer, Indian Chief," 351.

4. William S. Rubin, introduction to *"Primitivism" in 20th Century Art*, 7.

5. Araeen, "From Primitivism to Ethnic Arts."

6. The group's thirteen-point program included demands that artists retain control over their work after it left the studio and became the property of private collectors and museums. They wanted artist and staff participation in museum governance; free admission; and museum support for all artists, not only those with gallery representation. For a full version of the thirteen demands dated January 28, 1969, see Art Workers' Coalition, *Documents / Open Hearing*, 1969, n.p.

7. For a clear discussion of this issue and of the relationship between this ideology and the artists' artwork, see Bryan-Wilson, *Art Workers*.

8. Raphael Montañez Ortiz, interview by author, Highland Park, NJ, January 8, 2011.

9. In the 1960s, Raphael Montañez Ortiz went by the name Ralph Ortiz.

10. "Program for Change: Black and Puerto Rican Culture," John B. Hightower Papers, III.2.16, MoMA Archives, NY.

11. Over time the demands changed slightly, and by fall the number of signatures had grown to twenty. Yasmín Ramírez refers to the group as the PRAWC in her article "The Activist Legacy of Puerto Rican Artists in New York and *The Art Heritage of Puerto Rico*."

12. Bill Quinn, "Trace Culture, Art of the White World to African Aesthetic and Artistic Base," *Muhammad Speaks*, April 4, 1969.

13. Bill Quinn, "Amazing Art of 'Primitive' World through Black Eyes," *Muhammad Speaks*, February 14, 1969.

14. In reviewing the show, Thomas McEvilley made the astute assessment that "primitivism" was an attempt to thwart the threat of change that would undermine formalist modernism's claim to be above history—above, McEvilley writes, "the web of natural and cultural change." By the 1970s formalist modernism had lost its claim to universality and utopianism and become "just another style." McEvilley, "Doctor, Lawyer, Indian Chief," 340.

15. Lippard, "The Art Worker's Coalition," 171.

16. Carl Andre statement in Art Workers' Coalition, *Documents / Open Hearing*, 1969, n.p.

17. Wallace, "African People, Black Light," 43.

18. Andre, in *Documents / Open Hearing*, 1969, n.p.

19. Alex Gross, "The Artist as Nigger," *East Village Other*, December 22, 1970.

20. Julie Ault, Lucy Lippard, and Julia Bryan-Wilson have made significant contributions to the understanding of arts activism of the 1960s and '70s, particularly the activities of the Art Workers' Coalition, though none have explored the group's internal racial dynamics. See Bryan-Wilson, *Art Workers*; Ault, *Alternative Art New York, 1965–1985*.

21. Tom Lloyd quoted in "The Black Artist in America," 251.

22. This show circulated to six museums under the title *30 Black Contemporary Artists* and was expanded and circulated to an additional six museums under the title *Contemporary Black Artists*. See Ruder & Finn Fine Arts, *Contemporary Black Artists*.

23. The show was *Tom Lloyd: Kinetic Light Sculptures* (New York, November 2–23, 1968). Series 3 Exhibition Files, box 7, AAA, Howard Wise Gallery. Howard Wise also showed the artist Takis.

24. Benny Andrews, journal, p. 59, entry 442, November 29, 1968, EBA.

25. Benny Andrews, journal, p. 59, entry 442, November 29, 1968, EBA.

26. Ringgold, *We Flew over the Bridge*, 168.

27. Wallace, "American People, Black Light," 38.

28. Judson was the center of avant-garde art activity in New York for performers such as Carolee Schneeman, Allan Kaprow, Lil Picard, Kate Millet, Al Hansen, Charlotte Moorman, and Nam June Paik.

29. In his October 1967 performance at Judson Memorial Church, Ortiz filled the cellar gallery with blood, soapsuds, and burned food. His sacrifice of a chicken was stopped when an audience member intervened. Some of these elements were used in later GAAG actions. The gathering, DIAS USA '68, was scheduled for early April 1968 but was cancelled by the artists when Martin Luther King Jr. was assassinated. In an interview with the author on June 20, 2011, Hendricks remarked, "There was enough real destruction going on. . . . [The event] wasn't going to help."

30. See Yasmín Ramírez, "The Activist Legacy of Puerto Rican Artists in New York."

31. "Students and Artists United for a Martin Luther King, Jr. Wing for Black and Puerto Rican Art at the Museum of Modern Art in New York City," pamphlet, April 1969, reprinted in Art Workers' Coalition, *Documents / Open Hearing*, n.p.

32. Alfred Barr discusses the elasticity of the term "modern" in his essay "Modern and 'Modern,'" in Sandler and Newman, *Defining Modern Art*, 82–83. For a discussion of the history of MoMA's collecting philosophy, see Varnedoe, "The Evolving Torpedo."

33. Varnedoe, "The Evolving Torpedo," 15. In 1953, after deaccessioning several important works to the Met, most famously Picasso's *Woman in White* (1923), and after heated debate among members of the board of trustees, the museum changed its policy.

34. Hans Haacke, statement delivered at "An Open Hearing on the Subject: What Should Be the Program of the Art Workers Regarding Museum Reform and to Establish the Program of an Art Workers Coalition," New York, NY, April 10, 1969, in Art Workers' Coalition, *Documents / Open Hearing*, 1969, n.p.

35. Alfred H. Barr Jr., "The 1929 Multidepartmental Plan for The Museum of Modern Art: Its Origins, Development, and Partial Realization," August 1941, typescript prepared for A. Conger Goodyear (who was working on a history of the museum), Alfred H. Barr, Jr. Papers, 9a.15A, MoMA Archives, NY.

36. The Museum of Modern Art, Exh. #1, November 7–December 7, 1929. Many of the pieces were owned by the trustees themselves, especially Lillie P. Bliss. These works would form the core of the canon of MoMA's late twentieth-century brand of modernism.

37. Barr, "Modern and 'Modern,'" 82–83.

38. Barr, *Cubism and Abstract Art*, 11.

39. Barr, *Cubism and Abstract Art*, 11.

40. Alfred Barr Jr., "Loan Exhibitions" (1933), Alfred H. Barr, Jr. Papers [AAA: 2198;32], MoMA Archives, NY.

41. Quoted in Varnedoe, "The Evolving Torpedo," 21.

42. Quoted in Varnedoe, "The Evolving Torpedo," 21.

43. Quoted in Varnedoe, "The Evolving Torpedo," 21.

44. Flam, introduction to *Primitivism and Twentieth-Century Art*, 16, 21n12.

45. *American Sources of Modern Art (Aztec, Maya, Incan)*, Exh. #29, May 8–July 1, 1933. Cahill served as acting director of the museum in 1932 and 1933 while Barr was on leave of absence and also organized *American Folk Art: Art of the Common Man in America, 1750–1900*, Exh. #22, November 30, 1932–January 14, 1933, and a survey exhibition, *American Painting and Sculpture 1862–1932*, Exh. #20, October 31, 1932–February 11, 1933.

46. The Museum of Modern Art, press release for *American Sources of Modern Art*, May 7, 1933.

47. *African Negro Sculpture*, Exh. #39, March 18–May 19, 1935; *Prehistoric Rock Pictures in Europe and Africa*, Exh. #61, April 28–May 30, 1937; *Twenty Centuries of Mexican Art*, Exh. #106, May 15–September 30, 1940; *Indian Art of the United States*, Exh. #123, January 22–April 27, 1941; *Arts of the South Seas*, Exh. #306, January 29–May 19, 1946; and *Ancient Arts of the Andes*, Exh. #550, January 25–March 21, 1954. During preparations for the *Twenty Centuries of Mexican Art* exhibition, MoMA film curator Jay Leyda, who had taken an interest in Lawrence's work, introduced the young painter to José Clemente Orozco, who was at the museum painting a fresco portable mural for the show, *Dive Bomber and Tank*. See Hills, *Painting Harlem Modern*, 45.

48. See Webb, *Perfect Documents*, 15.

49. The Museum of Modern Art, *African Negro Art*, press release. The widespread interest in the aesthetics of African art is revealed by the breadth of the list of lenders: collectors Walter Arensberg, Frank Crowninshield, and Conger Goodyear; artists André Derain, Jacques Lipchitz, and Henri Matisse; art critic Félix Fénéon; poet Tristan Tzara; dealers Paul Guillaume and Daniel-Henri Kahnweiller; arts writer and gallerist Christian Zervos; and the Muséee d'Ethnographie, Palais du Trocadero, in Paris.

50. Sweeney, *African Negro Art*, 11.

51. We hear this statement resonate in Rubin's *"Primitivism"* catalogue introduction: "If, on the one hand, we accept that tribal art was the most important non-Western influence on the history of twentieth-century art, we must certainly, on the other, dismiss the often-heard claims that 'Negro art engendered Cubism,' or that 'Primitive art changed the whole course of modern art.' . . . The changes in modern art at issue were already under way when vanguard artists first became aware of tribal art." See Rubin, introduction to *"Primitivism" in 20th Century Art*, 11.

52. Barr's chart ultimately arrives at two modernist tendencies, one toward "non-geometrical abstraction" exemplified by German Expressionism, Dada, and Surrealism, and the other toward "geometrical abstraction" exemplified by Suprematism, Constructivism, and de Stijl. See Barr, *Cubism and Abstract Art*. The exhibition included no American artists, with the exception of Man Ray and Alexander Calder, a decision Barr justified by noting that there had been an exhibition of abstract art at the Whitney Museum of American Art the previous year.

53. Bearden and Henderson, *A History of African-American Artists from 1792 to the Present*, 247–50.

54. Lawrence reported that "the show made a great impression on me." Inspired by West African sculpture, Lawrence did a little bit of carving and, more importantly for the development of his work, began to depict figures in his paintings. Quoted in Bearden and Henderson, *A History of African-American Artists from 1792 to the Present*, 296.

55. Alain Locke, "African Art: Classical Style," *American Magazine of Art* 28 (May 1935): 270–78, reprinted in Stewart, *The Critical Temper of Alain Locke*, 149–55.

56. Locke, "African Art," 149.

57. Alain Locke, "A Note on African Art," *Opportunity* 2 (May 1924): 134–38, reprinted in Stewart, *The Critical Temper of Alain Locke*, 135.

58. Locke, "A Note on African Art," 135.

59. Locke, "Art Lessons from the Congo," *Survey Graphic* 57 (February 1, 1927): 587–98, reprinted in Stewart, *The Critical Temper of Alain Locke*, 137.

60. Porter, *Modern Negro Art*, 96.

61. Porter, *Modern Negro Art*, 96.

62. Goldwater, *Primitivism in Modern Painting*.

63. Romare Bearden, letter to Walter Quirt, January 20, 1942, quoted in Mercer, *Cosmopolitan Modernisms*, 129.

64. Porter, preface to *Modern Negro Art*, xviii.

65. Now called the Frobenius-Institut.

66. Alfred H. Barr Jr., preface and acknowledgment, in Museum of Modern Art, *Prehistoric Rock Pictures in Europe and Africa*, 10.

67. Making a reference to the Mural Division of the Federal Art Project, an agency run by Holger Cahill, Barr wrote, "Today walls are painted so that the artist may eat, but in prehistoric times walls were painted so that the community might eat." See the press release for *Prehistoric Rock Pictures in Europe and Africa*, Exh. #61 (April 28–May 30, 1937), April 28, 1937, MoMA Archives, NY.

68. Press release for *Prehistoric Rock Pictures in Europe and Africa*.

69. See Blier, "Africa and Paris."

70. See Sylvain, "KulturKreis to Kulturmorphologie."

71. See Barr, *Fantastic Art, Dada, Surrealism*. Despite Barr's seemingly ahistorical approach to the exhibition, his attentiveness to the historical record is evident. At the beginning of the book he offers a detailed chronology of the inception, growth, and development of the various Dada movements and Surrealism, identifying which artists participated in the movements.

72. This show included two works by Horace Pippin, *The End of the War: Starting Home* (1930–33) and *Shell Hole and Observation, Balloon Champagne Sector* (1931). The press release for the show characterized Pippin as a "disabled Negro war veteran." Barr's interest in folk art and "primitive" art was not unique at the time. Edith Halpert had been showing folk art at her Downtown Gallery since 1931, and Abby Aldrich Rockefeller was one of her biggest clients. See Pollock, *The Girl with the Gallery*, 130–34.

73. The Museum of Modern Art, press release for *New Acquisitions: Modern Primitives; Artists of the People*, Exh. #153, October 16, 1941–April 30, 1944, MoMA Archives, NY.

74. *Sculpture by William Edmondson*, Exh. #63c, October 20–November 4, 1937, Museum of Modern Art, New York.

75. The Museum of Modern Art, press release for *Sculpture by William Edmondson*, October 5, 1937, MoMA Archives, NY. Barr had learned of Edmondson's work by a circuitous route from his assistant, Tom Mabry, who in turn had heard about it from his friend the photographer Louise

Dahl-Wolfe. She had been introduced to Edmondson by a circle of friends and poets associated with Vanderbilt University in Nashville. See the exhibition catalogue published by Cheekwood Museum of Art in conjunction with the exhibition *The Art of William Edmondson*, January 28–April 23, 2000.

76. Cooks, *Exhibiting Blackness*, 30.

77. Pollock, *The Girl with the Gallery*, 233.

78. The Metropolitan Museum of Art also bought a painting of Lawrence's at this time, *Pool Parlor* (Arthur Hoppock Hearn Fund 42.147). Lawrence had won sixth prize in the Met's national *Artists for Victory* exhibition.

79. As Patricia Hills has pointed out, the warm reception of the work may be explained, in part, by a shared sense within the business community on the eve of World War II that racially integrated factories would be a necessary step toward having a plentiful labor force. See Hills, *Painting Harlem Modern*, 129.

80. Porter, *Modern Negro Art*, 151.

81. Registrar Exhibition Files, Exh. #262, MoMA Archives, NY. Lawrence was actually a specialist third class. The error in rank is attributable to the fact that African Americans in the Coast Guard were typically consigned to the role of steward's mate, first class, which meant waiting on tables and doing janitorial work. This was Lawrence's initial rank, but he was eventually reassigned to the USS *Sea Cloud*, the navy's first integrated ship. In September 1944, just before the MoMA show opened, he was promoted to specialist third class and assigned to public relations as an official combat artist. See Hills, *Painting Harlem Modern*, 150; Bearden and Henderson, *A History of African-American Artists from 1792 to the Present*, 301–3.

82. "Navyman Lawrence's Works at Modern Art," *New York World Telegram*, October 4, 1944, 9.

83. Elizabeth Catlett, "Artist with a Message," *People's Voice*, October 21, 1944, Exh. #61, MoMA Archives, NY.

84. *Young Negro Art: An Exhibition of the Work of Students at Hampton Institute*, MoMA Exh. #243, October 26–November 28, 1943.

85. The work acquired was Junius Redwood, *Night Scene*, 1941, oil on cardboard, 43⅜" × 33⅜", accession number 755.1943.

86. *The Bainbridge Mainsheet*, December 24, 1943, vol. 3, no. 6, in Department of Public Information Records, II [22;545], MoMA Archives, NY.

87. Bearden and Henderson, *A History of African-American Artists from 1792 to the Present*, 421–22.

88. See Lynes, *Good Old Modern*, 241.

89. Lynes, *Good Old Modern*, 241.

90. See Dizard, *Inventing Public Diplomacy*. Rockefeller's work in the Office of Inter-American Affairs would be the model for the cultural diplomacy created in 1955, the USIA, which would be instrumental in using art for diplomatic and propaganda purposes in the Cold War milieu. These exhibitions supplemented the museum's propagandistic photomural shows, including *Road to Victory*, Exh. #182, May 21–October 4, 1942; and *Airways to Peace*, Exh. #236, July 2–October 31, 1943.

91. Founded in 1933 in order to extend the museum's reach to other parts of the United States, the Circulating Exhibitions Department not only created a program of cultural exchange

with Latin American institutions but also developed exhibitions to tour in Europe for the United States Office of War Information. For a good description of the museum's International Program, see Franc, "The Early Years of the International Program and Council."

92. In these roles d'Harnoncourt continued to focus on Latin America; in December 1944 he embarked on a three-month trip to initiate a membership campaign for MoMA in Mexico, Peru, Chile, Argentina, Brazil, and Haiti.

93. From 1947 until he was appointed director in October 1949, Rene d'Harnoncourt served as director of the Curatorial Departments and chairman of the Coordinating Committee, an ad hoc group managing the museum.

94. Kate Ezra discusses differences between d'Harnoncourt/Rockefeller and Goldwater's approaches in "Collecting African Art at New York's Museum of Primitive Art."

95. Varnedoe, "The Evolving Torpedo," 14.

96. The exhibitions included *Paintings by Nineteen Living Americans* (1929); *Painting and Sculpture by Living Americans* (1930); *American Painting and Sculpture, 1862–1932* (1932); *Painting and Sculpture from 16 American Cities* (1933); *Rugs by American Artists* (1937); *Eighteen Artists from Nine States* (1942); *Fourteen Americans* (1946); *Twelve Americans* (1956); *New American Painting* (1959); *Sixteen Americans* (1959); and *Americans* (1963). Some of the folk artists listed as anonymous may have been African American.

97. *New Horizons in American Art*, Exh. #52 (September 16–October 12, 1936), consisted of work made under the WPA Arts Project and may have included artists of color; documentation does not include an artists list.

98. Barr's papers contain ephemera, correspondence, and writings on art of the 1960s, including a folder containing over fifteen items pertaining to the Art Workers' Coalition. Alfred H. Barr, Jr. Papers, 10.D.1 [AAA: 3266;163 and 3266;180–182], MoMA Archives, NY.

99. Warren M. Robbins, letter to Alfred Barr dated January 11, 1964, Alfred H. Barr, Jr. Papers [AAA: 2196;367], MoMA Archives, NY.

100. Ortiz told the author that his use of the axe in his *Piano Destruction* pieces was inspired, in part, by a violent scene in the Walt Disney movie version of Pinocchio when the evil Stromboli terrorizes Pinocchio by thrusting an axe at a wooden doll lying in wait to serve as firewood and cleaving his body in two. Like Barr, Ortiz drew on myriad sources, both popular and elite. Grace Glueck, "Barrio Museum: Hope Si, Home No," *New York Times*, July 30, 1970.

101. He was also exploring the idea of ritual sacrifice as a means of redemption, especially as it was expressed in the Old Testament in the book of Leviticus. At the time he encountered Ortiz's work Barr was also researching the relationship between art and religion, and was considering this as the theme for an exhibition. Barr had, on May 10, 1962, become the founding president of the Foundation for Arts, Religion, and Culture, a post he would hold until 1965. The purpose of the foundation was "to initiate and foster collaboration between religion and the arts in contemporary life." Foundation for Arts, Religion, and Culture, Certificate of Incorporation, Alfred H. Barr, Jr. Papers, 4.A.10. See also "Religion and Art" section of the Alfred H. Barr, Jr. Papers, 1.529 [AAA: 2197;119], MoMA Archives, NY.

102. For texts on Ortiz, see El Museo del Barrio, *Raphael Montañez Ortiz*, and Yasmín Ramírez, *Unmaking*.

103. Raphael Montañez Ortiz, interview by Yasmín Ramírez in *Unmaking*, 22.

104. These exhibitions were *Picasso: "Guernica" Studies and Postscripts,* Exh. #829, June 2, 1967–February 13, 1968; *The Sculpture of Picasso,* Exh. #841, October 11, 1967–January 1, 1968; and *Prints by Picasso: A Selection from 60 Years,* Exh. #842, October 11, 1967–January 1, 1968.

105. Beth Straus, 1970, quoted in Lynes, *Good Old Modern,* 409.

106. Lynes, *Good Old Modern,* 409.

107. Hans Haacke, statement delivered at "An Open Public Hearing on the Subject; What Should Be the Program of the Art Workers regarding Museum Reform and to Establish the Program of an Open Art Workers Coalition," New York City, April 19, 1969, published in Art Workers' Coalition, *Documents / Open Hearing,* n.p.

108. Alex Gross, "New Volcano Found under Modern Museum," *East Village Other,* March 14, 1969.

109. "Museum Demonstration Sunday," *East Village Other,* March 26, 1969, reprinted in Art Workers' Coalition, *Documents / Open Hearing,* n.p.

110. The Museum of Modern Art, press release for *The New City: Architecture and Urban Renewal,* January 24–March 13, 1967. The Harlem neighborhood was chosen as the area in which to explore these problems.

111. Rubin was an art historian who had done his graduate work at Columbia University with Mayer Shapiro and Millard Meiss. He taught full time at Sarah Lawrence College and had given a graduate seminar for the City University of New York. He was responsible for acquisitions, research, and writing on the collection. While working at the museum he taught a course at New York University's Institute of Fine Arts. He was a studious scholar but did not have the charisma, panache, or populist sensibility of Alfred Barr.

112. Rubin included some recent works with relationships to the historical works, but these relationships tended to be superficial, such as Konrad Klapheck's painting of a sewing machine entitled *Intriguing Women* (1964). The piece evokes Isidore-Lucien Ducasse's famous phrase "as beautiful as the chance encounter of a sewing machine and an umbrella on a dissecting table." Quoted in Rubin, *Dada, Surrealism, and Their Heritage,* 19.

113. See Rubin, *Dada, Surrealism, and Their Heritage.* The show contained forty-one works that, in Swenson's words, "direct questions, insults, and homages toward art," including Marcel Duchamp's *LHOOQ,* Robert Rauschenberg's *Erased de Kooning Drawing* (1953), and works by Juan Gris, Kurt Schwitters, Francis Picabia, Robert Indiana, Andy Warhol, and others. This show reiterated a theme that Swenson had addressed in a show he had organized at the Institute of Contemporary Art in Philadelphia entitled *The Other Tradition* at the ICA, Philadelphia, and held January 28–March 7, 1966.

114. See Rothkopf, "Banned and Determined," 142–45, 194. In February Swenson had begun a lone daily protest in front of the museum, walking back and forth carrying a sign in the shape of a question mark.

115. Rothkopf, "Banned and Determined."

116. Claes's brother, Richard, was the museum's director of publications. In November 1972 Richard was appointed director of the museum.

117. Jon Hendricks, interview by author, New York, NY, June 20, 2011.

118. Grace Glueck, "Hippies Protest at Dada Preview; 300 in Gentle Demonstration at Museum of Modern Art," *New York Times*, March 26, 1968.

119. When d'Harnoncourt left, so did board president Eliza Parkinson, who had served as a trustee since 1939. She was succeeded by William S. Paley, the chairman of CBS. Dorothy Miller, who had worked with Barr since 1934, left in 1969. Monroe Wheeler, who had first become involved with the museum as a guest curator in 1936 and was at various times a staff member and trustee, also stepped down.

120. Upon arrival, Lowry quickly announced three curatorial appointments: Kynaston McShine, Margaret Potter, and William Agee. The Museum of Modern Art, press release, July 3, 1968.

121. *In Honor of Dr. Martin Luther King, Jr.*, Exh. #873a, October 31–November 3, 1968.

122. A pamphlet distributed at the museum on April 4, 1969, by the Black and Puerto Rican Students and Artists for a Black Wing in Memory of Dr. Martin Luther King, Jr., an ad hoc group led by Faith Ringgold and Tom Lloyd, read: "On October 20th, 1968 at the Museum of Modern Art, prominent black artists were segregated in a back room at a memorial show in honor of Dr. Martin Luther King, Jr.—or rather, in contempt of Dr. Martin Luther King, Jr. Among those black artists subjected to this humiliating, racist cultural segregation were Jacob Lawrence, Charles White, Romare Bearden, and the late Bob Thompson." See "An Open Letter to Today's Visitors to the Museum of Modern Art," in Art Workers' Coalition, *Documents/Open Hearing*, 1969, n.p.

123. Bates Lowry, memo to the Staff of the Museum of Modern Art, in Art Workers' Coalition, *Documents/Open Hearing*, 1969, n.p.

124. "13 Demands," in Art Workers' Coalition, *Documents/Open Hearing, 1969*.

125. "13 Demands."

126. Bates Lowry, letter to the Gregory Battcock, Hans Haacke, Tom Lloyd, Willoughby Sharp, Takis Vassilakis, Wen-Ying Tsai, and John Perrault dated February 14, 1969, Alfred H. Barr, Jr. Papers [AAA: 2196;310], MoMA Archives, NY.

127. Bates Lowry, The Museum of Modern Art visitor handout, March 30, 1969, Alfred H. Barr, Jr. Papers [AAA: 2196;299–302], MoMA Archives, NY.

128. Bill Gordy quoted in Grace Glueck, "Dissidents Stir Art World," *New York Times*, April 12, 1969.

129. Alex Gross reported that none of the AWC's thirteen demands appeared to be controversial, "with the exception of the demand for a black artists' wing." See Alex Gross, "Black Art—Tech Art—Prick Art," *East Village Other*, April 2, 1969.

130. "Students and Artists United for a Martin Luther King, Jr. Wing for Black and Puerto Rican Art at the Museum of Modern Art in New York City," flyer in Art Workers' Coalition, *Documents/Open Hearing*, n.p.

131. "Students and Artists United for a Martin Luther King, Jr. Wing for Black and Puerto Rican Art at the Museum of Modern Art in New York City."

132. Bates Lowry, letter to Faith Ringgold and Tom Lloyd dated April 10, 1969, in Art Workers' Coalition, *Documents/Opening Hearing*, n.p.

133. Faith Ringgold, interview by author, Englewood, NJ, January 27, 2011.

134. For a discussion of the politics of placement, particularly this work, see Yau, "Please Wait by the Coatroom," 133–39.

135. John B. Hightower Papers, I.7.49, MoMA Archives, NY.

136. Fearless then, and since then, Wallace would publish her first smash success book, *Black Macho and the Myth of the Superwoman* (1978, reprinted by Verso in 1990). Her other essential volumes are *Invisibility Blues: From Pop to Theory* and *Dark Designs and Visual Culture*.

137. Sound Recordings of Museum-Related Events, 69.54, MoMA Archives, NY. The entire exchange, which took place at the September 30, 1969, meeting of the AWC and the museum staff, proceeded like this:

> MICHELE WALLACE: Excuse me, just one thing please. In October was it, last year? You had a Memorial exhibition here in this museum for Martin Luther King.
>
> ARTHUR DREXLER: That's right, a benefit.
>
> WALLACE: And a large group of us black artists, about twelve, fifteen of us were assembled in a back room together. Segregated in a back room.
>
> DREXLER: I think there's one thing that you don't understand. And that is what the basis of that particular exhibition was. Could somebody please clarify that? How the pictures were hanging for that exhibition?
>
> UNKNOWN SPEAKER: I'm sorry I was not here at the time.
>
> BILL RUBIN: Yes, they were selected by a group of various curators. Works of art donated by various artists to be sold for the benefit of the Southern Christian Leadership Conference.
>
> WALLACE: I know about that. I know.
>
> DREXLER: But the point I'm trying to make is that that exhibition did not—
>
> WALLACE: I'm aware of that.
>
> DREXLER: Maybe you are but I'd like to make sure everybody else is.
>
> WALLACE: Yes, we weren't told that we were going to be in one little room.
>
> RUBIN: It really was not the case.
>
> WALLACE: Excuse me, it wasn't?
>
> RUBIN: It was not the case.
>
> WALLACE: What was not the case?
>
> RUBIN: That all the black artists were segregated in one room.
>
> WALLACE: Oh my dear, it certainly was the case.
>
> RUBIN: No it wasn't.
>
> UNKNOWN SPEAKER: It really was not the case.
>
> UNKNOWN SPEAKER: This can be very easily resolved by showing the installation record.

DREXLER: We have a record of the exhibition and we will be glad to show it to anyone who wants to look at it.

WALLACE: I was there. I saw it. I was right there in the middle.

DREXLER: *He* installed it!

RUBIN: I installed it and I can show you my photographs.

WALLACE: My dear, you installed a segregated show. That's what you did.

138. Cintra Lofting, memo to Carroll Greene, October 23, 1968, in Curatorial Exhibition Files, Exh. #873a, MoMA Archives, NY.

139. A handful of white artists were also marked as "unknown."

140. Sound Recordings of Museum-Related Events, 69.54, MoMA Archives, NY.

141. Following Lowry's departure the museum was run by a committee composed of trustee Walter Bareiss, director of the Exhibition Program Wilder Green, and director of administration Richard Koch. See Lynes, *Good Old Modern*, 417.

142. Elizabeth Shaw, memo to Staff Executive Committee, November 3, 1969, John B. Hightower Papers, III.1.11.b, MoMA Archives, NY.

143. Included were Jo Baer, Betty Blayton, Mel Bochner, Jason Crum, Walter de Maria, Mark di Suvero, Melvin Edwards, Herbert Ferber, Dan Flavin, Adolph Gottlieb, Hans Haacke, Al Held, Peter Hutchinson, Jasper Johns, Don Judd, Alex Katz, Joseph Kosuth, Sol Lewitt, Roy Lichtenstein, William Majors, Robert Morris, Robert Motherwell, Kenneth Noland, Jules Olitski, Dennis Oppenheim, Ray Parker, Robert Rauschenberg, Richard Serra, Robert Whitman, and William T. Williams. Sound Recordings of Museum-Related Events, 69.66, MoMA Archives, NY.

144. Sgt. Ron Haeberle, having returned to his hometown of Cleveland, Ohio, after an honorable discharge, offered photographs of dead villagers killed at My Lai to the *Plain Dealer*. The newspaper published some of them on November 20, 1969. Haeberle soon after sold the photos to *Life* magazine, which published them in the December 1, 1969, issue. One of the photos of the massacre was used in the *And Babies?* poster.

145. For a description of this action, see *GAAG: The Guerrilla Art Action Group*, n.p.

146. The original goal of the AWC was to have the photo in front of *Guernica* published on as many magazine covers as possible, but only *Studio International* did so, with what has become an iconic image. See *Studio International* 180, no. 927 (November 1970).

147. At the meeting Tom Lloyd provoked an ugly confrontation with Betty Blayton, who had publicly praised the museum for the outreach program it had started in Harlem that she ran, the Children's Art Carnival. Sound Recordings of Museum-Related Events, 69.66, MoMA Archives, NY. Lloyd opposed this program. In a letter written to Bates Lowry on April 3, 1969, Lloyd had claimed that the Children's Art Carnival introduced irrelevant art that didn't satisfy children's need for "cultural identification." In Art Workers' Coalition, *Documents/Open Hearing*, n.p.

148. Benny Andrews, journal, p. 109, entry 733, December 10, 1969, EBA.

149. Lloyd organized nineteen artists to research eight communities and "investigate their needs, desires, and physical resources for a community cultural center." Tom Lloyd,

letter to Doris Freedman, n.d., John B. Hightower Papers, III.1.3, MoMA Archives, NY. The money granted by NYSCA passed through the Metropolitan Museum as the project's not-for-profit fiscal agent. This partnership would lead to the establishment of the Store-Front Museum in Jamaica, Queens, which Lloyd founded in 1971 and directed for sixteen years.

150. John Hightower, interview by author, Newport News, VA, August 2, 2004.

151. Sherman Lee quoted in " 'Today' Not for Museum, Lee Says," *Cleveland Plain Dealer*, March 1, 1969.

152. Sherman Lee quoted in John Canaday, "Definition of an Art Museum," *Cedar Rapids Gazette*, March 9, 1969.

153. Ringgold, interview.

154. By contrast, Alfred Barr, MoMA's founding director and artistic leader, had always been politically engaged. For example, he had helped artists escape from Nazi persecution in Europe and immigrate to the United States. Likewise, the museum in general had been a political player, mounting prowar propaganda exhibitions throughout the early 1940s to build support for U.S. participation in World War II and organizing cultural exchanges with Latin American governments as a form of cultural diplomacy on behalf of the U.S. government.

155. John Hightower, "The Museum of Modern Art Members Newsletter," November 1970 (New York: Museum of Modern Art), n.p., John B. Hightower Papers, I.8.64, MoMA Archives, NY.

156. See Grace Glueck, "Hightower Meets Museum's Critics," *New York Times*, March 4, 1970.

157. Oral History Program, Grace Glueck, 1997, p. 63, MoMA Archives, NY.

158. Hightower, interview.

159. Ortiz has told the author that although he was friends with Jon Hendricks and Jean Toche, their GAAG actions were too invasive for him.

160. For a description of this action, see *GAAG: The Guerrilla Art Action Group*, n.p.

161. The document was signed by Tom Lloyd, Faith Ringgold, Bob Carter, Todd Williams, Jack Hunte, Adrian Garcia, Ralph Ortiz, James Sepyo, Martin Rubio, Armando Soto, and Joan Barnes.

162. John B. Hightower Papers, III.1.9, MoMA Archives, NY. See also Ringgold, *We Flew over the Bridge*.

163. Benny Andrews, interview by author, Litchfield, CT, July 14, 1999.

164. Grace Glueck, "Modern Museum Adds 10 Trustees," *New York Times*, September 17, 1970.

165. James Thrall Soby, letter to David Rockefeller and William S. Paley, June 19, 1970, Alfred H. Barr, Jr. Papers [AAA: 2196;326], MoMA Archives, NY.

166. Minutes of the Trustee Executive Committee Meeting, June 25, 1970, Alfred H. Barr, Jr. Papers [AAA: 2196;329], MoMA Archives, NY.

167. Minutes of the Trustee Executive Committee Meeting, June 25, 1970, Alfred H. Barr, Jr. Papers [AAA: 2196;329], MoMA Archives, NY.

168. Minutes of the Trustee Executive Committee Meeting, June 25, 1970, Alfred H. Barr, Jr. Papers [AAA: 2196;329], MoMA Archives, NY.

169. John Hightower, Memo to the Trustees, June 29, 1970, Alfred H. Barr, Jr. Papers [AAA: 2196;327], MoMA Archives, NY.

170. James Thrall Soby, letter to Alfred H. Barr Jr., June 27, 1970, Alfred H. Barr, Jr. Papers [AAA: 2196;1009], MoMA Archives, NY.

171. Pindell had received her MFA at Yale University in 1967 and began working at MoMA shortly thereafter.

172. Howardena Pindell, interview by author, New York, NY, January 7, 2011.

173. Howardena Pindell, memo to Dr. Mamie Phipps Clark, October 23, 1970, John B. Hightower Papers, I.9.69, MoMA Archives, NY.

174. Report to the Byers Committee from Howardena Pindell, n.d., p. 2, John B. Hightower Papers, I.9.69, MoMA Archives, NY.

175. See Pindell, *The Heart of the Question*.

176. Hightower, interview.

177. Art Strike flyer, John B. Hightower Papers, III.1.13, MoMA Archives, NY.

178. *May 2–May 9*, Exh. #929, May 23–June 2, 1970, Museum of Modern Art, New York.

179. Hightower, interview.

180. Bill Lieberman, memo to Betsy Jones, July 21, 1970, Curatorial Exhibition Files, Exh. #968a, MoMA Archives, NY.

181. Exhibition proposal, John B. Hightower Papers, I.5.37, MoMA Archives, NY.

182. Lieberman, memo to Betsy Jones, July 21, 1970, Curatorial Exhibition Files, Exh. #968a, MoMA Archives, NY.

183. Doloris Holmes, Corinne Robins, Sara Saporta, Nancy Spero, letter to John Hightower, June 1, 1970, John B. Hightower Papers, I.6.38, MoMA Archives, NY.

184. John Hightower, Opening Remarks, Discussion–American Association of Museums Meeting held on June 1, 1970, at the Brooklyn Museum, John B. Hightower Papers, I.6.38, MoMA Archives, NY.

185. Oral History Program, interview with Walter Bareiss, 1991, p. 61, MoMA Archives, NY.

186. John B. Hightower Papers, III.1.6, MoMA Archives, NY.

187. Ringgold, interview.

188. Ringgold, *We Flew over the Bridge*, 171.

189. Ringgold, *We Flew over the Bridge*, 171.

190. Ringgold, *We Flew over the Bridge*, 172.

191. John Hightower, e-mail to author, April 8, 2008.

192. "Black American Artists for Whom Exhibitions Might Be Considered," Curatorial Exhibition Files, Exh. #959, MoMA Archives, NY.

193. *Romare Bearden: The Prevalence of Ritual*, Exh. #958, and *The Sculpture of Richard Hunt*, Exh. #959, were held at the Museum of Modern Art, March 25–June 9, 1971.

194. Hightower, e-mail to author.

195. From 1945 to 1948 he had shown at the Kootz Gallery and since 1960 with Michel Warren Gallery (later renamed Daniel Cordier & Michel Warren, and again renamed Cordier & Ekstrom Inc.). Bearden had had many museum and gallery exhibitions, including a show titled *Projections* at the Corcoran Art Gallery in 1965.

196. Faith Ringgold, interview by Cynthia Nadelman, September 6–October 18, 1989, AAA.

197. Greene, introductory essay in *Romare Bearden*, 3.

198. For a discussion of how Bearden "translates back and forth" between European modernism and African American traditions, see pages 148–49 of Mercer's "Diaspora Aesthetics and Visual Culture."

199. Museum of Modern Art, Advance Fact Sheet for *The Sculpture of Richard Hunt*, February 18, 1971, MoMA Archives, NY.

200. Museum of Modern Art, *The Sculpture of Richard Hunt*, press release, March 25, 1971.

201. Museum of Modern Art, *The Sculpture of Richard Hunt*, press release, March 25, 1971.

202. The museum purchased the piece right after it was made, in 1957.

203. Exhibition review, *Art in America* 59 (May–June 1971): 130–31.

204. Hilton Kramer, " 'Black Art' and Expedient Politics," *New York Times*, June 7, 1970.

205. Hilton Kramer quoted in Lieberman, essay in *The Sculpture of Richard Hunt*, 5.

206. Hilton Kramer, "Hunt Show Has 50 Sculptures, Drawing, and Prints," *New York Times*, March 24, 1971.

207. Hilton Kramer, "From Open-Form to the Monolithic Cube," *New York Times*, April 4, 1971.

208. Venues included the National Collection of Fine Arts, Washington, DC, July 16–September 12, 1971; the University Art Museum, Berkeley, October 25–December 5, 1971; the Pasadena Art Museum, December 20, 1971–January 30, 1972; the High Museum of Art, Atlanta, February 27–April 9, 1972; the North Carolina Museum of Art, Raleigh, May 1–June 11, 1972; and the Studio Museum in Harlem, July 16–September 30, 1972.

209. On June 15, 1971, Carolyn Lanchner spoke with Richard Hunt and expressed the museum's interest in buying one of the works in the show, *Wall Piece with Extending Form* (1960). Hunt agreed to a sale price of $2,500. Several months passed, but the museum neglected to follow up. No one made arrangements to transfer ownership of the work or to pay Hunt. The show toured to a second venue, the Art Institute of Chicago, and only when this show ended and arrangements were being made for return of the work did MoMA realize the oversights. On October 5, 1971, curator Betsy Jones had the unenviable job of writing to Hunt to explain the museum's mistakes. He declined to sell the work. Curatorial Exhibition Files, Exh. #959, MoMA Archives, NY.

210. Faith Ringgold, letter to John Hightower, October 14, 1970, Curatorial Exhibition Files, Exh. #959, MoMA Archives, NY. Incorrect punctuation in the original text has been corrected.

211. Tom Lloyd, statement during panel discussion, "The Black Artist in America," *Metropolitan Museum of Art Bulletin* 27, no. 5 (January 1969): 258. Two weeks later Ringgold, along with Iris Crump, Camille Billops, and Theresa Schwartz, sent David Rockefeller a letter containing a proposal for a conference on the role of women in art and an exhibition of work by women to be held concurrently with the Bearden and Hunt shows in spring 1971. Ringgold sent Hightower pages of data documenting the exclusion of women and African Americans in New York City's museums. The data pointed out that in the previous five years, MoMA had had seventy-

two solo shows: seventy-one men and one woman (no African Americans). The statistic went on to chronicle the records at the Met, the Whitney, and other museums; they looked at the records of African American group shows and noted the paucity of women. In books, magazines, conferences, and seminars, inclusion of African Americans was slight, and of women, particularly African American women, almost nonexistent. John B. Hightower Papers, III.1.7, MoMA Archives, NY.

212. Charles Allen, "Have the Walls Come Tumbling Down?," *New York Times*, April 11, 1971.

213. John Hightower, letter to Faith Ringgold, November 4, 1970, John B. Hightower Papers, III.1.7, MoMA Archives, NY. During this period of exchange between Hightower and Ringgold, the artist was also involved in organizing the *People's Flag Show* with Jon Hendricks and Jean Toche at the Judson Memorial Church. The show opened on November 9, 1970, and the three artists were arrested for desecration of the American flag on the show's closing day. They were convicted on May 14, 1971, and each was sentenced to a fine or one month in prison. Ringgold paid the fine. See Farrington, *Creating in Their Own Image*, 141; and Ringgold, *We Flew over the Bridge*, 181–86.

214. The museum's Projects series of small shows would feature a range of artists, including Sam Gilliam (1971), Raphael Ferrer (1974), Nam June Paik (1977), Shigeko Kubota (1978), Catalina Parra (1981), Houston Conwill (1990), Lorna Simpson (1990), Felix Gonzalez-Torres (1992), Gabriel Orozco (1993), and Carrie Mae Weems (1996). The group show *Dislocations*, organized by Robert Storr, included David Hammons and Adrian Piper, Exh. #1598 (October 19, 1991–January 7, 1992); and in 1995 the museum exhibited Jacob Lawrence's *Migration Series*.

215. *Projects 23: Lorna Simpson*, Exh. #1554, July 6–August 26, 1990, organized by curatorial assistant Jennifer Wells.

216. "The Report to the Trustees of the Museum of Modern Art from the Committee to Study Afro-American, Hispanic and Other Ethnic Art" (hereafter Byers Report), June 1971, pp. 6–8, Reports and Pamphlets: 1970's, MoMA Archives, NY.

217. Byers Report, 9.

218. Byers Report, 1.

219. Byers Report, 5–6.

220. Art historian and curator Mari Carmen Ramírez discussed this aspect of the Museum of Modern Art's history in a paper delivered at the Working Seminar "Contemporary Visual Art/Critical and Historical Interpretations," held at the Center for Curatorial Studies at Bard College, Annandale-on-Hudson, NY, February 1993.

221. This show's actual title was *African Textiles and Decorative Arts* (Museum of Modern Art, Exh. #1012c, October 11, 1972–January 31, 1973). *Twenty-Five Contemporary American Painters and Sculptors as Printmakers*, containing works selected by William S. Lieberman, circulated under the auspices of Mrs. George A. Morgan, wife of the U.S. ambassador to Ivory Coast, with cooperation of American Embassies in Africa. From 1966 through 1970 the exhibition was shown in Abidjan and Bouaké in Ivory Coast (Republic of Côte d'Ivoire); Contono, Dahomey (now Benin); Lomé, Togo; Accra, Ghana; Cairo, United Arab Republic (now Egypt); Monrovia, Liberia; Ouagadougou, Upper Volta (now Burkina Faso); Kampala, Uganda; Nairobi, Kenya; Dar es Salaam, Tanzania; and Mogadishu, Somalia. John B. Hightower Papers, I.9.69, MoMA Archives, NY.

222. Chon Noriega, letter to Elizabeth Sussman, February 5, 1993, International Center of the Arts of the Americas at the Museum of Fine Arts, Houston, doi: icaadocs.mfah.org /icaadocs/.

223. Byers Report, 8, Reports and Pamphlets: 1970's, MoMA Archives, NY.

224. Byers Report, 14.

225. Byers Report, 27.

226. Byers Report, 10.

227. Mildred Constantine, memo to the Byers Committee, October 29, 1970. Attachment to Byers Report, n.p., Reports and Pamphlets: 1970's, MoMA Archives, NY.

228. Byers Report, 30, Reports and Pamphlets: 1970's, MoMA Archives, NY.

229. Byers Report, 16.

230. Hightower, interview.

231. Rockefeller, *Memoirs*, 452. In a letter to the author dated December 21, 2004, Hightower noted that he found David Rockefeller's memoir "fascinating and troubling. From his perspective to find me 'courting' anti-Vietnam dissent is curious and distant. It does not help that he confuses me with Arthur Drexler who authorized copies of the My Lai poster sold in the shop."

232. Ortiz, interview.

233. Robert Malone, interview by author, New York, NY, August 25, 2013.

234. Miriam G. Cedarbaum, Minutes of the Annual Meeting of the Corporation of the Museum of Modern Art, November 8, 1972, p. 13, Alfred Barr, Jr. Papers [AAA: 2196;211], MoMA Archives, NY.

235. Flam, "Matisse and the Fauves," in *"Primitivism" in 20th Century Art*, 239n111.

236. Rubin, "Picasso," in *"Primitivism" in 20th Century Art*, 252–53.

237. The museum's scope would widen after Rubin's transition into the role of Director Emeritus of Painting and Sculpture in 1988, especially between 1989 and 1993. The first exhibition to be organized by curator Robert Storr, *Dislocations* (Exh. #1589, October 21–January 7, 1992), included artists Chris Burden, Sophia Calle, David Hammons, Ilya Kabakov, and Adrian Piper. In 1990 Kynaston McShine was responsible for acquiring two works by Melvin Edwards, both from the *Lynch Fragment Series*, *Katutura* (1986) and *Cup of?* (1988). In 1991 curator Carolyn Lanchner spearheaded the acquisition of *Emergency Room* (1989) by Robert Colescott. Though MoMA continues to collect works by artists of color, the holdings are thin and omissions are evident. A small sampling reveals that the museum owns only the single work by Robert Colescott mentioned above; one work by Sam Gilliam; one major work by Glenn Ligon; two sculptures by Martin Puryear despite the artist's having a retrospective there in 2007; one major work by Kara Walker; one major work by Carrie Mae Weems; two paintings by Jack Whitten; and one painting by Hale Woodruff acquired in 2015. Artists represented in somewhat greater depth include David Hammons, Alison Saar, and Charles White. MoMA owns no work by Charles Alston, Barbara Chase-Riboud, Aaron Douglas, Lois Mailou Jones, Archibald J. Motley Jr., Augusta Savage, Henry Ossawa Tanner, Alma Thomas, or Robert Thompson, and no major works by Emma Amos, Houston Conwill, Faith Ringgold, or Fred Wilson, among others.

238. Museum of Modern Art, *The Museum of Modern Art, New York*.

239. Barbara Rose, "People Are Talking About: The Man from MoMA," *Vogue*, August 1, 1984, 358. In a 1993 interview with Sharon Zane, Rubin reasserted his claim: "I was not to be Alfred's No. 2 man, I was to be his successor." Oral History Program, Williams S. Rubin, 1993, p. 25, MoMA Archives, NY.

240. Oral History Program, Walter Bareiss, pp. 58–59, MoMA Archives, NY.

241. The art critic Roberta Smith wrote in Rubin's obituary:

Some critics faulted Mr. Rubin's exhibitions and research for only rarely venturing beyond the parameters established by Barr, suggesting that this had a chilling effect on his department's involvement with new art and often made the museum seem obsessed with its own history. His painting and sculpture installations were generally formalist and chronological, with an emphasis on masterpieces, great artists and the French.

Yet Mr. Rubin's painstakingly worked-out presentations, especially those prepared after the Modern's 1984 expansion, told its version of modernism with a clarity and level of detail that many curators still consider unmatched.

Roberta Smith, "William Rubin, 78, Curator Who Transformed MoMA, Dies," *New York Times*, January 24, 2006.

242. Alfred Barr, letter to the editor, *New York Times*, September 25, 1960.

243. John Elderfield quoted in Roberta Smith, "William Rubin, 78, Curator Who Transformed MoMA, Dies."

244. Oral History Program, Betsy Jones, 1994, p. 19, MoMA Archives, NY.

245. Oral History Program, Walter Bareiss, 1991, p. 44, MoMA Archives, NY.

246. Robert Storr, interview by author, New Haven, CT, January 10, 2011.

247. Storr, interview.

248. Rubin quoted in Rose, "The Politics of Art," 361.

249. Oral History Program, Walter Bareiss, 1991, p. 65, MoMA Archives, NY.

250. See Gayle, *The Black Aesthetic*.

251. The Museum of Primitive Art had lent twenty-three works for exhibition at the Premiere Festival Mondial des Arts Nègres held in Dakar, Senegal, in 1966; see http://www .metmuseum.org/exhibitions/listings/2013/nelson-rockefeller/chronology. The Second World African Festival of Arts and Culture (FESTAC '77), in Lagos, Nigeria, was attended by thousands of artists of African descent, as well as by Africans. Curator Lowery Stokes Sims and artist/curator Howardena Pindell traveled to Egypt, Nigeria, Ghana, the Ivory Coast, and Senegal in 1973. Mel Edwards first traveled to Africa, to Nigeria and Ghana, in 1973; he went to Senegal and Ghana for the Conference on Philosophy and African Culture in 1982. He subsequently established a home in Senegal and now divides his time between there and New York City. In the United States, a new Pan-Africanism was evidenced by the 1976 African Diaspora Festival produced by the Smithsonian Institution. See Ruffins, "Mythos, Memory, and History," 575–80.

252. Varnedoe, "Issues and Commentary."

253. The Museum of Modern Art, press release for *Sculpture of William Edmondson*.

254. By contrast, the exhibition *African Art, New York, and the Avant-Garde* held at the Metropolitan Museum of Art, November 27, 2012–April 14, 2013, included Malvin Gray Johnson and mentioned Alain Locke. See "African Art, New York and the Avant-Garde," special issue, *Tribal Art*, no. 3 (2012).

255. Levin, " 'Primitivism' in American Art."

256. Gail Levin, interview by author, New York, NY, January 14, 2014.

257. Levin, interview.

258. Ringgold, interview with Moira Roth, 235.

259. Mercer, *Cosmopolitan Modernisms*, 7.

260. Flam, *Primitivism and Twentieth-Century Art*, 17.

261. See Mosquera, *Beyond the Fantastic*; the series of books in the Annotating Art's Histories series published by InIVA and edited by Kobena Mercer: *Cosmopolitan Modernisms* (2005), *Discrepant Abstraction* (2006), *Pop Art and Vernacular Culture* (2007), and *Exiles, Diasporas, and Strangers*, all copublished with MIT Press; Sims, *Wifredo Lam and the International Avant-Garde, 1923–1982*; Sims, *Challenge of the Modern*; and Nka: *The Journal of Contemporary African Art*.

262. These exhibitions and their accompanying publications include Powell and Bailey, *Rhapsodies in Black*; Sims, *Challenge of the Modern*; Mosaka et al., *Infinite Island*; Barson and Gorschülter, *Afro Modern*; and Sims and King-Hammond, *The Global Africa Project*. Noteworthy, though not hosted at any of the major museums, is *Caribbean*, a collaborative research and exhibition project organized by El Museo del Barrio in conjunction with the Queens Museum of Art and the Studio Museum in Harlem. See Cullen and Fuentes, *Caribbean*.

263. Perry, *More Beautiful and More Terrible*, 37.

EPILOGUE

1. *Alvin Loving: Paintings* (December 19, 1969–January 25, 1970); *Melvin Edwards: Works* (March 3–29, 1970); *Fred Eversley: Recent Sculpture* (May 18–June 7, 1970); *Marvin Harden* (January 5–February 4, 1971); *Malcolm Bailey* (March 16–April 15, 1971); *Frank Bowling* (November 4–December 6, 1971); *Rafael Ferrer* (December 9, 1971–January 1972); *Alma W. Thomas* (April 25–May 28, 1972); *Mahler Ryder* (November 8–December 9, 1973); *Jack Whitten* (August 20–September 22, 1974); *Betye Saar* (March 20–April 20, 1975); and *Minnie Evans* (July 3–August 3, 1975). In the main galleries, Jacob Lawrence was the subject of a survey exhibition (May 16–July 7, 1974). In addition, the museum's film and video program began in 1971, and curator John Hanhardt consistently showed media-based work by artists of color.

2. The artists were shown in 1973, 1974, 1977, and 1978, respectively.

3. During the 1990s, after the appointment of Robert Storr as curator in 1990, U.S.-based artists were shown more frequently, and recently the series has become more international.

4. The Metropolitan Museum of Art presented its first major exhibition of an African American artist in 1995 when it served as a venue for the traveling exhibition *I Tell My Heart: The Art of Horace Pippin*, organized by the Museum of American Art at the Pennsylvania Academy of the Fine Arts.

5. Benny Andrews, "Art in the Eateries: New York City's Kitchen Galleries," *New York Age*, June 22, 1974.

6. John Yau, "Please Wait by the Coatroom," in *Out There*, 133–39.

7. Newsome and Silver, *The Art Museum as Educator*.

8. See Wolcott, *Race, Riots, and Roller Coasters*.

9. Lowery Stokes Sims, interview by author, New York, NY, February 27, 2001.

10. These shows were held in May 1971, July 1971, and November–December 1971, respectively.

11. Quoted in Judith Mara Gutman, "Uncovering a Long-Lost Village," *New York Times*, February 22, 1976. The Community Programs Department was disbanded in 1978.

12. Though these terms are insufficient because they distort the fact that all museums are "culturally grounded," I use them to denote institutions that overtly declare the lenses through which they view art and history.

13. Michele Wallace and Faith Ringgold, interview by author, Englewood, NJ, January 27, 2011.

14. Some of the major institutions in New York City include the American Indian Community House (1969); Cinque Gallery (1969); El Museo del Barrio (1969); Taller Boricua (1970); AIR Gallery (1972); Jamaica Arts Center (1972); Institute of Contemporary Hispanic Arts (1973); the Nuyorican Poets Café (1973); Asian American Arts Centre (1974); En Foco (1974); Kenkeleba House (1974); the Association of Hispanic Arts (1975); the Caribbean Cultural Center (1975); the Alternative Museum (1975); Cayman Gallery (1976); Charas/El Bohio (1979); the New York Chinatown History Project (1980); and the Museum of Contemporary Hispanic Art (1985). See Rosati and Staniszewski, *Alternative Histories*; and Yasmín Ramírez, "The Activist Legacy of Puerto Rican Artists in New York," 46.

15. Araeen, "From Primitivism to Ethnic Arts," 23–24.

16. Until 1967 all of New York City's museums, with a few exceptions, such as the Brooklyn Museum and the Brooklyn Children's Museum, were located in Manhattan within a mile of each other: on the Upper East Side, the Metropolitan Museum of Art, the Frick Collection, the Museum of the City of New York, the Museum of Modern Art, and the Whitney Museum of American Art; on the Upper West Side, the New-York Historical Society and the Museum of Natural History. The Hispanic Society of America, founded in 1904, is located on Audubon Terrace between 155th and 156th Streets; the Asia Society on Park Avenue was founded in 1959.

17. The first exhibition organized by Irvine R. MacManus Jr. in collaboration with the Bronx Council on the Arts featured twenty-eight popular paintings from the American and European collections, including Vincent van Gogh's *Cypresses* (1889) and Edward Hicks's *Peaceable Kingdom* (ca. 1830–32). This was followed by *Games!!! ¡Juegos!*, a selection of works from a dozen curatorial departments that depicted games.

18. Later renamed the Queens Museum of Art.

19. In February 1971 Lloyd received permission from the City of New York to set up a storefront museum in a York College Renewal Site designated for development by City of New York in conjunction with the establishment in 1966 of York College, part of the City University

of New York system. Lloyd paid five dollars per month for the 12,000-square-foot building at 162-02/06 Liberty Avenue.

20. Even after achieving 501(c)3 status, the Store-Front Museum continued to turn to the Met for funds. On July 12, 1971, after the inaugural show closed, Lloyd wrote to Hoving: "I am appealing to you again in another emergency situation for support." In an astonishing show of stamina, Hoving noted to his staff on the bottom of the letter: "Let's go out and see it. And then hit the Foundation trail again." Office of the Secretary Records, MMAA.

21. El Museo had been founded in 1969 by Raphael Montañez Ortiz when parents in Central and East Harlem were pressuring the school district to incorporate Puerto Rican history and culture into the curriculum. With funds from the Community Education Center, a state agency set up to support educational enrichment programs in poor neighborhoods, the district superintendent had approached Ortiz, who was then teaching at the High School of Music and Art. Ortiz worked out of PS 125 at 425 West 123rd Street, which also housed the office of District 4 until the school district was split during a reorganization, and in fall 1970 the museum moved to PS 206, located at 508 East 120th Street and Pleasant Avenue. Tom Hoving learned of Ortiz's work and suggested to Community Programs staff member Irvine R. MacManus Jr. that he familiarize himself with the project.

22. Marta Moreno Vega, interview by author, New Haven, CT, July 11, 2011.

23. Harry S. Parker III, "The Training of Museum Educators," Ninth General Conference, 1971, mimeographed transcript quoted in Newsome and Silver, *The Art Museum as Educator*.

24. Ada Ciniglio, "Training for Museum Professionals—a Brief History," report from the Rockefeller Foundation Training Fellows in Museum Education at the Metropolitan Museum of Art, 1974/75 (New York: Metropolitan Museum of Art, n.d.), n.p., cited in Newsome and Silver, *The Art Museum as Educator*, 634.

25. Ciniglio, "Training for Museum Professionals—a Brief History," cited in Newsome and Silver, *The Art Museum as Educator*, 634.

26. Foucault, *The Order of Things*.

27. My own experience as an educator at the Museum of Modern Art working with New York City public high school students in the 1980s attests to this aspect of museum education programs: all groups were accompanied by security guards; no student was allowed to stray.

28. Marta Moreno Vega, who headed El Museo del Barrio from 1969 to 1974 and then founded the Caribbean Cultural Center, was also a participant in the program.

29. Linda Goode Bryant, interview by author, New York, NY, February 7, 2003.

30. Goode Bryant, interview.

31. Goode Bryant, interview. The name of the gallery was devised when Goode Bryant had intended to open it on Eighty-Sixth Street and Broadway. She liked the acronym JAM so much that she kept the name even though the gallery was initially located on Fifty-Seventh Street. After the gallery moved to Tribeca in 1980, Goode Bryant renamed the space Just Above Midtown/Downtown.

32. Sims, interview.

33. Sims, interview.

34. Sims, interview.

35. Sims, interview.

36. Sims would organize a traveling show of work by Chase-Riboud for the St. John's Museum of Art in Wilmington, North Carolina, that showed at the Met in 1999.

37. Lowery Stokes Sims, *Joaquín Torres-Garcia (1874–1949): Paintings Constructions and Drawings* (New York: Salander O'Reilly Galleries, 1981).

38. Her important exhibitions include *Challenge of the Modern: African American Artists, 1925–1945*, mounted at the Studio Museum in Harlem. Sims later served as a curator at the Museum of Art and Design in New York City.

39. Quoted in Charlayne Hunter-Gault, "Planned Move of Museum of Black Art from Harlem Stirs Dissension among Institution's Staff Members," *New York Times*, June 21, 1977, 37.

40. Quoted in Michael Goodwin, "Census Finds Fewer Blacks in Harlem," *New York Times*, May 30, 1981.

41. Goodwin, "Census Finds Fewer Blacks in Harlem."

42. Goodwin, "Census Finds Fewer Blacks in Harlem."

43. Mary Schmidt Campbell, interview by author, New York, NY, February 26, 2000.

44. Campbell, interview.

45. Gerald Fraser, "Studio Museum Finds a Harlem Home," *New York Times*, November 10, 1979.

46. Campbell, interview. The relocation of the museum, and whether to stay in Harlem or move downtown, was a subject of great debate. See Hunter-Gault, "Planned Move of Museum of Black Art from Harlem Stirs Dissension." The Studio Museum's efforts were aided by a new funding initiative of the National Endowment for the Arts. In 1980 the NEA offered its first Advancement Grants, ranging from $20,000 to $150,000, to a select group of arts organizations that had previously received Expansion Arts grants and were producing excellent work but needed "help to develop as institutions."

47. Kinshasha Holman Conwill, interview by author, Washington, DC, November 17, 2014.

48. See Sussman, *1993 Biennial Exhibition*.

49. See Danto, "The 1993 Biennial"; Kimball, "Of Chocolate, Lard, and Politics"; and Heartney, "Identity Politics at the Whitney." Around this time, there was also a resurgence in "ethnically based" survey exhibitions that echoed the structure of the Black Art shows of the 1970s, including *Hispanic Art in the United States: Thirty Contemporary Painters and Sculptors*, a traveling exhibition that originated at the Museum of Fine Arts in Houston in 1989 and was organized by John Beardsley and Jane Livingston; *Latin American Spirit, Art and Artists in the United States 1920–1970*, organized by Luis Cancel at the Bronx Museum of Art in 1988; and *Asia/America: Identities in Contemporary Asian American Art*, organized by Margo Machida at the Asia Society in 1994.

50. *Excellence and Equity*. W. Bell, former president of the American Association of Museums (now the American Alliance of Museums), proudly stated in the 2008 preface that "equity is a two-way street: If we want our communities to support us, to keep coming through our doors, we must ensure that we reflect their varied interests, that we tap everyone's strengths. We at AAM hope that this third edition of *Excellence and Equity*, reissued *virtually unchanged*, will continue to lead the field in pursuing these critical goals" (3; emphasis added).

51. These institutions include the California African American Museum, chartered in 1977 and opened in 1981; the National Museum of Mexican Art, founded in 1982 and opened in 1987; and the Japanese American National Museum, incorporated in 1985 and opened in 1992.

52. Enabling legislation for the National Museum of the American Indian was passed in 1989; one branch opened in New York City in 1992 and another in Washington in 1994. The legislation establishing the National Museum of African American History and Culture in 2004 also created a funding program for museums of African American culture, with an initial allocation of $15 million for that fiscal year. For a detailed history of this museum, see Ruffins, "Culture Wars Won and Lost, Part II." In addition to the Smithsonian Museums, the Japanese American National Museum opened in Los Angeles in 1992.

"African Art, New York, and the Avant-Garde." Special issue, *Tribal Art*, no. 3 (2012).

Afro-American Artists New York and Boston. Introduction by Edmund Barry Gaither. Boston: Museum of the National Center of Afro-American Artists, Museum of Fine Arts, and School of the Museum of Fine Arts, 1970.

Agee, William C. *The 1930's: Painting and Sculpture in America.* New York: Whitney Museum of American Art, 1968.

Albrecht, Donald, ed. *The Work of Charles and Ray Eames: A Legacy of Invention.* New York: Harry N. Abrams in association with the Library of Congress and the Vitra Design Museum, 1997.

Alloway, Lawrence. "Art." *The Nation*, November 18, 1968, 540.

———. "Harlem on My Mind." *The Nation*, February 3, 1969, 156–57.

Als, Hilton, Charles Gaines, Thelma Golden, Lizzetta LeFalle-Collins, Catherine Lord, Ben Patterson, Sandra Rowe, Gary Simmons, and Pat Ward Williams. "Roundtable Discussion." In *The Theater of Refusal: Black Art and Mainstream Criticism*, edited by Charles Gaines and Catherine Lord, 55–82. Irvine: Regents of the University of California and Fine Arts Gallery of the University of California, Irvine, 1993.

Anderson, Gail. *Reinventing the Museum: Historical and Contemporary Perspectives on the Paradigm Shift.* Lanham, MD: Altamira, 2004.

Andrews, Benny. "The B.E.C.C.: Black Emergency Cultural Coalition." *Arts Magazine* 44 (Summer 1970): 18–20.

Andrews, Benny, and Rudolf Baranik, eds. *Attica Book by the Black Emergency Cultural Coalition and Artists and Writers Protest against the War in Vietnam*. South Hackensack, NJ: Custom Communications Systems, 1972.

Araeen, Rasheed. "From Primitivism to Ethnic Arts." *Third Text* 1, no. 1 (1987): 6–25.

Art Workers' Coalition. *Documents/Open Hearing, 1969* (Facsimile). Seville, Spain: Editorial Doble J, 2009.

Atkinson, Edward J., ed. *Black Dimensions in Contemporary American Art*. New York: Plume Books, 1971.

Ault, Julie, ed. *Alternative Art New York, 1965–1985*. Minneapolis: University of Minnesota Press, 2002.

Banks, James. "Approaches to Multicultural Curriculum Reform." *Multicultural Leader* 1, no. 2 (1988): 1–4.

Baraka, Imamu Amiri. "Counter Statement to Whitney Ritz Bros." In *Black Art Notes*, edited by Tom Lloyd. N.p., 1971.

Barr, Alfred H., Jr. *Cubism and Abstract Art*. New York: Museum of Modern Art, 1936. Reprinted in 1966.

————, ed. *Fantastic Art, Dada and Surrealism*. New York: Museum of Modern Art, 1936.

Barson, Tanya, and Peter Gorschülter. *Afro Modern: Journeys through the Black Atlantic*. Liverpool: Tate Liverpool, 2010.

Barthes, Roland. *Mythologies*. New York: Hill and Wang, 1987. First published 1957 by Editions du Seuil, Paris. Translation by Jonathan Cape, Ltd., 1972.

Baur, John I. H. *Revolution and Tradition in Modern American Art*. Cambridge, MA: Harvard University Press, 1951; New York: Frederick A. Praeger, 1967.

Bearden, Romare. "The Negro Artist and Modern Art." *Opportunity* 12 (December 1934): 371–72. Reprinted in Gary A. Reynolds and Beryl Wright, *Against the Odds: African American Artists and the Harmon Foundation*, 41. Newark: Newark Museum, 1989.

Bearden, Romare, and Harry Henderson. *A History of African-American Artists from 1792 to the Present*. New York: Pantheon, 1993.

————. *Six Black Masters of American Art*. Garden City, NJ: Doubleday and Co., 1972.

Bee, Harriet S., and Michelle Elligott. *Art in Our Time: A Chronicle of the Museum of Modern Art*. New York: Museum of Modern Art, 2004.

Bell, Gregory. *In the Black: A History of African Americans on Wall Street*. New York: John Wiley and Sons, 2002.

Benjamin, Walter. "The Work of Art in the Age of Mechanical Reproduction." In *Illuminations: Essays and Reflections*. Edited and with an introduction by Hannah Arendt, translated by Harry Zohn, 217–51. New York: Schocken, 1985. First published in 1936.

Berman, Avis. *Rebels on Eighth Street: Juliana Force and the Whitney Museum of American Art*. New York: Atheneum, 1990.

Biddle, Flora Miller. *The Whitney Women and the Museum They Made: A Family Memoir*. New York: Arcade, 1999.

Biddle, Livingston. *Our Government and the Arts: A Perspective from the Inside*. New York: ACA Books/American Council for the Arts, 1988.

Birt, Rodger C. "A Life in American Photography." In *VanDerZee, Photographer 1886–1983*, edited by Deborah Willis-Braithwaite, 57–73. New York: Harry N. Abrams in association with the National Portrait Gallery, Smithsonian Institution, 1993.

"The Black Artist in America: A Symposium." *Metropolitan Museum of Art Bulletin* 27, no. 5 (January 1969): 245–60.

Blayton-Taylor, Betty. Presentation in "When That Time Came Rolling Down: Panel 1" and "When That Time Came Rolling Down: Panel 2." *Artist and Influence* 3 (1985): 143–49.

Blier, Suzanne Preston. "Africa and Paris: The Art of Picasso and His Circle." In *The Image of the Black in Western Art*, vol. 5, part 1, *The Twentieth Century: The Impact of Africa*, edited by David Bindmand and Henry Louis Gates Jr., 77–98. Cambridge, MA: Belknap Press of Harvard University Press, 2014.

Blinkiewicz, Donna M. *Federalizing the Muse: United States Arts Policy and the National Endowment for the Arts: 1965–1980*. Chapel Hill: University of North Carolina Press, 2004.

Brenson, Michael. *Visionaries and Outcasts: The NEA, Congress, and the Place of the Visual Artist in America*. New York: New Press, 2001.

Brown, H. Rap. *Die Nigger Die!* New York: Dial, 1969.

Brown, Kay. "The Weusi Artists." *Harlem Magazine* (1995): 36–37.

———. "The Weusi Artists." *Nka: Journal of Contemporary African Art*, no. 30 (Spring 2012): 60–67.

Bryan-Wilson, Julia. *Art Workers: Radical Practice in the Vietnam War Era*. Berkeley: University of California Press, 2009.

Cahan, Susan. "Performing Identity and Persuading a Public: The *Harlem on My Mind* Controversy." *Social Identities* 13, no. 4 (July 2007): 423–40.

Calo, Mary Ann. *Distinction and Denial: Race, Nation, and the Critical Construction of the African American Artist, 1920–40*. Ann Arbor: University of Michigan Press, 2007.

Campbell, Mary Schmidt, ed. *Tradition and Conflict: Images of a Turbulent Decade 1963–1973*. New York: Studio Museum in Harlem, 1984.

Cannato, Vincent J. *The Ungovernable City: John Lindsay and His Struggle to Save New York*. New York: Basic Books, 2001.

Carson, Juli. "On Discourse as Monument: Institutional Spaces and Feminist Problematics." In *Alternative Art New York, 1965–1985*, edited by Julie Ault, 121–57. Minneapolis: University of Minnesota Press, 2002.

Cazenave, Noel. *Impossible Democracy: The Unlikely Success of the War on Poverty Community Action Programs*. Albany: SUNY Press, 2007.

Cheekwood Museum of Art. *The Art of William Edmondson*. Nashville: Cheekwood Museum of Art; Jackson: University Press of Mississippi, 1999.

City University of New York. *The Evolution of Afro-American Artists: 1800–1950*. New York: City College, 1967.

Clark, Kenneth B. *Dark Ghetto*. New York: Harper and Row, 1965.

Clark, Kenneth B., and Jeannette Hopkins. *A Relevant War against Poverty*. New York: Harper and Row, 1968.

Clarke, John Henrik, ed. *Harlem: A Community in Transition*. 2nd ed. New York: Citadel, 1969.

———, ed. *Harlem U.S.A.* New York: A&B, 1971.

———, ed. *Malcolm X: The Man and His Times.* New York: Collier, 1969. 2nd ed., Trenton, NJ: Africa World Press, 1990.

Coleman, A. D. *Light Readings.* New York: Oxford University Press, 1979.

Collins, Lisa Gail, and Margo Natalie Crawford, eds. *New Thoughts on the Black Arts Movement.* New Brunswick, NJ: Rutgers University Press, 2006.

Collins, Thom, and Tracy Fitzpatrick, eds. *African People, Black Light: Faith Ringgold's Paintings of the 1960s.* Purchase, NY: Neuberger Museum of Art, 2010.

Colomina, Beatriz. "Enclosed by Images: The Eameses' Multimedia Architecture." *Grey Room 2* (Winter 2001): 6–29.

Cooks, Bridget R. *Exhibiting Blackness: African Americans and the American Art Museum.* Amherst: University of Massachusetts Press, 2011.

Corrin, Lisa, ed. *Mining the Museum: An Installation by Fred Wilson.* New York: New Press, 1994.

Crow, Thomas. *The Rise of the Sixties: American and European Art in the Era of Dissent.* New Haven, CT: Yale University Press, 1996.

Cullen, Deborah, and Elvis Fuentes, eds. *Caribbean: Art at the Crossroads of the World.* New York: El Museo del Barrio; New Haven, CT: Yale University Press, 2012.

Danto, Arthur C. "The 1993 Biennial." *The Nation,* April 19, 1993, 533.

Dávila, Arlene. *Culture Works.* New York: New York University Press, 2012.

Dávila, Arlene, and Agustín Laó-Montes. *Mambo Montage: The Latinization of New York.* New York: Columbia University Press, 2001.

The Decade Show: Frameworks of Identity in the 1980s. New York: Museum of Contemporary Hispanic Art, New Museum of Contemporary Art, and Studio Museum in Harlem, 1990.

DeCarava, Roy, and Langston Hughes. *The Sweet Flypaper of Life.* New York: Simon and Schuster, 1955.

DeCarava, Sherry Turner. "Pages from a Notebook." In *Roy DeCarava: A Retrospective,* edited by Peter Galassi, 40–60. New York: Museum of Modern Art, 1996.

DiMaggio, Paul, and Francie Ostrower. *Race, Ethnicity and Participation in the Arts.* National Endowment for the Arts, Research Division Report No. 25. Washington, DC: Seven Locks Press, 1992.

Dizard, Wilson P., Jr. *Inventing Public Diplomacy: The Story of the U.S. Information Agency.* Boulder, CO: Lynne Rienner, 2004.

Donaldson, Jeff R. "AfriCOBRA and Transatlantic Connections." *Nka: Journal of Contemporary African Art* , no. 30 (Spring 2012): 84–89; doi:10.1215/10757163-1496498.

———. "AfriCOBRA Manifesto? 'Ten in Search of a Nation.' " *Nka: Journal of Contemporary African Art,* no. 30 (Spring 2012): 76–83.

Doty, Robert. *Contemporary Black Artists in America.* New York: Whitney Museum of American Art, 1971.

———. *Extraordinary Realities.* New York: Whitney Museum of American Art, 1973.

———. *Human Concern / Personal Torment: The Grotesque in American Art.* New York: Whitney Museum of American Art, 1969.

————. *Photo-Secession: Photography as a Fine Art*. Rochester: George Eastman House, 1960.

Doty, Robert, and Diane Waldman. *Adolph Gottlieb*. New York: Whitney Museum of American Art, 1968.

Dowell, John, Sam Gilliam, Daniel LaRue Johnson, Joe Overstreet, Melvin Edwards, Richard Hunt, and William T. Williams. "Politics." *Artforum* 9, no. 9 (May 1971): 12.

Dubin, Steven. *Displays of Power: Memory and Amnesia in the American Museum*. New York: New York University Press, 1999.

Duganne, Erina. "Transcending the Fixity of Race: The Kamoinge Workshop and the Question of a 'Black Aesthetic' in Photography." In *New Thoughts on the Black Arts Movement*, edited by Lisa Gail Collins and Margo Natalie Crawford, 187–209. New Brunswick, NJ: Rutgers University Press, 2006.

Duncan, Carol. *Civilizing Rituals: Inside Public Art Museums*. New York: Routledge, 1995.

English, Darby. *How to See a Work of Art in Total Darkness*. Cambridge, MA: MIT Press, 2007.

Excellence and Equity: Education and the Public Dimension of Museums. Washington, DC: American Association of Museums, 1992.

Ezra, Kate. "Collecting African Art at New York's Museum of Primitive Art." In *Representing Africa in American Art Museums: A Century of Collecting and Display*, edited by Kathleen Bickford and Christa Clarke, 122–49. Seattle: University of Washington Press, 2011.

Failing, Patricia. "Black Artists Today: A Case of Exclusion." *ARTNews* 88 (March 1989): 124–31.

Faith Ringgold: Twenty Years of Painting, Sculpture, and Performance, 1963–1983. New York: Studio Museum in Harlem, 1984.

Farrington, Lisa E. *Creating in Their Own Image: The History of African-American Women Artists*. New York: Oxford University Press, 2004.

Fifteen under Forty; Paintings by Young New York State Black Artists. Albany: Division of the Humanities and the Arts, 1970.

Fine, Elsa Honig. *The Afro-American Artist: A Search for Identity*. New York: Holt, Rinehart and Winston, 1973.

Fine, Ruth. *The Art of Romare Bearden*. Washington, DC: National Gallery of Art; New York: Harry N. Abrams, 2003.

Five Famous Black Artists. Roxbury, MA: National Center of Afro-American Artists, 1970.

Flagg, Barbara J. "The Transparency Phenomenon, Race-Neutral Decision Making, and Discriminatory Intent." In *Critical White Studies: Looking behind the Mirror*, edited by Richard Delgado and Jean Stefancic, 220–26. Philadelphia: Temple University Press, 1997.

Flam, Jack, ed., with Miriam Deutch. *Primitivism and Twentieth-Century Art: A Documentary History*. Berkeley: University of California Press, 2003.

Flomenhaft, Eleanor, ed. *Faith Ringgold: A 25 Year Survey*. Hempstead, NY: Fine Arts Museum of Long Island, 1990.

Foucault, Michel. *The Order of Things: An Archeology of the Human Sciences*. New York: Vintage, 1973.

Franc, Helen. "The Early Years of the International Program and Council." In *The Museum of Modern Art at Mid-Century: At Home and Abroad*, edited by John Elderfield, 109–49. New York: Museum of Modern Art, 1994.

Fusco, Coco. "Fantasies of Oppositionality." *Afterimage* 16, no. 5 (December 1988): 6–9.

GAAG. *GAAG: The Guerrilla Art Action Group, 1969–76: A Selection*. New York: Printed Matter, 1978.

Gaines, Charles, and Catherine Lord, eds. *The Theater of Refusal: Black Art and Mainstream Criticism*. Irvine: Regents of the University of California and Fine Arts Gallery of the University of California, Irvine, 1993.

Gaither, Edmund Barry. *Afro-American Artists: New York and Boston*. Boston: Museum of the National Center of Afro-American Artists, Museum of Fine Arts, and School of the Museum of Fine Arts, 1970.

———. "Hey! That's Mine." In *Museums and Communities: The Politics of Public Culture*, edited by Ivan Karp, Christine Muller Kreamer, and Steven D. Lavine, 56–64. Washington, DC: Smithsonian Institution Press in cooperation with American Association of Museums, 1992.

Galassi, Peter, ed. *Roy DeCarava: A Retrospective*. New York: Museum of Modern Art, 1996.

Gammon, Reginald. Two Interviews with Camille Billops. In *Artist and Influence* 15 (1996): 100–121.

Gangitano, Lia, and Steven Nelson, eds. *New Histories*. Boston: Institute of Contemporary Art, 1996.

Gates, Henry Louis. "Black Anti-Semitism." In *Let Nobody Turn Us Around*, edited by Manning Marable and Leith Mullings, 601–6. Lanham, MD: Rowman and Littlefield, 2000.

———. "Harlem on Our Minds." In *Rhapsodies in Black: Art of the Harlem Renaissance*, edited by Richard J. Powell and David Bailey, 160–67. Berkeley: University of California Press, 1997.

Gayle, Addison, Jr. *The Black Aesthetic*. Garden City, NJ: Doubleday, 1971.

Geldzahler, Henry. *New York Painting and Sculpture: 1940–1970*. New York: E. P. Dutton and Co. in association with the Metropolitan Museum of Art, 1969.

Genovese, Eugene D. "An Historian Looks at Hoving's Harlem: Harlem on His Back." *Artforum* 7, no. 6 (February 1969): 34–37.

Gibson, Ann Eden. *Abstract Expressionism: Other Politics*. New Haven, CT: Yale University Press, 1997.

Glazer, Nathan, and Daniel Patrick Moynihan. *Beyond the Melting Pot*. Cambridge, MA: Joint Center for Urban Studies, 1963.

Glueck, Grace. "New York: Big Thump on the Bass Drum." *Art in America* 59, no. 3 (May–June 1971): 128–32.

Goldwater, Robert. *Primitivism in Modern Art*. New York: Vintage, 1967.

———. *Primitivism in Modern Painting*. New York: Harper and Brothers, 1938.

Goodrich, Lloyd, and John I. H. Baur. *American Art of Our Century*. New York: Praeger, 1961.

Grillo, Jean Bergantino. "The Studio Museum in Harlem—a Home for the Evolving Black Esthetic." *ARTnews* 72 (October 1973): 47–49.

Gross, Alexander. *The 'Sixties Book: Inside the 'Sixties: What Really Happened on an International Scale*. Online book, 2000. Accessed December 23, 2002. http://language.home.sprynet.com/otherdex/6os-comm.htm.

Gruber, J. Richard. *American Icons: From Madison to Manhattan, the Art of Benny Andrews, 1948–1997*. Augusta, GA: Morris Museum of Art, 1997.

Gunn, Theodore. *Harlem Artists 69*. New York: Studio Museum in Harlem, 1969.

———. Presentation in "When That Time Came: Panel 1." *Artist and Influence* 3 (1985): 157–58.

Guzzardi, Walter, Jr. *The Henry Luce Foundation, a History: 1936–1986.* Chapel Hill: University of North Carolina Press, 1988.

Hall, Stuart, ed. *Representation: Cultural Representations and Signifying Practices.* London: Sage Publications in association with Open University, 1998.

"Harlem: A State of Mind." *Camera*, no. 6 (July 1966): 4–25.

Harper, Donald, prod. *Harlem on My Mind: A History in Voices and Music.* Hank Johnson with the Jazz Heritage Ensemble. Metropolitan Museum of Art, New York, 1969. Stereo LP.

Harris, Jay, and Cliff Joseph. *Murals of the Mind: Image of a Psychiatric Community.* New York: International Universities Press, 1973.

Harvey, Emily Dennis, and Bernard Friedberg, eds. *A Museum for the People: A Report of the Proceedings at the Seminar on Neighborhood Museums.* New York: Arno, 1971.

Hatch, James V. "From Hansberry to Shange." In *A History of African American Theater*, edited by Errol G. Hill and James V. Hatch, 375–429. Cambridge: Cambridge University Press, 2010. First published in 2003.

Heartney, Eleanor. "Identity Politics at the Whitney." *Art in America* 81, no. 5 (May 1993): 42–47.

Hess, Thomas B. "Editorial: The Studio Museum in Harlem." *ARTnews* 67 (Summer 1968): 23.

Hills, Patricia. *Painting Harlem Modern: The Art of Jacob Lawrence.* Berkeley: University of California Press, 2009.

Hogu, Barbara Jones. "Inaugurating AfriCOBRA: History, Philosophy, and Aesthetics." *Nka: Journal of Contemporary African Art*, no. 30 (Spring 2012): 90–97.

Hoving, Thomas P. F. *Making the Mummies Dance: Inside the Metropolitan Museum of Art.* New York: Touchstone, 1994.

Jacobs, Jay. "What the Federal Arts Program Really Means." *Art in America* 55, no. 2 (March–April 1967): 28.

Jones, Kellie, ed. *Energy/Experimentation: Black Artists and Abstraction, 1964–1980.* New York: Studio Museum in Harlem, 2006.

———. "It's Not Enough to Say 'Black Is Beautiful': Abstraction at the Whitney, 1969–1974." In *Discrepant Abstraction*, edited by Kobena Mercer, 154–80. London: InIVA; Cambridge, MA: MIT Press, 2006.

———. *Now Dig This: Art and Black Los Angeles 1960–1980.* Munich: Delmonico Books–Prestel, 2011.

Jones-Henderson, Napoleon. "Remembering AfriCOBRA and the Black Arts Movement in 1960s Chicago." *Nka: Journal of Contemporary African Art* , no. 30 (Spring 2012): 98–103.

"Kamoinge." Special issue, *Nueva Luz* 7, no. 1 (2001).

The Kerner Report: The 1968 Report of the National Advisory Commission on Civil Disorders. New York: Pantheon, 1988. First published in 1968.

Kimball, Roger. "Of Chocolate, Lard, and Politics." *National Review*, April 26, 1993, 54.

Kramer, Hilton. *The Age of the Avant-Garde: An Art Chronicle of 1956–1972.* New York: Farrar, Straus and Giroux, 1973.

———. Letter to the editor. *Artforum* 7, no. 7 (March 1969): 3.

Kuh, Katharine. "The Fine Arts—What's an Art Museum For?" *Saturday Review*, February 22, 1969, 58–59.

Leach, Richard H. "The Federal Role in the War on Poverty Program." In *Anti-Poverty Programs*, edited by Robinson O. Everett, 18–38. Dobbs Ferry, NY: Oceana, 1966.

Lennon, Mary Ellen. "A Question of Relevancy: New York Museums and the Black Arts Movement, 1968–1971." In *New Thoughts on the Black Arts Movement*, edited by Lisa Gail Collins and Margo Natalie Crawford, 92–116. New Brunswick, NJ: Rutgers University Press, 2006.

Levin, Gail. " 'Primitivism' in American Art: Some Literary Parallels of the 1910s and 1920s." *Arts* 59, no. 3 (November 1984): 101–5.

Lewis, Samella, and Ruth Waddy, eds. *Black Artists on Art*. Vol. 1. Rev. ed. Los Angeles: Contemporary Crafts, 1976. First published in 1969.

———. *Black Artists on Art*. Vol. 2. Los Angeles: Contemporary Crafts, 1971.

Lippard, Lucy. "The Art Worker's Coalition: Not a History." *Studio International* 180 (November 1970): 171–74.

Lipstadt, Hélène. " 'Natural Overlap': Charles and Ray Eames and the Federal Government." In *The Work of Charles and Ray Eames: A Legacy of Invention*, edited by Diana Murphy, 160–66. New York: Harry N. Abrams in association with the Library of Congress and the Vitra Design Museum, 1997.

Lloyd, Tom, ed. *Black Art Notes*. N.p., 1971.

Lubiano, Wahneemah, ed. *The House That Race Built*. New York: Vintage, 1998.

Lynes, Russell. *Good Old Modern: An Intimate Portrait of the Museum of Modern Art*. New York: Atheneum, 1973.

Mainardi, Patricia. "The Political Origins of Modernism." *Art Journal* 45, no. 1 (Spring 1985): 11–17.

Marable, Manning, and Leith Mullings, eds. *Let Nobody Turn Us Around*. Lanham, MD: Rowman and Littlefield, 2000.

Mayor's Advisory Panel on Decentralization of the New York City Schools. *Reconnection for Learning: A Community School System for New York City*. New York, 1967.

McEvilley, Thomas, William S. Rubin, and Kirk Varnedoe. "Doctor, Lawyer, Indian Chief: 'Primitivism' in Twentieth Century Art at the Museum of Modern Art." Series of individually authored articles reprinted in *Discourses: Conversations in Postmodern Art and Culture*, edited by Russell Ferguson, William Olander, Marcia Tucker, and Karen Fiss, 339–405. New York: New Museum of Contemporary Art; Cambridge, MA: MIT Press, 1990. Reprinted from *Artforum* (November 1984): 54–60; (February 1985): 42–51; and (May 1985): 63–71.

McKinzie, Richard D. *The New Deal for Artists*. Princeton, NJ: Princeton University Press, 1973.

Mercer, Kobena, ed. *Cosmopolitan Modernisms*. Annotating Art's Histories. London: InIVA; Cambridge, MA: MIT Press, 2005.

———. "Diaspora Aesthetics and Visual Culture." In *Black Cultural Traffic: Crossroads in Global Performance and Popular Culture*, edited by Harry Justin Elam and Kennell A. Jackson, 141–61. Ann Arbor: University of Michigan Press, 2005.

———. *Discrepant Abstraction*. Annotating Art's Histories. London: InIVA; Cambridge, MA: MIT Press, 2006.

———. *Exiles, Diasporas, and Strangers*. Annotating Art's Histories. London: InIVA; Cambridge, MA: MIT Press, 2008.

———. *Pop Art and Vernacular Culture*. Annotating Art's Histories. London: InIVA; Cambridge, MA: MIT Press, 2007.

The Metropolitan Museum of Art Bulletin 26, no. 5 (January 1968).

The Metropolitan Museum of Art Bulletin 27, no. 5 (January 1969).

Meyer, Richard. *What Was Contemporary Art?* Cambridge, MA: MIT Press, 2013.

Minneapolis Institute of Arts. *30 Contemporary Black Artists*. Minneapolis: Minneapolis Institute of Arts with the assistance of Ruder & Finn, New York, 1968.

Mirzoeff, Nicholas, ed. *Diaspora and Visual Culture: Representing Africans and Jews*. London: Routledge, 2000.

Morrow, Lance. *The Henry Luce Foundation 1936–1996, Sixtieth Anniversary Report*. New York: Henry Luce Foundation, 1996.

Mosaka, Tumelo, ed. *Infinite Island: Contemporary Caribbean Art*. New York: Brooklyn Museum in association with Philip Wilson, 2007.

Mosquera, Gerardo, ed. *Beyond the Fantastic: Contemporary Art Criticism from Latin America*. London: InIVA, 1995.

El Museo del Barrio. *Raphael Montañez Ortiz: Years of the Warrior, Years of the Psyche, 1960–1988*. New York: El Museo del Barrio, 1988.

The Museum of Modern Art. *The Museum of Modern Art, New York: The History and the Collection*. New York: Harry N. Abrams in association with the Museum of Modern Art, 1984.

———. *Prehistoric Rock Pictures in Europe and Africa*. New York: Museum of Modern Art, 1937.

Neal, Larry. *Visions of a Liberated Future: Black Arts Movement Writings*. New York: Thunder's Mouth, 1989.

Neal, Larry, and LeRoi Jones, eds. *Black Fire: An Anthology of Afro-American Writing*. Baltimore: Black Classic, 2007. First published in 1968.

Neuhart, John, Marilyn Neuhart, and Ray Eames. *Eames Design: The Work of the Office of Charles and Ray Eames*. New York: Harry N. Abrams, 1994. First published in 1989.

New Black Artists. Foreword by Edward K. Taylor. New York: Harlem Cultural Council in cooperation with the School of the Arts and the Urban Center, Columbia University, 1969.

Newkirk, Pamela. "Searching for the Black Audience." *ARTnews* (May 2001): 184–87.

New Muse Community Museum of Brooklyn. *Black Artists in the WPA 1933–1943*. Brooklyn: New Muse Community Museum of Brooklyn, 1976.

Newsome, Barbara Y., and Adele Z. Silver, eds. *The Art Museum as Educator: A Collection of Studies as Guides to Practice and Policy*. Berkeley: University of California Press, 1978.

New York State Council on the Arts. "Planning and Operation of Neighborhood Museums." Seminar sponsored by the New York State Council on the Arts and the New York City Department of Cultural Affairs, November 20–22, 1969. Sound tapes and transcript. Archives of American Art, Washington, DC.

New York State Council on the Arts Annual Report 1965–66. Syracuse: New York State Council on the Arts, 1966.

New York State Council on the Arts Annual Report 1966–67. Syracuse: New York State Council on the Arts, 1967.

New York State Council on the Arts Annual Report 1967–68. Syracuse: New York State Council on the Arts, 1968.

New York State Council on the Arts Annual Report 1968–69. Syracuse: New York State Council on the Arts, 1969.

New York State Council on the Arts Annual Report 1969–70. Syracuse: New York State Council on the Arts, 1970.

Nka: A Journal of Contemporary African Art, no. 30 (Spring 2012).

"Not a Rhyme Time." Episode 5 from season 1 of *I'll Make Me a World.* New York: Blackside Films, produced in association with Thirteen/WNET New York, 1999.

Ogbar, Jeffrey O. G. *Black Power: Racial Politics and African American Identity.* Baltimore: Johns Hopkins University Press, 2004.

Olin, Margaret. *Touching Photographs.* Chicago: University of Chicago Press, 2012.

Olugebefola, Ademola. "Weusi History: Selected Highlights." *Nka: Journal of Contemporary African Art,* no. 30 (Spring 2012): 68–75.

Omi, Michael, and Howard Winant. *Racial Formation in the United States from the 1960s to the 1980s.* New York: Routledge, 1990. First published in 1986 by Routledge and Kegan Paul.

Ortiz, Ralph [Raphael Montañez Ortiz]. "Culture and the People." *Art in America* 59 (May/June 1971): 27.

Perez-Torres, R. "Nomads and Migrants: Negotiating a Multicultural Postmodernism." *Cultural Critique* 26 (1994): 161–90.

Perry, Imani. *More Beautiful and More Terrible: The Embrace and Transcendence of Racial Inequality in the United States.* New York: New York University Press, 2011.

Pincus-Witten, Robert. "Reviews." *Artforum* 7, no. 6 (February 1969): 64–67.

Pindell, Howardena. "Artist's Statement" (interview by Helen Ramsaran). In *High Times, Hard Times: New York Painting, 1967–1975,* edited by Katy Siegel, 105. New York: Independent Curators International, 2006.

———. "Art World Racism." *Third Text* 3, no. 4 (Spring/Summer 1988): 157–90.

———. *The Heart of the Question: The Writings and Paintings of Howardena Pindell.* New York: Midmarch Art, 1997.

Pollock, Lindsay. *The Girl with the Gallery: Edith Gregor Halpert and the Making of the Modern Art Market.* New York: Public Affairs, 2006.

Porter, James A. *Modern Negro Art.* 1943. Reprint, with an introduction by David Driskell. Washington, DC: Howard University Press, 1992.

Powell, Richard J. "Re/Birth of a Nation." In *Rhapsodies in Black: Art of the Harlem Renaissance,* edited by Richard J. Powell and David Bailey, 14–33. Berkeley: University of California Press, 1997.

Powell, Richard J., and David Bailey, eds. *Rhapsodies in Black: Art of the Harlem Renaissance.* Berkeley: University of California Press, 1997.

Powell, Richard J., David Bailey, and Petrine Archer-Straw. *Back to Black: Art, Cinema and the Racial Imaginary.* London: Whitechapel Gallery, 2005.

Powell, Richard J., and Jock Reynolds. *To Conserve a Legacy: American Art from Historically Black Colleges and Universities.* Cambridge, MA: MIT Press, 1999.

Ramírez, Mari Carmen, Tomás Ybarra-Frausto, and Héctor Olea, eds. *Resisting Categories: Latin American and/or Latino?* Vol. 1 of *Critical Documents of 20th-Century Latin American and Latino Art.* Houston: International Center for the Arts of the Americas at the Museum of Fine Arts, Houston, 2012.

Ramírez, Yasmín. "The Activist Legacy of Puerto Rican Artists in New York and *The Art Heritage of Puerto Rico.*" Documents of 20th-Century Latin American and Latino Art Working Papers, International Center for the Arts of the Americas at the Museum of Fine Arts, Houston, no. 1 (September 2007): 46–53.

———. *Unmaking: The Work of Raphael Montañez Ortiz.* Jersey City, NJ: Jersey City Museum, 2007.

Rebuttal to Whitney Museum Exhibition: Black Artists in Rebuttal at Acts of Art Gallery, NYC. New York: Acts of Art, 1971.

Reed, Adolph L., Jr. "Black Particularity Reconsidered." *Telos* 39 (Spring 1979): 86.

Reynolds, Gary A., and Beryl Wright. *Against the Odds: African American Artists and the Harmon Foundation.* Newark: Newark Museum, 1989.

Ringgold, Faith. Interview with Moira Roth. *Artist and Influence* 15 (1996): 220–37.

———. *We Flew over the Bridge: The Memoirs of Faith Ringgold.* Boston: Little, Brown, 1995.

Robinson, Dean E. *Black Nationalism in American Politics and Thought.* Cambridge: Cambridge University Press, 2001.

Rockefeller, David. *Memoirs.* New York: Random House, 2002.

Rogin, Michael Paul. *Ronald Reagan, the Movie.* Berkeley: University of California Press, 1987.

Romare Bearden: The Prevalence of Ritual. Introductory essay by Carroll Greene Jr. New York: Museum of Modern Art, 1971.

Rosati, Lauren, and Mary Anne Staniszewski, eds. *Alternative Histories: New York Art Spaces, 1960–2010.* Cambridge, MA: MIT Press, 2012.

Rose, Barbara. "The Politics of Art." *Artforum* 6, no. 6 (February 1968): 31–32.

Rothkopf, Scott. "Banned and Determined: Scott Rothkopf on Gene Swenson." *Artforum International* 40, no. 10 (Summer 2002): 142–45, 194.

Rubin, William S. *Dada, Surrealism, and Their Heritage.* New York: Museum of Modern Art, 1968.

———, ed. *"Primitivism" in 20th Century Art: Affinity of the Tribal and the Modern.* 2 vols. New York: Museum of Modern Art, 1984.

Ruder & Finn Fine Arts. *Contemporary Black Artists.* New York: Ruder & Finn, 1969.

Ruffins, Fath Davis. "Culture Wars Won and Lost, Part II: The National African-American Museum Project." *Radical History Review* 70 (1998): 78–101.

———. "Mythos, Memory, and History: African American Preservation Efforts, 1820–1990." In *Museums and Communities: The Politics of Public Culture,* edited by Ivan Karp, Christine Muller Kreamer, and Steven D. Lavine, 506–611. Washington, DC: Smithsonian Institution Press in cooperation with the American Association of Museums, 1992.

Ryder, Mahler. Presentation in "When That Time Came: Panel 1." *Artist and Influence* 3 (1985): 152–56.

Sandeen, Eric J. *Picturing an Exhibition: "The Family of Man" and 1950s America.* Albuquerque: University of New Mexico Press, 1995.

Sandell, Richard, ed. *Museums, Society, Inequality.* New York: Routledge, 2002.

Sandler, Irving, and Amy Newman, eds. *Defining Modern Art: Selected Writings of Alfred H. Barr, Jr.* New York: Harry N. Abrams, 1986.

Schoener, Allon. "Art without Pedestals." *Zodiac* 7 (1960): 22–29.

———, ed. *Harlem on My Mind: Cultural Capital of Black America, 1900–1968.* Preface by Thomas P. F. Hoving; introduction by Candice Van Ellison. New York: Random House, 1968.

———, ed. *Harlem on My Mind: Cultural Capital of Black America, 1900–1978.* Introduction by Nathan Irvin Huggins. With an updated chapter on the period from 1969 to 1978. New York: Dell, 1979.

———, ed. *Harlem on My Mind: Cultural Capital of Black America, 1900–1968.* 2nd ed. With a new introduction by Allon Schoener and a new foreword by Henry Louis Gates Jr. New York: New Press, 1995.

———, ed. *Harlem on My Mind: Cultural Capital of Black America, 1900–1968.* 3rd ed. With a new foreword by Congressman Charles Rangel. New York: New Press, 2007.

———. "The New Aesthetic: Process Prevails (Art and the Environments)." *Art Voices* (Fall 1968): 34–43.

———, ed. *Portal to America: The Lower East Side 1870–1925.* New York: Holt, Rinehart and Winston, 1967.

———. "Television in the Art Museums." *Quarterly Journal of Film, Radio and Television* 11, no. 1 (1956): 70–86.

Schoonmaker, Trevor, ed. *Barkley L. Hendricks: Birth of the Cool.* Durham, NC: Nasher Museum of Art at Duke University, 2008.

Schwartz, Therese. "The Politicalization of the Avant-Garde." *Art in America* 59, no. 6 (November–December 1971): 97–105.

———. "The Politicalization of the Avant-Garde, II." *Art in America* 60, no. 2 (March–April 1972): 70–79.

The Sculpture of Richard Hunt. New York: Museum of Modern Art, 1971.

Siegel, Katy, ed. *High Times, Hard Times: New York Painting, 1967–1975.* New York: Independent Curators International, 2006.

Sims, Lowery Stokes. *Challenge of the Modern: African American Artists, 1925–1945.* New York: Studio Museum in Harlem, 2003.

———. "Cultural Pluralism versus the American Canon: The Aesthetic Dialogue for the 1990s." In *The Decade Show: Frameworks of Identity in the 1980s,* 140–45. New York: Museum of Contemporary Hispanic Art, New Museum of Contemporary Art, and Studio Museum in Harlem, 1990.

———. *Joaquín Torres-Garcia (1874–1949): Paintings Constructions and Drawings.* New York: Salander O'Reilly Galleries, 1981.

———. *Wifredo Lam and the International Avant-Garde, 1923–1982.* Austin: University of Texas Press, 2002.

Sims, Lowery Stokes, and Leslie King-Hammond. *The Global Africa Project*. New York: Museum of Art and Design; Prestel, 2010.

Smethurst, James Edward. *The Black Arts Movement: Literary Nationalism in the 1960s and 1970s*. Chapel Hill: University of North Carolina Press, 2005.

Spriggs, Edward S. "Field Notes: Raising the 'Studio' at Studio Museum." *Nka: Journal of Contemporary African Art 2011*, no. 29 (2011): 72–77.

Staniszewski, Mary Ann. *The Power of Display: A History of Exhibition Installations at the Museum of Modern Art*. Cambridge, MA: MIT Press, 1998.

Steichen, Edward. *The Family of Man*. Prologue by Carl Sandburg. New York: Simon and Schuster in collaboration with Maco Magazine Corporation, 1955.

Steinberg, Leo. *Other Criteria: Confrontations with Twentieth-Century Art*. New York: Oxford University Press, 1972.

Steinberg, Stephen. "The Liberal Retreat from Race during the Post–Civil Rights Era." In *The House That Race Built*, edited by Wahneemah Lubiano, 13–47. New York: Vintage, 1998.

Stewart, Jeffrey C., ed. *The Critical Temper of Alain Locke*. New York: Garland, 1983.

Stowe, Harriet Beecher. *Uncle Tom's Cabin, or, Life among the Lowly*. New York: Penguin, 1981. First published in 1852.

The Studio Museum in Harlem. *Explorations in the City of Light: African-American Artists in Paris, 1945–1965*. New York: Studio Museum in Harlem, 1996.

The Studio Museum in Harlem Annual Report 1968–1969. New York: Studio Museum in Harlem, 1969.

Sussman, Elizabeth, ed. *1993 Biennial Exhibition*. New York: Whitney Museum of American Art in association with Harry N. Abrams, 1993.

Sweeney, James Johnson. *African Negro Art*. New York: Museum of Modern Art, 1935.

Sylvain, Renee. "KulturKreis to Kulturmorphologie." *Anthropos* 91, nos. 4/6 (1996): 483–94.

Szwed, John F. *Space Is the Place: The Lives and Times of Sun Ra*. New York: Pantheon, 1997.

"Taking Stock on Wall Street." *Black Enterprise* 10 (March 1980): 37–43.

Tompkins, Calvin. *Merchants and Masterpieces: The Story of the Metropolitan Museum of Art*. New York: E. P. Dutton, 1970.

Van Deburg, William L., ed. *Modern Black Nationalism: From Garvey to Louis Farrakhan*. New York: New York University Press, 1997.

Varnedoe, Kirk. "The Evolving Torpedo: Changing Ideas of the Collection of Painting and Sculpture of the Museum of Modern Art." In *The Museum of Modern Art at Mid-Century: Continuity and Change*, edited by John Elderfield, 12–73. New York: Museum of Modern Art, 1995.

———. "Issues and Commentary: On the Claims and Critics of the 'Primitivism' Show." *Art in America*, May 1985, 11–12.

Vincent, Rickey. *Funk: The Music, the People, and the Rhythm of the One*. New York: St. Martin's Griffin, 1996.

Wallace, Michele. "American People, Black Light: Faith Ringgold's Paintings of the 1960s." In *American People, Black Light: Faith Ringgold's Paintings of the 1960s*, edited by Thom Collins and Tracy Fitzpatrick, 15–51. Purchase, NY: Neuberger Museum of Art, 2010.

———. *Black Macho and the Myth of the Superwoman*. London: Verso, 1990.

———. *Dark Designs and Visual Culture*. Durham, NC: Duke University Press, 2004.

———. *Invisibility Blues: From Pop to Theory*. London: Verso, 1990.

Wallis, Brian. *Hans Haacke: Unfinished Business*. New York: New Museum of Contemporary Art; Cambridge, MA: MIT Press, 1986.

Watts, Jerry Gafio. *Amiri Baraka: The Politics and Art of a Black Intellectual*. New York: New York University Press, 2001.

Webb, Virginia-Lee. *Perfect Documents: Walker Evans and African Art, 1935*. New York: Metropolitan Museum of Art, 2000.

Whitney Museum of American Art. *The Whitney and Its Collection*. New York: Whitney Museum of American Art, 1954.

———. *The Whitney Review, 1961/62*. New York: Whitney Museum of American Art, 1962.

———. *The Whitney Review, 1963/64*. New York: Whitney Museum of American Art, 1964.

———. *The Whitney Review, 1964/65*. New York: Whitney Museum of American Art, 1965.

———. *The Whitney Review, 1966/67*. New York: Whitney Museum of American Art, 1967.

———. *The Whitney Review, 1967/68*. New York: Whitney Museum of American Art, 1968.

———. *The Whitney Review, 1968/69*. New York: Whitney Museum of American Art, 1969.

Wilding, Faith. *By Our Own Hands: The Woman Artist's Movement, Southern California, 1970–1976*. Santa Monica, CA: Double X, 1977.

Williams, William T. Presentation in "When That Time Came: Panel 1." *Artist and Influence* 3 (1985): 162.

Willis-Braithwaite, Deborah, ed. *VanDerZee, Photographer 1886–1983*. New York: Harry N. Abrams in association with the National Portrait Gallery, Smithsonian Institution, 1993.

Wolcott, Victoria W. *Race, Riots, and Roller Coasters: The Struggle over Segregated Recreation in America*. Philadelphia: University of Pennsylvania Press, 2012.

Women Artists in Revolution. *A Documentary Herstory of Women Artists in Revolution*. New York: Women Artists in Revolution, 1971; reprint, Pittsburgh: Women's Interart Center, 1975.

Yau, John. "Please Wait by the Coatroom." In *Out There: Marginalization and Contemporary Cultures*, edited by Russell Ferguson, Martha Gever, Trinh T. Minh-ha, and Cornel West, 133–39. New York: New Museum of Contemporary Art; Cambridge, MA: MIT Press, 1990.

Ybarra-Frausto, Tomás. "The Chicano Movement/The Movement of Chicano Art." In *Exhibiting Cultures: The Politics and Poetics of Museum Display*, edited by Ivan Karp and Steven D. Lavine, 128–50. Washington: Smithsonian Institution Press, 1991.

Yee, Lydia, ed. *Division of Labor: "Women's Work" in Contemporary Art*. New York: Bronx Museum of the Arts, 1995.

Zabunyan, Elvan. *Black Is a Color (A History of African American Art)*. Paris: Éditions dis Voir, 2005.

AUTHOR INTERVIEWS

Andrews, Benny. Litchfield, CT, July 14, 1999.

Blayton, Betty. New York, NY, June 29, 2011.

Campbell, Mary Schmidt. New York, NY, February 26, 2000.

Conwill, Kinshasha Holman. Washington, DC, November 17, 2014.

Gaither, Edmund Barry. Boston, MA, February 22, 2006.

Goode Bryant, Linda. New York, NY, February 7, 2003.

Hendricks, Jon. New York, NY, June 20, 2011.

Henry, Janet. Jamaica, NY, March 19, 2013.

Hightower, John B. Newport News, VA, August 2, 2004.

Kramarsky, Werner. New York, NY, November 15, 2000.

Levin, Gail. New York, NY, January 14, 2014.

Malone, Robert. New York, NY, August 25, 2013.

Ortiz, Raphael Montañez. Highland Park, NJ, January 8, 2011.

Overstreet, Joe, and Corrine Jennings. New York, NY, April 12, 2006.

Parker, Harry S., III. San Francisco, CA, July 19, 1999.

Pindell, Howardena. New York, NY, January 7, 2011.

Ringgold, Faith. Englewood, NJ, January 27, 2011.

Rosenblatt, Arthur. New York, NY, February 27, 2000.

Schoener, Allon. Grafton, VT, December 17, 1998.

Sims, Lowery Stokes. New York, NY, February 27, 2001.

Storr, Robert. New Haven, CT, January 10, 2011.

Vega, Marta Moreno. New Haven, CT, July 11, 2011.

Wallace, Michele. Englewood, NJ, January 27, 2011.

INDEX